JANET MALCOLM

# *The Purloined Clinic*

Janet Malcolm's previous books are *Diana and Nikon, Psycho-analysis: The Impossible Profession, In the Freud Archives,* and *The Journalist and the Murderer.* Born in Prague, she grew up in New York and lives there now with her husband.

*The Purloined Clinic*

# The Purloined Clinic

*Selected Writings*

*by*

## JANET MALCOLM

*Vintage Books*

A DIVISION OF RANDOM HOUSE, INC.

NEW YORK

FIRST VINTAGE BOOKS EDITION, NOVEMBER 1993

*Copyright © 1992 by Janet Malcolm*

All rights reserved under International and Pan-American Copyright Conventions.
Published in the United States by Vintage Books, a division of
Random House, Inc., New York, and simultaneously in Canada by
Random House of Canada Limited, Toronto. Originally published in hardcover
by Alfred A. Knopf, Inc., New York, in 1992.

The following pieces originally appeared in *The New Yorker*, in slightly
different form:

"The One-Way Mirror" (A Reporter at Large), 1978
*"Six roses ou Cirrhose?"* (Review of *Narrative Truth and Historical Truth*
by Donald P. Spence), 1983
"A Girl of the Zeitgeist" (Profile of Ingrid Sischy, parts I and II), 1986
"J'appelle un Chat un Chat" (now titled "Dora") (Reflections), 1987
"The Purloined Clinic" (Books), 1987
"The Window Washer" (A Reporter at Large), 1990

Owing to limitations of space, acknowledgments for permission to
reprint previously published material may be found on page 385.

Library of Congress Cataloging-in-Publication Data
Malcolm, Janet.
The purloined clinic: selected writings / by Janet Malcolm. — 1st Vintage Books ed.
p.    cm.
Originally published: New York: Knopf, 1992.
ISBN 0-679-74810-5
I. Title.
[AC8.M315    1993]
081—dc20          93-7859
CIP

*Manufactured in the United States of America*
10   9   8   7   6   5   4   3   2   1

To G.B.

# Contents

*The Purloined Clinic*

# Preface

THE essays, reviews, and reports in this book are a selection from work done largely in the past decade, and almost all were first published either in *The New Yorker* or *The New York Review of Books*. The selections reflect what I was thinking and how I was writing at the time, and I leave them in their original state, as the traces of a particular moment. They are arranged in what I hope is a rational and inviting order. But they constitute a miscellany and may be read in any sequence.

The book opens with an essay on Freud's Dora case and ends with a semi-autobiographical report on a trip to post-Communist Prague and an encounter with a Czech-Jewish former dissident, in whom I recognized a sort of double. In between, there are articles and reviews that touch on, among other subjects, the New York art world, family therapy, Bloomsbury, autobiography, architecture, and fiction. I have chosen the title of one of the pieces, a review of Michael Fried's *Realism, Writing, Disfiguration: On Thomas Eakins and Stephen Crane*, as the title of the collection, because in Fried I recognized another sort of double: a critic whose imagination I found almost uncannily familiar and congenial, and who caused me to see that I had been thinking like a deconstructionist for a long time without knowing it, like Molière's M. Jourdain, who discovered that he had been speaking in prose all his life.

I am deeply grateful to Robert Gottlieb, Barbara Epstein, and William Shawn for giving these pieces a home, and for their encouragement and always helpful criticism; to Barbara Bristol and Joan Keener for making the stately process of book publication a great pleasure; and to Mary Quaintance for her sharp-eyed and elegant reading of the final text.

J.M.

# *Part* I

# Dora

TODAY, everyone knows—except possibly a few literary theorists—that the chief subject of the psychoanalytic dialogue is not the patient's repressed memories but the analyst's vacation. As our therapeutic community grows, as more and more of us participate in the cultural ritual known as "going to the shrink," the popular view of psychoanalysis as a kind of surrealistic agon has given way to the less theatrical, more domesticated vision of the analytic encounter as a proving ground for the concept of transference. "The patient does not *remember* anything of what he has forgotten and repressed, but *acts* it out," Freud wrote in "Remembering, Repeating, and Working-Through" (1914). "He reproduces it not as a memory but as an action; he *repeats* it, without, of course, knowing that he is repeating it. For instance, the patient does not say that he remembers that he used to be defiant and critical towards his parents' authority; instead, he behaves in that way to the doctor." Psychoanalysis is the wary (ultimately weary) examination by patient and analyst of the patient's behavior toward the analyst. Out of this absurdist collaboration—the tireless joint scrutiny of the patient's reactions and overreactions to the analyst's limited repertoire of activity in the sphere of fees, hours, waiting-room etiquette, and, above all, absences—come small, stray self-recognitions that no other human relationship yields, brought forward under conditions of frustration (and gratification) that no other human relationship could survive.

The patient leaves the analysis older, and wiser about analysis. It is finally borne in on him that the object of analysis is not to make sense of his life but to make nonsense of his neurosis. Through repetitive enactment of the neurosis in the transference, the neurosis loses its edge. Psychoanalysis is a process of blunting. From its earliest period, long before Freud knew what he was doing or where he was going, he used the metaphor of wearing away to express the therapeutic effect of the talking cure. Freud's concept of the unconscious is poised on an opposition between the durable and the mutable. What is unconscious is timeless, of stone, forever, while what is conscious is transient, ephemeral, written in water. Freud's early flounderings with hysterical patients, in which, following Josef Breuer's flounderings with Anna O., he did what he called "cathartic therapy," were posited on the theory that hysteria is caused by "forgotten memories" of trauma, which have "been acting like foreign bodies in the mind." This figure of the oxymoronic irritant appears in Freud's 1897 abstract of earlier writings on hysteria. He continues:

> The memories which are revealed as "pathogenic," as the roots of hysterical symptoms, are regularly "unconscious" to the patient. It seems that by thus remaining unconscious they escape the wearing-away process to which psychical material is normally subject. A wearing-away of this sort is brought about by the method of "abreaction."

In 1909, when Freud wrote his "Notes Upon a Case of Obsessional Neurosis," popularly known as the Rat Man case, psychoanalytic theory as we now know it was in place, and clinical practice was a far cry from its earliest manifestation, which has been wonderfully characterized by Leo Stone as "a sort of unwitting, sometimes grudging patient participation, like the bringing of urine to be analyzed, or enduring the expression of pus." But the distinction between what is conscious and what is unconscious remained, and remains, a kind of lodestar of psychoanalytic thought (or, to use Freud's own figure of speech in 1923, "our one beacon-light in the darkness of depth psychology"), and the wearing-away metaphor retained its authority as other figures of pre-psychoanalysis lost theirs. In the

Rat Man case, indeed, Freud gave the wearing-away metaphor its fullest and most poetic expression:

> At the next session the patient showed great interest in what I had said, but ventured, so he told me, to bring forward a few doubts.—How, he asked, could the information that the self-reproach, the sense of guilt, was justified have a therapeutic effect?—I explained that it was not the information that had this effect, but the discovery of the unknown content to which the self-reproach was really attached.—Yes, he said, that was the precise point to which his question had been directed.—I then made some short observations upon *the psychological differences between the conscious and the unconscious*, and upon the fact that everything conscious was subject to a process of wearing-away, while what was unconscious was relatively unchangeable; and I illustrated my remarks by pointing to the antiques standing about in my room. They were, in fact, I said, only objects found in a tomb, and their burial had been their preservation: the destruction of Pompeii was only beginning now that it had been dug up.

However, Freud, with his characteristic refusal to make things easy for his interpreters, elsewhere in his writings uses the analogy of the archaeological relic to make an altogether different and seemingly contradictory point. In his late paper "Constructions in Analysis" (1937), and also in the Dora case, Freud employs the analogy of the archaeological relic not to illustrate the destructive action of psychoanalysis on pathogenic thought, like the corrosive effect of air and light on long-buried objects, but, rather, to legitimate the making of "constructions"—i.e., the analyst's conjectures about fateful events in the patient's psychic life during early childhood:

> Just as the archeologist builds up the walls of the building from the foundations that have remained standing, determines the number and position of the columns from depressions in

the floor, and reconstructs the mural decorations and paintings from the remains found in the debris, so does the analyst proceed when he draws his inferences from the fragments of memories, from the associations, and from the behavior of the subject of the analysis.

The apparent contradiction between analysis as destruction and analysis as construction is resolved in the next paragraph in the "Constructions" paper, in which Freud notes that "the main difference" between the analyst and the archaeologist "lies in the fact that for the archaeologist the reconstruction is the aim and end of his endeavors, while for analysis the construction is only a preliminary labor." He continues, "The analyst finishes a piece of construction and communicates it to the subject of the analysis so that it may work upon him." In the case of the Rat Man, Freud's constructions "worked upon" the patient so well that his symptoms were relieved before the whole story of his infantile neurosis could be pieced together. "It was impossible to unravel this tissue of fantasy thread by thread," Freud writes in a footnote, because

the therapeutic success of the treatment was precisely what stood in the way of this. The patient recovered, and his ordinary life began to assert its claims: there were many tasks before him, which he had already neglected far too long, and which were incompatible with a continuation of the treatment. I am not to be blamed, therefore, for this gap in the analysis. The scientific results of psychoanalysis are at present only a by-product of its therapeutic aims, and for that reason it is often just in those cases where treatment fails that most discoveries are made.

The Rat Man's crippling obsessional neurosis—his tormenting idea that the woman he loved and also his (dead!) father were being subjected to a horrible Turkish torture—was gradually "worn away" during analysis as his unconscious hatred for his father came into consciousness. But, Freud writes, "it was only along the painful road of transference that he was able to reach a conviction that his relation to his father really necessitated the postulation of this unconscious complement," and he goes on to describe the rather comical as-if form of the Rat Man's transference:

> Things soon reached a point at which, in his dreams, his waking fantasies, and his associations, he began heaping the grossest and filthiest abuse upon me and my family, though in his deliberate actions he never treated me with anything but the greatest respect. His demeanour as he repeated these insults to me was that of a man in despair. "How can a gentleman like you, sir," he used to ask, "let yourself be abused in this way by a low, good-for-nothing fellow like me? You ought to turn me out: that's all I deserve." While he talked like this, he would get up from the sofa and roam about the room—a habit which he explained at first as being due to delicacy of feeling: he could not bring himself, he said, to utter such horrible things while he was lying there so comfortably. But soon he himself found a more cogent explanation, namely, that he was avoiding my proximity for fear of my giving him a beating. . . . His father had had a passionate temper, and sometimes in his violence had not known where to stop. Thus, little by little, in this school of suffering, the patient won the sense of conviction which he had lacked—though to any disinterested mind the truth would have been almost self-evident.

Dora, the eighteen-year-old subject of Freud's first major case history (written in 1901 and published in 1905, under the title "Fragment of an Analysis of a Case of Hysteria"), never gained the Rat Man's sense of conviction about the unconscious. After three months spent in complaining angrily about her dire family situation and listening skeptically to Freud's incredible dream interpretations and improbable constructions about her infantile sexuality, she abruptly quit the analysis, her hysteria intact— and thus provided Freud with the instructive failure that he spoke of so wistfully in the Rat Man case. She has also provided our Freud-obsessed age with a kind of marvelous fetish: we cherish the Dora case, because it proves that Freud, who told us such unpleasant truths about ourselves, was himself just another pitiful, deluded, dirty-minded neurotic. The Dora case shows us a Freud out of control, a Freud whose genius has gone awry, a Freud who can be likened to an analytic patient in the grip of a powerful regressive transference. Or, perhaps more to the point of our own transference relationship to Freud, he is like an analyst who has slipped up and at last given the patient something "real" to work with in his desperate struggle against his interlocutor's maddening disinterestedness.

A recently published anthology called *In Dora's Case: Freud —Hysteria—Feminism*, which was edited by Charles Bernheimer and Claire Kahane (Columbia University Press, 1985) and is largely devoted to writings of the past ten years by young and youngish literary critics who teach English and comparative literature at American and English universities, put me in mind of a scene in Virginia Woolf's *The Years*—the scene that forms the novel's symbolic center—where two little girls excitedly dance and leap around a bonfire lit for the older girl's birthday. These new writings—feminist, deconstructive, and Lacanian, for the most part—have a wild playfulness and a sort of sexual sparkle that flicker through their academic patois and give them an extraordinary verve. (There are also writings from the fifties and sixties by three psychoanalysts—Felix Deutsch, Erik Erikson, and Lacan himself—who form a sort of subdued elder-statesman group, with a transferential agenda different from that of the contemporary lit-crit contributors.) These New Critics of psychoanalysis worry Freud's text as if it were a metaphysical poem and, adroitly using Freud's own weapons against him, find example upon example of unconscious self-betrayal. A telltale passage on which a number of them pounce is the paragraph that follows Freud's interpretation of Dora's nervous cough: it is, he tells her, the hysterical representation of an unconscious fantasy in which she pictures her father's mistress, Frau K., performing fellatio on the father. Freud anticipates the "astonishment and horror" of the reader at his "daring to talk about such delicate and unpleasant subjects to a young girl," and goes on, rather preposterously:

It is possible for a man to talk to girls and women upon sexual matters of every kind without doing them harm and without bringing suspicion upon himself, so long as, in the first place, he adopts a particular way of doing it, and, in the second place, can make them feel convinced that it is unavoidable. A gynaecologist, after all, under the same conditions, does not hesitate to make them submit to uncovering every possible part of their body. The best way of speaking about such things is to be dry and direct; and that is at the same time the method furthest removed from the prurience with which the same subjects are handled in "society," and to which girls and women alike are so thoroughly accustomed. I call bodily organs and processes by their technical names, and I tell these to the patient if they—the names, I mean—happen to be unknown to her. *J'appelle un chat un chat.*

Jane Gallop, in an essay entitled "Keys to Dora," charmingly points out:

At the very moment he defines non-prurient language as direct and non-euphemistic, he takes a French detour into a figurative expression. By his terms, this French sentence would seem to be titillating, coy, flirtatious. And to make matters more juicy (less "dry"), *chat* or *chatte* can be used as vulgar (vulvar) slang for the female genitalia. So in this gynecological context, where he founds his innocence upon the direct use of technical terms, he takes a French detour and calls a pussy a pussy.

The fellatio interpretation itself becomes the object of ribald one-upmanship among the new commentators. Toril Moi, in her essay "Representation of Patriarchy: Sexuality and Epistemology in Freud's Dora," writes that "it would not be difficult to detect in Freud a defensive reaction-formation." She continues:

It is little wonder that he feels the need to defend himself against the idea of fellatio, since it is more than probable that the fantasy exists, not in Dora's mind, but in his alone. Freud has informed us that Dora's father was impotent, and assumes this to be the basis of Dora's "repulsive and perverted phantasy." According to Freud, the father cannot manage penetration, so Frau K. must perform fellatio instead. But as Lacan has pointed out, this argument reveals an astonishing lack of logic on Freud's part. In the case of male impotence, the man is obviously much more likely, *faute de mieux*, to perform cunnilingus. As Lacan writes: "Everyone knows that cunnilingus is the artifice most commonly adopted by 'men of means' whose powers begin to abandon them."

Neil Hertz, in his essay "Dora's Secrets, Freud's Techniques," also quotes Lacan's magisterial line, and wryly remarks, "It is hard to guess what Freud would have made of this note of high Parisian *savoir vivre;* whatever everyone else knew, he seems to have taken for granted the more phallic—and phallocentric—option." Hertz goes on to play with the conceit of "oral intercourse in the other sense of that term"—i.e., the verbal one—and to propose that as "Dora refuses to 'know' that when she coughs she is picturing to herself a scene of oral gratification," so "Freud has every reason to deny that his own conversations with girls like Dora are titillating."

Like the perverse fantasies and dreams about Freud and his family that enabled the Rat Man to tell his analyst of his hatred (and love) of him, the sex-playful explications of Gallop, Moi,

Hertz, et al. (and also, of course, my own explication of their explications) carry an unmistakable transferential weight. Like the Rat Man's dead father, the dead father of psychoanalysis still "lives" in our imagination as a sort of superstar professor, whose classes are so big that in order to attract his attention we practically have to make public nuisances of ourselves. "I believe that Freud would have been the first to be amused by the observation that in this splendid extended declaration about plain speech . . . he feels it necessary to disappear not once but twice into French," Steven Marcus writes in his anthology essay "Freud and Dora: Story, History, Case History," making manifest what the other commentators carefully leave latent. (We are back in the passage about calling a cat a cat. Freud's second disappearance into French, a paragraph later, is *"Pour faire une omelette il faut casser des oeufs."*)

In addition to the father/naughty-children transference, there are sibling transferences, which carry the book into yet another emotional field. Toril Moi's unpleasant remark about a fellow contributor's essay—that Maria Ramas's " 'theoretical' inquiry advances little beyond a scrupulous, somewhat tedious résumé of Freud's text"—has some of the atmosphere of a waiting-room encounter between a departing analytic patient and an arriving one. Claire Kahane, in her introduction, administers a kind of watchful child's justice in pointing out Marcus's (unacknowledged) intellectual debt to Philip Rieff, who "already in 1962 . . . had emphasized . . . the literary nature of the case history as a genre" and had likened "Fragment of an Analysis"—in its labyrinthine narrative structure—to a work of modernist fiction.

Marcus's elaboration of Rieff's suggestion is the matrix of his influential *Freud and Dora: Story, History, Case History* (1974). In it, he characterizes the Dora case as "a great work of literature" and sees Freud as a sort of unwitting modernist master; he writes of the case history's "innovations in formal structure," its "Nabokovian frame," and its "unreliable narrator." But an unwitting modernist is a contradiction in terms, if by modernist literature we mean a certain kind of acutely self-aware writing. In back of every unreliable narrator of modernist fiction stands a reliably artful author. In Dora, however, the Freud who is writing the case history and the Freud who is narrating it are one and the same person. If *Pale Fire* had been *written* by the madman Charles Kinbote as well as narrated by him, there would be an analogy between Nabokov's novel and Freud's case history. Marcus struggles manfully with the contradiction but cannot resolve it: "If Freud communicates in this piece of writing a less than complete understanding of himself . . . like any great writer he provides us with the material for understanding some things that have escaped his own understanding, for filling in some gaps, for restoring certain fragments into wholes." It is in his analysis of Freud as madman rather than as modernist that Marcus makes his most valuable contribution. (As if to blunt his transgression, Marcus constantly calls Freud a "genius" and a "great writer," and wherever he directly challenges Freud he hastens to perform a little caper of propitiation—one recalls the Rat Man's nervous scurryings away from the couch lest Freud hit him—speaking of "this great text," "this passage of unquestionable genius," "an extraordinary piece of writing," "a masterpiece," "a scene that Freud orchestrates with inimitable richness," "the tact and sense of form that one associates with a classical composer of music." The younger siblings who follow in Marcus's footsteps evidently feel none of Marcus's need to appease the father; they attack the father with cool impunity—more confident of his love, perhaps.) Marcus draws attention to the "weirdness and wildness" of Freud's text and notes that it is the analyst rather than the patient who is its true subject: "The case history belongs progressively less to her than it does to him," and by the end "it is his *own* mind that chiefly matters to him."

Following Marcus's cue, the recent commentators place themselves at the head of the couch on which Freud has, so to speak, flung himself in writing the case history and, with an analyst's closely hovering attention, seek to catch the drift of his deeply stirred-up unconscious. Toril Moi performs an arresting feat of interpretation when she connects Freud's recurrent frettings about the fragmentary, incomplete, gap-filled state of his text to his "deeply unconscious patriarchal ideology." She quotes a famous passage from the Dora "Fragment," which contains yet another use by Freud of his beloved archaeological metaphor:

> In the face of the incompleteness of my analytic results, I had no choice but to follow the example of those discoverers whose good fortune it is to bring to the light of day after their long burial the priceless though mutilated relics of antiquity. I have restored what is missing, taking the best models known to me from other analyses; but like a conscientious archaeologist, I have not omitted to mention in each case where the authentic parts end and my construction begins.

She then points out what else it is that Freud is talking about:

> "The priceless though mutilated relics of antiquity" are not only Dora's story: they are Dora herself, her genitals and the feminine epistemological model. Freud makes sure that the message here is clear: "mutilated" is his usual way of describing the effect of castration, and "priceless" also means just what it says: price-less, without value. For how can there be value when the valuable piece has been cut off? The relics are mutilated, the penis has been cut. Freud's task is therefore momentous: he must "restore what is missing"; his penis must fill the epistemological hole represented by Dora.

Neil Hertz's fine-tuned third ear picks up Freud's fear not only of actual sexual entanglement with Dora but of "epistemological promiscuity in which the lines would blur between what Dora knew and what Freud knew, and, consequently, in which the status of Freud's knowledge, and of his professional discoúrse, would be impugned." This fear, of course, haunts every analysis, enters the transference as well as the counter-transference, and is inextricably bound up with the analytic fee. For what the analyst is "selling" is precisely the difference of his psychoanalytic discourse from the discourses of ordinary, conscious life and common sense. If the analyst is to earn his fee, and the talking cure isn't to be mere talk, only the uncommon sense of the patient's symptoms and behaviors may be allowed status in the analysis. Freud seemed to be groping his way toward an understanding of the necessary epistemological inequality between the analytic interlocutors when, in the chapter on the psychotherapy of hysteria in *Studies on Hysteria* (1893–95), he wrote, "It is of course of great importance for the progress of the analysis that one should always turn out to be in the right vis-à-vis the patient, otherwise one would always be dependent on what he chose to tell one."

Jane Gallop examines the lopsided patient-analyst relationship in terms of the analyst's economic dependence on the patient. The starting point of her very original discussion of the analyst as paid servant is the scene in "Dora" where the girl walks into Freud's office and announces that this is her last session. Freud unemotionally asks her when she formed her resolve to quit the analysis. She replies, "A fortnight ago, I think," and he tartly comments, "That sounds just like a maid-servant or a governess—a fortnight's warning." Gallop pauses before the comment's manifest ambiguity—"Is the servant giving two weeks' notice before quitting, or is the master giving the servant two weeks' notice"—and opts for the latter reading, an interpretation that one intuitively feels is indeed the one Freud "meant." "Identification between Freud and a governess, maid, or nurse is not restricted to the confines of the Dora case but has a decisive, structural relation to psychoanalysis in general," Gallop writes. She correctly identifies the analytic fee as the fulcrum of transference interpretation—"The money proves that the analyst is only a stand-in"—and continues, "Rather than having the power of life and death like the mother has over the infant, the analyst is financially dependent on the patient. But, in that case, the original 'analyst,' the earliest person paid to replace the mother, is that frequent character in Freud's histories, the nursemaid/governess." In the Dora analysis, however, Freud was not entirely willing to accept the humble role of the servant: he struggled against its alterity; he wanted "in"—he wanted, as Gallop puts it, "to be the Mother (the phallic mother, Lacan's Other, the subject presumed to know, the Doctor) rather than the nurse"—and this was his undoing with Dora, just as every analyst is undone when he wants to move into the patient's family, when he doesn't know his place, which is outside. When we speak of the analyst's countertransference, we refer to some such breaching of "class" lines.

TODAY, analysts enjoy so much social prestige, have so much money, and are so pompous that the governess/nurse figure—the analyst as Jane Eyre—seems very figurative indeed. But when the metaphor is applied to Freud of the 1880s, 1890s, and early 1900s, it is less farfetched. At the time Freud was doing cathartic and then early analytic therapy, he was such an irregular sort of doctor (according to Peter Swales's recent study *Freud, His Teacher, and the Birth of Psychoanalysis*, he was known as "*der Zauberer*," the magician, by the children of Anna von Lieben, a rich patient whom he treated at home in the 1880s) that it isn't even certain he was always admitted by the front door when he made house calls. From *Studies on Hysteria* (to which Swales's study forms a valuable pendant), we gain a sense not only of the wild, ad hoc nature of Freud's early therapy but of the marginality of his social position. He was more like one of today's mildly disreputable alternative-medicine men than like a "real" doctor. In the Frau Emmy von N. case, we read of Freud's twice-a-day visits to the sanitarium where his hysterical patient was staying—of his massages, his pacifying hypnotic suggestions, and his nannylike interest in whether she ate her dessert or threw it out the window. Another of his patients—a young Englishwoman, Lucy R.—was actually a governess herself, and one is struck by the tone of cordiality, almost of collegiality, that creeps into Freud's account of his treatment of her. Like him, and in marked contrast to the idle rich women like Emmy von N. and Cäcilie M. (as Freud called Anna von Lieben in *Studies*), Lucy R. had to earn her living and was dependent on the goodwill, and frequently on the whim, of her employer. (In *Studies*, Freud writes with similar friendliness of the eighteen-year-old Katharina, another "service industry" colleague, who waited on table at her mother's mountain inn—Freud stayed there during a vacation—and whose anxiety attacks he traced to an incident of childhood sexual molestation. "I owed her a debt of gratitude for having made it so much easier for me to talk to her than to the prudish ladies of my city practice, who regard whatever is natural as shameful," he wrote.) Lucy R.'s chief hysterical symptom was the loss of her sense of smell, accompanied by a persistent imaginary smell of burnt pudding. Freud traced the latter to a nursery incident in the house where she was working—some pudding had actually burned—and eventually to the fact that she was in love with her employer, the widowed director of a factory in Outer Vienna. Freud writes:

I said to her, "I cannot think that these are all the reasons for your feelings about the children. I believe that really you are in love with your employer, the Director, though perhaps without being aware of it yourself, and that you have a secret hope of taking their mother's place in actual fact. . . ." She answered in her usual laconic fashion: "Yes, I think that's true."—"But if you knew you loved your employer, why didn't you tell me?"—"I didn't know—or rather I didn't want

to know. I wanted to drive it out of my head and not think
of it again; and I believe latterly I have succeeded."

In a footnote, Freud remarks of this answer, "I have never
managed to give a better description than this of the strange
state of mind in which one knows and does not know a thing
at the same time . . . that blindness of the seeing eye which is
so astonishing in the attitude of mothers to their daughters,
husbands to their wives and rulers to their favorites." However,
contrary to Freud's expectations, his interpretation did not then
and there cure Lucy of her bizarre symptom. In the next few
weeks, the smell of burnt pudding gradually receded, only to
be replaced by the smell of cigar smoke. "It had been there
earlier as well, she thought, but had, as it were, been covered
by the smell of the pudding. Now it had emerged by itself."
Lucy was one of the first patients on whom Freud tried his
"pressure technique," in the place of hypnosis (which he apparently wasn't too adept at), to elicit the desired "forgotten
memory"; he would place his hand on the patient's forehead,
or take her head in his hands, and say, "You will think of it
under the pressure of my hand. At the moment at which I relax
my pressure, you will see something in front of you, or something will come into your head. Catch hold of it. It will be what
we are looking for." Using this technique, he traced the cigar
smoke to a scene at the end of a luncheon at the house of the
Director/Mr. Rochester, when the men were smoking cigars
and the Director had shouted at a poor accountant for kissing
the children. This scene led Freud back to the Ur-scene of
Lucy's hysteria, a traumatic incident in which the Director,
having lashed out at Lucy herself for allowing a visitor to
kiss the children on the mouth, had mortifyingly crushed
her hopes of his love. This time, the therapy took. Two days
later, a radiantly happy Lucy walked into Freud's consultation room. "She was as though transfigured," Freud writes, and
continues:

She was smiling and carried her head high. I thought for a moment that after all I had been wrong about the situation, and that the children's governess had become the Director's fiancée. But she dispelled my notion. "Nothing has happened. It's just that you don't know me. You have only seen me ill and depressed. I'm always cheerful as a rule. When I woke yesterday morning, the weight was no longer on my mind, and since then I have felt well."—"And what do you think of your prospects in the house?"—"I am quite clear on the subject. I know I have none, and I shan't make myself unhappy over it." . . . "And are you still in love with your employer?"—"Yes, I certainly am, but that makes no difference. After all, I can have thoughts and feelings to myself."

As this remarkable passage suggests, Freud's identification with the governess had become so nearly complete that it is he, the doctor, who articulates the fantasy of the governess who becomes the Director's fiancée, and she, the patient, who, in a wonderful kind of reversal, has to remind Freud that when hysterical misery has been transformed into common unhappiness (or, as the case may be, stiff-upper-lip cheerfulness), there is reason enough for rejoicing. *Studies on Hysteria* is full of such reversals; the book as a whole could be characterized as the story of the gradual transformation of a naively blundering hypnotist into the composed founder of psychoanalysis. The Freud who emerges from the book is startlingly young and tentative; if he already exhibits the intellectual agility of the mature Freud, he has none of the latter's magisterial, somewhat grumpy manner. The mature Freud was always defending himself against "the opponents of psychoanalysis"; the young Freud could hardly flatter himself on having opponents, since no one had even heard of him, and he didn't himself yet really know what he was doing. Each of the cases in *Studies* is a humble little progress report on the education of the first psychoanalyst, whose only claim to cleverness was that he didn't pretend to know more than he did, but knew enough to learn from un-expected sources of knowledge. Readers of the mature Freudian texts will recognize what Neil Hertz calls the pose of "the Impressionable Junior Colleague," whose credulity is both a shield against vulgar error and a weapon that penetrates to the truth of things. In "On the History of the Psychoanalytic Movement" (where Freud recounts anecdotes about himself vis-à-vis his mentors Charcot and Breuer, thus giving Hertz his tag), Freud looks back on the period of his " 'splendid isolation' "—"those lonely years, away from the pressures and confusions of today"—when "I was not subject to influence from any quarter; there was nothing to hustle me," and "I learnt to restrain speculative tendencies and to follow the unforgotten advice of my master, Charcot: to look at the same things again and again until they themselves begin to speak."

This piece of naive empiricism cannot itself be taken at face value. Freud knew quite as well as we do that nothing "speaks" but men's theories; he opens his paper "Instincts and Their Vicissitudes" (1915) with an almost Kuhnian discussion of the relationship of theory to observation in scientific method:

Even at the stage of description it is not possible to avoid applying certain abstract ideas to the material in hand, ideas derived from somewhere or other but certainly not from the new observations alone. Such ideas—which will later become the basic concepts of the science—are still more indispensable as the material is further worked over. They must at first necessarily possess some degree of indefiniteness; there can be no question of any clear delimitation of their content. So long as they remain in this condition, we come to an understanding about their meaning by making repeated references to the material of observation from which they appear to have been derived, but upon which, in fact, they have been imposed. Thus, strictly speaking, they are in the nature of conventions—although everything depends on their not being arbitrarily chosen but determined by their having significant relations to the empirical material, relations that we seem to sense before we can clearly recognize and demonstrate them.

His insistent depiction of himself as a sort of irrepressible stumbler upon solid scientific fact ("There I go, discovering something again!") was a kind of necessary alibi for the promoter of a therapy whose most salient feature was its erotic potential. Freud grasped that if psychoanalysis—with its love-affair-like privacy, intimacy, and intensity—wasn't going to be disreputable it was going to have to be severely depersonalized and firmly relabeled as a science. In their original and underrated book, *The Therapeutic Revolution, from Mesmer to Freud*, Léon Chertok and the late Raymond de Saussure trace a line from the "universal fluid" theory of the eighteenth-century magnetists to the Freudian concept of transference, finding the latter a kind of culminating prophylaxis against the sexual temptations of psychotherapy—a sort of duenna that hovers over the therapeutic pair and keeps them from overstepping the bounds of propriety. But long before Freud developed the full-blown concept of transference he was an adept of the "dry" manner of which he speaks in the Dora case. One has only to compare Freud's cases in *Studies* with Breuer's case of Anna O. to see the distance that Freud had gone beyond his mentor in learning how to play with fire without burning the house down. That the Anna O. case would end as it did—with the frightened doctor fleeing from the lovesick patient—could have been predicted from the start: Breuer's fondness for the girl, his loverlike attentivenesses, and his admiration of her person were the mechanisms of cure, and once these were withdrawn she could only fall ill again. Freud clearly realized that such a state of affairs had to be avoided at all costs; his tone toward the women in *Studies* is consistently and entirely asexual. But it was Freud's genius to presently see (as none of his predecessors had seen) that for sex to be kept at bay in therapy, only *one* member of the therapeutic pair—namely, the doctor—has to behave himself. When Freud gave his female patients permission to declare their love for him (and his male patients permission to abuse him), psychoanalysis proper was under way. Before that moment, Freud only obscurely understood the newness and bizarreness of the psychoanalytic relationship, its utter unlikeness—in its antinomies of silence and speech, reticence and abandon, veiledness and nakedness—to any other relationship in life. At the time of *Studies*, Freud knew how to behave correctly but didn't yet know how to think analytically; by the time of the Dora case, he was on the verge of becoming a psychoanalyst. He was discovering the devilish complexity of this thing he had "stumbled" upon, and how inadequate the straightforward narrative form of the rudimentary *Studies* cases was for representing cases of more fully developed analysis. "I was trained to employ local diagnoses and electro-prognosis, and it still strikes me myself as strange that the case histories I write should read like short stories and that, as one might say, they lack the serious stamp of science," Freud writes in the Elisabeth von R. case in *Studies*. He goes on, "I must console myself with the reflection that the nature of the subject is evidently responsible for this, rather than any preference of my own. The fact is that local diagnosis and electrical reactions lead nowhere in the study of hysteria, whereas a detailed description of mental processes such as we are accustomed to find in the works of imaginative writers enables me, with the use of a few psychological formulas, to obtain at least some kind of insight into the course of that affection." In the Dora case, this pleasant and easy literary formula no longer suffices, and Freud repudiates it thus:

I must now turn to consider a further complication, to which I should certainly give no space if I were a man of letters engaged upon the creation of a mental state like this for a short story, instead of being a medical man engaged upon its dissection. The element to which I must now allude can only serve to obscure and efface the outlines of the fine poetic conflict which we have been able to ascribe to Dora. This element would rightly fall a sacrifice to the censorship of a writer, for he, after all, simplifies and abstracts when he appears in the character of a psychologist. But in the world of reality, which I am trying to depict here, a complication of motives, an accumulation and conjunction of mental activities—in a word, overdetermination—is the rule.

The complication that was turning Freud's dry Viennese *Liaisons Dangereuses* into a Swiftian nightmare of bed-wetting, thumb-sucking, fellatio, masturbation, venereal disease, vaginal discharge, and gastric pain was Freud's libido theory. Writing of the case of Emmy von N., in the *Studies*, Freud recalled that at the time (1889), "I regarded the linking of hysteria with the topic of sexuality as a sort of insult—just as the women patients themselves do." By the time of the Dora case, Freud regarded the linking of hysteria with sexuality as a sine qua non. In the Freud-Fliess letters, we can trace the evolution of Freud's thinking from his idea of the mid-1890s—that hysteria could always be traced to an episode or episodes of sexual abuse in early childhood (the "seduction theory")—to his gradual realization that child molesters weren't required for the stunting of a person's psychosexual development; the potential for psychosexual catastrophe lies in wait for us all in the ordinary vicissitudes of infantile life. In the Clark Lectures of 1909, Freud noted, "People are in general not candid over sexual matters. They do not show their sexuality freely, but to conceal it they wear a heavy overcoat woven of a tissue of lies, as though the weather were bad in the world of sexuality." Just how bad this weather was was indicated in *Three Essays on the Theory of Sexuality*, published in 1905 (the same year the Dora case was published). To accomplish the feat of becoming a "normal" sexually active adult was, in Freud's view, about as probable for most people as winning the lottery. The path from the polymorphous perversity of infancy to the missionary position of adulthood is littered with obstacles; in moving from the oral to the anal and on to the genital stages of infancy (and we are talking here about the mewling, puking, sucking, defecating, rhythmically rocking, touching, stroking infant's *imagination* in relation to these activities and to interferences with them), the individual invariably gets a little or very stuck, and in the genital, or Oedipal, period he or she suffers wounds that never heal. Whether one becomes a pervert or a neurotic depends on constitution and circumstance, and is a kind of six-of-one, half-a-dozen-of-the-other "choice," according to the *Three Essays*. When Freud was treating Dora, he was forming this dour view of sexuality and, most daunting of all, the conviction that this misery-filled aspect of the human condition was its central fact. He was coming to see that the scenes he worked so hard to elicit from his patients in the *Studies*—the burnt-pudding scene in Lucy R., or the scene in the Elisabeth von R. case in which she comes to her sister's deathbed and has the "pathogenic" (i.e., morally unacceptable) idea that now that her sister is dead her brother-in-law is free to marry her—were not the final destination of the psychoanalytic journey. He understood that he had to go beyond the novelistic plots and characters of the patient's present life and recent past, cross the river Lethe, and penetrate the obscure, inchoate, shade-populated region of infant sorrow where the patient was still haplessly living. In the Wolf Man and the Rat Man cases, Freud makes this crossing; in the writing of both case histories he eliminates almost everything pertaining to the patient's adult biography and confines himself to the exotic inner world of the Oedipal and pre-Oedipal child. The only fully alive contemporary character in the Wolf Man and Rat Man cases is Freud, the narrator. The patient isn't there; he is like an anesthetized body on which an operation is being performed. The Dora case—where Freud has not yet arrived at his final vision of the psychoanalytic case history and is still rendering the patient as a character in a nineteenth-century novel, and also as the host of a kind of operable cancer—reads like an account of an operation being performed on a fully awake patient. Thus its agony and its horror. Every reader of "Fragment of an Analysis" comes away with the feeling that something awful has been done to the girl. The Dora case is known as the case that illustrates Freud's failure to interpret the transference in time; even more, it illustrates a failure of narration. Freud tells the novelistic story of Dora so well that the psychoanalytic story—the narrative of the analyst's probe into the patient's unconscious being—reads like an assault, almost like a rape; we cannot but feel outraged as Freud describes the girl's desperate attempts to elude him while he obscenely moves in on her. (In the Rat Man and the Wolf Man cases, where we follow the surgeon's movements as he cuts into a small area of flesh surrounded by surgical drapery, we feel no such outrage.)

Moreover, and paradoxically, the superlative telling of the novelistic story of Dora has made Freud more vulnerable to the charges of misogyny and sexism that are regularly leveled at him than he might have been if he had been a less gifted writer. In the standard feminist version of the Dora case, the attractive, spirited, intellectually precocious eighteen-year-old hysterical girl is a victim both of a society that gives women no opportunities to use their minds and of a particularly nasty family constellation—a "charmless circle," as Philip Rieff has memorably described it, of "a sick daughter, [who] has a sick father, who has a sick mistress, who has a sick husband, who proposes himself to the sick daughter as her lover." Dora's father and Herr K., the mistress's husband, have a sinister unspoken pact whereby Dora is to be handed over to Herr K. in exchange for his toleration of the father's affair with Frau K. When Dora refuses to play the game, and slaps Herr K.'s face in answer to a proposition he makes her during a walk beside a lake, Herr K. and the father attempt to browbeat her into admitting that the proposition was never made but was a product of her sexually overheated fancy. Freud is enlisted by the father as an ally in the subduing of the rebellious daughter; the girl is handed over (Freud's term in both cases) to him for indoctrination. Though Freud's natural tendency is to side with respectable grown men against irritating hysterical girls, he is obliged to see that in this instance it is the girl who is telling the truth and the men who are lying to save their reputations. He reluctantly declines to be part of the male plot against the girl.

This gynophilic account, as it happens, is also Freud's own account of Dora's life situation—and, indeed, it is the *only* account of it we have. But such are Freud's narrative powers, and so compelling is the verisimilitude he achieves, that, like the Greek artist Zeuxis, who painted such realistic grapes that birds pecked at them, Freud fools us into believing that we are in the face of unmediated reality. Even a reader as sophisticated as Steven Marcus falls into the trap. Early in his essay, he writes, "It may be helpful for the reader if at the outset I briefly review some of the external facts of the case"—as if such "facts" could be looked up in some archive. But there is no archive. Everything we know about Dora and her father and the K.s is what Freud has chosen to tell us, and everything we think and feel about them is what Freud has directed us to think and feel. The "fact" that Herr K. propositioned Dora and then lied is Freud's "fact." Before writing the case history, Freud had made up his mind that the scene by the lake was not a fantasy, and his "fair-minded" account ("I had resolved from the first to suspend my judgment of the true state of affairs") was written under and shaped by this conviction. For all we know, however, the actual, historical Dora may have invented the scene by the lake, and the actual, historical Herr K. may have been telling the truth. Another writer could have made the episode an illustration of how hysterical, lying women can bring trouble upon innocent, respectable men. But as Freud structured his account of it, the truth and goodness of the girl and the falsity and badness of the father and Herr K. are as unarguable as are the traits of princesses and ogres in fairy stories. The feminists who innocently peck at Freud's grapes (I am not talking about the savvy feminist writers of *In Dora's Case*)—who charge Freud with insufficient understanding of and sympathy for the beleaguered girl's plight at the hands of the creepy men around her—should understand the extent to which their own understanding of and sympathy for the girl are artifacts of Freud's rhetoric.

STANLEY FISH, in his beguiling essay "Withholding the Missing Portion: Power, Meaning, and Persuasion in Freud's 'The Wolf-Man' " (*Times Literary Supplement*, August 29, 1986), characterizes the Wolf Man case as a dazzling rhetorical exercise, and Freud as the most exquisitely artful of persuaders, who is able to palm off on the reader, as he was evidently able to palm off on the patient, a mad, weird story about a neurosis based on a one-and-a-half-year-old child's witnessing of parental intercourse "*a tergo*"—a story that has nothing "out there" to support it and is fueled only by the power of Freud's "continual need to control, to convince, and to seduce, in endless vacillation with the equally powerful need to disclaim any trace of influence, and to present himself as the passive conduit of forces that exist independently of him." Far from being critical of Freud's spurious positivism, Fish believes that "were we to fault him . . . and accuse him of bad faith we would be committing a deep philosophical mistake, the mistake of thinking that our convictions can and *should* be shaken by the knowledge that they are unsupported by anything external to themselves." Fish's discussion is part of—lies in the most nihilistic corner of—the larger debate on the nature of knowing, which touches every field of discourse today; and in its own rhetorical incandescence it powerfully illuminates the deconstructive epistemology. But it is riddled by a problem of logic, a paradox—namely, that in persuading us of the daftness and preposterousness of Freud's narrative, Fish defeats his own claim that Freud is persuasive. If Freud is so persuasive, why does Fish remain unpersuaded? Why does he retell Freud's story of the Wolf Man's infantile neurosis with the irony of a skeptic rather than with the credulity of one on whom rhetoric has done its work? Is it possible, then, that Fish is mistaken, and that "The Wolf Man" is *not*, after all, a great masterpiece of rhetoric?

It has long been my own belief that Freud's three major case histories (I omit "Little Hans" and "Schreber," because they are not about patients whom Freud saw himself) are indeed rhetorically ineffectual—neither great literature nor great psychoanalysis but a kind of doomed literary experiment in a genre whose center cannot hold. Freud himself understood the impossibility of the task he had set himself, and began each case with a disclaimer. "Analyses such as this are not published in order to produce conviction in the minds of those whose attitude has hitherto been recusant and skeptical," he writes in the Wolf Man case, adding, "The intention is only to bring forward some new facts for investigators who have already been convinced by their own clinical experiences." In the Dora case, Freud warns the reader who is not familiar with his theory of dream interpretation that he will find "only bewilderment in these pages instead of the enlightenment he is in search of, and . . . will certainly be inclined to project the cause of his bewilderment onto the author and to pronounce his views fantastic." In the Rat Man case, Freud apologizes for his "disconnected statements of an aphoristic character" and the mere "crumbs of knowledge" he offers instead of a full, coherent narrative. After 1918, Freud stopped writing full-scale case histories, and later analysts have not revived the form. However, in recent years the major Freudian case histories have taken on a new life as sorts of "found objects" of the literary academy. Removed from their own contexts and placed in that of literary modernism, they have undergone the transformation that patchwork quilts, Shaker chairs, Yale locks, and other vernacular and folk-art forms underwent when removed from their context and scrutinized in the light of twentieth-century Functionalism. As these objects took on a beauty that their makers never intended them to have, and that was not apparent to their original users, so the Wolf Man, the Rat Man, and the Dora cases have acquired a kind of poetry they did not have when they were read only by bored candidates at psychoanalytic institutes. Today, they are rich, mysterious, wild, infinitely ambiguous texts, which seem to restore to dull, medicalized, suburbanized American psychoanalysis some of its original radical strangeness—which appear to cut through the antiseptic blandness of ego psychology and penetrate to the hard, sharp, bleeding core of (as Lacan called it) "*la chose Freudienne*" itself. But in fact the core of the Freudian thing lies elsewhere. In his prefatory remarks to the Dora case, Freud explains that he has deliberately excluded from his account almost all mention of what he calls "the technique of the analytic work." We now know, as Freud was on the verge of knowing, how crucial this excluded portion is. It is in the particular, idiosyncratic, ineffable encounter between patient and analyst that the "story" of an analysis is lodged. The Rat Man's transferential wanderings around the consultation room and Freud's countertransferential "dry" manner with Dora are what constitute the "plot" of an analysis, and it is in his papers on technique—"The Dynamics of Transference" (1912), "Recommendations to Physicians Practising Psychoanalysis" (1912), "On Beginning the Treatment" (1913), "Remembering, Repeating, and Working-Through" (1914), and "Observations on Transference Love" (1915)—that Freud codifies the clinical theory he has hitherto scattered piecemeal through his writings. The technical papers are the poetics (as well as the nursing manual) of psychoanalysis. A reading of these laconic, deceptively straightforward essays quickly dispels the misconception that Marcus, among other literary Freudians, has given currency to—that psychoanalysis is a sort of cure by narrative. Peter Brooks, in his book *Reading for the Plot: Design and Intention in Narrative*, writes:

There is in Freud's case histories an underlying assumption that psychic health corresponds to a coherent narrative account of one's life. As Steven Marcus notes in his discussion of the case history of Dora, "Human life is, ideally, a connected and coherent story, with all the details in explanatory place, and with everything (or as close to everything as is practically possible) accounted for, in its proper causal or other sequence. And inversely illness amounts at least in part to suffering from an incoherent story or an inadequate narrative account of oneself."

But this "underlying assumption" is nowhere to be found in Freud's writings. Quite on the contrary, as we have seen in the footnote in the Rat Man case, Freud distinguishes between narrative closure and therapeutic benefit. Moreover—as both Brooks and Marcus refuse to notice—the protagonist of the Freudian case history is not an analytic patient trying to make a narrative of his life but a small child struggling (and tragically failing) to fathom the actions of his parents. Brooks trivially but seriously misreads Freud when he writes, "The modernist thirst for myth, for explanatory and justificatory masterplots, which we find not only in Joyce, Mann, Faulkner, but also in Yeats, Eliot, Gide, Kafka, Giraudoux, and so many others, is suggested in Freud's comment that a person 'catches hold of this phylogenetic experience where his own experience fails him. He fills in the gaps in individual truth with prehistoric truth.' " For what Freud wrote in the Wolf Man case was not that a person but that a *child* catches hold of this phylogenetic experience—in this instance, a one-and-a-half-year-old infant. These powerful, magical stories that we as infants tell ourselves are never outlived or forgotten. They remain in unconscious thought, and they cause us poignant suffering throughout our conscious lives. Psychoanalysis seeks to mitigate our sufferings by loosening the hold of these stories on us—by convincing us, through the transference, that they are stories, and not the way things "are." At the same time—and this is why psychoanalysis has never recommended itself to certain precise and orderly minds and will always appeal to poets and other mentally lax types—these stories are not dismissed, dispatched, destroyed. They are regarded with awe. In Freud's metaphor of wearing away, there is tacit recognition of the durability of neurosis and the modesty of the program of psychotherapy. As Freud realized that neurosis was the human condition—that the people with florid symptoms who came to him for treatment were only a little further along a continuum—he came to understand that every analysis is a failure. It has to be. A "successful" analysis would be monstrous. In "On Transference Love," Freud writes of the female patient's need to "acquire the extra piece of mental freedom which distinguishes conscious mental activity—in the systematic sense—from unconscious" in order to overcome her obsessive, desperate, crazy, sick love for her analyst. But, as the paper acknowledges, there is no difference between the patient's love for the analyst and anyone else's love for anyone—it is the nature of passionate love to be obsessive, desperate, crazy, sick. Freud, after admonishing the novice analyst to stand firm and not let the patient "bring him down to the level of a lover," concedes that "sexual love is undoubtedly one of the chief things in life, and . . . when a women sues for love, to reject and refuse is a distressing part for a man to play; and, in spite of neurosis and resistance, there is an incomparable fascination in a woman of high principles who confesses her passion." Freud's understanding of the flickering and fleeting bulb life of "the extra piece of mental freedom" from which reason and autonomy derive gives his writings their tension and irony. That post-structuralist literary theorists should find prefigurations of their weltanschauung in Freud's texts is not surprising, and if, in the fading light of the end-of-the-century Freudian dusk, they are sometimes misled into calling a dog a cat—well, *c'est la vie*.

*The New Yorker*, 1987

# Six Roses ou Cirrhose?

THERE is a magnificent and deplorable tradition of *de haut en bas* in psychoanalysis. From its earliest days to the present, following the example of the first psychoanalyst, the psychoanalytic movement has exuded an insufferable air of impregnability, which has driven its opponents to extremes of pettishness. "Movement" may no longer be the word for the association of bland suburban practitioners who have come to largely constitute the profession in America since its medicalization, but "arrogance," "complacency," "self-righteousness," "tactlessness," and "condescension" continue to characterize its tone. Freud started it all. He would dismiss all objections to psychoanalysis as the irrational maunderings of weak minds— minds not ready for the threatening theory of sexual drives and the chastening hypothesis of unconscious motivation. "Society makes what is disagreeable into what is untrue," Freud wrote in the *Introductory Lectures* of 1916–17. "It disputes the truths of psychoanalysis with logical and factual arguments; but these arise from emotional sources, and it maintains these objections as prejudices, against every attempt to counter them." Earlier, in the 1909 Clark Lectures, he had likened the opponents of psychoanalysis to patients in analysis: "Psychoanalysis is seeking to bring to conscious recognition the things in mental life which are repressed; and everyone who forms a judgment on it is himself a human being who possesses similar repressions and may perhaps be maintaining them with difficulty. They are therefore bound to call up the same resistance in him as in our patients; and that resistance finds it easy to disguise itself as an intellectual rejection." Freud even went so far as to complain to his patients about his detractors. The poet H.D., in her memoir of her analysis with Freud in 1933–34, "Tribute to Freud," reports that Freud once said to her, "Please, never —I mean, never at any time, in any circumstance—endeavor to defend me if and when you hear abusive remarks made about me and my work. . . . You will do no good to the detractor by mistakenly beginning a logical defense. You will drive the hatred or the fear or the prejudice in deeper. . . . You will do no good to me and my work, for antagonism, once taking hold, cannot be rooted out from above the surface, and it thrives, in a way, on heated argument and digs in deeper." This sort of near-paranoid thinking continues to hold sway among analysts; and the idea of psychoanalysis as a special and innately inviolate discipline, somewhere between medicine and philosophy (as Freud situated it in his paper "A Difficulty in the Path of Psychoanalysis"), continues to have currency in the orthodox establishment. A sort of *cordon sanitaire* surrounds the profession. Those within the pale regard their critics with a dubiety that resembles nothing so much as the Transylvanian attitude toward the undead: What can you expect of such people? They haven't even been analyzed.

During the last two decades, a number of analysts restive under the hermetic tradition of their elders have called for a remodeling of the decrepit mansion of psychoanalysis. They have said, in effect, "Let's stop conducting our clinical and theoretical enterprise as if it were a Greek mystery cult. Let's pull up the shades and see what we have here. Let's put our data on the table, just as everybody else does. Instead of dismissing the objections of our critics, let's meet them. Let's see what else is going on in the twentieth century. And, above all, let's stop treating Freud as if he were the dead Albert and we were the widowed Victoria." One of the most trenchant and influential documents of this movement of middle-aged Turks is a 1973 paper by the late George Klein called "Two Theories or One?" Klein proposes that psychoanalysis rid itself of that most difficult and uncongenial part of Freud's writings known as his metapsychology, which discusses mental phenomena in terms of energies, forces, cathexes, mechanisms, apparatuses, and other analogies drawn from the physical sciences. Not only is the metapsychology an embarrassing holdover from the nineteenth-century positivism to which Freud was helplessly wedded, Klein writes, but it is utterly irrelevant to the clinical encounter. The true core of psychoanalysis is the clinical theory that rules the analytic situation. Roy Schafer's *A New Language for Psychoanalysis*, published three years later, pursues the implications for psychoanalysis of the jettisoning of metapsychology and proposes a new "action language" to replace the old metaphors from physics, chemistry, and biology. Psychoanalysis should be considered "an interpretive discipline, not a natural science," he writes. Analysts, instead of speaking—and, more important, writing—in terms of impersonal forces that cause people to act passively and irresponsibly ("My unconscious made me do it, so don't blame me"), should confine themselves to verbs and adverbs that express the *active* character of unconscious thought ("You finally acted angrily after all this time" instead of "It was an old anger you finally got out") and that restore to the patient responsibility for his intentions and actions, which the old mechanistic locutions degradingly robbed him of.

In *Narrative Truth and Historical Truth* (Norton, 1982), Donald P. Spence, the latest contributor to the genre of psychoanalytic refurbishment, has dared to do something no previous remodeler has done. He has actually ventured into the inner sanctum—the consultation room itself—and disdainfully indicated that all *its* appurtenances are hideously outmoded: they, too, will have to go, just as metapsychology went. Spence's "sympathetic critique of psychoanalysis," as the jacket of his book calls it, makes the notorious hatchet job on psychoanalysis that the neo-Freudophobe Frederick Crews performed in the July 1980 issue of *Commentary* look like a testimonial for the American Psychoanalytic Association. For here is a *psychoanalyst* saying all the things that the tendentious, irrational, unanalyzed (or unrepentantly analyzed) detractors of psychoanalysis have been saying—that it's not a science, that it has no truth, that it's a lot of made-up stories, that analyst and patient are kidding themselves, that theory and practice have no connection, that there are no "data," that whatever efficacy it has comes from suggestion and manipulation—and saying them with erudition and grace. The picture of the author that emerges from the book is that of the ideally civilized psychoanalyst whom Freud, arguing against the medical requirement, wistfully describes in "The Question of Lay Analysis." There is scarcely a page in *Narrative Truth* without its quotation from or allusion to an advanced novelist, philosopher, literary critic, or art critic. (Marcel Proust, Henry James, Roland Barthes, Michel Foucault, Paul Ricoeur, Maurice Merleau-Ponty, Harold Rosenberg, E. H. Gombrich, Hannah Arendt, Jonathan Culler, and George Steiner are among them.) If Spence's book does nothing else, it will treat the analytic community to a tantalizing sampling of some of the dominant intellectual perspectives of our time—the structuralist one in particular. Whether the book will also succeed in shaking up psychoanalytic orthodoxy, causing analysts to trade their dog-eared Freud, Abraham, Fenichel, Hartmann, Kris, Loewenstein, Arlow, and Brenner cards for the crisp new ones of the de Saussure, Jakobson, Derrida, Barthes, Lacan, Todorov, and Kristeva roster remains to be seen.

Spence's argument goes like this: There are two kinds of truth—narrative truth and historical truth—the first being the truth of literary art and the second the truth of actuality, of what *really* happened. Psychoanalysis is supposed to deal in historical truth, in accordance with Freud's metaphor of the analyst as archaeologist unearthing the traumatic events of the patient's past, but, Spence says, it actually deals largely, if unwittingly, in narrative truth. Patient and analyst, naively assuming that they are recovering the truth of the patient's past, are in fact merely concocting a story about him that hangs together and makes the kind of aesthetic sense that literary narratives do. The long shadow of Freud's case histories (which "possess an important literary quality that can best be defined as a masterful control of style and content," according to Spence) hovers over the analytic encounter and heavily influences the analytic dialogue. "If our goal is to discover the underlying thread of the patient's story and eventually to be in a position to match Freud's examples of narrative persuasion, we necessarily will listen with an ear tuned to sequence, coherence, and transformation," Spence writes. He goes on, "The narrative tradition has also had a significant influence on our patients. Some may even feel that they are competing with Freud's more famous cases and have fantasies of seeing their own history in published form; as a result, their effort to associate freely may always be tinged with an effort to show their best narrative voice and thus ensure their place among the clinical immortals." In Spence's view, the covert collaboration of would-be Freuds and their would-be Doras and Wolf Men succeeds *in spite of* the free-association rule and its complementary injunction to the analyst to listen with "evenly suspended attention."

The classical formulation of free association (the "fundamental rule" of analysis) was set down by Freud in 1913 in his paper "On Beginning the Treatment." Addressing a hypothetical patient, he said:

What you tell me must differ in one respect from an ordinary conversation. Ordinarily, you rightly try to keep a connecting thread running through your remarks, and you exclude any intrusive ideas that may occur to you and any side-issues, so as not to wander too far from the point. But in this case you must proceed differently. You will notice that as you relate things, various thoughts will occur to you which you would like to put aside, on the ground of certain criticisms and objections. You will be tempted to say to yourself that this or that is irrelevant here, or is quite unimportant, or nonsensical, so there is no need to say it. You must never give in to these criticisms, but must say it in spite of them—indeed, you must say it precisely *because* you feel an aversion to doing so. . . . Act as though, for instance, you were a traveller sitting next to the window of a railway carriage and describing to someone inside the carriage the changing views which you see outside.

"Evenly suspended attention" was described thus in an article that Freud wrote for a German encyclopedia in 1923:

The attitude that the analytic physician could most advantageously adopt was to surrender himself to his own unconscious mental activity, in a state of *evenly suspended attention*, to avoid as far as possible reflection and the construction of conscious expectations, not to try to fix anything that he heard particularly in his memory, and by these means to catch the drift of the patient's unconscious with his own unconscious.

Spence maintains that the complementary relationship of free association and evenly suspended attention is a myth, arguing that the two are incompatible. He likens the listening analyst and the speaking patient to the reader and the writer of a text. How the analyst "reads" the patient's utterances will depend on how well or badly "written" they are. When the patient is obeying the fundamental rule and talking in a fragmented, disconnected, inchoate manner, Spence says, the analyst cannot listen in the laid-back way of Freud's instruction. He can't let his mind drift, he can't surrender himself to his unconscious; he has to *work* to make sense of what he hears, since "a truly free and spontaneous piece of association corresponds to a hasty piece of writing and can only be understood by active and constructive listening." Only when the patient is disobeying the fundamental rule—is attending to the connecting thread of his thoughts and is artfully ordering what he says for the benefit of the listener—can the analyst afford to listen with the passive enjoyment experienced by the reader of a great work of literature. When the patient *narrates*, the analyst listens with free-floating attention; when the patient free-associates, the analyst must listen actively. (Spence divides literature into works that can be read with "a minimum of effort and struggle," because they are "well crafted," and those that have to be worked at, because they are "badly crafted"—a somewhat odd view of literature for a fancier of structuralist obscurantism.)

According to Spence, the pressure on the patient to narrate rather than to free-associate is great, since he is always struggling with "the conflict between what is true and what is describable." The true memory or dream or thought is often so unformed and murky and inchoate that it cannot be expressed except by resort to narrative description, which somehow falsifies it. For it is in the very nature of speech to form, rather than to express, thought. "The thought is in the mouth," as Tristan Tzara once absently, unforgettably put it. Spence, drawing on Merleau-Ponty's similar observation that "to speak is not to put a word under each thought," challenges Freud's analogy of the passenger on the train. "Speech is an active task that, as Merleau-Ponty is fond of pointing out, never quite succeeds," he writes, adding, "Much more than simply reporting on what is 'outside the window,' speech may be necessary for the speaker to know what he thinks. . . . The mind is often empty of words until the patient makes an effort to find them. Silence, in this view, is therefore not a resistance but the baseline condition; to be a truthful reporter, putting a strict meaning on *truthful*, the patient might not speak at all." Thus, the obdurately silent patient who truculently replies "Nothing" to the analyst's "Tell me what comes to mind" is a person of preternatural truthfulness—an epistemologist, a Cordelia. The typical patient, however, is a Regan or Goneril, for he is only too willing to betray truth as he glibly fills the analyst's ear with what he thinks the analyst wants to hear. "Under the press of a strong transference—either positive or negative—what the patient is saying about the past must be translated into what he is demanding of the present," Spence writes. He continues, "If he needs to be pitied, for example, he might exaggerate the misery of his childhood; if he wants to be praised for being an exceptional analytic patient, he might generate a crystal-clear memory of an infantile event. These reports have nothing much to do with the past as experienced or with other reports of the same event at different times in the analysis. Rather, they are tokens in a conversational exchange designed to win some kind of response from the analyst. As in any bargaining session, truth takes the back seat; to treat these reports as faithful accounts of some earlier time is to overemphasize the historical side of the analytic process and to underplay its conversational overtones."

While the patient is evading historical truth in these and other ways, the analyst is contributing his share to what Spence calls the "mischief" of the analytic encounter. For as the analyst listens to the patient's incoherent wanderings, as he "reads" the ill-written text of his associations (there are times, evidently, when the patient *does* obey the fundamental rule, though Spence's argument for the inherent difficulty, if not impossibility, of free association is so compelling, is nailed down so firmly from so many perspectives, that one wonders how this eventuality can ever occur), he silently imposes assumptions, notions, preconceptions, memories, theories, and even wishes of his own on the material in order to make sense of it. These "unwitting interpretations" are often unjustified, irrelevant, and even outright false—based on the mishearing of a word, for example. In normal conversation, such misapprehensions would be corrected on the spot, but in analysis, where they are unspoken, they may remain uncorrected forever, eventually forming the basis of unwarranted formal interpretations. But the formal interpretation itself is in any case almost bound to be nonveridical. For if the analyst escapes the snare of unwitting interpretation, it is only to fall into the trap of the meretricious pattern match. Like the patient, the analyst, caught in the conflict between what is true and what can be described, opts for the describable. Inevitably, Spence writes, "in making a formal interpretation we exchange one kind of truth—historical truth—for the truth of being coherent and sayable—narrative truth." In other words, if you can say it you are not being truthful, since the truth is unsayable, like the word for God.

In the closing chapters of the book, after trashing the scientific credibility of psychoanalysis and, *en passant*, pointing out the necessarily spurious character of analytic theorizing and the ineptitude of analytic writing in general, Spence surprisingly *defends* the status quo of analytic practice. Instead of dismissing psychoanalysis as a pseudoscience and predicting, as Crews did, that it will "fade away just as mesmerism and phrenology did," Spence holds it up as a kind of marvelous, high-class entertainment that not only gives the patient an unforgettable aesthetic experience for his money but has therapeutic value for him as well. The analyst's interpretations are "artistic creations" that invest the untidy bits and pieces of the patient's life with the form and structure of art; further, they are "pragmatic statements" that influence the future course of his life. As an example of a pragmatic statement, Spence cites a politician's claim that he is going to win next Tuesday's election: "He makes the statement not because he *knows* the outcome but because he wishes to *influence* the outcome. If he says he will win, he may persuade the voters still in doubt." In the same way, the most off-the-wall of the analyst's interpretations may become true simply by having been stated with conviction. To illustrate "interpretation as an aesthetic creation," Spence cites a dream interpretation by the French analyst Serge Viderman, reported in a 1979 paper entitled "The Analytic Space." The patient dreamed of being in a garden with his father and of offering him a bouquet of six roses. Viderman, recalling that the patient's father had died of alcoholism, delivered his interpretation in the form of a question: "*Six roses ou cirrhose?*" Now, it can be objected—and many, probably most, analysts would so object—that Spence has got things by the wrong handle here. Surely it wasn't Viderman who was the creator of the brilliant play on words; it was the patient. The analyst had merely "got" the pun that the patient's unconscious, doing its While-U-Sleep dreamwork, had wittily made. He had acted merely as an interpreter—a decoder, if you will—of a message from the unconscious; he wasn't its author. Similarly, Spence's above-mentioned discussion of transference as an obstacle in the way of the true report of the patient's life story will cause analyst readers to shake their heads in disbelief at what they are hearing from a colleague, since in the psychoanalytic view the transference *is* the life story. When Spence writes, "What the patient is saying about the past must be translated into what he is demanding of the present," he is committing a psychoanalytic solecism. For what the patient is demanding of the present—that is, of the analyst—constitutes the most authoritative statement about the past that the patient can make. To complain (as Spence does) about the deterioration of the "truth value" of what a patient says when, in the grip of transference, he tries "to win some kind of response from the analyst" is simply to miss the point of the concept of transference.

Elsewhere, writing of the misunderstandings that may occur between an analyst and a patient who have selected different "genres" in which to perform their respective roles, Spence cites the hypothetical case of a patient who "remembers incessantly, and with unbelievable detail, remarkable scenes from early childhood." He goes on:

> Suppose the memories are, in fact, true. But suppose, in addition, that the analyst makes the assumption that memories of this kind suggest the failure of early repressive defenses; he therefore chooses not to respond. The patient, feeling

slighted and perhaps misunderstood, tries to better his position by increasing the number of memories and perhaps adding details that he knows are false but that he hopes will elicit a more favorable response. The analyst, for his part, hears the change as proof of his early diagnostic impression and decides to test the issue by querying the patient at length about one of the fabricated memories. When it turns out that the fabrications were consciously supplied by the patient, the analyst becomes even more convinced that the patient is untreatable and decides to cut short the analysis.

The impasse just described is not the typical kind of countertransference complication caused by the acting out of unanalyzed impulses; rather, the analyst believes he is behaving properly by not giving too much reassurance too soon. But the meaning of this forbearance is perceived differently by the patient, and in his determination to win more approval, he ends up by losing the analyst's trust.

Here again, one feels that one is being served up a peculiar version of psychoanalysis. Since when do analysts penalize their patients for lying by cutting short their analyses? On the contrary, lies are of the deepest interest to analysts. They are like dreams: they mean something, they lead somewhere. That a patient would lose his analyst's trust is an absurdity, since he never had his analyst's trust to begin with, if the analyst was doing his job. Mistrust is the analyst's stock-in-trade, an attitude from which he must never relent. For by not taking at face value anything the patient says or does—even his lies, which are examined for their underlying "truth"—the analyst is able to wrest him from his habitual ways of thinking and impel him into the unfamiliar mode of psychoanalytic thought. This mode of thought, which was Freud's essential contribution to the history of ideas, cuts through all the conventional discourses on truth and deals with a special variety of truth, which is neither the truth of what happened in the past (historical truth) nor the truth of what might have happened (narrative truth) but the truth of what the present betrays about the past (psychoanalytic truth). The present ("the here and now" of the analytic encounter, as the analyst Merton Gill likes to call it) is the true focus of psychoanalysis—not (as is popularly assumed and as Spence assumes) the past. The patient's task is not to strain to remember what happened in his childhood and then tell his story in a way that will both render justice to reality and make sense to the analyst. For it isn't the story he tries to tell but the story he tells *in spite of himself* that the analyst listens for. The analyst is only minimally interested in the story the patient is trying to tell him. What he is really after is the story behind the story—the story that the patient is not telling him—and this he can infer only from the patient's behavior toward him (transference) and from his manner of disobeying the fundamental rule of free association (resistance). To compare the "work" of free association with that of writing is to misunderstand the purpose and the rationale of free association. Although it often seems hard going to the patient, free association is actually no work at all; what work is done in the analysis is done by the analyst, and whether the analysis succeeds or founders depends on his interpretive skills, coupled with the susceptibility of the patient's problems to analytic therapy. No narrative skills such as Spence demands are required of the patient. All he has to do is lie there and talk—or not talk. Everything he says and does, or doesn't say and doesn't do, expresses something true about him. He can't help but betray himself. This is the essence of the clinical theory of psychoanalysis; this is what Freud discovered after abandoning the hypnotic method and its successor, the urging method, and introducing the laissez-faire technique of analysis proper. That the fundamental rule is impossible for the patient to carry out to the letter—or even to carry out at all in some cases—was hardly Spence's discovery. No sooner had Freud established the rule (to, as he thought, facilitate the flow of reminiscence) than he had to face the fact that not a single patient obeyed it. He faced this revelation with characteristic equanimity. He had already noted in the patients on whom he was visiting his urging technique that they always experienced difficulty in remembering the distressing events that had evidently precipitated their hysterical symptoms. From these difficulties Freud inferred a force, which he called "the resistance," that was keeping these mortifying memories out of consciousness and was clearly another face of the force that had *put* them out of consciousness in the first place. ("The resistance" is a key target of Schafer's attack on the reified, anthropomorphic, spatial language of metapsychology. In action language, one may say only that a patient resists. But resists against what? Schafer explores the question in a dense, complex chapter of *A New Language* entitled "The Idea of Resistance.") Now Freud began to consider the possibility that the resistance itself might be at least as worthy of analytic scrutiny as the material it was warding off. Although all patients resisted, no two patients resisted alike. Each had a characteristic mode of evasion, marked by a kind of timeless implacability. The patients' silences, recalcitrances, obduracies, forgettings, lies, inarticulatenesses, circumlocutions, intellectualizations, and rationalizations were like fossils of behavior from an earlier time. Freud dated the origin of these "defense mechanisms" in the Oedipal period, between the ages of three and six; many subsequent analysts have set them farther back —some as far back as the first months of life. But there is agreement that "analysis of the resistance" coupled with (and merging into) "analysis of the transference" constitutes the basis of psychoanalytic therapy. Novice psychoanalysts learn to handle these double-edged power tools of the trade by applying them gingerly to practice patients; they do not, as Spence suggests, go to Freud's case histories for instruction. Spence holds up a piece of fudging that Freud did in the Wolf Man case— where a supposition that a patient once micturated on the floor becomes, a few pages later, an assertion that he definitely did so—as an example of the specious "narrative closure" that analysts are prone to impose on the patients' utterances. But Freud's case histories are full of this sort of thing—in fact, they *are* this sort of thing. Of all Freud's writings, they are the most dated and quaint, the most vulnerable, the least instructive, certainly the least literary. Have the people who exclaim over the "novelistic" quality of Freud's case histories actually read them? And do patients actually exist who (as Spence writes) secretly aspire to seeing their cases written up in the *Psychoanalytic Quarterly?* If they do, analysis can't help them.

PEOPLE go into analysis because they are in pain. Analysis proposes to relieve mental pain by the homeopathic method of applying more of the same; analysis is itself a painful emotional experience. Nowhere in Spence's book is there any account of the emotion inherent in analysis. In his version of analysis —the calm collaborative effort of patient and analyst to transform the unkempt *fabula* of actuality into the orderly *sjužet* of narrative art—emotion has no place. But emotion is the center of analysis. It is the fulcrum of the patient's "conversion" to the psychoanalytic view of reality and to its basic doctrine that life is lived on two levels of thought and act: one in our awareness and the other only inferable, from dreams, slips of the tongue, and inexplicable behavior. It is from the strength of the feelings aroused in the patient by the analyst—a person about whom the patient knows next to nothing, who hardly ever speaks, who wants nothing for himself from the encounter, who hands him a bill every month—that the patient gains a conviction of the insistence with which the past intrudes on the present. It is in the way he makes himself at home, as it were, in the totally alien environment of the analyst's consultation room, treating the analyst as if he were some sort of close, difficult relative, friend, or lover rather than the innocuous, well-meaning stranger he is, that the patient receives a shocking recognition of himself as someone who behaves and feels not in accordance with the claims of outer, material reality but with the demands of inner, psychic reality. Of course, not every analysis engenders such convictions and recognitions. There are inept analysts; there are horrendous analysts; there are unfortunate combinations of analyst and patient; there are patients for whom analysis is the wrong therapy. But when analysis works, it makes an indelible impression on the patient. It has been said that devotees of analysis are like members of a religious sect—people bound together by a mysterious experience yielding esoteric knowledge that no one outside the sect is privy to. There is truth in this description. The person who has spent several years (or maybe just several weeks) participating in the bizarre relationship of analysis, which is unlike any relationship in life (or even in art, with the possible exception of Marcel and Albertine), *does* possess a form of esoteric knowledge. To this extent, some of the "if you unbelievers only *knew*" attitude of analysts is justified. Spence himself uses the term "believing analysts" about himself and his colleagues. Only, he doesn't believe the same things they do.

His view of the analyst's interpretations as "artistic creations" imposed on the messy, meaningless contents of the patient's mind can be maintained only in contradistinction to the most fundamental assumption of psychoanalysis—that of psychic determinism, which invests the most random-seeming of our actions, the most incomprehensible of our symptoms, the most inchoate of our dreams with the coherence and elegance of art. "The psychoanalytic view transforms all men into poets— incurable symbolists, betraying unknown secrets with every word," Philip Rieff writes in *Freud: The Mind of the Moralist*. The Spence view returns man to his pre-psychoanalytic condition of psychic chaos and divests analytic therapy of its raison d'être. Far from presenting the patient with a well-made story, analysis seeks to destroy the story that the patient has for a long time believed to be the story of his life. Like a police investigator bent on breaking down the alibi of a stubborn suspect, the analyst doggedly whittles away at the patient's story through evidence that the patient unwittingly provides. Nor does analysis replace the old story with a new one. It emboldens the patient to live without a story. It permits him to see that his life is at once more disorderly and risky and interesting and free than he had dared to imagine. Our lives are not like novels. In postulating the pleasure and reality principles, Freud was expressing his rueful sense of the difference between life and art. Psychoanalysis seeks to acquaint us with and free us from the tyranny of the artist within us, who insists on an impossible order, who schemes and arranges to make things come out right, who commits us to a foolish, sometimes even dangerous adherence to *l'art pour l'art*. That it never completely (or perhaps even noticeably) does so is a reflection less on the insufficiency of analysis than on the obduracy of human nature.

In his intemperate paper "On the History of the Psychoanalytic Movement" (1914), written to put the secessionists Jung and Adler in their place, Freud once again equated those resistant to "the unwelcome truths of analysis" with patients in analysis. "One may have succeeded in laboriously bringing a patient to grasp some parts of analytic knowledge and to handle them like possessions of his own, and yet one may see him, under the domination of the very next resistance, throw all he has learned to the winds and stand on the defensive, as he did in the days when he was a carefree beginner," Freud wrote, and added, "I had to learn that the very same thing can happen with psychoanalysts as with patients in analysis." But there are patients and patients. Spence is not a Jung or an Adler. He is no revisionist; he is not out to found his own school of psychoanalysis; he offers no new system or terminology. Rather, he is like one of a special group of "good patients" whom the analyst Martin Stein described in his 1981 paper "The Unobjectionable Part of the Transference" (*Journal* of the American Psychoanalytic Association): patients who are "likable, attractive people, cultivated and often gifted . . . highly rational, demonstrating excellent judgment about most matters . . . cooperative, interesting, and very adept at the analytic process" —and, of course, as Stein is quick to add, just as desperately and aggressively resistant, in their charming way, as their more floridly and disagreeably resistant fellow patients. At the core of Spence's likable, attractive, cultivated, and professedly pro-psychoanalytic book lies a profound antipathy to psychoanalytic thought. All the vigor of his argument and all the grace of his writing cannot obscure (let alone resolve) this paradox.

*The New Yorker*, 1983

# The Patient Is Always Right

> Does psychoanalysis remain a dialectical relation in which the non-action of the analyst guides the subject's discourse towards the realization of his truth, or is it to be reduced to a phantasmatic relation in which "two abysses brush against each other" without touching, while the whole gamut of imaginary regressions is exhausted—like a sort of "bundling" pushed to its extreme limits as a psychological experience?
>
> —*Jacques Lacan, "The Function and Field of Speech and Language in Psychoanalysis"*

FREUD stumbled on the concept of transference while desperately casting about for an antidote to the epidemic of iatrogenic lovesickness that had spread through his practice in the 1890s. When, one by one, all of his women patients stopped doing the work of free association that they had at first enthusiastically taken up and began shyly and then importunely to declare their love for him, he shrewdly surmised that it was not "the charms of my person" that were the cause of the disturbance but, rather, that the women were in a state of readiness to fall in love, and he was simply Bottom to their Titania. Freud's clear-sightedness about the profound impersonality of romantic passion was not an original insight—it is one that

❧ ANALYSIS OF TRANSFERENCE AND TECHNIQUE, 2 vols.: Vol. I, THEORY AND TECHNIQUE (New York: International Universities Press, 1982), by Merton M. Gill; Vol. II, STUDIES OF NINE AUDIO-RECORDED PSYCHOANALYTIC SESSIONS (New York: International Universities Press, 1982), by Merton M. Gill and Irwin Z. Hoffman.

poets have long been privy to. Where Freud's genius came into play was in his extension of the metaphor of unseeing, solipsistic passion to the whole of human interaction. It began to dawn on Freud that it is not only love that is blind—*all* our feelings toward and ideas about one another are marked by a magnificent obliviousness to reality. Like the chains of the prisoners in Plato's cave, which prevented them from turning their heads to distinguish shadow from substance, the shackles of transference keep us in a state of perpetual misprision. Freud's modest program of fending off his importunate patients with some sort of tactful and professional-sounding formula—"We overcome the transference by pointing out to the patient that his feelings do not arise from the present situation and do not apply to the person of the doctor, but that he is repeating something that happened to him earlier," Freud wrote in the *Introductory Lectures* of 1917—flowered into a powerful and subtle theory of personal relations, which soon became the center of analytic therapy. According to the theory, we spend our lives playing out the same internal drama—that of our earliest parental and sibling relationships—indiscriminately casting the people we meet in the leading roles and doing our own rote performance of the part of the child, like an actor in a play with a very long run who years ago outgrew his part but whom nobody has thought to replace. Analysis proposes to show the patient (whose reason for seeking help is inevitably bound up with problems in his personal relations) that he doesn't have to play this part anymore—that other parts are available to him now that he is an adult. The success of the demonstration is thought to depend on how well the analyst plays *his* role, which was specially written for the drama of the analytic encounter and has no model in life outside analysis. It partakes of some of the qualities of oracles, lawyers, and hairdressers—the detachment of the first, the acuity of the second, and the intimacy of the third—but has a character (or one could say characterlessness) all its own. In the analysis, as the patient trots out his stale play and absently casts the analyst in the usual parental and sibling roles, the analyst does not react in the way that people in normal life react—which is to trot out their own stale plays—but in a manner the patient has never before encountered. The analyst does not respond in kind to anything the patient says or does; he does not reveal his feelings; he does not talk about anything the patient hasn't brought up first; he never interrupts the patient; he never argues with him; he never defends himself; he doesn't want anything from the patient; he talks very little. He is so utterly unlike anyone the patient has ever met—his behavior is so manifestly bizarre—that the patient is ultimately forced to acknowledge that he has made a mistake in thinking about and acting toward the analyst as he would toward a normal person, with the feelings, desires, and flaws that normal people have. As the patient examines his thoughts about and behavior toward the analyst in the light of the actuality of the analyst's conduct and sees how far off the mark they are, he is compelled to consider the possibility that his thoughts about and behavior toward people outside the analysis are similarly skewed. The analyst's performance of his role of nonperson is known as analytic technique.

The performance is extremely hard to sustain. The analyst, being a member of a culture that values sympathy, warmth, compassion, kindliness, spontaneity, and sincerity, can never be comfortable playing a part from which these qualities are conspicuously absent, and he is constantly tempted to temporize, to admit some culturally approved behavior into his performance, to let some evidence of his niceness come through to the patient. At the same time—being a member of a species locked in perpetual internal combat between the lofty ideals of society and the pitiful realities of human nature—he is in constant danger of unwittingly wandering off analytic course in the opposite direction—that of cruelty, vengefulness, envy, spite, and petty tyranny. (Analysts use the term "countertransference" to refer to—and help forgive themselves for—lapses of either sort.)

A further difficulty in the way of the analytic performance is the ever lengthening duration of analysis. When Freud wrote his papers on technique (between 1911 and 1915), analysis lasted from a few weeks to a year; today, analysis lasts an average of ten years. Freud's hard-edged metaphors for the analyst—in the technical papers, he described him as a surgeon, a soldier, and a mirror—are plausible enough for a short course of treatment but seem strained for a lengthy analysis: an operation, a battle, and a look in the mirror can go on only so long. "Our patients become gradually better analyzed than we are," Sandor Ferenczi wryly noted in 1933. Like children who hang around the house too much and become morbidly attuned to the moods and quirks of their parents, long-term analytic patients get to know their analyst so well that his protestations that there is nothing there for them to know become increasingly hollow.

Throughout the history of psychoanalysis there have been analysts—starting with Ferenczi—who have openly scoffed at the idea that a man can ever abjure his humanity, and who have repudiated the ideal of analytic neutrality not only as impossible but as full of hubris. The analysts belonging to this humanistic tradition have disavowed Freud's harsh metaphors and have tinkered with the analyst's role to make it less Wizard of Oz–like and more avuncular. They have argued that the analysts who erect a wall of silence and unresponsiveness between themselves and their patients are being not neutral but simply unpleasant, and that the patient's reaction to such behavior is not transference but realistic outrage. This school is marked by a spirit of moral reform and has some of the character of a patients'-lib movement. Its members would like to sweep analysis clean of the hypocrisy that they believe pervades it and free patients from the "cold" and "rigid" analysts of the authoritarian old school, who keep them in a condition of cowed resentment like that of Butler's Ernest Pontifex. Some brilliant and rigorous writing has been produced by this school (Ferenczi and Leo Stone are two of its literary ornaments), and so has some very poor and lax writing, by authors who are under the impression that the constant use of the word "empathy" absolves them from any obligation to think. A recent contribution to the genre, Merton Gill's two-volume *Analysis of Transference*, scarcely suffers from lack of thought, and firmly belongs among its most distinguished productions.

The book, indeed, is so far from being simpleminded—is so alive to the maddening complexity of the subject and pursues such high epistemological goals—that it suffers the fate of all obsessively honest intellectual works: it is riddled with contradiction. It reflects the dilemma of a moralist who is trying to remain a Freudian analyst. Gill's sympathies are clearly with the patient who is being covertly bullied by an authoritarian analyst, but he is equally concerned with the predicament of a profession that is always perilously on the edge of losing its privileged status as a science (of sorts) and becoming just another feel-good therapy. In Volume I of *Analysis of Transference*, Gill attempts to build a theoretical framework for doing analysis in a more conversational and fraternal way than orthodoxy would allow; and in Volume II (prepared with the collaboration of Irwin Z. Hoffman, a candidate at the Chicago Institute of Psychoanalysis), he illustrates both the old and the new techniques by transcribing sessions with nine different patients, tape-recorded by five different analysts. In Volume I, Gill argues that old-school analysts do not, on the one hand, pursue transference vigorously enough and are not alert enough to the subtle references to themselves that the patient constantly makes while appearing to be talking about other matters; and, on the other, do not take sufficient account of the influence of their own behavior on the patient's perceptions of them. "It is the analyst's task constantly to tear the patient out of his menacing illusion and show him again and again that what he takes to be new life is a reflection of the past," Freud wrote in 1938 in *The Outline of Psychoanalysis*, maintaining to the end his idea of transference interpretation as a report from outside the cave. Gill absolutely denies the traditional concept of transference as a kind of delusion. He repudiates Freud's Platonism and maintains that there is always some truth to the patient's perceptions, because the analyst is always doing *something* on which these perceptions must be based. Even when (or as Gill would argue, especially when) the analyst remains silent, he is acting on the patient in a way that will influence his feelings and ideas about the analyst. There is no way, Gill argues, that the analyst's behavior can be eliminated from the equation. "The realistic situation cannot be made to disappear," he writes, and adds, "The analytic situation *is* real."

Gill accordingly recommends that analytic technique be emended so as to embrace the "new life" that is the actuality of analysis, and he counsels analysts to let no opportunity go by for discussing the effect that their behavior is having on their patients. In denying that transference is a distortion of reality, he writes,

> A more accurate formulation than "distortion" is that the real situation is subject to interpretations other than the one the patient has reached. The analyst suggests that the patient's conclusions are not unequivocally determined by the real situation. Indeed, seeing the issue in this way rather than as a "distortion" helps prevent the error of assuming some absolute external reality of which the "true" knowledge must be gained.

It is a measure of the treacherousness of the ground on which discussions of transference are held that Gill can simultaneously believe in a "real situation" and not believe in an "absolute external reality." But more to the point, perhaps, is the inescapable impression of Gill's own stern absolutism regarding proper and improper analytic conduct that one receives from a reading of the annotated transcripts of Volume II. Gill has divided the five analysts into two groups—those who have been schooled in his theories and techniques and those who have not—and he begins the book with four sessions conducted by the unindoctrinated analysts. The first session, dramatically, is one in which the analyst never utters a single word. As the patient wanders from subject to subject like a Scheherazade desperately searching for a story that will entertain her dangerously restive interlocutor, Gill and Hoffman, like annotators of a wretchedly played chess game, interject their disapproval of the analyst's unrelenting silence—which they see as the real subject of the patient's discourse. The silent session offers the *ad absurdum* example of what Gill calls "enactment of the transference," whereby analysts unwittingly lapse into the very behavior that patients "imagine" of them. When the patient tells the silent analyst a story about how she took a sick cat to the ASPCA, where it died because "they fooled around for a few days" instead of operating immediately, she is (according to the annotators) alluding to her fear that she herself has fallen into the hands of a negligent practitioner who "fools around," saying nothing instead of decisively intervening with interpretations. And by remaining silent in the face of the patient's persistent efforts to move him to speech, the analyst at least partially corroborates the patient's fantasy of mistreatment. For by letting all opportunities go by for a transference interpretation— for allowing the patient to equate silence with malpractice—he is in fact falling down on his job as analyst. In a session with another benighted practitioner, a patient becomes angry when the analyst brings up, obviously not for the first time, the subject of her penis envy. "You know, I'm getting sick of this," she says emotionally, adding, "I'm thinking of knocking all the books off the wall again." The transcript continues:

ANALYST: What about knocking all the books off there?

PATIENT: It's, I'm getting mad. I'm lying here getting mad and I'm afraid to move because I'm mad. I mean, what it seems like—and I know it's worked—but what it seems like is that you're always, no matter what I say, you're always bringing it back to this, you know—my thing about something being wrong with me. And then we just get to that, and then nothing fucking happens. We just end up saying, "Well, you think there's something wrong with you." So big fucking deal. What about it? You know, when are we going to get away from the illness and onto the cure?

ANALYST: I take the idea about knocking all the books off the wall as if you wanted to knock my penis off.

Gill and Hoffman hasten to register their outrage at this "almost unbelievably pat interpretation." They go on to say, "Instead of finding out what she means by wanting to knock down his books, the analyst uses what she has said to reiterate his fixed conviction, which—however correct it may be—she had just characterized as unhelpful. It is far more likely that her conscious experience is that he is repeating a formula from his books and that that is why she wants to knock them down." The dialogue goes on:

P: You do?

A: Yes, I do.

P: [laugh]

A: That your reaction to my saying it is to want to do that.

P: Is to want to be [inaudible]—what?

A: Is to want to do that.

P: Well, if that's what getting mad is.

A: It wasn't just getting mad. It was also knocking all the books off the wall.

P: But why, but why are books a penis now? [sigh] Huh? Yeah, I think I always thought they were. That's why I read so much. I'm serious and I'm saying it sarcastically, but think back about trying to be smart.

A: Yeah, I know.

P: [inaudible]—OK. Well, I'm admitting it ruefully, but I'm admitting it pissed-offedly. [inaudible] If I can't have one, you can't have one either? And if you won't give me one, then you can't have yours. But it's still the same question. And it's still the same feeling.

At the end of the session, which has continued in the above vein, the annotators write:

Whatever the truth about the role of penis envy in her neurosis, it cannot be gotten at usefully by eliding the transference. The patient experiences the relationship as one in which a tyrannical male forces his will on her without any genuine understanding of what she is feeling. She is left in part submissive and in part raging and distrustful. The analyst fails to see . . . how his behavior only reinforces how the patient experiences him, and probably strengthens her convictions about what men in general are like. The neurosis has been enacted, not analyzed.

When Gill and Hoffman turn to the work of the "good" analysts—those who are "consciously attempting to employ our point of view"—they find them, astonishingly enough, screwing up just as badly as, and sometimes even worse than, the "bad" analysts. It is immensely to Gill's credit (in fact, it authoritatively removes his book from the category of polemic and raises it to the status of a work of true research) that he has permitted the chips to fall where they may, at whatever cost to his thesis. He and Hoffman are just as hard on the new-school analysts when they lapse as they were on the old-school ones. When a new-school analyst says to a patient, "I can understand that you essentially experience me as putting you down, so, presumably, you must feel I have a purpose in doing that," they sternly point out that the analyst is indeed putting the patient down: "That he says you 'essentially experience me' suggests, again, a hyperbole—that there is no basis for the patient's feeling. This disguise of an attack as empathy makes it all the more difficult for the patient to assert his anger." In another session, the analyst asks the patient, "What did I do last week that gave you the feeling that I'm not strong enough? My tiredness, perhaps, or other things?" The patient replies, "Maybe your tiredness. . . ." When the analyst interpolates, "That is to say, what you thought was tiredness," the annotators disgustedly comment, "As has happened repeatedly in the hour, a promising start in exploring the patient's perceptions of the analyst is followed by an abrupt, defensive, and gratuitous emphasis on the subjectivity of the patient's impressions." As Gill and Hoffman hold up example after example of "enactment of the transference" (which increasingly sounds like their euphemism for bullying), one begins to wonder whether Gill's active technique isn't itself at fault—whether it doesn't invite the very abuses it is designed to protect the patient against. Is not the persistent minute examination of what is going on between patient and analyst that Gill recommends a kind of trap? Isn't the analyst—once he starts squabbling with the patient about whether it was really two o'clock or two-fifteen—lost? In his paper "On Beginning the Treatment: Further Recommendations on the Technique of Psycho-Analysis (I)," Freud advises analysts not to behave like "the other member of a married couple." The following exchange, which is typical of the dialogue of the last five "good" sessions, illustrates (among other things) the wisdom of Freud's advice:

A: I was late three times?

P: Mmm-hmm. According to the clock in the hall. You weren't today.

A: Which clock—downstairs?

P: No. This one.

A: That one? Oh . . .

P: That—but I don't think that's a big thing. The first two days, as I said, I was relieved because I was late myself, so . . . [pause]

A: You don't think it's a big thing, but it sounds like you noticed it and added them up.

P: I noticed it. Yes.

A: Yes.

P: I guess that's because it's become pretty—you know, it's become an issue for me to get here on time so I do watch the clock pretty, pretty closely.

A: Well, when you said three days in a row . . .

P: Mmm-hmm.

A: . . . I thought you meant I was late two minutes.

P: You—that's right, but I mean, I'm watching the clock so I'm sensitive . . .

A: How did you know I was, if you were late? I'm not clear.

P: Because I got here and it was two minutes after . . .

A: Oh, you got here and I still . . .

P: And you hadn't opened your door.

A: Oh. [pause] You mentioned it only one time, is that right?

P: Mmm-hmm.

A: Why did you not tell me the other times?

P: Because I didn't think it was worth mentioning.

A: Why not?

P: Because . . .

A: You noticed it.

P: That's right. But, I mean, I notice a lot of things and . . .

A: You attributed some important significance to it.

P: I don't think I did.

A: Oh, you don't think so. You think, maybe retrospectively, these things started to pile up, is that it?

P: Yes.

A: I see. [pause] And what, then, did they mean—I'm losing interest in you, or what?

P: You didn't want to see me.

A: I didn't want to see you because . . .

P: 'Cause it's going to be such a struggle.

One question naturally arises: How representative of the profession at large are the analysts in Gill's book? If they are merely exceptionally inept, then the transcripts are merely illustrations of poor analysis rather than documentation of common problems and pitfalls of analysts and of the relative merits of the orthodox and new techniques. Much depends on the answer, but unfortunately the answer is not forthcoming, because the majority of analysts refuse to tape-record their work, and so there is no material to which the Gill transcripts can be compared. It would be nice to think that there are wiser and larger-souled people doing analysis than those in Gill's book, but until they identify themselves and produce examples of their work, Gill's analysts will have to be accepted as not uncharacteristic and their work as standard. Certainly the self-congratulatory clinical histories in the analytic literature cannot be accepted as evidence of anything beyond the writers' self-regard.

If Gill's new technique leaves intact the Gordian knot of the unplayability of the analytic role—as we have seen, it seems simply to allow analysts more scope for petty tyranny than did the old technique—its effect on the associations of patients is momentous. "Associations," indeed, is hardly the term for the few words the patient manages to get in edgewise before the new-school analyst engages him in interminable discussion of the "here and now" of the analysis. Gill's dislike of analytic silence—"sustained silence is a very powerful stimulus, the effect of which will, by definition, pass uninterpreted and probably unrecognized as long as the analyst refrains from speaking"—has had the paradoxical but predictable result of muffling almost to inaudibility the voice of the unconscious. In fact, it is only from the early "bad" sessions that one can gain any sense whatever that psychoanalysis is the study of unconscious rather than of conscious mental life. Gill's idea—that in order to determine what is irrational and past-ridden in the patient's attitude toward the analyst, one must first be clear about the inevitable "real" contribution of the analyst to this attitude—is commendably logical, admirably fair-minded, but utterly unpsychoanalytic. The business of analysis is to acquaint the patient with the parts of himself he is least eager to know and has hidden most cleverly from himself. Gill's obsessive examination of the actuality of the analysis—of the rights and wrongs of the patient's beliefs and feelings about the analyst—effectively prevents this business from ever going forward. "The patient does not *remember* anything of what he has forgotten and repressed, but *acts* it out," Freud wrote in "Remembering, Repeating, and Working-Through," adding: "He reproduces it not as a memory but as an action; he *repeats* it, without, of course, knowing that he is repeating it." In the Gill version of analysis, the memory that is being reproduced as an action is never pursued to its source. The analysis remains frozen in the present. The session ends, and analyst and patient are still quarreling about what time it is. Gill's valiant attempt to solve the conundrum of the analyst-patient relationship—to cut through what Philip Rieff has called "the profound and true absurdity of psychoanalysis"—has led to the even greater absurdity of analysis whose hidden agenda is to corroborate the patient in his conscious perceptions of the analyst.

The analyst who told the patient, "I take the idea about knocking all the books off the wall as if you wanted to knock my penis off," may be the tyrannical prig the annotators say he is, but he could also be a perfectly workmanlike analyst who—following Freud's directive to listen with "closely hovering attention" in order to "put himself in a position to make use of everything he is told for the purposes of interpretation and of recognizing the concealed unconscious material"—had "heard" the patient's unconscious message and reported it accurately. While the literal meaning of the interpretation is outlandish, there is plenty of support, not only in psychoanalytic case material but in mythology, anthropology, art, and literature, for the theory that a woman's unconscious life is beset by a profound sense of powerlessness, a gnawing dissatisfaction—a feeling for which the term "penis envy" is thoroughly inadequate, not to say extremely irritating to women. In reading the transcript of the session with the angry patient, one cannot but recall the famous last section of Freud's "Analysis Terminable and Interminable," in which he holds up what he sees as the two most troublesome complaints of patients ("in the female, an envy for the penis—a positive striving to possess a male genital—and in the male, a struggle against his passive or feminine attitude to another male") and confesses his pessimism about the power of analysis to cure them:

> We often have the impression that with the wish for a penis and the masculine protest we have penetrated through all the psychological strata and have reached bedrock, and that thus our activities are at an end.

In Gill's optimistic belief that the feeling of defeat and hopelessness on the part of the angry patient derives from the way her analyst is treating her—and that if only he behaved better she would feel better about herself—he is leaving psychoanalytic theory far behind. This is surely not what he intends to do. His critique in Volume I of contemporary clinical theory and practice is offered in a spirit of deference and constructiveness. He is proposing to restore and modernize the sagging and peeling mansion of psychoanalysis, not to demolish it and put up a skyscraper. But the "improvements" of Volume II only show how delicately poised the whole thing is, and how easy it is to bring it crashing down with a few large, ill-considered movements.

*The New York Review of Books,* 1984

# The Seven-Minute Hour

FOR an ordinary literate person, reading the French psychoanalyst Jacques Lacan is like being trapped in a cave whose entrance is blocked by a huge rock. Outside, one hears the hammerings and heavings of the rescue mission that has rushed to the scene—the explicators and annotators of Lacan's texts, who wield the heaviest of modern intellectual equipment (the structural linguistics of Saussure and Jakobson, the structural anthropology of Lévi-Strauss, the philosophy of Hegel and Heidegger, the metapsychology of Freud)—but which makes no headway against the monolith of Lacan's magisterial hermeticism. For if the general reader hasn't the omniscience to read Lacan unaided, neither has he the will to follow Lacan's explicators in their slow and hesitant unknottings of the enigma of his beautiful and *meshuggeneh* prose. At the end of John P. Muller and William J. Richardson's *Lacan and Language: A Reader's Guide to* Ecrits, one of the more approachable of the textual analyses, the authors themselves nervously concede that if understanding Lacan "is not exactly guesswork," it is "nonetheless, a highly precarious business, and sharing our impressions with the reading public may be utter folly. After all, it exposes us to the embarrassment of being told how wrong we are, especially when the master's many disciples are there to say, 'that's not what he meant at all.' "

In this context of doubt and difficulty, Stuart Schneiderman's brilliant and confident book about Lacan, which one reads in a single avid and effortless sitting, comes almost as a shock.

✤ JACQUES LACAN: THE DEATH OF AN INTELLECTUAL HERO (Cambridge, Mass.: Harvard University Press, 1983), by Stuart Schneiderman.

Schneiderman writes like someone who has arrived in a room slightly out of breath, with so much to say that he doesn't even take off his coat. He is a former academic who in 1973 did what no other Lacan-struck American had thought to do: He picked up and went to Paris to be analyzed by Lacan and to receive analytic training at Lacan's École freudienne. "I decided that it would be contradictory for me to continue explicating texts when I knew nothing of the experience from which the texts were drawn," Schneiderman writes. "Thus I left Buffalo and a career as professor of English to become a Lacanian psychoanalyst."

Schneiderman stayed in Paris for four years, and returned to America even more enamored of Lacan and Lacanism than he had been as a mere befuddled reader of *Ecrits*. His book has some of the enthusiasm common to analytic patients in the first fine, careless rapture of early analysis, before the dog days— or, rather, the dog years—of analysis proper set in. The exalted and excited vision of psychoanalysis that Schneiderman derived from his analysis with Lacan is in some respects no different from the vision he might have derived had he stayed in Buffalo and gone into analysis with a drab local practitioner. Analysis is a profound imaginative experience, and for a professor of literature it is apt to have special poignancy; the lunatic, lover, and poet present in every analysand are doubtless specially vivid to the analysand who has taught Shakespeare. In blurring the distinction between what was uniquely Lacanian in his analysis and what is common to every analysis, Schneiderman gives a somewhat exaggerated notion of Lacan's unearthly potency in the consulting room. He makes Lacan sound more like an enchanter than like an analyst. (When writing of Lacan's inability to establish an orderly succession, he calls him a failed Prospero.) One can't help wondering whether Schneiderman's perception of his late analyst isn't somewhat skewed by his continuing transference. Anticipating this suspicion, Schneiderman writes, "In normal circumstances and according to psychoanalytic common sense, this would be a valid objection. With Lacan, though, there are no normal circumstances, and common sense, psychoanalytic and otherwise, is thoroughly unreliable."

For, evidently, Lacan "was not an analyst just like the others; he was an aristocrat, even a tyrant, possessing a theoretical mind the likes of which the psychoanalytic world had not seen since Freud." Moreover, Schneiderman writes, he was "strange, bizarre, insolent, and at times outrageous," adding, "He was prone to making scenes in public, to being abrupt and rude, to expressing his amorous intentions toward women in flagrant ways. (Once, it is told, a taxi driver was so impressed by a love scene between Lacan and a woman in the back seat of his cab that he called for an appointment the next morning and went on to spend several years in analysis with Lacan." The story would seem to reveal more about Paris taxi drivers than about Lacan.)

Schneiderman reports that "on the one occasion when Lacan appeared on television, he said that he would not alter his notoriously impenetrable style because he simply did not care to speak to idiots: my discourse, he said, is for those who are not idiots." Schneiderman nevertheless believes that "if his theory has validity, one should be able to articulate it with clarity and precision," and he does a remarkable job of placing Lacan's thought, if not exactly within the grasp of the nonspecialist reader, at least within waving distance. He does this partly by writing like an American or an Englishman (that is, by tempering theory with analogy, rather than, as the French do, with more theory) and partly by giving an idiosyncratic version of Lacanian theory. He has singled out for special emphasis the symbolization of death in psychoanalysis—a subject that engaged Lacan's attention, but not nearly as obsessively as it engages Schneiderman's.

Schneiderman sees death everywhere: in the "deathlike silence of the analyst"; in the "death mask" the analyst wears during sessions; in a dire rite of passage called "the pass," which Lacan instituted at the École freudienne to separate the men from the boys and which Schneiderman likens to the Last Judgment; in the case of Anna O., whose hysterical neurosis began at the bedside of her dying father; in Lacan's notorious innovation, the short session (it was one of the reasons he was thrown out of the International Psychoanalytic Association), which had "something of the horror of death" for Schneiderman, when he experienced it during his analysis. Although he allows that Lacan "did not shrink before theorizing about death . . . and was one of the few post-Freudian analysts who did not write off the death drive," Schneiderman believes that he "did not take things far enough," adding, "To do so he would have run up against the medical juggernaut with its passion for life, for saving life, for prolonging life, for beating death. The great advantage . . . to making symbolism sexual is that it favors the production of life, and even the advancement of the quality of life." Schneiderman firmly maintains that "psychoanalysis ought to get out of the business of thinking about how people live their lives, about how they behave." He goes on, "What this means, perhaps unexpectedly, is that analysis has as its major task the repairing of the relationships people have, not with other people, but with the dead."

If Lacan did not go as far as Schneiderman would have liked him to go in transforming psychoanalysis into a thanatology, he did not disappoint his exactingly radical disciple's expectations in the area of analytic technique, which he transformed —some people would say mauled—almost beyond recognition. Lacan behaved quite as oddly during his analytic sessions as he did outside them. For example, he would sit at his desk arranging piles of banknotes—a gesture Schneiderman construed to mean just the opposite of what most people would think it meant, seeing it as a sign of Lacan's *indifference* to the patient's money (since he already had a lot of it) and as his way of pointing the patient "beyond signs" to the question of desire.

As for the infamous short session, Schneiderman devotes a long, dense, and ultimately unsatisfying chapter to it. He begins with an amusing account of his own first experience with the short session. He had been coming to see Lacan for leisurely preliminary afternoon sessions, during which Lacan behaved like a friendly and gracious host (once he even went so far as to serve his supine guest a glass of Jack Daniel's), lulling him into a state of pleasurable self-absorption. One day, all unsuspecting, Schneiderman arrived for his session full of interesting things to tell his analyst, and after delivering himself of a little prologue, proceeded to speak of the matter close to his heart on which he had prepared to discourse that day. At that moment, Lacan abruptly rose from his chair and pronounced the session to be over. "And he did this unceremoniously with a total lack of the good manners to which one [was] accustomed," Schneiderman writes, evidently still feeling a little outraged. He adds, "The ending of the session, unexpected and unwanted, was like a rude awakening, like being torn out of a dream by a loud alarm. (One patient likened it to *coitus interruptus*.)"

Analysis is a bizarre human encounter, and the short session greatly accentuates its "Otherness," as they say in Lacan-speak. It removes analysis from everyday life more decisively than does the traditional analytic hour and imparts to the relationship between analyst and patient an extra dimension of alienation. When the analyst says at the end of fifty minutes, "I'm afraid that our time is up," he is behaving like an ordinary human being, whereas, as Schneiderman points out, when he suddenly and whimsically ends the session after five minutes, he "adopts a role like that of a god." The problem of the "real," or non-transference, relationship between patient and analyst, which has engaged some of the ablest minds in contemporary psychoanalysis, simply doesn't arise when the analyst persists in behaving like a somewhat mad Assyrian minor deity. After his initial shock and disbelief, Schneiderman came to appreciate the short session enormously, and is now a big apologist for it. He feels that it expedites access to the unconscious, forcing the patient out of the trite, long-winded discourse of everyday life into the witty ellipses of dreams, jokes, and aphorisms. "The combined pressure of the shortness of the sessions and the unpredictability of their stops creates a condition that greatly enhances one's tendencies to free-associate," Schneiderman writes. "Almost by definition, the ego can never be the master of the short session." An even more compelling advantage of the short session is that it spares the analyst hours of listening to things that bore and irritate him. According to Schneiderman,

> When Lacan talked about why he invented the short session, he referred in particular to this question. He said that some analysands, knowing that they were guaranteed fifty minutes no matter what, used their sessions to discuss things that did not interest them in the least. If they had something important to say, they would wait for the last few minutes of the session to broach it. Lacan reasoned that such analysands were using the fifty-minute hour as a resistance, as an excuse to waste time—in particular to waste the analyst's time, to make him wait for them. This is a neurotic form of abuse that finds a home in the fifty-minute hour. It is also called procrastination. The short session responds that the time being wasted is the analyst's and that he has some say in how he spends his time.

In traditional analysis, the analyst has no say in how he spends his time. He has leased it—all fifty minutes of it—to the analysand and has given him carte blanche to do what he likes with it: to be as dull, witless, verbose, evasive, phony, sleepy, uncooperative, uptight, or silent as he pleases. On his side, the analyst has the privilege of studying the patient from a special and not uninteresting point of view known as analysis of resistance. According to this perspective, the patient's elaborate and inevitable attempts to circumvent the fundamental rule of analysis—to say whatever comes to mind without premeditation—are no less expressive of his unconscious motives than are his (rare) compliances with the rule. When Freud switched from hypnosis to psychoanalysis, he understood that what he had done was to obstruct the pathway to the unconscious that he had opened with the earlier talking cure. It was his genius to see that it is in the very area of the falling short of the ideal of free association—in the resistance—that the big payoff lies for the investigator of unconscious conflicts. This insight of Freud's, coincident with his discovery of the transference, has been a cornerstone of analytic therapy since the turn of the century. The short session, in eliminating the resistance, does away with a fundamental structure of analysis. Lacan's self-proclaimed "return to Freud" would seem to be a return to the clinician of the prehistorical period of analysis.

Schneiderman tries to address himself to the analytical issues raised by the short session, but quickly becomes distracted. He plunges, instead, into a discourse on procrastination and "death's desire," culminating in an existential analysis of Hamlet. During this discourse, the mild intellectual discomfort that one has experienced throughout the book becomes more pronounced. The gap that one has felt to exist between Lacanian and non-Lacanian thought widens, and the unwelcome suspicion that the non-Lacanians are talking about horses (resistance) while the Lacanians are responding about oranges (existence) can be suppressed no longer. Lacan once told a seminar, "If they knew what I was saying, they would never have let me say it." Perhaps Schneiderman's game attempt to extract the plain meaning of Lacan's thought from the murky poetry of his style was bound to come to grief. When brought out into the light of day—at least as Schneiderman brings them out—Lacan's ideas seem to have little real bearing on psychoanalysis. In fact, they often irreverently remind one of the solemn metaphysical absurdities expounded by the characters in Thomas Love Peacock's novels. Earlier in the book, discussing the "theoretical wasteland" that psychoanalysis threatens to become through its exclusion of nonmedical people, Schneiderman disdainfully writes, "Bringing a group of physicians together to discuss questions that have for centuries been posed and debated by philosophers might produce some amusing moments, but it is inconceivable that such untrained people will say anything new and original about these questions, unless they are in constant interaction with people whose preanalytic training is broader and more intellectually oriented." From Schneiderman's book, the *nekulturny* M.D.'s of American psychoanalysis will comprehend the full measure of their intellectual insufficiency. They will marvel at the bigness of the thinking of the Lacanians, in contrast to the pettiness of their own theoretical concerns. In an effort at self-betterment, they may even be driven to attempt to grasp the writings of the master himself. But to negotiate this feat they will probably have to follow Schneiderman to Paris.

*The New York Times Book Review*, 1983

# *Part* II

# The Quarterly Affair

LIFE, after dealing him an unspeakable blow at the age of seven with the death of his mother, was very good to Edmund Gosse; but posterity has not been kind to him. T. S. Eliot, Evelyn Waugh, and Virginia Woolf (among others) have left memorably snotty epithets. Eliot, reviewing Evan Charteris's official biography, *The Life and Letters of Sir Edmund Gosse*, in the *Criterion* in 1931, wrote:

> The place that Sir Edmund Gosse filled in the literary and social life of London is one that no one can ever fill again, because it is, so to speak, an office that has been abolished. . . . I will not say that Sir Edmund's activity was not a very useful activity, in a social-literary world which is rapidly receding into memory. He was, indeed, an amenity, but not quite any sort of amenity for which I can see any great need in our time.

In his memoirs of 1964, Waugh wrote:

> His eminence sprang from his sedulous pursuit of the eminent, among whom he was more proud of his intimacy with people of power and fashion than with artists. . . . I saw Gosse as a Mr. Tulkinghorn, the soft-footed, inconspicuous, ill-natured habitué of the great world, and I longed for a demented lady's maid to make an end of him.

✣ EDMUND GOSSE: A LITERARY LANDSCAPE, 1849–1928 (Chicago: University of Chicago Press, 1984), by Ann Thwaite.

In her diary, Woolf described a gathering in 1926 at which Vita Sackville-West "was fawned upon by the little dapper grocer Gosse," and five years later, in a review of the Charteris biography, she said of Gosse:

> It was no wonder that he overshot the mark, never quite got his equilibrium at parties which he loved, required to know the maiden names of married guests, and observed formalities punctiliously which are taken as a matter of course by those who have never lived in dread of the instant coming of the Lord, and have ordered their clothes for generations in Savile Row.

Perhaps the unkindest cut of all was the release in 1975 of Arthur Benson's secret journal, which runs to over four million words, a great many of which are about Gosse—more than any other contemporary ever wrote about him, according to Gosse's latest biographer, Ann Thwaite. While Gosse was busy sucking up to the English aristocracy, Benson was darkly watching him and going home at night to record in his diary every last undignified thing Gosse did. For one of numerous examples quoted by Thwaite:

> the difference of his behaviour when he is with people of consequence and when he is not is terrible. At the Ribblesdales, the Newtons, the Eltons he was all wreathed in smiles, jesting, on tiptoe, bowing. Yesterday he took offence at something at Lis Escop and stalked about pouting, looking gloomily at things, brooding. It is this awful *valuation* of people, thinking whether it is worthwhile being civil to them, demanding recognition from them, which sickens me. . . .

Gosse is remembered today because, in 1907, he wrote *Father and Son*, a memoir of his childhood, which was immediately acclaimed as a minor masterpiece, and which continues to exert a strong and strange power over all who read it. Gosse wrote nearly fifty other books—of criticism, biography, literary history, fiction, and verse—but none of them are read today; only in *Father and Son* does he rise above his usual mushy urbanity ("the peculiar combination of suavity, gravity, malignity, and common sense always repels me," Virginia Woolf wrote) and strike the pure note of durable English prose.

Edmund was the son of Philip and Emily Gosse, a pair of educated, genteelly poor fanatical Calvinists, whose favorite recreation was to interpret the Book of Revelation together (they thus diverted themselves in the evening as other Victorian couples played cards or the piano) and whose expectation for Edmund was that he would either die and go to heaven (he was a sickly child) or become a fundamentalist minister, like his father. Instead, the mother died of cancer, and the boy's life, which hitherto had been merely narrow and odd and utterly dominated by religion (he had no playmates, no storybooks, no secular amusements), now became pitiably sad and bleak. The circumstances of the mother's death were harrowing. She had fallen into the hands of a quack, who for four months subjected her to the most painful of futile treatments; in order to receive the treatments, she had moved to a house in Pimlico near the quack, taking her son with her. Remembering this period bitterly, Gosse writes in *Father and Son*, "Let those who take a pessimistic view of our social progress ask themselves whether such tortures could to-day be inflicted on a delicate patient, or whether that patient would be allowed to exist, in the greatest misery, in a lodging with no professional nurse to wait upon her, and with no companion but a little helpless boy of seven years of age."

Soon after the mother's death, the father suffered a lesser, but in some ways more permanently devastating, blow. Philip Gosse was a religious fundamentalist by calling but a scientist by profession. He was a naturalist of some eminence, who had published works of zoology, ornithology, natural history, and marine biology, belonged to the Royal Society, and was the inventor of the marine aquarium. Like other Christian intellectuals of the time (the 1850s), but more acutely than most, he was racked by the contradiction between the theory of evolution, which was inexorably emerging from the work of Darwin, Wallace, Hooker, Lyall, et al., and the scriptural account of creation. As Edmund writes, "Every instinct in his intelligence went out at first to greet the new light." But "it had hardly done so, when a recollection of the opening chapter of 'Genesis' checked it at the outset."

In 1857, Philip Gosse published a book called *Omphalos: An Attempt to Untie the Geological Knot*, which offered an ingenious way out of the theological dilemma posed by the existence of fossils and which he confidently thought would bring him universal gratitude for its reconciliation of science and religion. Philip Gosse proposed that when the world was created in six days it was created with fossils already embedded in the rocks—just as Adam was created with *his* insignia of previous life that had never been lived: the navel—and as trees were created with marks of sloughed bark and fallen leaves that had never existed, animals with teeth worn away by exercise never taken, and so on for all living forms. Some ninety years later, Jorge Luis Borges was to write of the "monstrous elegance" of Philip Gosse's thesis and to link it with the metaphysics of Augustine, Heraclitus, and Spinoza, among others. But in 1857 the book was a dismal failure. "Atheists and Christians alike looked at it and laughed, and threw it away," Edmund writes in *Father and Son*. And

as his reconciliation of Scripture statements and geological deductions was welcomed nowhere; as Darwin continued silent, and the youthful Huxley was scornful, and even Charles Kingsley, from whom my Father had expected the most instant appreciation, wrote that he could not "give up the painful and slow conclusion of five and twenty years' study of geology, and believe that God has written on the rocks one enormous and superfluous lie"—as all this happened or failed to happen, a gloom, cold and dismal, descended upon our morning teacups.

This atmosphere pervades *Father and Son* and inevitably brings *The Way of All Flesh* to mind. But there is a crucial difference between the two accounts of childhood in clergymen's households (which were published within four years of each other). Unlike Theobold Pontifex, whose special combination of stupidity and sadism makes him one of the most chilling villains of Victorian literature, Philip Gosse, as depicted by his son, is a remarkable and lovable man, if a stubbornly willful and extreme one. While Gosse is no fonder of religion than Butler—*Father and Son* is written from the viewpoint of a man who considers fundamentalist religion fanatical and repellent—his affection and admiration for his father gleam through the bleak pages of his autobiography and give it its unique pathos. (The passages in *Father and Son* devoted to expeditions to tidal pools on the Devonshire coast, where the naturalist and his little boy went in quest of specimens of sea anemones and where, Gosse recalls, "my father became most easy, most happy, most human," form some of the book's most potent images.)

Ann Thwaite's researches among unpublished family documents, to which she was given access by Gosse's granddaughter, corroborate the son's idealization of the father and, indeed, suggest that the actuality of Gosse's childhood was somewhat more benign and "normal" than the autobiography would have us believe. Thwaite points out that Edmund *did* play with other children, when he claims he never did, and says it was not true that he was his mother's only companion during her ordeal in Pimlico: evidently a Mrs. Hislop had been there, too.

Thwaite's attention to these discrepancies recalls Gosse's review of Henry Festing Jones's biography of Samuel Butler, in which he refuses to believe that Butler's father was the monster that is Theobold Pontifex and chastises Butler for being "incapable of confronting the incidents of his own life without colouring them, and without giving way to prejudice in the statement of plain facts." Gosse's strange and unconvincing insistence that Canon Butler wasn't all that bad ("if Samuel Butler was really tormented at home, as Ernest Pontifex was, it is odd that some note of hostility should not have crept into his juvenile correspondence," Gosse writes, and a few pages later adds, "After all, when the worst of Canon Butler is admitted, he was a Christian and a gentleman by the side of the appalling Pauli") must spring from some personal motive, some anxious need to see his own father as good.

Thwaite's underscorings of disparities between Gosse's narrative and the "plain facts" have a different purpose. She has constructed the first half of her very intelligent and very readable biography to lead up to a dramatic incident in Gosse's life—a searing humiliation he suffered in October 1886, which, like his father's Calvary, was over a book. In this case, however, the difficulty was not a fantastical thesis but horrendous factual error. And so Thwaite foreshadows the coming debacle with example after example of what Henry James called Gosse's "genius for inaccuracy." Gosse simply couldn't—or wouldn't —get facts straight. Even when he has his own journal in front of him while writing an account of a trip to Norway, he gets dates wrong, Thwaite notes, adding, "It was as if he wearies of accuracy."

GOSSE had come to London from Devonshire at the age of seventeen to work as a junior assistant in the cataloguing department of the British Museum—a position procured for him by his father, through the intervention of Kingsley—and to try to make a name for himself as a poet. (The father appears to have accepted the son's lack of a religious vocation, though for years after Edmund left home he was subjected to the almost daily "torment of a postal inquisition" by his father regarding the state of his soul.) Gosse's verse was feeble (to put it charitably), and eventually he had to put his poetic ambitions to rest;* but he became successful in a field—that of literary criticism—for which he had even less apparent qualification.

Gosse had no university education; he had gone to not very good boarding and day schools, chosen by his father for the piety of the headmasters; and perhaps most significant of all, as a child he had not been permitted to read any fiction, so that when once—as he records in a famous passage in *Father and Son*—while exploring a garret he came across a trunk lined with sheets of a sensational novel, he never doubted that what he read was an account of actual events, since the genre of invented events was simply unknown to him. In their preface to *Transatlantic Dialogue: Selected American Correspondence of Edmund Gosse* (1965), the scholars Paul F. Mattheisen and Michael Millgate attribute Gosse's improbable success in a field that he had no business entering ("he was clearly ill-equipped to undertake full-scale critical work on major literary figures," Mattheisen and Millgate sternly write) to his ingenious choice of areas of study where little, if any, scholarly work had been done and which, further, abounded in minor figures who lent themselves to the "personal and discursive" treatment that was Gosse's stock-in-trade. Scandinavian literature and seventeenth-century English literature were two such areas.

Perhaps even more remarkable, considering his solitary and odd childhood, was the young Gosse's rapid, Norman

---

* Though as late as 1894 he was publishing stuff like this:

*Thank God, that, while the nerves decay / And muscles desiccate away, / The brain's the hardiest part of men, / And thrives till threescore years and ten;*

*That, tho' the crescent flesh be wound / In soft unseemly folds around, / The heart may, all the days we live, / Grow more alert and sensitive.*

(from "In Russet and Silver")

Podhoretz–like conquest of literary London. He made it first with the Pre-Raphaelites (Ford Madox Brown, William Morris, and the Rossettis were among his earliest catches), then with Algernon Swinburne, Robert Browning, Coventry Patmore, Alfred, Lord Tennyson, and Robert Louis Stevenson, followed by Sidney Colvin, William Archer, John Addington Symonds, Henry James, and Thomas Hardy—to mention only the most luminous of the literary figures by whom Gosse was taken up and to whom, in many cases, he formed close, lifelong attachments. When, three years before the disaster of 1886, he became a candidate for the newly founded Clark Lectureship at Cambridge, no lesser personages than Matthew Arnold, Tennyson, and Browning wrote warm letters of recommendation.

In assigning a first cause to the disaster, it is perhaps to this candidacy—and to the hubris behind it—that we should look. For if Gosse's error-ridden book *From Shakespeare to Pope: An Inquiry into the Causes and Phenomena of the Rise of Classical Poetry in England* had not issued from a university press, it might not have provoked the devastating review it received in the August–October *Quarterly Review*, and certainly it would not have given the anonymous reviewer his first deadly sentence: "That such a book as this should have been permitted to go forth to the world with the *imprimatur* of the University of Cambridge, affords matter for very grave reflection." (Gosse had been beaten out, by one vote, for the Clark Lectureship by Leslie Stephen—a defeat he took with equanimity because of the distinction of his rival—but then, to his delight, he was offered the job a year later, when Stephen dropped out. *From Shakespeare to Pope* was a book of the lectures that Gosse gave at Cambridge in 1884 and repeated on an American tour.)

Had Gosse not ventured into the academy, had he been content to remain in the world of amateur belles-lettres, his "literary felonies" (as K.R. Eissler characterized the errors in a similar case of scholarly insufficiency) might well have gone forever undetected. Such crimes are committed every day—as everyone knows who has ever done research in a library. Carelessness, sloppiness, misinformation, misquotation, and fudging of fact are commonplaces, not extraordinary occurrences. What is not commonplace is a wrathful Defender of the Spirit of Fact who occasionally comes forward to catch out an unfortunate wretch. Such a recent defender was Eissler, who, angered by what he saw as a slur on the name of Sigmund Freud, devoted a whole book, *Talent and Genius* (1971), to demonstrating the errors in Paul Roazen's book *Brother Animal* (1969). And such a defender, in 1886, was John Churton Collins, the writer of the anonymous review in the *Quarterly* of Gosse's book, whose identity was an open secret from the start but whose motives were never entirely clear.

Collins was a man of Gosse's age—at the time of the attack, Collins was thirty-eight and Gosse was thirty-seven—and the two had been friends a few years earlier but had drifted apart. Collins had all the qualifications for a career in literary scholarship that Gosse lacked: he had gone to Oxford, he had the instincts of a scholar, and he wrote with Leavis-like acerbity and authority. (Eliot, in his 1930 essay on Cyril Tourneur, characterized Collins's introduction to the 1878 edition of Tourneur's works as being "by far the most penetrating interpretation of Tourneur that has been written.") But he was a luckless man. Where Gosse glided easily through life—he went from his job at the British Museum to one as a translator at the Board of Trade, which permitted him leisure for reading and writing and brought in enough money to comfortably maintain his wife and three children in a pleasant London house—Collins had to struggle to stay above water. He was like a character in a Gissing novel—a harried, unfortunate man, with a wife and seven children to support; with no money except what he earned from teaching Greek and Latin in a cram school, from writing reviews, and from giving lectures for the University Extension Society; and with a disposition to depression, which grew worse as the years of overwork and disappointment continued.

Gosse had evidently only to walk into a room and charm everyone in it, while poor Collins would write in his journal after a dinner party, "The most striking figure there was, of course, Robert Browning, to whom I was not introduced and who had, of course, forgotten me." (The journal entry is reprinted in a biography of Collins written by his son Laurence in 1912; except for a few letters scattered in university libraries and occasional references in contemporary letters and memoirs, this inept and inadequate exercise in filial piety is our sole source of biographical information about Collins.) Along with the social mortification that Collins had to swallow, he had to endure professional rebuffs. He was repeatedly passed over for academic positions: the Merton Chair of Language and Literature at Oxford, which he had helped to establish and confidently applied for in 1885, went, instead, to a philologist; it wasn't until 1904 that he got a professorship at the University of Birmingham. His relations with editors were no less unhappy. A pathetic correspondence has been preserved by the National Library of Scotland (which I happened on, years ago, while doing some research on Gosse and Collins), in which Collins sends letter after letter to the editor of *Blackwood's* magazine, inquiring after the fate of an article. ("This is the *third* or *fourth* letter I have written *begging* you to send me just one line to tell me what has become of my 'Athenaeus Oxoniensis,' " he writes in 1877, and continues, "I really think an author who has taken such trouble as I have done to please you is not being exacting when after a piece has been retained *three* years . . . he ventures modestly to enquire after his bantling. I cannot reproach myself with impertinently and intrusively *bothering* you and I am sure there was nothing in the tone of my repeated letters which could in any way have annoyed. . . .") Was it any wonder that Gosse's appointment to the Clark Lectureship should have galled Collins and that he should have seized an opportunity to savage Gosse's very vulnerable book with special, ill-concealed joy?

But lucklessness is like a disease for which there is no cure, and among the many ironies of "the *Quarterly* affair," as it came to be called, is the devastating effect it had on the fortunes of Collins while leaving Gosse relatively unscathed. Like F. R. Leavis's famous attack on C. P. Snow in 1962—where it was generally felt that while Leavis was "right," he had been wrong to attack Snow in the intemperate way he did—Collins's attack on Gosse illustrates the thanklessness and ill-advisedness of the task of the self-appointed guardian of truth and morals. To be right at the expense of another is one of the most unfortunate positions one can find oneself in, since, at bottom, it is the position of the tattling child. One of the earliest lessons we learn as children (it may be our earliest experience of paradox) is that tattling goes unrewarded and thus is profitless. The "Look what he did!" atmosphere of Collins's review gives it its bracing edge and piques our *Schadenfreude* (the pleasure of the other children listening to the tattler enumerate the sins of the naughty child), but eventually it sours on us.

Although the review caused a flurry of interest and excitement (the *Pall Mall Gazette* and the *World*, adopting the role of the excited siblings, took Collins's side and pilloried Gosse daily in editorials), it brought Collins no real glory and, in fact, shoved him the more decisively and irrevocably off to the side of the arena in which late-nineteenth-century literary life was being played out. The literary establishment—the grownups—closed ranks around its favored child, knowing full well how naughty he had been but declining to be dictated to by an impertinent outsider. Cambridge stood staunchly behind Gosse (what else could it do?), as did James, Symonds, Swinburne, Tennyson, Colvin, Stevenson, Archer, Howells, Browning, Hardy, and others, whose letters, carefully preserved by Gosse, form an authoritative primer on how to write comforting bullshit on demand.

On the other hand, poor Collins contrived, in the course of the *Quarterly* affair, to lose the single illustrious friend he had.

In replying in the *Athenaeum* to Gosse's reproach that "there are no stabs like those which are given by an estranged friend," Collins had the unhappy inspiration of citing Swinburne, whom he had savaged in the *Quarterly* the previous year, as an example of someone who didn't take criticism personally. "I believe, rightly or wrongly, that Mr. Swinburne's critical opinions are often wild, unsound, and even absurd; that his prose style is still oftener intolerably involved, florid and diffuse; and that he has in consequence exercised a most pernicious influence on contemporary style and on contemporary literature. . . . But I have yet to learn that Mr. Swinburne considers me 'no gentleman,' " the ever luckless Collins boasted—little knowing that Swinburne's preternatural calm and forbearance under attack came of the fact that he had simply never read (or even heard of) the article in question. Once alerted to it, he let out a howl of outrage in the *Athenaeum*, calling Collins, among other things, "the pertest of all pupil teachers" and the *Quarterly* a "*journal pour rire*, graver at once and duller than its fellows of the more professionally comic press. . . ."

Gosse, bloody but unbowed (one of his sharpest critics had been the author of "Invictus" himself, who, under the initials H.B., wrote a series of Letters from London for the American journal *The Critic*, giving jocular blow-by-blow descriptions of "the scandal of the year"), went on to spend thirty more years writing, lecturing, and socializing, gradually becoming the venerable institution that it behooved the younger generation to want to knock down, and finally getting knighted, in 1924. Collins, meanwhile, went on slaving and struggling and getting nowhere, and finally, in 1904, during an episode of depression, he drowned in a canal. Even in death he came off without dignity. During the inquest on his body (as reported by the London *Times*), a physician friend of Collins, attempting to convince the jury that Collins had not committed suicide, argued that he could have fallen into the canal accidentally "while performing a necessary function."

．　．　．

THAT Gosse made appalling mistakes in *From Shakespeare to Pope* is beyond question—but what these mistakes were about, psychologically speaking, remains somewhat mysterious. Ann Thwaite's account of the *Quarterly* affair is very spirited, amused, and amusing—she has a sharp eye for the ludicrous and moves easily through the masses of documentation that the incident threw up, to create a brisk, farcical narrative—but it doesn't answer the question of why Gosse did this thing to himself. Thwaite's incuriosity about Gosse's proneness to error—her treatment of it as if it were some sort of regrettable but not very interesting constitutional debility, like nearsightedness—leaves a hole in her narrative where one had confidently expected a mountain. Thwaite simply declines to examine Gosse's errors. "It would be tedious to go through all his [Collins's] objections in any detail," she says offhandedly.

In one sense, of course, Thwaite's implicit notion, that literary error is so common and universal that instances of it do not require special psychological explanation, is correct. The fact that all writers constantly make mistakes of fact and transcription is attested to by the professions of proofreader and fact checker. The checking departments of modern magazines routinely work with manuscripts that are as factually porous as Gosse's. To quote a passage from a text and get every word right seems utterly beyond the capacity of all but the most nuttily obsessive among us. Thwaite herself, for example, in transcribing an eleven-line excerpt from a letter of 1890 from Gosse to Symonds (which I happen to have a copy of in holograph), makes *five* errors, most of them trivial, but one rather serious (she skips several pages and creates a sentence Gosse never wrote), and another that ruins Gosse's grammar. It is as if we all need in some way to take possession of whatever passes through our hands, to leave our mark, to show that we have been there. What may look like mere sloppiness is in (unconscious) fact a studied assertion of personality.

But there are also errors animated by more specific and less innocent wishes than the general desire to be onstage all the time. These are the tendentious errors that twist facts in a way favorable to the writer's thesis and are rightly called "felonies" (or, in Collins's term, "delinquencies"), because of the way they undermine the foundation of fact on which the world of ideas is poised. Such an error, for example, was Gosse's assertion that Edmund Waller was the first English poet to write in distichs (heroic couplets that contain complete thoughts); as Collins nastily pointed out, numerous English poets (Nicholas Grimoald, Robert Greene, George Sandys, among others) had written in distich years before Waller did. But since Gosse had declared Waller to be "the hero of this whole volume"—a study of the classical reaction to the "hysterical riot of the Jacobeans"—the reason for his "ignorance" of the work of Waller's predecessors, which takes some of the luster off Waller's heroism, is not hard to fathom.

To Gosse's credit, most of his literary offenses are more gratuitous than felonious. I cannot resist quoting an example of the former (one that Thwaite omits), which gives a rich sense both of the extraordinary lengths Gosse went to to ball everything up and of the icy savagery of Collins's attack. Collins writes:

In the life of Waller, Mr. Gosse finds this sentence: "Mr. Saville used to say that no man in England should keep him company without drinking but Ned Waller." This becomes, in Mr. Gosse's narrative, "George Savile, Lord Halifax, the famous *viveur*, and a pupil of Waller's, in verse, said," &c. (p. 236). It would be difficult to match this. Nearly every word is a blunder. Indeed, we will boldly say that, if our own or any other literature were ransacked, it would be ransacked in vain for a sentence which condenses so many errors and so much of that *crassa negligentia*, which is as reprehensible in writers as it is in lawyers and doctors. George Savile, Lord Halifax, who is apparently known only to Mr. Gosse as "the famous *viveur*," was, as we need scarcely say, one of the most distinguished statesmen of the seventeenth century. He was in no sense of the word a *viveur*. He was not a pupil of Waller. He never, so far as is recorded, wrote a line of verse in his life. But there was another Lord Halifax, who might perhaps be known to Mr. Gosse only in connection with his convivial habits and his bad poetry, but who is known to everyone else as the Originator of the National Debt, as the Founder of the Bank of England, and as the most eminent financier in English history. It is this Lord Halifax who might, as the author of a copy of verses on the death of Charles II, be described as a pupil of Waller. And it is of this Lord Halifax that Mr. Gosse is probably thinking. But the name of this Lord Halifax was, unfortunately for Mr. Gosse, Charles Montague. The "Mr. Savile" alluded to, was in truth neither George Savile, Marquis of Halifax, nor Charles Montague, Earl of Halifax, but Henry Savile a younger son of Sir William Savile, and a younger brother of the Marquis.

That the strictly reared son of a fundamentalist minister should produce a book of such florid unreliability is ironic, indeed, but perhaps only inevitable. The fanatical concern of Edmund's parents with literal truth, which led them to forbid him any nonfactual literature (the Bible, of course, was considered factual), may have been the very wellspring of his "genius for inaccuracy." In *Father and Son*, Gosse quotes a passage from the diary of his mother regarding a secret sin she had struggled against since childhood—the sin of inventing stories. "The longing to invent stories grew with violence," the mother wrote. "Everything I heard or read became food for my distemper. The simplicity of truth was not sufficient for me; I must needs embroider imagination upon it, and the folly, vanity, and wickedness which disgraced my heart are more than I am able to express. Even now [at the age of twenty-nine], tho' watched, prayed and striven against, that is still the sin that most easily besets me." "This is, surely, a very painful instance of the repression of an instinct," Gosse writes, and goes on to speculate whether his mother had not been "intended by nature to be a novelist."

In his own case, the repressed instinct for invention surfaced in the form of made-up facts. That factual truth was an issue for Gosse is clear from such passages as the following, from *From Shakespeare to Pope*: "Here again, as everywhere where we look closely into the historic development of literature, we see the value of dates, and the paramount importance of a clear chronological sequence." (Which in no way prevented Gosse —such is the power of the repressed to cloud men's minds— from, for example, giving the date of Waller's poem "To the King on His Navy" as 1621, even though the date 1626 appears as part of the poem's full title.) "Never, in all my early childhood, did anyone address to me the affecting preamble, 'Once upon a time!'" Gosse wistfully recalls in *Father and Son*. "I was told about missionaries, but never about pirates; I was familiar with humming-birds, but I had never heard of fairies." Perhaps in recompense, the grown-up Gosse filled his books of criticism and biography with *viveurs* who never lived, events that never took place, and chronologies that invested the dry world of literary history with the timelessness of never-never land.

SINCE the publication, in 1964, of Phyllis Grosskurth's biography of John Addington Symonds, *The Woeful Victorian*, Gosse is commonly believed to have been a secret homosexual. Grosskurth published part of a letter of Gosse's to Symonds (the mistranscribed letter of 1890 mentioned above—Grosskurth made only two mistakes in her extract), in which Gosse all but spelled out his personal knowledge of the "problem" by which Symonds was beset. In the letter, Gosse wrote:

I know all that you speak of—the solitude, the rebellion, the despair. Yet I have been happy, too; I hope you also have been happy,—that all with you has not been disappointment & the revulsion of hope? Either way, I entirely & deeply sympathise with you. Years ago, I wanted to write to you about all this, and withdrew through cowardice. I have had a very fortunate life, but there has been this obstinate twist in it. I have reached a quieter time—some beginnings of that Sophoclean period when the wild beast dies. He is not dead, but tamer; I understand him & the trick of his claws. . . .

One of the surprises of Thwaite's biography is its dearth of corroborative evidence for Gosse's homosexuality; twenty years have elapsed since the publication of Grosskurth's book, and the 1890 letter remains the single piece of hard evidence for the view of Gosse as a closet invert. Either he covered his traces extraordinarily well or the whole thing has been a misunderstanding. Leon Edel has argued for the latter view in the fourth volume of his biography of Henry James (*The Treacherous Years, 1895–1901*), writing that the 1890 Gosse letter "has been grossly misinterpreted as an admission by him of his own homosexuality" and going on to say that although "Gosse did say to Symonds in this letter that there was an 'obstinate twist' in his life . . . the fuller text of the letter shows that he was alluding not to inversion but to his 'cowardice' in not taking originally a large-minded and generous view of Symonds's 'problem.' "

At the risk of sounding—and ending up—like Collins (and also marveling at the amount of scholarly trouble the adventitious appearance of a holograph can stir up), I must rebuke the admirable biographer of James for talking through his hat. There is *nothing* in the fuller text of the letter to substantiate Edel's interpretation; if anything, the fuller text—which partly deals with a "beautiful study," probably of a nude male model, that Symonds had sent Gosse and which contains the statement "I have come out of the fire absolutely clear in conscience and without the shadow of a doubt as to right & wrong"—gives even greater credence to the Grosskurth view than does the extract alone.

Ann Thwaite writes, "When someone once asked Lytton Strachey whether Gosse was a homosexual, Strachey replied, 'No, but he's Hamo-sexual.'" The reference is to Hamo Thornycroft, a sculptor of Gosse's age, with whom Gosse had a passionate friendship for many years and to whom Thwaite believes Gosse was referring when he wrote to Symonds of the "obstinate twist" in his life and of "the wild beast." Gosse's letters to Thornycroft (which were preserved by Thornycroft) are clearly love letters, but they are letters that can also be read (and were written to be read) as the letters of one married man writing to another. There was never anything clandestine about the relationship. Gosse would go alone with Thornycroft on walking tours and fishing trips and boating excursions—which we know about today because of the letters Gosse wrote home to his wife, describing the banks of calamus on which he and his friend lay, the naked bathing they did, the alfresco meals they prepared, etc. Thwaite uses her eyes and ears and instinct to pick up the homoerotic atmosphere of the friendship, but she doesn't go beyond the evidence. The question of Gosse's homosexuality remains unanswered, but Thwaite's delicate, sympathetic, and clear-sighted treatment of the Thornycroft friendship has somehow laid it to rest.

In Ann Thwaite, altogether, Gosse has found a biographer of special temperamental affinity who, like himself, is more drawn to men's "fireside ways" than to their unsheltered, inchoate public or private dramas and who has filled her long biography with the sort of domestic details and anecdotes that Gosse's own writings are filled with. In saying this, I do not in any way want to suggest that Thwaite's book is superficial or overlong. I think her approach is right. If it faltered in the *Quarterly* affair—Gosse's single larger-than-life appearance—it has served her admirably everywhere else. Gosse is one of life and literature's Prufrocks, and to write about him as if he were

Hamlet wouldn't do at all. "I see his faults clearly, but am very deeply attached to him, by a kind of insoluble tie, like relationship," Benson wrote of Gosse, and this could describe Thwaite's attitude toward her subject. Her portrait of this touchy, feline, ambitious, cautious, snobbish, self-stroking, vivacious, generous, warmhearted, and *interesting* man is an authoritative and just one. I recommend it to students of the art of biography as well as to aficionados of the Victorian literary scene.

*The New York Review of Books*, 1985

# What Maisie Didn't Know

IN the spring of 1914, Vanessa Bell playfully wrote to Maynard Keynes, who was then subletting Asheham House, in Sussex, from her:

> Did you have a pleasant afternoon buggering one or more of the young men we left for you? It must have been delicious out on the downs in the afternoon sun—a thing I have often wanted to do but one never gets the opportunity and the desire at the right moment. I imagine you, however, with your bare limbs entwined with his and all the ecstatic preliminaries of sucking sodomy—it sounds like the name of a station. . . . How divine it must have been.*

Vanessa at this time was no longer living regularly with her husband of eight years, Clive Bell; was getting tired of her lover of two years, Roger Fry; and was falling desperately in love with the homosexual Duncan Grant, who had been a lover of Keynes and Lytton Strachey, and was now involved with, among others, her brother Adrian Stephen. At the end of 1914, Duncan began an affair with David Garnett, known as Bunny, "whose tastes were only temporarily homosexual" (as Angelica Garnett, his second wife, has written) but were to last the duration of the First World War, which Duncan and Bunny spent working as conscientious-objector farm laborers and sleeping together in one or another spare bedroom provided by Vanessa. She had humbly accepted the presence of Bunny in

✤ DECEIVED WITH KINDNESS: A BLOOMSBURY CHILDHOOD (San Diego: Harcourt Brace Jovanovich, 1987), by Angelica Garnett.
* Quoted by Frances Spalding in *Vanessa Bell* (Ticknor & Fields, 1983).

order to be near Duncan, and her forbearance was occasionally rewarded: "I copulated on Saturday with her with great satisfaction to myself physically," Duncan wrote in his diary in February 1918, during an absence of Bunny's, and added, somewhat incoherently, "It is a comfortable way the females of letting off one's spunk and comfortable. Also the pleasure it gives is reassuring. You don't get this dumb misunderstanding body of a person who isn't a bugger."*

It is to one such coitus of convenience that the author of the memoir under review owes her life, which began on Christmas Day, 1918, at Charleston, the Sussex farmhouse that Vanessa had rented in 1916 for her and Duncan and Bunny, and where she and Duncan were to intermittently live (with and without his various boyfriends) for the next forty years. The child was given the name Angelica Bell—the ever genial (and almost ever absent) Clive had agreed to be the putative father—and was not told the truth about her parentage until she was seventeen. On the night of Angelica's birth, Frances Spalding reports, Vanessa's other children, Julian and Quentin Bell, aged ten and eight, "scuttled about like mice, until distracted by stockings and presents; Duncan and Bunny sat up all night talking with the doctor. Bunny was surprised that the perfectly formed baby already exhibited signs of intelligence and independent will. . . . 'Its beauty is the remarkable thing about it,' he wrote to Lytton on Christmas Day, adding the afterthought 'I think of marrying it; when she is twenty I shall be 46—will it be scandalous?' "

It is common for children to think of their parents' lives as divided into two discrete parts, the dividing line being their own birth. In the photographs they see of their parents as young people and in the stories they hear about their parents' youth, children simply do not recognize the heavy, monolithic, often oppressive presences that—such being the condition of helpless dependency into which we are born—parents become in the

---

* Frances Spalding again.

imaginations of their offspring and never entirely leave off being, however lovingly and intelligently, and even gaily, family life is conducted. Angelica Garnett expresses this universal fantasy when she writes that after reading her mother's letters to Virginia Woolf and to Clive Bell, "I was astonished by a vitality that I had not known was there," and that the person who emerged from the letters "was a woman that I could see through the much darker personality of the later Vanessa, which lay far more heavily on my consciousness." But in her case, as in that of other children of famous parents writing their almost inevitably aggrieved memoirs, there is an added pathos to the feelings both of having arrived on the scene too late to know her parents at their most wonderful and of disbelief in the wonderfulness itself.

These books by the children of the celebrated are poised on a painful paradox. Their authors say they want to be free of their parents, and yet they can think of no better way of achieving an identity than to retail to a callous and indifferent world the intimate secrets of their families. Acting as posterity's spies, rather than as characters in their own dramas, these oppressed and obsessed offspring write with the self-effacement of the biographer rather than with the egotism of the autobiographer. Imagine a book written after the deaths of Anna and Vronsky by their illegitimate daughter, Annie, in which she expresses her resentment at being treated as a cipher (how many readers of *Anna Karenina* even remember the child's name?) but simply cannot reinvent herself. Angelica Garnett, similarly, cannot get out from under the weight of the monumental novelistic work that the writings of the Bloomsbury diarists, letter writers, memoirists, autobiographers, and biographers have collectively become (and of which her own memoir now becomes a part), and she remains a figure with practically no distinguishing characteristics—something she notices herself: in an epilogue she writes, "To me no one appears more shadowy than myself, or more questionably portrayed in my book."

Vanessa, in contrast, is vividly (if savagely) portrayed. Frances Spalding's affectionate and admiring biography gave us the portrait of a beautiful and talented woman who lived her life bravely, gamely, and unconventionally; who achieved a balance between her considerable artistic achievement and her even more extraordinary personal relations; and who, without having any of today's feminist consciousness, created an existence for herself that any feminist might envy for its freedom from social constraint and its serene dedication to the daily, unremitting making of art. Spalding's evaluation of Vanessa may be summed up in the following passage she quotes from an unpublished letter that Vanessa's discarded lover, Roger Fry, wrote to her:

> Oh why do I admire you—my dear it would take ages to tell you all I do admire you for but you see I think you go straight for the things that are worthwhile—you have done such an extraordinarily difficult thing without any fuss, but thro' all the conventions kept friends with a pernickety creature like Clive, got quit of me and yet kept me your devoted friend, got all the things you need for your own development and yet managed to be a splendid mother. . . . You give one a sense of security of something solid and real in a shifting world. Then to [sic] your marvellous practical power wh. has of course really a quality of great imagination in it, because your efficiency comes without effort or worry or fuss. No I don't think you need ever doubt yourself. You have genius in your life as well as in your art and both are rare things.

In *Deceived with Kindness*, Angelica offers us the unpleasant underside of this idealization. She does not consider Vanessa a splendid mother. She writes sinisterly of Vanessa's intrusiveness—"long straight fingers [which were] too apt to find their way into every crevice of my body." On the other hand, she felt frustrated in her child's desire for discipline:

95

My earliest sensations were of her propitiatory attitude, as though I held a weapon in my small, fat hands. Anxious not to provoke, she continually soothed and lulled me into acceptance. Cries, screams or the sight of tears upset her; if she could buy peace she was satisfied. I longed for her to want me to be strong and independent, whereas apparently all she desired was to suffocate me with caresses.

As a girl and an adolescent, she continued to feel oppressed and somehow cheated. She reproaches Vanessa for denying her proper schooling—"Convinced that I was going to be an artist, she decided that I needed no more education than she had had herself. Seeing also that I had showed promise of being good-looking, she thought that I would 'get along all right' without training of the mind: such indeed was her attitude of laissez-faire that one sometimes had the impression that she despised the intellect—or perhaps she only denied my right to develop mine, since she certainly admired the erudition of many of her friends, including her sister"—and she writes bitterly of her experience at a sort of progressive girls' school named Langford Grove, whose headmistress, known as Curty, was so enamored of Vanessa and Bloomsbury that she permitted Vanessa to dictate the terms of her daughter's education:

She persuaded Mrs. Curtis to let me drop any subject I found difficult. Latin, arithmetic and allied subjects, games and some other disciplines were successively crossed off my time-table until, in addition to music and the arts, I learnt only history, French and English. True, I would never have shone at any of the discarded subjects, except perhaps for Latin—but it was the demoralisation of not being put to the test like everyone else that was insidious and harmful. I did not realise what it was at the time, but this misplaced permissiveness ate into my morale like a beetle into a honeycomb.

The glorious artistic and intellectual household of Charleston—"Each year the house and garden grew lovelier, more adorned, more imbued with associations," Spalding rhapsodizes; "It exerted a potent spell on all who visited it, spinning an invisible net of contentment over its occupants"—was perceived a little differently by its youngest member. Recalling the obscure shame about her sloppy appearance she was made to feel during a visit to the utterly conventional middle-class household of a schoolmate, the grown Angelica reflects:

> At home what did it matter if my legs were bare or my clothes in holes, so long as I was busy and happy? No one ever noticed whether I brushed my hair or cleaned my fingernails—if Mrs. Carr had used the word "slut" she would have been nearer the truth. Vanessa frowned on convention, and we imitated her, mentally elbowing out those who valued cleanliness and tidiness, as though there was no room in the world for both points of view. In our world indeed there hardly was—Mrs. Carr would not have survived for five minutes—but no one seemed to think this might be our loss rather than hers. The walls round us were high and the conditions inside the castle odd. Though we were unbrushed, unwashed and ragged, our carpets and curtains faded and our furniture stained and groggy, appearances of a purely aesthetic kind were considered of supreme importance. Hours were spent hanging an old picture in a new place, or in choosing a new colour for the walls.

Of Vanessa's relationship with Duncan, which Spalding characterizes as a "lasting creative union" and sees as a triumph of womanly forbearance over homosexual inconstancy ("By avoiding confrontation, mitigating disturbance and by silently absorbing her suffering into herself, she had emerged from these difficult early years at Charleston with the elusive Duncan still at her side. Where Lytton, Maynard, Adrian, and Bunny had failed, Vanessa had created a loving relationship that, however delicately balanced, had survived"), Angelica writes with a kind of pitying contempt:

> According to Paul Roche, in 1918, the year of my birth, Duncan had told Vanessa that he felt incapable of having further sexual relations with her. Thus her victory, if it was one, in keeping Duncan for herself was at best pyrrhic, gained at a cost she failed to assess. She seems to have accepted it as a necessary sacrifice for the privilege of living with this immensely attractive yet incomplete human being, to whom she was so passionately attached, and there must have been a strong element of masochism in her love for him, which induced her to accept a situation which did permanent harm to her self-respect.

A similar severity informs Angelica's view of her parents' obviously well-intentioned, though probably ill-judged, decision to shield her from the problems of being illegitimate by pretending that she was not. She sees the decision as an irresponsible and unloving act. Of Duncan, she writes in a prologue, "It has taken me all these years to realise how much I resent his neglect of me, divesting himself of all responsibility, as though I were an object rather than a human being," and later in the memoir Vanessa is charged with the same affront: "She never realised that, by denying me my real father, she was treating me even before my birth as an object, and not as a human being." Angelica was told the truth by Vanessa when she was seventeen, but she had already obscurely known it for a long time (a schoolmate had once actually accused her of being Duncan's daughter, and while denying it, "a flash of clairvoyance told me it was true"), and it changed nothing. Good old Clive was not even informed of Angelica's enlightenment—which only compounded the genial falseness of their relationship—and the charmingly flaky Duncan* could scarcely have been expected to acquire the characteristics of a paterfamilias on the spot. In fact, "being told the truth made the world seem less and not more real," she writes.

> No one seemed capable of talking openly and naturally on the subject: Vanessa was in a state of apprehension and exaltation, and Duncan made no effort to introduce a more frank relationship. They gave the impression of children who, having done something irresponsible, hope to escape censure by becoming invisible.

But Angelica's greatest bitterness is reserved (as well it might be) for her marriage to David Garnett. The cradleside prophecy came true. When she was eighteen and a timid student of acting in London, the forty-four-year-old Bunny began to court her. Angelica's account of Bunny's relentless pursuit of her has something of the atmosphere of doom and horror, tinged with a sense of nameless sexual awfulness, that surrounded marriages between innocent girls and corrupt older men in nineteenth-century novels—Isabel Archer and Gilbert Osmond, for instance, or Gwendolen Harleth and Grandcourt. "I was as putty in his hands," Angelica writes, still hating the man's guts. "I was . . . in the grip of a personality a hundred times more powerful than my own."

Of the characters who make up the cast of the Bloomsbury *Dynasty*, Bunny Garnett emerges as one of the least prepossessing. The son of Edward and Constance Garnett, he trained as a botanist and then became the author of some very successful, now outdated but not discreditable, novels. He was

---

* In his biography of Lytton Strachey, Michael Holroyd characterizes Grant thus: "As a youth he often wore a dirty collar, usually upset his afternoon tea, and never knew what time it was. When he spoke he blinked his eyes, and generally carried on in such an irresponsible fashion as to convince his uncle, Trevor Grant, that he was a hopeless and possibly certifiable imbecile."

said to be very good-looking, was a chronic womanizer, and was the friend of many gifted men and women; evidently he had qualities that made people love him in spite of his faults, but they have not survived. He cuts a very poor figure now, and, perhaps more than any other testimony, it is his own preposterously pompous three-volume autobiography (*The Golden Echo*, *The Flowers of the Forest*, and *Familiar Faces*)* that diminishes him in the eyes of posterity, though Virginia Woolf's diaries don't help his image much, either. "Poor lugubrious Bunny," she calls him, or "lumpish Bunny."

On learning of the affair that Bunny and Angelica started in the spring of 1940, a concerned Virginia wrote: "Pray God she may tire of that rusty surly slow old dog with his amorous ways & his primitive mind. . . . What can she be feeling, in the train to Yorkshire this sullen May night? All the nightingales singing from that rusty canine jaw?" Later that year, after Virginia and Leonard had lunched with Angelica and Bunny, Virginia lamented, "A.'s position, with B. as her mentor, struck us both as almost grotesque—a distortion: a dream; for how can she endure Bottom. And when will she wake?"

By the time Bunny and Angelica married, in the spring of 1942, Angelica was already fully awake to the dank gloom of her predicament in marrying a man she didn't love (and who, she now believes, married her for the sickest of unconscious reasons: to revenge himself on Vanessa for once refusing to sleep with him by carrying off the chief prize of her union with his ex-lover), but it wasn't until she had borne him four daughters and was well into middle age that she was able—emboldened by a chance encounter with the writings of Karen Horney—to leave her creepy Mr. Knightely. We get a glimpse of Angelica as a young married woman, running a large, cold country household, with little help and perpetually ill small children, driving herself also to paint and sing and play the violin and piano, and going to bed every night "almost giddy

* "Ye olde Cocke and Balls," Lytton Strachey once said of Garnett's style.

with exhaustion." Visitors would come, and "seeing my life through their eyes, I built up an image of myself as the perfect young mother-housewife-hostess, and spent much of my energy living up to it."

Angelica says she was "unable to imagine anything more original than actually becoming a second Vanessa," and consequently never became anybody at all, until a mental breakdown in 1975 propelled her into the rueful self-awareness that permeates her memoir, and without which it doubtless would never have been written. But unlike other women of her generation who have lately been fretfully reexamining their lives, it never occurs to Angelica to look outside her family and to wonder whether at least some of her unhappiness might not have had to do with the particularly difficult moment in social history with which her coming of age coincided. Roger Fry characterized the Bloomsbury group as "the last of the Victorians." Vanessa's bohemianism and artiness and bawdiness were played out against a reassuring background of middle-class philistinism; and her painting, with its Postimpressionist palette and sometimes somewhat spurious modernist air, remained securely anchored in the English academy. Vanessa and Virginia and the other unconventional young women of Bloomsbury were like Rosalinds dressed in men's clothes, slipping back and forth between the men's world and the women's world, delighting equally in the masquerade and the unmasking. By the time of Angelica's marriage, the borders between the two worlds, disconcertingly, were at once dissolving and being more heavily patrolled. The postwar period tried and confused the souls of young married women in a way that no other period had (or has since); the desperate domesticity that Angelica describes was hardly unique to her: when she writes of herself as "a domestic slave, giving up, in practice if not in theory, any claim to [a] brilliant future," she could be writing about a whole generation of educated, or—as they actually found it amusing to call themselves—overeducated women. At the same time, of course, few women came out of a family situation as rum as Angelica's—or were surrounded from birth by such crushingly remarkable people.

Angelica grew up feeling that she did not come up to scratch. She believed that her aunt Virginia was disappointed in her. Of all the Bloomsbury people, it was the upright Leonard—who unapologetically called her on misbehavior—with whom she felt most easy. As she presents herself, we get the picture of a child of ordinary abilities and somewhat weak will who didn't quite belong among the extraordinary and willful people of Bloomsbury. While *Deceived with Kindness* acknowledges the privilege of a childhood spent among artists and writers of the caliber of Virginia Woolf, Leonard Woolf, Duncan Grant, Vanessa Bell, Clive Bell, Lytton Strachey, and Roger Fry—and gives us some wonderful vignettes of them at Charleston—it seems to suggest that Angelica would have been better off in a more regular, if less interesting, family. Her people may have been brilliant, but they didn't know the first thing about raising a child—this is the book's repeated refrain, and its pathos is finally wearisome. Angelica's psychological insights seem half-baked (significantly, they are almost always insights into the motives of others), and the discussion of her complicated relationship with her mother—though it forms the matrix of the book—remains on a vague, platitudinous level. As it must remain. It is only behind the doors of analysts' consultation rooms or between the covers of great novels that these mysteries of family love and hatred receive their deeper elucidation. Angelica Garnett modestly says of herself that she is no professional writer (in her innocence, she believes that this fact and the fact that her book took seven years to write are connected), and her memoir, though many cuts above the usual amateurish mess produced by relatives of the famous under the cynical proddings of publishers, is the work of a talented but untrained writer. How much of the gaping hole of self at the book's center is due to the writer's insufficient grasp of the autobiographical form, and how much to her incomplete self-knowledge, can only be surmised.

*The New York Review of Books*, 1985

# School of the Blind

We are forever telling stories about ourselves.

—*Roy Schafer, "Narration in the Psychoanalytic Dialogue"*

EVERY good autobiography raises the question of whose story to credit—that of the intelligent, critically observing, narrating adult or that of the uncomprehending, dumbly accepting, experiencing child. In *Vedi*, Ved Mehta's extraordinary memoir of the four years he spent as a young child in an appalling place in Bombay called the Dadar School for the Blind, the tension between the two "I"s is particularly pronounced. The adult "I" is outraged by what his father did to him when he abruptly removed him—a blind child not yet five—from his affectionate and comfortable middle-class home in the Punjab and sent him a thousand miles away to an orphanage for destitute blind children located in a mosquito-ridden industrial slum, where he was to contract typhoid within three months (and suffer repeated bouts of it) and where he lived for four years under the harshest of physical conditions and received the most pitifully rudimentary of educations. But the child "I" is unconcerned about the things that pain and appall the grown-up "I." He is a high-spirited, strong-willed, eager little boy, so intent on exercising his child's prerogative of enjoyment that he seems almost unaware of the cruelty and difficulty of his predicament. In George Orwell's bitter memoir of his boarding school days, "Such, Such Were the Joys . . . ," the narrating adult dwells on the gratuitous sufferings of children caused by their ignorance of reality. The child Orwell cringes and cowers before the ghastly couple who run the

✤ VEDI (New York: Oxford University Press, 1982), by Ved Mehta.

school Crossgates, seeing them as all-powerful monsters rather than as the mere "silly, shallow, ineffectual people" they are. But in young Mehta's case, the reality is *worse* than the child knows. Thus, in *Vedi*, paradoxically, it is the knowledgeable narrator who suffers over the monstrous events of the story, while the ignorant child at their center accepts them with composure and even, amazingly, a kind of gaiety.

In *Vedi*, for the first time in his mature writing, Mehta writes from the perspective of total blindness. The book is entirely without visual descriptions. We follow the blind child into the orphanage, and, like him, we never learn what the place or any of the people in it looked like. We hear, we feel, but we see nothing. We are dislocated and disoriented. As the child misses the familiar persons and things of home, so the reader misses the customary visual clues of literature. One feels a kind of sensory deprivation throughout the book—almost a lack of enjoyment—even as one experiences the excitement that an original work engenders. Not the least of *Vedi*'s originality is this very stylistic denial, which amounts to an approximation of the experience of blindness. As we grope through the early sections of the book, trying to get our bearings in its alien literary environment, we are like tourists in a foreign country who have to struggle with themselves not to commit the absurdity of rejecting the very foreignness they have traveled to experience. The country of the blind is exotic indeed, and Mehta takes us to places in its bleak, impassable terrain that no one from the sighted world has previously penetrated. (The term "sighted world" is itself newly learned from the book—being a term for which there is no need outside the community of the blind, in the way that the term "goyim" has no currency among non-Jews.) Mehta relates, for example, how

> All of us totally blind boys were constantly hitting ourselves against something or other. We would feel each other's bumps and injuries, and we would joke about them. "Let me feel,"

we would say. "Is it on your hood or your mudguard? Or is it the wheel again?" "Hood" was our slang for a forehead, "mudguard" for an eyebrow, and "wheel" for a shin. . . . Even as we made light of our injuries, we endowed whatever we hit—or whatever hit us, as we came to think of it—with the malevolence we attributed to the entire sighted world. It seemed to us that a stationary object, like a wall, no less than a familiar object in an unfamiliar place, like a chair that had been moved, would willfully loom out of the sighted world to vex us. Whenever we hurt ourselves on anything at all, we would kick it and beat it and cry out, "The sighted bastards!"

The principal of the school, Mr. Ras Mohun, though sighted, was somehow exempted from the resentment and fear that the blind children extended to the sighted world, perhaps because of his benignity and genuine interest in the blind. He was a man in his early thirties, a Bengali Christian convert, who had worked with missionaries among the blind and the deaf and had studied at the Perkins Institution for the Blind in America. His wife, who "was the same height he was," was a little less kind, though hardly a villainess. The villains of the book are poverty, disease, and blindness. Vedi arrived at the school a healthy, sturdy little boy, with fat cheeks that the other children kept pulling at in wonder. "At five, I was the youngest boy in the boys' dormitory, and the other boys could not understand why I seemed so healthy: why they never heard me scratch my head, why I never coughed at night, why I never complained of a stomach ache in the morning—above all, why I never had a fever. The boys kept coming up and touching my forehead and exclaiming, 'He still doesn't have a fever.' "

In a few months' time, Vedi became as sickly and fever-ridden as the rest, and when he went home for Christmas vacation, his parents removed him from the school. Unaccountably, they sent him back a year later, and once again he fell into a brutal physical decline. When he came home for his second Christmas vacation, his clothes hung from him and his head was so severely infested with ringworm that his father, a doctor, decided to risk baldness, and even brain damage, by having him undergo X-ray treatments, then the only remedy for the condition. Years later, Mehta writes, his father confessed, "Looking back, I blame myself for not having gone to the school and seen for myself the conditions there." But he still justified his decision to send the small boy away from home. "When you lost your sight, I didn't know anything about the blind," he told his grown son, who became blind at the age of four after an attack of meningitis. The father continued:

"Like everyone else, I had, of course, often seen blind people stumbling along, groping their way down a city street. They usually carried a staff in one hand and a tin cup in the other. Also, as a public-health officer, I had visited many villages and seen blind villagers being cared for by the joint-family system, which in those days took in any and all relatives. But all those blind people lived little better than wounded animals. I made up my mind that my blind son would never have to depend on the charity of relatives. I wanted you to be independent, like your sisters and brother. I wanted you to be able to hold your head high in any company. I started looking around for a school for you. . . ."

The irony was, of course, that the school the father selected (after some perfunctory correspondence with its head) plunged the boy into the very society—the indigent blind—that the separation from home was supposed to protect him from. In his books about his parents, *Daddyji* (1972) and *Mamaji* (1979), which form a trilogy with *Vedi*, Mehta draws a sharp contrast between his rational, decisive, tough-minded, Western-educated, physician father and his superstitious, backward, uneducated, childish, tenderhearted mother. Typically, when her son went blind, the mother refused to accept the fact and dragged him around to faith healers and quacks, in the confident belief that the blindness was a temporary punishment for some transgression in this or a previous life. And typically, the father clutched at the idea of "progressive, Western methods of educating the blind" as the answer to his son's tragic predicament (for which, as Mehta unhappily suggests in *Daddyji*, recounting the events that led up to the loss of his eyesight, he may have been responsible).

But, paradoxically, it was the emotional, irrational, childish, fanciful, "Indian" parts of Ved Mehta's nature that were his strongest defense against the harsh actuality of Dadar. The Western values and qualities that his father represented, and that he mistakenly believed the school to embody—realism, pragmatism, stoicism, common sense—had little survival value in the extreme situation where the five-year-old blind child was placed. The following passage, about Vedi's first bath at the school, wonderfully illustrates the power that the childish imagination may exert over an unpleasant reality.

The ayah had me sit under a tap. The water was cold and came out in a strong jet, making me shiver all over. I howled. I begged for a bucket of hot water and a dipper, as at home, so that I could wet myself slowly.

The ayah held me fast under the tap and said, "Come on now, Vedi, be a brave boy."

"No, I don't want to!" I cried.

"It's just like going out in the rain," she said.

I thought a moment, and then laughed.

The ayah let go of me.

"Rain, rain!" I yelled, and turned on the tap full blast. The water poured out in a heavy stream and splashed all around me on the cement floor.

I ran to the ayah, who wrapped me in a little towel.

"Brave boy," she said, hugging me.

Because of his family's superior status—and, more to the point, the money that his father sent every month—Vedi received special treatment at the school. He ate his meals with the Ras Mohuns, instead of with the other children, and was exempted from chair-caning instruction. But Mrs. Ras Mohun found it inconvenient to honor the agreement that he also sleep in the principal's quarters, and so he was put into the boys' dormitory, though he was given a special bed, with a mattress and mosquito netting; the other boys slept on bare wood slats, unprotected from mosquitoes. The move to the dormitory was a fortunate one: it brought the child into the life of the school, its real life of mischief, gossip, fighting, ghost-story telling, sex play (called "boy mischief"), cruelty, savagery, camaraderie. His special situation as a boy who wore silk shirts, ate toast and mutton, and slept on a soft mattress was apparently accepted without rancor—perhaps because these things did not spare him the common lot of disgusting sanitary conditions, pitiful educational facilities, disease, and blindness.

It is again interesting to contrast the situation of Vedi at Dadar with that of the young George Orwell at Crossgates, who, as a boy from a relatively poor family among well-to-do boys, was subjected to humiliating distinctions made between scholarship boys and those whose parents paid. But Vedi, no less than the young Orwell, wanted what the rest had, and just as Orwell recalls with bitter rue the longings of his younger self for the small treats and privileges so cruelly and unnecessarily denied him, so Mehta writes with mild irony of the hankerings of *his* younger self after the harsh food that the indigent orphans ate and of his desire to learn to cane chairs and to play the musical instruments that many of them would end up playing on the streets of Bombay.

Irony of a sharper character is reserved for the efforts of Mrs. Ras Mohun to educate Vedi in what she believed to be refined behavior. At table, she taught him to ask for food and water by raising his hand with the fourth and the little finger held up when he wanted food, and just the little finger held up when he wanted water. When he was asked "How are you?" he was to answer, "I'm quite well and happy, thank you," and smile pleasantly, and when he laughed, he was to cover his mouth with his hand. Mrs. Ras Mohun's stock response to behavior that displeased her was to say, "Don't be a jungly boy," or "That's what jungly boys do." There is a very funny scene at the Mehta home during Christmas vacation, when Vedi, at the dinner table, holds up his hand and raises this finger and that one, with nobody taking the slightest heed of him. Finally his sister Umi says, "What do you think you are doing? Why are you holding your hand up in that absurd way?"

"Water and vegetables," I whispered. "Little finger for water, both fingers for water and food."

"Speak up," she said. "Why are you whispering? Why don't you say, 'I want water and vegetables?' "

"That's what jungly boys do."

THERE is a scene toward the end of the book that freezes the blood. It takes place at Dadar in the boys' dormitory, and it concerns Jaisingh, a boy who is blind, deaf, dumb, and retarded—a large, helpless, miserable, barely human creature, whom Mr. Ras Mohun calls "the Dadar School's Helen Keller" and whom the other children dislike. "In fact, we scorned him, as we imagined that the sighted scorned all of us," Mehta writes. Jaisingh is given to crying at night, making eerie moaning and wailing sounds, and when this happens, the Sighted Master, who is in charge of the boys' dormitory, subdues him by beating him with a shoe. The Sighted Master is a sinister, shadowy figure without name or any other characteristics besides his brutality and lowness. One night, both Jaisingh and another pathetic child, named Ramesh, begin howling together, awakening everyone in the dormitory. Vedi hears the Sighted Master get up, and as he passes his bed he hears him mutter, "I will finish Ras Mohun's Helen Keller." Vedi hears the Sighted Master walk toward the howling boys and hears him remove a plank from one of their beds. As Vedi and the other boys listen in terror, first Ramesh's howling and then Jaisingh's abruptly stop. The next day, both Ramesh and Jaisingh are gone. They are never seen again at Dadar. Whether the Sighted Master actually killed the two boys—as the other boys speculate—is unclear. What really happened is never known.

*What really happened?* This is the question that impels every autobiographer and that gives autobiography its special epistemological interest. In Mehta's taut, strong, ironic memoir, he restively ponders the question of what his experience at the Dadar School had been, worrying it and turning it this way and that and finally letting it lie there in all its unanswerability—like the question of what happened to Ramesh and Jaisingh, like the question, perhaps, of what happened to all of us in our childhoods. The retrieval of childhood experience is one of the most mysteriously unpropitious of human endeavors; memory is the most feckless and epistemologically useless of our psychic faculties. Neither of the two "I"s through which the story of a childhood is told is trustworthy: the testimony of the child, who was there, is lacking in understanding; the testimony of the adult, who is omniscient, is lacking in authenticity. At best, an uneasy truce between the child (memory) and the man (understanding) is achieved. In an epilogue, Mehta states the problem of the two "I"s with almost shocking explicitness. As an adult, he returns to the school and finds it unchanged in its dirtiness but changed in its occupants. He reports:

> The school and the entire building now housed only girls and women, with thin, shrinking, demented voices—it was as if the new residents were not only blind but also retarded. This made me wonder whether the school of my childhood had had the same atmosphere. The thought was depressing—the more so because I knew there was no way I could dispose of

the question to my satisfaction, since the answer was a matter not of memory but of judgment and experience, which, as a boy, I could not have had.

He learns that many of his classmates had died of consumption at an early age. He reports a depressing meeting with Deoji, his best friend at the school, who "confirmed this fact and that fact, but what he really succeeded in confirming was the divide between us—both before, during, and after our first meeting, when I was a child, and before, during, and after our last meeting, when I was a man." His final encounter is with Rajas, a girl at the school, now a destitute woman living in a squalid tenement in Dadar. He does not remember her at all. He presses her for details about himself at the school. To the narrator's disappointment—and to the reader's elation—she has only one thing to say about him: "I remember that you were a very jolly child."

*The New York Review of Books*, 1982

# A Problem of Growth

EARLY in this chilling novel about a Jewish boy named Maciek and his aunt Tania, who survive the Nazi years in Poland by acquiring false Aryan papers, the question of the child's circumcised penis is raised. As the narrator dryly points out, Jewish women could represent themselves as Aryans easily enough, but

> with men, there was no cheating, no place for Jewish ruses. Very early in the process would come the simple, logical invitation: If Pan is not a kike, a *zidlak*, would he please let down his trousers? A thousand excuses if we are wrong.

"With his old man's flabby skin," the boy's grandfather "might even pass the trousers test if he was careful. It was possible, with surgical glue, to shape and fasten enough skin around the gland to imitate a real uncut foreskin. Grandfather was duly equipped with such glue." But for the boy, only surgery with skin grafts could achieve the desired effect, an alternative considered by the aunt and the grandparents and ultimately rejected. For, in addition to the risk of infection and of the graft not taking,

> there was the problem of growth. My penis would become longer but the grafted skin would not keep pace. I would have trouble with erections. This last consideration tipped the scales. They decided to leave me as I was.

♣ WARTIME LIES (New York: Alfred A. Knopf, 1991), by Louis Begley.

The passage is typical of the book's irony and metaphoric proficiency. As the narrative unfolds, we see that "the problem of growth" extends beyond the operation of decircumcision and is the problem of the book. What happens to a child's soul when he lives his childhood in constant fear for his life and witnesses atrocities that no child should know of, much less witness? In a prologue, the narrator—who is the adult the child has become, "a man with a nice face and sad eyes, fifty or more winters on his back, living a moderately pleasant life in a tranquil country"—refers to skin that covers another part of the anatomy. The man is "a bookish fellow," a Latinist who "reveres" the *Aeneid* because "that is where he first found civil expression for his own shame at being alive, his skin intact and virgin of tattoo, when his kinsmen and almost all the others, so many surely more deserving than he, perished in the conflagration." Between the images of the tattooed arm and the erect penis Begley has situated his austere moral and psychological fable of survival. Like other contributors to what Lawrence Langer has called the literature of atrocity, Begley writes with a kind of muted and stunned air, as if the words are sticking in his throat. The exquisite soft note of the master writer of the genre, Primo Levi, is sometimes heard in the novel, and Levi's bitter reflection (so quietly murmured, in *The Drowned and the Saved*, that it goes by almost unnoticed) that "the worst survived, that is, the fittest; the best all died" has not gone unremarked by Begley. The thought inhabits the novel and gives it its pervasive atmosphere of moral anxiety.

It is a woman, the aunt Tania, who is the instrument of survival and who is equipped by character and temperament to take the assertive measures necessary to cheat death in the time of its near-total ascendancy. To create his remarkable heroine, Begley has drawn on ancient and modern literary models: the character has the courage and selflessness of Alcestis, the brilliance and inventiveness of the Duchessa Sanseverina, the hardness of Becky Sharp. He has also drawn on Freud for his elucidation of the remarkable psychological situation in which his fable is set—the situation of a boy upon whom dire circumstances have imposed the fulfillment of a child's headiest Oedipal wishes. The father is absent—he disappears into Russia at the beginning of the novel—and the grandparents also disappear from the boy's childhood as part of the strategy of survival whereby Jewish families with false papers split up in order to be less conspicuous. Tania, who has been Maciek's surrogate mother all his life (the real mother died in childbirth), briefly provides him with a surrogate father when she takes up with an influential German officer named Reinhard, a kind of Mosca *manqué*, but he, too, passes out of the picture, and the field is left to the nine-year-old Maciek. The aunt and the boy move from place to place with their false identities, never daring to stay anywhere too long (blackmailers, who bleed Jews dry and then turn them over to the Gestapo, lurk like sharks throughout Nazi-occupied Poland); they are like a pair of traveling charlatans, working in ever more perfect sync and becoming intimate in ways that people who do not lie together (the pun serves the idea) possibly never know. Near the end of the book, the boy begins to feel the debit side of sleeping with his mother. (Although, as it happens, the pair sleep in the same bed throughout most of the novel, they do not literally breach the incest barrier or come anywhere near breaching it; but the relationship is nevertheless incestuous.) He articulates what all children who are brought into arousing relationships with adults must obscurely feel: the sense of the relationship's crushing inequality and of their own powerlessness. "I admired and loved my beautiful and brave aunt with increasing passion," Maciek says.

> Her body could never be close enough to mine; she was the fortress against danger and the well of all comfort. . . . I waited impatiently for the nights when I knew she would come to bed wearing only a slip so that I could feel closer to her.

And yet:

> I had never seen Tania naked. Tania undressed was Tania in
> her slip or Tania in her long nightgown. Her bodily functions
> were private, even under the most constraining conditions.
> On the other hand, my nakedness and my bowel and bladder
> movements continued to be subject to question, inspection
> and comment.

In the mind of the boy (as recollected by the man), he himself
is a poor, weak creature (there are echoes of the sickly and
coddled young Marcel in the self-representation), while the aunt
is a being of almost mythic powerfulness, an androgynous god-
dess embodying the paternal as well as the maternal principles,
both *fortress* and *well*. Her audacity and guile know no bounds;
in a scene in the latter half of the novel, her mission-impossible
capacities reach a thrilling culmination. It is the summer of
1944, and the pair have escaped detection as Jews only to find
themselves trapped in a roundup of Poles at the central railroad
station in Warsaw following the premature, ill-fated uprising
of the Polish resistance. Begley has rendered the scene like an
immense narrative painting. As far as the eye can see, frightened
men, women, and children, who have been marched to the
station and assembled in columns, wait to board trains to Auschwitz; Ukrainian guards with whips and dogs savagely herd people onto the trains as Wehrmacht and SS officers look on
impassively. We glimpse Tania and Maciek in the crowd. At
the start of the march the previous day, Tania had smeared her
face with soot and walked bent over like an old woman so as
to escape notice by the Ukrainians, who were raping and sometimes, for good measure, bayoneting attractive young women.
Now, as the column approaches the station, she undergoes
another transformation:

> Over my tearful protests she had used our remaining water
> to wash our faces and hands. She brushed the dust off her

clothes and mine and straightened them. Then she combed my hair, and, with great concentration, peering into the pocket mirror, combed her own hair and put on lipstick, studied the result, and made little corrections. I was astonished to see how she had transformed herself. The stooped-over, soot-smeared old woman of the march from the Old Town had vanished. Instead, when we entered the station, I was holding the hand of a dignified and self-confident young matron. Unlike the day before, she was not hanging back, trying to lose us in the crowd; she pushed her way to the outside row and, holding my hand very tight, to my horror, led me away from the column so that we were standing, completely exposed, in the space on the platform between the rest of the people and the train. Despite my panic, I began to understand that Tania was putting on a very special show. Her clear blue eyes surveyed the scene before her; it was as if she could barely contain her impatience and indignation. I thought that if she had had an umbrella she would be tapping the platform with it.

Pulling the boy behind her, Tania strides over to a fat Wehrmacht captain standing on the platform, and

addressing him in her haughtiest tone, she asked if he would be kind enough to tell her where these awful trains were going. The answer made my legs tremble: Auschwitz. Completely wrong destination, replied Tania. To find herself with all these disreputable-looking people, being shouted at by drunk and disorderly soldiers, and all this in front of a train going to a place she had never heard of, was intolerable. She was a doctor's wife from R., about two hours from Warsaw; she had come to Warsaw to buy dresses and have her son's eyes examined; of course, everything she bought had been lost in this dreadful confusion. We had nothing to do with whatever was going on here. Would he, as an officer, impose some order and help us find a train to R.? We had spent almost all our money, but she thought she had enough for a second-class compartment. The captain burst out laughing. My dear lady, he said to Tania, not even my wife orders me about quite this way. Could Tania assure him her husband would be glad to have her return? And where had she learned such literary turns of expression? After he had an answer to these basic questions he would see about this wretched train business. Tania blushed. Should I tell you the truth, even though you won't like it? Naturally, replied the captain. I think my husband doesn't mind my being sometimes hot tempered. I learned German in school and probably I managed to improve it by reading, especially everything by Thomas Mann I can find in the original—not much in R., but quite a lot in Warsaw. It's a good way for a provincial housewife to keep occupied. I know Mann's work is forbidden in the Reich, but that is the truth. I am not a party member, merely a railroad specialist, announced the captain still laughing, I am glad you have chosen a great stylist. Shall I get someone to carry your suitcases while we look for transportation to R.?

IN A review in the *Times Literary Supplement* of October 14, 1983, Gabriel Josipovici severely criticized a book called *Hasidic Tales of the Holocaust* for the simpleminded note of rejoicing it struck in recounting stories of successful survival through luck, quick-wittedness, or the intervention of the Almighty. Holding up for special disapprobation a tale in which a rabbi survives a mass shooting because he is wearing a garment with apparent magical properties, Josipovici icily asks, "What kind of God is this who saves those with magic cloaks and not others? What kind of faith is this that rejoices in personal safety and spares no thought for those who did not get up?"

Josipovici's question rings throughout *Wartime Lies*. The account of the aunt's brilliant charade of "identification with the aggressor" is told in full awareness of its moral ambiguity. The image of "those awful trains" haunts the book, as do the shades of "those who did not get up." The foreground fairy story of survival is but a prism through which the horror story of the Holocaust is refracted. In the relationship of the boy and the aunt we see a kind of distorting mirror image of the relationship of the Jew and the Nazi. Although the aunt is "good," her methods have a heart-freezing Teutonic efficiency, and the boy's abject dependence on her has a chilling pathos. Embedded in Begley's narrative of the boy's ambivalence toward his too powerful and too desirable protectress and of his, perforce, weak struggle to free himself from her iron hold—since his life depends on strict obedience and adherence to her program of survival—is a meditation on authoritarianism of great subtlety and originality.

THE author is a fifty-seven-year-old New York lawyer who has not previously written fiction. He and I have been friends for years. I have known that he spent the war years in Poland, but until reading this book, I did not know anything about his wartime experiences; he never spoke of them. After reading it, I begin to know what he must have experienced, since a book like this could not have been written except out of firsthand knowledge of the history it chronicles. The Holocaust is permanently lodged in the unconscious memory of our time; we cannot free ourselves of our grief and anger. *Wartime Lies*, even as it brings these emotions to the surface, denies us the solace of catharsis. The crime was too great, the motive unfathomable.

*The New York Review of Books*, 1991

# Schneebaum's Confessions

TOWARD the end of this memoir of homoerotic experience in the jungle of New Guinea, a Dutch missionary's wife makes a brief appearance. When the author and two European male companions arrive by canoe at the minister's house, the wife, standing on the banks of the river, tells them that her husband is "working on his sermon for Sunday and cannot be wasting time with visitors." Schneebaum notices the woman's "faded print dress, stockings, and shoes" and the "deep crevices of bitterness on her face." One of his companions strides up to her and says unpleasantly, "We don't ask anything of you. We don't need you." The missionary suddenly appears and takes the men into the house, over the wife's protests, and the woman vanishes from the book, dispatched by a single pettish sentence: "In spite of her antagonism, she made tea and offered delicious-looking cookies that we left untouched."

The incident jars one into a recognition of the author's antipathy to women that one had hitherto only obscurely felt. Earlier in the book, Schneebaum has spoken of his sense of alienation from heterosexual men and women, who, he feels, cannot know

what it is like to be homosexual. . . . They do not know that particular form of deception and pain, what it is always to be on guard, always to be afraid of being laughed at, sneered at, hated, repelling people, angering people. It doesn't matter that attitudes sometimes appear to be in change; what matters

✤ WHERE THE SPIRITS DWELL: AN ODYSSEY IN THE NEW GUINEA JUNGLE (New York: Grove Press, 1989), by Tobias Schneebaum.

is that I raised myself to relate to that intolerance and have lived my life as an undesirable.

In fact, however, Schneebaum has vividly communicated "what it is like" to be obsessed by male sex; in each of his three books—*Keep the River on Your Right* (1969), *Wild Man* (1979), and the present book—he draws the reader into his universe of homosexual desire the way every strong writer draws the reader away from his own fantasies and into those of another for the duration of his act of reading. As Nabokov, in *Lolita*, draws the nonpedophilic reader into an imaginative sharing of Humbert Humbert's lust for a twelve-year-old girl, so Schneebaum, with his rhapsodic accounts of sex with cannibals and head-hunters, expands the heterosexual reader's consciousness of erotic possibilities. Only occasionally, as in the incident of the missionary's wife, is one recalled, with a sort of start, to who one is: in this case, another middle-aged woman who wears stockings and shoes, if not faded print dresses, and has a little trouble entering into the spirit of the gynophobia that Schneebaum has briefly allowed to surface.

He was born in 1922 in a tenement on the Lower East Side, the son of Polish-Jewish immigrants. His father was a pushcart peddler, eventually the owner of a small grocery store in Brooklyn, and his mother a janitor, who, the day after giving birth to each of the two older of her three sons, was back in the cellar shoveling coal. The father was strict, rough, cruel; the mother was gentle, and died of uterine cancer at the age of thirty-eight. In *Wild Man*, Schneebaum records a memory of getting up in the middle of the night during the period when his mother was dying at home, and seeing, through the open door of his parents' bedroom, his father "on top of her, being cruel to her, hurting her in some way, for each time he pressed down, she let out an agonizing groan." Schneebaum went to City College, majoring in math and taking art courses; during the Second World War, he was a radar technician at an army base in Indiana. After the war, he studied painting with the Mexican artist Rufino Tamayo at the Brooklyn Museum Art School and then went to live in Mexico. In the village of Ajijic, he fell in with a group of expatriate artists and bohemians and remained there for four years, painting and becoming the confidant but not the bedmate of two attractive young homosexuals named Lynn and Nicolas; finally, in a fit of despairing jealousy, he took the obligatory, gestural overdose of sleeping pills and endured the obligatory, humiliating aftermath.

Schneebaum had never been attracted to girls and was drawn to men from an early age (in boyhood, he had been seduced by an older male relative), but he believed himself to be ugly and puny ("some half-creature, thin and weak, not frail but vaguely feminine," he writes of himself in *Wild Man*) and felt as much a sexual as a social outcast. It was only in his thirties, in a village in the jungle of Peru, where he had traveled on a Fulbright, that Schneebaum found a fulfilling sexual relationship with a group of Akarama tribesmen, who let him sleep with them at night in a tangled heap on the floor of a hut, and who fed him, on one festive occasion, the roasted flesh of neighboring tribesmen they had killed the day before. Schneebaum tells of his adventures among the Peruvian cannibals in *Keep the River on Your Right*, the most lyrical, Lawrencian, and cohesive of his works. After traveling for many days alone through the jungle below the Andes, he arrives at a desolate mission, where he finds a crazed old priest, a hunchback, and, incredibly, an alter ego—Manolo, a Spanish homosexual with vague literary leanings and a mysterious, romantic aura. But the mission is only a way station in Schneebaum's quest for exotic erotic experience, which he finally finds deeper in the jungle, among the naked, painted Akaramas, who, inexplicably, do not kill and eat him but welcome him with hugs and shouts of laughter, as if they were at a California love-in:

> All weapons had been left lying on stones and we were jumping up and down and my arms went around body after body and I felt myself getting hysterical, wildly ecstatic with love

for all humanity, and I returned slaps on backs and bites on hard flesh, and small as they were, I twirled some round like children and wept away the world of my past.

A group of five young men become his special friends and lovers; he goes around naked, learns to shoot a bow and arrow, and lives as if in paradise. "I know finally that I am alive," he exults in his journal. The idyll ends when one of the young men, Darinimbiak, becomes ill with dysentery. Schneebaum takes him back to the mission for medicine and there finds that Manolo has disappeared; he had decided to follow Schneebaum's example and go live among the cannibals, but evidently didn't go over so big with them: his head is found impaled on a stake, and his body, of which no trace remains, is assumed to have been eaten. In a love letter left behind for Schneebaum, Manolo writes with bizarre prescience:

> I've always wanted myself to be really useful in some way, and frankly I'd have liked it to be in a loving, sensual way, almost in the way that the body of Christ is used in communion. . . . I want, for a change, instead of someone else filling me with love, for me to fill someone completely, even if it literally means that my flesh and blood must enter into another body. . . . I've had dreams of my body being eaten by men and it thrilled me in such an indescribable way that I had an orgasm before I realized what was going on inside of me.

One begins to wonder whether anything in *Keep the River* is true—whether it isn't all some sort of poetic/pathological daydream (known as a novel)—and in *Where the Spirits Dwell* Schneebaum confirms one's intuition. "The book I wrote on Peru had its exaggerations," he confesses. "I wrote it as I felt it, changing time elements and adding to the number of those my friends had killed." In the new book, he presumably writes it as it was, and has equipped the work with such emblems of authenticity as poor photographs of bare-breasted native women, ancestor poles, bamboo huts, etc.; a bibliography of anthropological texts; and a glossary of Asmat and Indonesian words, in which terms for (male) sexual practices receive the sort of rapt overattention that the arcana of tipping and checking-in receive in vocabularies for tourists. ("*Ndo tsjemen afai towai*—I give my penis into the ass; to be the active partner in sodomy" or "*Yipit a minau tamen emefafarimis*—to peel back the foreskin of one's penis; to masturbate.")

As in *Keep the River on Your Right* (which also has photographs, but of a dark, murkily arty sort), the narrative begins at a mission—this one run by mod Catholic priests from the Midwest (when we first meet Father Frank Trenkenschuh, he is wearing shorts and a T-shirt that says SHIT)—and again, when Schneebaum ventures into the unexplored jungle, he achieves immediate rapport with the naked savages he encounters. In the early work he had pondered on this capacity:

> What smell did I exude that allowed them to accept me? It was in Borneo that Mathurin Daim had said, "You are the only Westerner whose smell I have ever been able to bear." There, I knew well that having lived for so long among his people, eating their foods, my body smells were like his own. But here, it is something else, something to do with the fact that I came as I did, that I came alone and in need. I knew that they recognized me, that we recognized each other.

Now, in the Asmat village of Otsjenep, having just watched two young tribesmen, who are bond friends, unselfconsciously bugger each other after a bathe in the river, he feels a similar affinity. There was "something about me that the men recognized, some overt gesture on my part, some restlessness seen in my eyes or filtering through my skin," he writes. "In acting out their desires so spontaneously with me looking on, Amer and Kokorai demonstrated that they knew I was sympathetic, possibly a participator." In time, Schneebaum acquires a bond friend of his own, Akatpitsjin, who gives him "a sense of myself that liberated me from the neuroses that had originally forced me into my search" and introduces him to *faper ameris* ("reciprocal sodomy"), which Schneebaum finds electrifying. But nothing he tells us about the relationship quite accounts for its momentous impact on him, and he tells us nothing about Akatpitsjin that makes him in any way distinguishable from any of the other primitive men we have met in this and the other of Schneebaum's books. They all melt and merge into one idealized construct. As Montaigne, in "Of Cannibals," enlisted primitive man into his polemic against cruelty, ironically comparing the savages of Brazil—who eat human beings after they are dead—with the civilized men of France, who horribly torture people while they are still alive, so Schneebaum uses the Akaramas and Asmats as foils in his polemic against homophobia. But where Montaigne saw primitive men (among whom he never lived) as embodiments of the highest potentialities of man, and bemoaned the fact that Plato and Lycurgus didn't know about them, in Schneebaum's version they seem scarcely men at all, but more like tamed wild animals—one thinks of the otters in *Ring of Bright Water* and the lions of *Born Free*. Schneebaum's remarkable talent for getting primitive men to trust and like (no less to *faper*) him is like the talent of Gavin Maxwell or Joy Adams for forging trans-species relationships. But Schneebaum lacks Maxwell's and Adams's talent for observation. His savages never come to life. He may sleep pressed up against them, but when it comes to rendering their portraits and conveying a sense of their everyday life, he is like someone taking pictures from too far away. In his three books, the only character who emerges in any depth and detail is Schneebaum himself. Impelled by his sense of alienation to leave Western culture and travel to primitive societies, he returns to write books about *his own otherness*. Schneebaum is one of the purest exponents of the autobiographical impulse to come along in a long time. The child's delusion of being freakishly different from everybody else, a feeling most of us outgrow, is the feeling that an autobiographer must summon and fan back into life in order to do his work of creating a literary character out of the unpromising material of himself. Rousseau's is the clearest expression of the mind-set of specialness on which all depends in the autobiographical enterprise. "I am unlike anyone I have ever met," he writes on the well-known first page of his *Confessions*. "I will even venture to say I am like no one in the whole world. I may be no better, but at least I am different. Whether nature did well or ill in breaking the mold in which she formed me is a question which can only be resolved after the reading of my book."

The *Confessions* amply bears out Rousseau's estimate of his outlandishness, and so, in their way, do Schneebaum's writings bear out his. If they are negligible as anthropology—Schneebaum can't get outside himself long enough to tell us the things we want to know about the places he has been to (anyone who attends a cannibal feast and brings back no gastronomical information whatever can hardly call himself a social scientist)— they are fascinating as autobiography (or maybe even as case history). They give us a portrait of a man who has spent his adult life trying to come to grips with crippling personal problems; but instead of doing it on a couch on East Ninety-sixth Street, he has done it on distant islands and in remote rain forests, endowing his relationships with primitive men with the same magic with which the analysand endows his relationship with the analyst. Schneebaum's three books are like the three stages of an analysis. (I have said little about the second work, *Wild Man*, which gives an overview of several decades of travel to Mexico, India, Bali, Libya, Peru, and New Guinea, among other places, and, like the middle game of analysis, is the longest and slowest-moving of the three.) Through their different narrative strategies and atmospheres, and their contradictions, we may track the uneven progress of Schneebaum's soul on its self-obsessed journey. From their relentless emphasis on sex, we may adduce, too, their status as inscriptions of the unconscious rather than transcriptions of what Schneebaum actually thinks about and does all day. No one—neither analysand nor analyst, including the first analyst—has written about the experience of analysis in a way that communicates its strangeness and uncanniness and remoteness from real life. The poet H. D. came close in her strange, uncanny little book *Tribute to Freud*, and so, curiously, does Tobias Schneebaum, in the three books of his autobiography.

*The New York Review of Books*, 1988

# Wolfe in Wolfe's Clothing

"I'VE got Europe off my back. You've no idea how it simplifies things and how jolly it makes me feel. Now I can live, now I can walk. If we wretched Americans could only say once for all, 'Oh, Europe be hanged!' we would attend much better to our proper business." So declares Marcellus Cockerell, a young American in Henry James's early comic story-in-letters "A Point of View," who has just returned from a long obligatory trip abroad. Over there he felt "bored and bullied," and this has only confirmed him in his feeling that "the future's here, of course. But it isn't only that—the present's here as well." Tom Wolfe, in his jolly new polemic against modern architecture, attributes the rise of the International Style in America to our chronic inability to say no to the Europeans. If only we had said "Europe be hanged!" when Walter Gropius and his Bauhaus colleagues Marcel Breuer, Lazlo Moholy-Nagy, Mies van der Rohe, Joseph Albers, and Herbert Bayer, fleeing Hitler, appeared here in the late thirties with their Teutonic good looks and their *sachlich* carpetbags, how differently things might have turned out. We might have been spared the "row after Mies van der row of glass houses," the "worker housing" that has spread over our land like the elm blight. Instead, as Wolfe writes with delicious malice:

> The reception of Gropius and his confreres was like a certain stock scene from the jungle movies of that period. Bruce Cabot and Myrna Loy make a crash landing in the jungle and crawl

✦ FROM BAUHAUS TO OUR HOUSE (New York: Farrar, Straus and Giroux, 1981), by Tom Wolfe.

out of the wreckage in their Abercrombie & Fitch white safari blouses and tan gabardine jodhpurs and stagger into a clearing. They are surrounded by savages with bones through their noses—who immediately bow down and prostrate themselves and commence a strange moaning chant.

*The White Gods!*
*Come from the skies at last!*

Already in the twenties, impressionable young Americans touring Europe were being beguiled by the avant-garde groups—or "art compounds," as Wolfe calls them—that were producing the new painting, sculpture, literature, music, architecture, and design. Wolfe believes, or affects to believe, that it was simply the desire to confound the bourgeoisie and to show off to one another that impelled the members of the compounds to modernism. The showing off at the Bauhaus, the most powerful of the architecture-and-design compounds, was especially dazzling to American architects making the grand tour. "The height of excitement in American architectural circles was those brave new styles, North Shore Norman and Westchester Tudor, also known as Half-timber Stockbroker," Wolfe writes. "What a goal to aspire to . . . as compared to . . . *re-creating the world.*"

By 1929, the Europhilia had reached such a pitch here that even the rich, who should have known better, were jumping on the bandwagon of modernism, some going as far as to found a Museum of Modern Art in which to display their chic buys from abroad. In 1932, the museum put on a show introducing the new architecture to its public, accompanied by Henry-Russell Hitchcock and Philip Johnson's essay "The International Style," which Wolfe characterizes as "one of the most dotty and influential documents in the entire history of the colonial complex" and credits with preparing the ground for the apotheosis of the exiled Silver Prince (as Wolfe likes to call

Gropius, after an unfortunate remark of Paul Kle.
court of Bauhaus masters.

Gropius was promptly installed as head of the Harvard
School of Architecture, where Breuer joined him. Moholy-
Nagy started his New Bauhaus in Chicago, Albers found a
niche in Black Mountain, and Mies became dean of architecture
at the Armour Institute, in Chicago. "Within three years the
course of American architecture had changed, utterly," Wolfe
writes. "It was not so much the buildings the Germans designed
in the United States, although Mies' were to become highly
influential a decade later. It was more the system of instruction
they introduced. Still more, it was *their very presence.* The most
fabled creatures in all the mythology of twentieth-century
American art—namely, those dazzling European artists poised
so exquisitely against the rubble—they were . . . *here!* . . . *now!*
. . . in the land of the colonial complex . . . to govern, in person,
their big little Nigeria of the Arts."

Wolfe believes that modern architecture is utterly alien to
and inexpressive of America of the twentieth century—"the
century in which she became the richest nation in all of history" and "the American liquor-store deliveryman's or cargo
humper's vacation was two weeks in Barbados with his third
wife or his new cookie." He continues, "This has been America's period of full-blooded, go-to-hell, belly-rubbing wahoo-
yahoo youthful rampage—and what architecture has she to
show for it? An architecture whose tenets prohibit every manifestation of exuberance, power, empire, grandeur, or even high
spirits and playfulness, as the height of bad taste." At this point
(we are about halfway through the book) Wolfe's own high
spirits and playfulness, which have been carrying forward a
thesis that one would have thought it impossible to sustain for
more than a sentence, begin to flag, and the thesis collapses like
a soap bubble.

Modern architecture was not only not imposed on us by the
Europeans, it was, as Wolfe fails to understand, in no small

measure derived from us. The Bauhaus's plain forms and egal-itarian rhetoric were hardly foreign to the nation that had pro-duced Abraham Lincoln and the Yale lock. We laid out the red carpet for the Bauhaus refugees precisely because they repre-sented something we knew and understood and, in our better moments, valued. Our unselfconscious vernacular forms, as John Kouwenhoven revealed them to us in his classic study *Made in America*, both foreshadowed and helped to shape the studied designs of the Bauhaus.* A hundred years before the Bauhaus, our own pioneers of modern design, the Shakers, were building "worker housing" that was as austere as Mies's. On his visit to the Shaker society at Mount Lebanon in 1874, the journalist Charles Nordhoff, struck by "the homeliness of the buildings, which mostly have the appearance of mere factories or human hives," asked the elder showing him around whether,

> if they were to build anew, they would not aim at some architectural effect, some beauty of design. He replied with great positiveness, "No, the beautiful, as you call it, is absurd and abnormal. It has no business with us. The divine man has no right to waste money upon what you would call beauty, in his house or his daily life, while there are people living in misery."

Then, as now, not everyone was up to such radiant social idealism. Nordhoff clearly wasn't about to run home and strip the gingerbread off his own house. But he gave the Shakers their due: he took their answer at face value, and he reported

---

* The formative influence of the vernacular is also forcefully demonstrated in *Nineteenth Century Modern: The Functional Tradition in Victorian Design*, by Herwin Shaefer, who draws on European as well as American examples of nineteenth-century tools, machines, furniture, and objects of daily use that presage twentieth-century modernism. Shaefer challenges Nikolaus Pevsner's thesis, advanced in *Pioneers of Modern Design, from William Morris to Walter Gropius*, that modern ar-chitecture and design came out of the Victorian design-reform movement. The true fulcrum of modernism, Shaefer says, was the industrial, scientific, and do-mestic vernacular.

it accurately. Wolfe, cynically dismissing the ideology of the twentieth-century modernists as a pose, writes about modern architecture as if it were something that had been put on earth simply to irk him, with no social and cultural history. His theory of the art compound—which reduces the modernist revolution in art, literature, music, design, and architecture to the status of a junior high school afternoon program taken over by cliques of exhibitionistic bohemians—isn't merely preposterous; it's worrisome. When someone as smart as Wolfe feels that it's OK to come out publicly with views as retrograde as his in this book (and in a previous one about abstract art), it's time to start wondering about what is going on with us. A few years ago, cultural backwardness like Wolfe's would have been an embarrassment; today, it is evidently just another manifestation of the New Mood.

Wolfe insidiously enlists the enlightened critical opinion of the last two decades to serve his yahoo-wahoo disdain for the whole of modern architecture. The unsuccessful buildings that Lewis Mumford and Ada Louise Huxtable ruefully held up as warnings that modern architecture can go awry Wolfe gleefully holds up as evidence of modernism's fundamental hollowness. (Peter Blake's *Form Follows Fiasco—Why Modern Architecture Hasn't Worked* and Charles Jencks's *The Language of Post-Modern Architecture* paved the way for Wolfe's polemic in their immoderation—but stopped short of Wolfe's nihilism.) Wolfe makes no distinction between the buildings that fail because they are aesthetic or functional disasters and successful buildings. As far as he's concerned, the ugly 666 Fifth Avenue, the notorious Pruitt-Igoe housing project in St. Louis (which so aggravated the misery it was designed to alleviate that it had to be blown up), and the elegant John Hancock Building in Boston are all "worker housing." Everything in Wolfe's "case against modern architecture" was said in 1962 by Lewis Mumford in his pessimistic essay of that title. But where Mumford's critique belongs to a great and passionate lifework, an encyclopedic meditation on the dilemmas of the modern age, Wolfe's gibe at modernism seems to come out of nothing but a penchant for gibing.

The mired issue of functionalism fuels Wolfe's irrepressible cynicism. He cites a much-cited example of Mies's hypocrisy: the corner of the Seagram Building, to which Mies appended a characteristic, elegant arrangement of non-load-bearing beams to "express" the load-bearing beams that fire laws had obliged him to bury in concrete. "Was there any way you could call such a thing *functional?*" Wolfe taunts, and goes on, "No problem. At the heart of function, as everyone knew, was not *function* but the spiritual quality known as *nonbourgeois*."

At the heart of the issue of functionalism is the fact that no one in the modern movement—from William Morris to Walter Gropius to the anonymous architect of McDonald's hamburger houses—was ever willing to scuttle beauty (or style, as we prefer to call it today) and go all the way with utility. (Even the Shakers, as we can see today better than their contemporaries could, sneaked subtle decorative elements into their austere artifacts.) If the plain forms of the industrial and domestic vernacular dovetailed with the agenda of the modernist reformers, they were by no means the only influence at work. The "cultivated tradition" was just as powerfully present—it was, after all, the tradition in which they themselves had been nurtured. The people who launched the design revolution were upper-class artists, designers, architects, and writers, not carpenters, masons, inventors, manufacturers; the Bauhaus was an art school, not a trade school; the Arts and Crafts Movement was the creation of a Pre-Raphaelite, not of a craftsperson. Aestheticism was so integral a part of modernism that as late as 1936, in an essay called "The New Architecture and the Bauhaus," Gropius could write:

> The liberation of architecture from a welter of ornament, the emphasis on its structural functions, and the concentration on concise and economical solutions, represent the purely

material side of that formalizing process on which the *practical* value of the New Architecture depends. The other, the aesthetic satisfaction of the human soul, is just as important as the material.

Which is nothing very different from what Ruskin was saying in *The Stones of Venice* when he distinguished between the structural elements of a building ("the signs of man's own good work") and its ornament ("the expression of man's delight in better work than his own"). "We are done with heavy stones and hard lines. We are going to be happy," Ruskin promises at the start of his chapter on ornament.

Indeed, the ideal of pure functionalism—the ideal that critics now pillory modern architecture for betraying—was never in the modernist canon at all. "Form follows function" was the formulation not of the Bauhaus but of the nineteenth-century sculptor Horatio Greenough. The functionalists whom Henry-Russell Hitchcock and Philip Johnson snub in "The International Style" for their crude utilitarianism—for being mere builders rather than true architects—were straw men. (To these dour, imaginary Marxists Hitchcock and Johnson ascribe the credo that "the modern world has neither the time nor the money required to raise building to the level of architecture" and then turn around and protest, preposterously, that outside Russia, "whether they ought to or not, many clients can still afford architecture in addition to building.")

However, to recall the aesthetic orientation of the early modernists should not be to forget or underestimate the force of the social and economic pressures that destroyed the status quo of Beaux-Arts eclecticism. When architecture was "liberated from a welter of ornament," it was in the manner of a woman on the edge of financial ruin "liberating" herself from her rings and necklaces. What impelled the modernists to break with the historical styles of the nineteenth century was not their burning desire to "baffle the bourgeoisie," as Wolfe explains it; plain buildings didn't arise because the compounds had impulsively decided that ornament was too middle class. They evolved out of the depressed and growing realization that, as Adolf Loos put it, "ornament is crime." In his brilliant, weird essay of 1908, Loos got to the crux of the design revolution:

> Conditions in the woodcarving and turning trades, the criminally low prices paid to embroiderers and lace makers, are well known. The producers of ornament must work twenty hours to earn the wages a modern worker gets in eight. . . . If I pay as much for a smooth box as for a decorated one, the difference in labor time belongs to the worker. And if there were no ornament at all—a circumstance that will perhaps come true in a few millennia—a man would have to work only four hours instead of eight, for half the work done at present is still for ornamentation.

Wolfe wistfully enumerates the absence from modern architecture of "quoin and groin and pediment and lintel and rock-faced arch, cozy anthropomorphic elements such as entablatures and capitals, pilasters and columns, plinths and rusticated bases . . . spires, Spanish-tile roofs, bays, corbels" but never stops to wonder why "all this had to go." "The main thing was not to be caught designing something someone could point to and say of, with a devastating sneer: 'How very bourgeois,' " he says with a sneer. Wolfe can and does dismiss the whole question in a sentence, but the fact is that it was only after tremendous self-struggle and with the greatest reluctance that Loos's point was taken and ornament was jettisoned by advanced practitioners. For the reform of design and architecture had begun as the reform of ornament.

Morris, following Ruskin, sought to create a single meaningful, Gothicized style of ornament as an alternative to the jumble of post-Renaissance styles that constituted Victorian design. It is a common misconception that Morris and his fellow reformers were seeking to replace machine-made ornament with hand-crafted examples, for in fact practically all ornament that was made throughout the nineteenth century was made by hand. Rather, it was Ruskin's and Morris's association of certain kinds of smooth, bland, refined, evenly executed ornament with machine production that led them to idealize Gothic crudeness, bluntness, idiosyncrasy, and heavy-handedness, and to use the doctrine of imperfection as a form of protest against the cruelties of laissez-faire capitalism and the hideous conditions in English factories. Herwin Shaefer is right to point out that the productions of the "medievalizing" Morris and his colleagues had little influence on the rise of modern architecture and design.

But if Morris the wallpaper-pattern maker and furniture designer belongs to the history of Art Nouveau, Morris the moralist and socialist surely has a place in the annals of modernism. Morris's tragedy wasn't that he was dreamily oblivious of the contradiction between the egalitarianism he espoused as a socialist and the elitism he practiced as an affluent post-artist-designer-entrepreneur. Like James's Hyacinth Robinson in *The Princess Casamassima*, he was all too *conscious* of the dilemma of the lover of beautiful things in a world of ugly social and economic fact, and, like Hyacinth, he finally understood that no resolution was possible: you go one way or the other. The way that Morris and company went caused C. R. Ashbee, in his unpublished memoir of the Arts and Crafts Movement, to write bitterly: "We have made of a great social movement a narrow and tiresome little aristocracy working with great skill for the very rich." But in Morris's quixotic attempt to forge beauty itself into a weapon against human misery, modernism found a rationale that sustained it in its formative years and continues to sustain it in its so-called present-day decline.

Wolfe has little to say about the prehistory of modern architecture except to credit the Vienna Secession with being the first of the "bourgeois-proofed" art compounds. He condenses the fourteen years of the Bauhaus into a single (admittedly, very funny) paragraph about a garlic-flavored vegetable mush that was served there and that inspired Alma Mahler Gropius to remark that "the most unforgettable characteristic of the Bauhaus style was 'garlic on the breath.' " He chronicles the bleak years during which the architecture departments of American universities were in the iron grip of the European International Stylists and their benighted American yes-men like Louis Kahn. He pauses to commiserate with "apostates" like Edward Durrell Stone, Eero Saarinen, Morris Lapidus, and Frank Lloyd Wright—who were either banished from the university compounds or never made it into them—and to take a few more swipes at rabid Europhile modernists in other fields, like John Szarkowski of the Museum of Modern Art photography department, and George Balanchine.

Arriving at the present, he extends his guarded approval to Robert Venturi's aggressive, stylish writings about architecture, which seem sufficiently antimodernist to him, but he finds Venturi's own modest, featly buildings disappointingly "timid"— in fact, just as bad as any modernist's. He juxtaposes a photograph of Venturi's Guild House of 1963 in Philadelphia with one of Bruno Taut's Berlin housing project of 1926, and jeers in the caption, "It took us thirty-seven years to get *this* far." One of the most unsettling things about Wolfe's book is the illustrations: he shows you one example after another of perfectly good-to-great modern architecture with the air of one displaying atrocity pictures from factory farms. Gropius's Dessau Bauhaus, Corbusier's Villa Savoye, Reitveld's Shroeder House, Mies's Seagram Building, and Meier's Douglas House are among the terrible sights in *From Bauhaus to Our House*.

Surprisingly, Wolfe has as little use for the postmodernists as he has for the modernists. One would have thought that some of the recent efforts to ameliorate the coldness of the International Style, to rethink public housing, to rehabilitate old buildings for new uses, would have struck responsive chords in the populist, corbel-loving Wolfe. But to Wolfe, postmodernism is no improvement on modernism, it's just more of the same—more compound "clerisy," more "worker housing." And he's right, of course. Postmodernism is a misnomer. The architects and urban planners laboring under its rubric haven't abandoned modernism but have continued to work serenely in its idiom. What Wolfe calls "that glass of ice water in the face, that bracing slap across the mouth, that reprimand for the fat on one's bourgeois soul, known as modern architecture" remains the architecture of our time. In its best forms, it expresses the decency, generosity, pragmatism, and common sense that inform our vernacular. In its worst forms, it reflects the grandiosity, the narcissism, the privatism, the "lurid, creamy, preposterous" hedonism that Wolfe considers our national character—the national character that he reproaches our architecture for not grotesquely expressing.

*The New York Review of Books*, 1981

# The Purloined Clinic

MICHAEL Fried's *Realism, Writing, Disfiguration: On Thomas Eakins and Stephen Crane* opens with quiet allurement, like a nineteenth-century novel that establishes in its first paragraph that a carriage bearing a veiled lady and an elderly companion has arrived in the town of N——. Fried writes, "When Thomas Eakins in March or early April 1875 began work on *The Gross Clinic* he was thirty years old and had reached a stage in his early career when for the first time he was prepared to attempt a painting of major artistic and intellectual scope," and then chronicles the trouble that the painting—today considered one of the masterpieces of American realist art—ran into among contemporary exhibition juries and critics because of its disturbing subject matter: an operation on a man's thighbone, depicted at a moment of maximum goriness. Next, Fried cites the art-historical writings—notably those of Lloyd Goodrich and Elizabeth Johns—that have shown the influence on *The Gross Clinic* of Eakins's own experience of dissecting and operating rooms when he was an art student, as well as that of earlier art, such as Rembrandt's *The Anatomy Lesson of Dr. Nicolas Tulp* and F.N.A. Feyen-Perrin's *The Anatomy Lesson of Dr. Velpeau*. Suddenly, a shot rings out. A dashing stranger on horseback gallops up to the carriage, and as his armed accomplices hold pistols to the heads of the coachman and the elderly companion, he drags the (not very seriously protesting) veiled lady from the carriage and rides off with her slung across his saddle. In some such fashion does Fried arrive

❧ REALISM, WRITING, DISFIGURATION: ON THOMAS EAKINS AND STEPHEN CRANE (Chicago: University of Chicago Press, 1987), by Michael Fried.

on the scene of his own book, and proceed to wrest *The Gross Clinic* from its previous stodgy commentators, whose "blandly normalizing" discourse, as he disdainfully calls it, has simply failed "to come to grips with [the painting] with anything like the energy of imagination and complexity of purpose that it displays towards us." Fried's own energy of imagination and complexity of purpose are of such vast, some might even say monstrous, proportions that Eakins's work positively shrinks before the onslaught of so many almost menacingly fanciful and intricate ideas. Fried's strange thesis is that Eakins's art is an especially acute and conspicuous example of the struggle between two modes of representation—the "pictorial" and the "graphic"—by which the enterprise of painting is ineluctably riven, and that *The Gross Clinic* is an (unconscious) allegory of that struggle, and as Fried develops it one begins to wonder whether his book is not itself a (conscious) allegory of the enterprise of criticism. When one reaches the second part of the book, devoted to Stephen Crane, in which Fried ascribes the peculiarities of Crane's "impressionist" prose style to Crane's preternatural sensitivity to the materiality of writing—to the sight of actual inked letters on the page—and reads Crane's recurrent images of disfigured upturned faces of dead or unconscious men as (again unwitting) allegorizations of the "excruciating" act of inscription, the suspicion becomes a certainty.

*The Gross Clinic* is a huge, dramatically horrific work, set in a nineteenth-century operating amphitheater, which shows the surgeon Samuel D. Gross, scalpel in hand, pausing to stare meditatively into the middle distance as surgical assistants work on a deep, bleeding incision, from which Gross's right fingers are still shiningly bloody. One of the assistants probes the wound with a long, thin wooden implement and two others hold the wound open with metal retractors; a fourth assistant holds down the patient's legs, while a fifth applies a chloroform-soaked cloth to the patient's face. Gross is wearing a dark business suit and vest and cravat—as are the assistants and also the students who form a shadowy audience in the background of steeply raked rows of seats—whose somber propriety brings into shocking relief the brightly blood-smeared hand holding the bloody scalpel. Behind Gross, another assistant sits at a table recording the proceedings, and to Gross's right is the figure of a woman dressed in black, who is cringing in horror, holding her hands in front of her eyes, in a kind of anticipatory mimesis of the feelings the painting will arouse in the viewer.

Traditional criticism has attributed the painting's power to its "uncompromising realism"—to Eakins's willingness to paint things as they are, however brutal and unpleasant, and at whatever sacrifice of compositional harmony and lucidity. (On one's first view of the work, for example, it is hard to make out the position of the patient's body on the operating table, or to account for a pair of hands holding retractors, which turn out to belong to an assistant seated behind Gross and almost completely obscured by him.) Fried challenges the presupposition that lies behind this criticism—the assumption of an original scene of which the painting is a doggedly faithful transcription. He argues that the only evidence for the existence of such a scene is the painting itself, which gives the *illusion* of being a rendering of actuality that was forced upon the painter but in fact is something that the painter chose to paint in a particular way. Moreover, he writes, "the features of *The Gross Clinic* we have been discussing [the odd disposition of the patient's body, the eclipsing of the assistant holding the retractors, and other of the painting's "affronts to seeing"] are all in different ways manifestly so excessive and provocative that the traditional argument from reality seems particularly inappropriate to their case." Fried's bearing down on this point, his insistence that the painting is the exclusive responsibility of the painter and is in no way beholden to anything outside the painter's imagination, is crucially relevant to his own enterprise (one that he has been carrying forward since the mid-sixties, both as a writer about contemporary art and as an art historian) of criticism practiced as a form of imaginative writing and as an exercise in excess and provocation.

In his previous book, *Absorption and Theatricality: Painting and Beholder in the Age of Diderot* (1980), Fried wrote of a desideratum of eighteenth-century French art criticism (as articulated largely by Diderot): that paintings should erect a kind of wall between themselves and their beholders, as actors in a play erect a wall between themselves and their audience in order to appear to be completely oblivious of it. Fried held up example upon example of historical and genre paintings whose characters are so intensely absorbed in each other and in what they are doing as to maintain "the supreme fiction" that the beholder does not exist. The issue of the relationship of art to beholder was already present for Fried in the criticism of contemporary art he wrote in the sixties, notably in his essay "Art and Objecthood," in which (as he sums it up in his introduction to *Absorption and Theatricality*) "I argued that much seemingly difficult and advanced but actually ingratiating and mediocre work sought to establish what I called a theatrical relation to the beholder, whereas the very best recent work—the paintings of Louis, Noland, Olitski, and Stella, and the sculptures of Smith and Caro—were, in essence, *anti*-theatrical, which is to say that they treated the beholder as if he were not there." The value of antitheatricality which Fried extols (note the yoking of "ingratiating" with "mediocre," as if the one inevitably followed the other) is, of course, a fundamental human value. We cherish the idea of doing things for themselves rather than for the purpose of showing off; the ideals of sincerity, authenticity, spontaneity—all derive from the bias against the theatrical. The paradigmatic image of the theatrical is the crying child peeping through the fingers he holds in front of his presumably tear-filled eyes, to see if he is being observed and what effect he is producing on the beholder. Or, rather, this is the paradigmatic image of the insufficiently artful: as clever children gain confidence in their powers of manipulation and perfect their performances, so do artists work out the strategies needed to obscure the fundamental hypocrisy that lies at the heart of their enterprise, and to strengthen the illusion that art is as natural and involuntary as breathing rather than as wrought and as willed as cheating at cards.

In *Realism, Writing, Disfiguration*, just below the surface of the narrative proper, which concerns the conflictive character of the painting of Eakins and the writing of Crane, lies another, related narrative, which concerns the relationship of the critic to the reader. On the face of it, it would seem impossible for a critic to establish the sort of distance between himself and the reader that novelists and poets establish simply by following the conventions of their genres. (The novelistic convention of dialogue, for example, puts the reader in the position of someone overhearing a conversation.) Since the function of the critic is to persuade, how can he pretend that there isn't someone there *to* persuade? Isn't criticism inherently and inescapably theatrical? Isn't the critic like the actor standing at the front of the stage after the play is over, reminding the audience—in the most blatantly theatrical gesture of all—that it's only a play? Fried's extraordinary achievement in *Realism, Writing, Disfiguration* is to show how the best criticism, like the best painting, sculpture, and literature, transcends its theatricality and creates (as Fried writes in *Absorption and Theatricality* of a painting by Joseph-Marie Vien) "a lucid and hermetic structure of absorptive relations . . . a closed system which, in effect, seals off [its] space or world." In the work of certain quirky painters, like Eakins, and quirky writers, like Crane, and quirky critics, like Fried, the contours of the struggle to maintain the supreme fiction are more visible than in that of others—they form part of the signature of the work—and thus provide the instructive abnormal case from which the structure of the normal may be adduced. Freud, in writing of the light that psychosis sheds on normal mental processes, offers the analogy of a broken crystal that has fractured along fault lines revealing the basic structure of crystal. Fried, similarly, uses what appear to be faults of his own character to elucidate the character of the critical enterprise. He presents himself as a person of unbounded conceit and arrogance; there may be more "I"s in this book than in any work of criticism hitherto published. At every turn, Fried brings himself into the discourse:

> To strengthen my case, let me introduce in this context a painting Eakins appears to have started. . . .
>
> I shall have more to say about this device further on. . . .
>
> So far I have said nothing about the precise articulation of writing and painting in *The Gross Clinic*, but rather than confront that issue directly I want to approach it in stages. . . .
>
> I shall have a lot more to say about the relationship between horizontality and verticality in Eakins's art before I am through. . . .
>
> This isn't crucial to my present argument but worth mentioning. . . .
>
> At this juncture I want to take up several cruxes barely touched upon earlier. . . .
>
> I shall soon claim that her refusal may not be as unequivocal as this implies. . . .
>
> Later in this essay I shall argue that the images of serpents and fire that turn up frequently in Crane's texts belong essentially to a metaphorics of writing. . . .
>
> But I hope that enough has been said to allow me to take the next step in my argument. . . .
>
> And this leads me, reading backward as it were, to find another emblem of disinterestedness. . . .

There is so much of this in the book that one quickly realizes it is hardly a matter of naive self-betrayal. It is, rather, deliberate strategy: by creating a larger-than-life, even somewhat grotesque, persona for himself, Fried brings into relief a characteristic of criticism that is not so easy to see in more "normal" examples of the genre but is the key to its potential for anti-theatricality. This is the absorptive, dialogistic character of the form. The Platonic dialogue remains the model for critical writing. If actual dialogue has been abandoned, there remains an implicit dialogue between a Socratic teacher-hero and a cast of colleagues and students who form the hermetic world of the text that the reader holds in his hand but is not himself a part of. The ontological situation of criticism, indeed, resembles that of *The Gross Clinic*, with its heroic master-teacher addressing an imaginary audience painted within its own frame, rather than the flesh-and-blood audience standing outside. And the sense of urgency and seriousness conveyed by the Eakins work—its atmosphere of tense risk: who knows whether the patient will live or die?—is paralleled (you could almost say parodied) by Fried's intensity and gravity as he performs, step by step, *his* critical operation, drawing the colleagues and students of *his* imagined universe into a spell of tense attentiveness. Occasionally (notably in the latter pages of the Crane essay), Fried more resembles the Ancient Mariner clutching at the coat of the reluctant guest as he tells him a mad story than the august master-teacher in dignified command of his audience—but this, too, is part of Fried's allegory of criticism, taking us to the edge that criticism skirts and inviting us to look into the abyss of delusion it has gamely pitched its tent right next to.

Perhaps the most conspicuous feature of the critical persona (as Fried invites us to regard it)—even more conspicuous than its magisterial egotism—is its hyperactivity. The critic of *Realism, Writing, Disfiguration* is never still; he is like a waiter rushing from table to table, with so much to do, so many orders to fill, that he is barely able to restrain himself from simply dumping food down on the table, instead of abiding by the proper waiter's stately protocol. But the critic must—and does—restrain himself, because that's the whole point, that's what criticism is: a process, a progress over time, not a mere blurting out of conclusions. Note, in Fried's prodigal use of the personal pronoun, how he is always involved with time:

I shall soon claim . . .
Later in this essay I shall argue . . .
At this juncture I want to take up . . .
So far I have said nothing about . . .

On almost every page of Fried's book there is a sense of how much of the energy of criticism goes into holding back what the critic knows but what the interlocutor is not yet ready to grasp. But even as Fried speaks of what he is not yet doing he darkly alludes to the countervailing forces that are impelling him toward the inexorable conclusions that he can only so long hold out against. For example (italics mine):

. . . he seems to me largely to escape the play of forces that eventually *we shall have to trace* . . .
The figures of Eakins and of the patient being operated on . . . *make it inevitable* that *The Gross Clinic* be construed, sooner or later, in Freudian terms. . . .
. . . before this essay is done, *we shall have to consider* the implications . . .
Coming to Eakins from that prior involvement has had the virtue of *forcing me* to register important differences . . .

It is here that Fried's allegory assumes its most complex and paradoxical guise. For, of course—as Fried knows better than anyone—there are no actual "forces," "inevitabilities," or "necessities" impinging on his freedom of action. Fried doesn't *have* to do any of the things he says he must do. These imperatives are fictions as bald as the fiction of the nonexistent beholder. Fried is no more obliged to speak of *The Gross Clinic* in Freudian terms than Emma Bovary was obliged to sleep with Rodolphe. In each instance, a choice was made, though made in such a way and in such a context as to seem to be the only choice possible. As Flaubert's realism creates the illusion that his characters behave as people in real life must, so does Fried ground his critical inventions in a sort of magnetic field of positivist factuality, thus creating *his* illusion of the unarguably self-evident. (Along with dozens of black-and-white and color reproductions in the Eakins essay and massive quotation in the Crane one, there are over forty pages of notes, in which Fried carries on a kind of sotto-voce conversation with colleagues and the most advanced of his students, on whose shoulders his crushingly heavy erudition will conceivably rest more lightly than on those of the regular students to whom the more coarse-grained main text is addressed.) Conversely, as a novel's structure of necessity can crumble at the prodding of one of its vulnerable nodes (of, say, coincidence or improbability), so can the structure of a work of criticism collapse under the strain of an acutely skeptical reading. That Fried's structure does and doesn't collapse—that his wild and farfetched arguments stand as wobbly, crumbling, but still bravely upright monuments to the autonomous imagination—is what gives his book its high tension. Although he never uses the term "deconstruction," it hovers over his work like a halo over a saint's head. References to Jacques Derrida, Paul de Man, Harold Bloom, Neil Hertz, and Walter Benn Michaels (among other deconstructionists) and to such staple subjects—"topoi"—of deconstructive writing as the sublime and "the scene of writing" signal Fried's involvement with this French intellectual import, which has improbably flourished in our heavy native clay as if it were goldenrod. Or not so improbably. Another major topos of deconstruction (one that Fried doesn't happen to mention) is Edgar Allan Poe's "The Purloined Letter," which since Jacques Lacan's resurrection of it in the sixties has steadily glowed in the poststructuralist firmament like a kind of lodestar. Fifty-four years before Freud wrote *The Interpretation of Dreams* (and a hundred thirty years before Derrida arrived at Yale), Poe had composed what must be the quintessential allegory of both psychoanalytic therapy and deconstructive critical theory. As the detective Dupin went straight for the most negligently obvious place that the government minister could have selected for the "concealment" of the compromising letter, so do the analyst and the deconstructionist know that the secrets of human nature and of works of art lie on the surface and in the margins, and that the metaphors of depth, delving, unearthing, plumbing, penetrating are irrelevant to their work. Fried's dismissal of the "normalizing" commentators on *The Gross Clinic*—his disdainful exclamation that "we shall find the usual techniques of arthistorical inquiry to be of little use" in getting at the painting's secret—is like Dupin's contemptuous dismissal of the "usual" methods of the Paris police, who have twice searched the minister's house with insane thoroughness, removing every floorboard, peering into every hollow table leg, and finding nothing. Fried, with Dupin-like cool perversity, begins his analysis of *The Gross Clinic* by tearing his gaze away from the lurid center of the painting and letting it alight on the marginal figure of a man in the audience who sits hunched over a pad and pencil; this is Eakins himself, sketching and/or taking notes on the scene he will eventually paint. Fried connects this shadowy figure with the three more prominent figures in the painting who wield pencil-like implements: the doctor recording the proceedings, the surgical assistant probing the wound, and Gross himself, holding the scalpel. Fried goes on to speak of other works by Eakins in which a "thematics of writing" is overtly or covertly present; he reminds us that Eakins was a teacher of penmanship and drawing before he became a painter, and that his father was a writing master and an engrosser of documents. From all these and other clues that no one has hitherto noticed he builds up a case for his bizarre notion that the secret energy of Eakins's art lies in Eakins's unconscious conflict over whether to write and draw or to paint—a case that it may take years for Fried's fellow art historians, using their clumsy "usual" techniques, to break down. In the second essay, Fried similarly distances himself from all previous commentary on Crane as he unfolds his remarkable narrative of a writer for whom the act of writing was so threatening that he wrote about wars and disfiguring deaths in order to express his horror at what he was doing when he wielded a pen. Criticism as radical as this is rare, but only when criticism is radical does it stand a chance of being something more than a pale reflection of the work of art that is its subject. By disfiguring the work of art almost beyond recognition, Fried forces us to imagine it anew—not a bad achievement for a critic.

*The New Yorker*, 1987

# Kundera's Legerdemain

ONE of the four central characters of Milan Kundera's brilliant new novel is a Czech painter named Sabina, who leaves Prague for Geneva around the time of the Russian invasion of 1968 and finds herself in a perpetual struggle against the unbearable banality of her situation as an émigré artist.

Sabina had once had an exhibit that was organized by a political organization in Germany. When she picked up the catalogue, the first thing she saw was a picture of herself with a drawing of barbed wire superimposed on it. Inside she found a biography that read like the life of a saint or martyr: she had suffered, struggled against injustice, been forced to abandon her bleeding homeland, yet was carrying on the struggle. "Her paintings are a struggle for happiness" was the final sentence.

She protested, but they did not understand her.

Do you mean that modern art isn't persecuted under Communism?

"My enemy is kitsch, not Communism!" she replied, infuriated.

From that time on, she began to insert mystifications in her biography, and by the time she got to America she even managed to hide the fact that she was Czech. It was all merely a desperate attempt to escape the kitsch that people wanted to make of her life.

Kitsch is the enemy of every artist, of course, but it has special menace for the artist who has made his way out of the abyss

✤ THE UNBEARABLE LIGHTNESS OF BEING (New York: Harper & Row, 1984), by Milan Kundera, translated by Michael Henry Heim.

of "totalitarian kitsch" (as Kundera calls it), only to find himself peering into the chasm of Western anticommunist kitsch. Kundera, who left Czechoslovakia in 1975, after he was expelled from the Communist Party for the second time and could no longer publish or teach there, now lives in Paris and works in an increasingly—what to call it?—abstract, surreal, "poetic" idiom. His need to experiment with form is surely connected to his personal vendetta against the puerilities of "socialist realism" and its "free world" counterparts. In an interview with Philip Roth which appears in the Penguin edition of Kundera's previous novel, *The Book of Laughter and Forgetting* (1980), Kundera spoke of his great fondness for Diderot and Laurence Sterne, citing them as "the greatest experimenters of all time in the form of the novel." "Sterne and Diderot understood the novel as a *great game*," he told Roth. But writers for whom the issue of artistic freedom hasn't the urgency it has had for Kundera do not play the game of the novel quite as close to the edge as he has played it.

His novels have all the unpredictability and changeability of mountain weather and are marked by an almost compulsive disregard for the laws of genre. Like a driver who signals right and promptly turns left, Kundera repeatedly betrays the reader's trust in the conventions that give him his bearings in a novel. In Kundera's farcical fairy tale *The Farewell Party* (1976), for example, a character named Jakub, who possesses a poison pill that he counts on for instant death in the case of arrest, finds a vial of pills, which are some kind of tranquilizer, left on a table in the cafeteria of a health spa and noticing that they are the same color blue as his own pill, he idly—just to see how closely the colors match—slips the lethal pill into the vial. Suddenly, the owner of the tranquilizers—Ružena, a vulgar nurse at the spa—bursts into the cafeteria, grabs her vial, and treats Jakub's attempts to covertly retrieve his own pill with such rude unpleasantness that finally, in mute protest, he simply lets her walk out with the vial intact.

For the next sixty pages, the reader is kept in a state of pleasurable suspense—not over whether the nurse will die or not (how can she, since *The Farewell Party* is a comedy?) but over the way Kundera will resolve the wonderfully insane situation he has contrived. Jakub, after eighteen hours of rather lackluster search for the nurse, finally learns that she is alive, sighs with relief, and concludes (as the clever reader has already done) that the doctor who had promised to supply him with a lethal pill must have actually given him a harmless one. As Jakub drives away from the spa, he meditates on the philosophical implications of his action. He decides that even though the nurse is unharmed, he must count himself no less a murderer than Raskolnikov—since he gave a stranger what he believed to be poison and had made no real attempt to save her. Marveling at his odd detachment, he calmly drives on, and out of the novel. Meanwhile, back at the spa, Ružena, in a moment of discomposure, has popped a pill in her mouth, clutched her stomach, and fallen dead to the ground.

In *The Joke* (1967), Kundera uses another bottle of mislabeled pills for another of his wild veerings of emotional direction—this time to give a potentially tragic situation a "comic" twist. The reader will understand the quotes around "comic" when he learns that the situation involves a desperately humiliated woman's decision to end her life with an overdose of analgesics that she finds in a friend's overcoat pocket—which turn out to be laxatives.

Near the end of his novel *Life Is Elsewhere* (1969), Kundera steps out from behind the curtain of his narrative—the sardonically told story of a mama's boy, a young poet who develops into a monstrosity of totalitarian kitsch—and speaks of his restiveness under the constraints of the novel form. "Just as your life is determined by the kind of profession and marriage you have chosen, so our novel is limited by our observatory perspective. . . . We have chosen this approach as you have chosen your fate, and our choice is equally unalterable," Kundera says ruefully, and then goes on to wonder whether maybe the novelist cannot welsh on his commitment after all: "Man cannot jump out of his life, but perhaps a novel has more freedom. Suppose we hurriedly and secretly dismantled our observatory and transported it elsewhere, at least for a little while?" Kundera then proposes to write a chapter that will be to the main narrative what a small guesthouse is to a country manor, and suddenly, without warning, the reader is thrust into one of the most lyrical and heartrending scenes in contemporary fiction —a scene between a red-haired girl and a middle-aged man (who appears in the novel for the first time) that is of almost unbearable sadness and tenderness. The girl had told a small, gratuitous lie that had had enormous tragic consequences, and the middle-aged man—her sexual initiator when she was seventeen, whose character is a Nabokovian blend of cynicism and compassion—now comforts her as one comforts a hurt child. Kundera describes the scene as "a quiet interlude in which an anonymous man unexpectedly lights a lamp of kindness," and it fades out of the book (which is interesting and sometimes very funny but otherwise never very affecting) like one of those mysterious distinct sounds one hears at dawn and supposes one has dreamed.

In his next two novels—*The Book of Laughter and Forgetting* and *The Unbearable Lightness of Being*—Kundera attempts to recapture this emotional tone while simultaneously experimenting with surrealist techniques. It stubbornly eludes him in the first book, whose surrealism seems somewhat pathetic and outdated, and whose pathos has an "as if" quality: instead of being moved, one is aware of being *cued* to be moved. But in *The Unbearable Lightness of Being* Kundera succeeds in actually creating the work of high modernist playfulness and deep pathos that he had merely projected in the earlier book.

Like *Ulysses*, it is a book entwined with another book—in this case *Anna Karenina*, a copy of which Kundera, with his characteristic directness, puts under the arm of his heroine, Tereza, as she enters the novel. He draws on *Anna Karenina* not in a literal sense—his Tereza and Tomas and Sabina and Franz in no way "equal" Anna and Vronsky and Levin and Kitty. It is the existential dilemma at the core of *Anna Karenina* that he plucks from the Russian novel and restates in terms of the opposition between heaviness and lightness. When Tolstoy wrote of the vacuous and senseless life of Vronsky and Anna in the country after their forced retreat from society (a life that he had the inspiration of showing through the eyes of the care-worn, child-burdened, "*excessivement terre-à-terre*" Dolly, as Vronsky dismissively calls her), he was writing about the un-bearable lightness of being. We keep this state at bay with our marriages, friendships, commitments, responsibilities, loyalties and ties to family, culture, and nation; and we float up toward it every time we commit adultery, betray a friend, break ranks, defy authority, sever a family bond, leave a homeland, or (as Kundera goes beyond Tolstoy in suggesting) attempt to create a work of art. "What then shall we choose?" Kundera writes. "Weight or lightness?"

Tomas, a middle-aged Prague surgeon and an unregenerate womanizer, meets Tereza, a simple, mild, somewhat pitiful, immensely touching young woman who works as a waitress in a small town he is visiting, and realizes that she is his fate. Tereza is the embodiment of all the things on the "heavy" side of the ledger: she is like a marble statue entitled *Fidelity* or *Constancy*. Passive, conservative, tradition-bound, she expresses our deepest atavisms of attachment and rootedness; and she inspires profound, compassionate love in Tomas. He cannot help loving her—any more than he can help sleeping with other women. Tomas and Tereza marry, and shortly after the Russian invasion they emigrate to Zurich. Sabina, who is one of Tomas's mistresses, has already left Czechoslovakia and is living in Ge-neva. She is the dazzling embodiment of lightness. As dégagé as a cat, she goes her own way and keeps her own counsel; she is ironic, perverse, and beautiful. She comes to Zurich for a tryst with Tomas; afterward Tomas "thought happily that he carried his way of living with him as a snail carries his house. Tereza and Sabina represented the two poles of his life, separate and irreconcilable, yet equally appealing." His satisfaction is short-lived, however. One evening, he comes home and finds a letter from Tereza saying that she has gone back to Prague. She needs to return; it is not in her nature to live in exile. For a few days, Tomas experiences "the sweet lightness of being." He breathed "the heady smell of his freedom. New adventures hid around each corner. The future was again a secret. He was on his way back to the bachelor life, the life he had once felt destined for, the life that would let him be what he actually was." Then:

> On Monday, he was hit by a weight the likes of which he had never known. The tons of steel of the Russian tanks were nothing compared with it. For there is nothing heavier than compassion. Not even one's own pain weighs so heavy as the pain one feels with someone, for someone, a pain intensified by the imagination and prolonged by a hundred echoes.

Tomas accepts his fate and makes the irrevocable border crossing back into Czechoslovakia.

The narrative here shifts to Sabina and her lover, the "heavy" Franz—a decent, good, intelligent man, a professor attracted to leftist causes, who is married to a woman he doesn't love and who finally does "the right thing" of telling his wife the truth and moving out of their apartment. This causes Sabina, for whom fecklessness is a kind of personal ethic and who is "charmed more by betrayal than by fidelity," to leave Franz.

In Prague, Tomas is faced with a choice: the chief surgeon at his hospital tells him that he must retract an impudent political article he published in a newspaper during the Prague Spring or lose his job.

"You know what's at stake," said the chief surgeon.

He knew, all right. There were two things in the balance: his honor (which consisted in his refusing to retract what he had said) and what he had come to call the meaning of his life (his work in medicine and research).

In following Tereza back over the border, like Alcestis following Admetus into Hades, Tomas had chosen heaviness over lightness, and now he again chooses the apparently heavy alternative. He refuses to retract the article, is promptly dismissed from his post, is forced to work in worse and worse clinics, is hounded by the secret police for a retraction, and finally, in desperation, voluntarily descends to a rung so far down on the social ladder that the police no longer find him interesting: he becomes a window washer. Now comes another of Kundera's astonishing and witty reversals. In choosing honor over expediency Tomas has actually chosen lightness: his new profession proves to be not a degradation and a punishment but a lark and a holiday. Tomas spends his days genially screwing the women whose windows he has come to wash. His libertinism is presented as a kind of libertarianism—a form of research into the variety and idiosyncrasy of human nature. He is what Kundera calls an "epic womanizer" as opposed to the "lyrical womanizer," who merely, rigidly and bleakly, seeks the ideal woman. Earlier in the book, Kundera has written of Tomas's trick of making himself interesting to women by suddenly commanding, "Strip!"

That was Tomas's way of unexpectedly turning an innocent conversation with a woman into an erotic situation. Instead of stroking, flattering, pleading, he would issue a command, issue it abruptly, unexpectedly, softly yet firmly and authoritatively, and at a distance: at such moments he never touched the woman he was addressing.

This is like the script of a wet dream. But Kundera gets away with it. In the context—a brilliantly bizarre scene in which Sabina and Tereza alternately take nude photographs of each other and Sabina unwittingly betrays her relationship to Tomas by commanding Tereza to strip—the silliness of the passage goes unnoticed. "Read!" Kundera commands, and we humbly and gratefully obey.

*The Unbearable Lightness of Being* has a kind of charmed life. It is like a performance that has gotten off on the right foot. Every door Kundera tries opens for him. In the earlier books, one felt like a passenger in a small plane, swooping and dropping precipitately and heading straight for a mountain; in the present book, one travels by steady jumbo jet. The heavy/light polarity acts as a kind of fixative for Kundera's special sensitivity to the ambiguities and ironies of the position of the Janus-faced political émigré, and to its potentialities as a universal metaphor. When Tomas decides to follow Tereza back into Czechoslovakia, he commits an act of radical antiromanticism. It is as if Anna had decided to go back to Karenin. (Tomas and Tereza actually name their dog Karenin.) Tomas's erotic idyll as a window washer reveals the lightness that may lurk even in the most lumpishly heavy of existences—the heady freedom that totalitarianism paradoxically bestows on those of its victims who have nothing left to lose. (Solzhenitsyn introduced this profound paradox in *The First Circle*.) Tomas and Tereza move to the country—a further slide down the social scale—and are killed in an automobile accident, crushed under the weight of a truck. We learn of their deaths early in the book; most of their story is narrated in the shadow of this knowledge.

Sabina, who has chosen the artist's condition of "silence, exile and cunning," bows under the almost equally crushing weight of her alienation. She moves from city to city, from Europe to America, in a state of depression and indifference. We see her disappear somewhere in the expanse of America—a small, gallant, forlorn figure. Before she fades from view, we see her standing at dusk on the lawn of a white clapboard house belonging to an aging couple who have taken her up. She is moved by the sight of two lighted windows, which evoke the sentimental image of home: "all peace, quiet, and harmony, and ruled by a loving mother and wise father." Sabina briefly warms herself in the glow of this image—"Had she then, herself on the threshold of old age, found the parents who had been snatched from her as a girl?"—but quickly pulls back.

She was well aware it was an illusion. Her days with the aging couple were merely a brief interval. The old man was seriously ill, and when his wife was left on her own, she would go and live with their son in Canada. Sabina's path of betrayals would then continue elsewhere, and from the depths of her being, a silly mawkish song about two shining windows and the happy family living behind them would occasionally make its way into the unbearable lightness of being.

Though touched by the song, Sabina did not take her feeling seriously. She knew only too well that the song was a beautiful lie. As soon as kitsch is recognized for the lie it is, it moves into the context of non-kitsch, thus losing its authoritarian power and becoming as touching as any other human weakness. For none among us is superman enough to escape kitsch completely. No matter how we scorn it, kitsch is an integral part of the human condition.

If Sabina is the novel's artistic conscience, Tereza is its emotional center. She is like Tamina of *The Book of Laughter and Forgetting*—a silently suffering woman living in exile and cleaving to the memory of her dead husband—whose anguish and desolation are rendered in mysterious, fantasy-laden, and somewhat artificial passages whose status as dreams or "sur-reality" Kundera leaves ambiguous. Such passages recur in *The Unbearable Lightness of Being*, but here they are clearly identified as Tereza's dreams. They are deeply disturbing dreams of naked women, cats, corpses, interrogations, executions, mass exterminations, whose horror is overlaid with a mysterious beauty. In waking life, Tereza often uses the term "concentration camp" to express her sense of life's oppressiveness and her feelings of weakness and defenselessness. (One hears in her name the echo of the Czech concentration camp Terezin.) As a child, she was victimized by her mother—a fierce, coarse Queen of the Night (as the earlier Tamina invites us to see her)—and she has never lost her air of victimization, her posture of a cringing child.

Franz is the least vivid figure of the four. Near the end of the novel, Kundera makes an authorial appearance to confide that "the characters in my novels are my own unrealized possibilities. That is why I am equally fond of them all and equally horrified by them. Each one has crossed a border that I myself have circumvented. It is that crossed border (the border beyond which my own 'I' ends) which attracts me most. For beyond that border begins the secret the novel asks about." Franz seems less close to his creator, less densely conceived, than the others; he is more abstract and schematic. His culminating "heavy" action—he joins a mordantly described left-wing international mission of mercy to Cambodia, made up of "twenty doctors and about fifty intellectuals (professors, writers, diplomats, singers, actors, and mayors) as well as four hundred reporters and photographers"—seems to arise as much from his creator's sense of the fatuity of political activism as from any internal necessity of character.

In the novel's final section the narrative suddenly narrows, to become the story of the mortal illness and death of the dog Karenin. The self-reflexiveness of the book here gives way to the simplest naturalism, and as we cry for poor Karenin and for the couple who mark the passage of ten years of their relationship in the ebbing life of their dog, we may feel—as Sabina felt while regarding the two lighted windows—that our tears are cheap, that this is kitsch of the most insidious kind, sentimentality at its most invasive. However Kundera, always a few jumps ahead of us, redeems his descent into kitsch with a message of remorseless pessimism—one that another great émigré writer, Isaac Bashevis Singer, has already delivered—on mankind's prospects in the light of its pitiless treatment of animals:

> Tereza kept stroking Karenin's head, which was quietly resting in her lap, while something like the following ran through her mind: There's no particular merit in being nice to one's fellow man. She had to treat the other villagers decently, because otherwise she couldn't live there. Even with Tomas, she was *obliged* to behave lovingly because she needed him. We can never establish with certainty what part of our relations with others is the result of our emotions—love, antipathy, charity, or malice—and what part is predetermined by the constant power play among individuals.
>
> True human goodness, in all its purity and freedom, can come to the fore only when its recipient has no power. Mankind's true moral test, its fundamental test (which lies deeply buried from view), consists of its attitude towards those who are at its mercy: animals. And in this respect mankind has suffered a fundamental debacle, a debacle so fundamental that all others stem from it.

Michael Henry Heim's translation of *The Unbearable Lightness of Being* is very distinguished; its distinction lies in the clean precision and elegant leanness of diction through which the novel's taut modernist tone is rendered. In her novel *Pitch Dark*, Renata Adler asks (in the voice of the book's narrator), "Do I need to stylize it, or can I tell it as it was?" To point out that "telling it as it was" is itself another stylization is only to restate the question that has haunted fiction throughout this century. In *Life Is Elsewhere*, Kundera used Rimbaud's line "*Il faut être absolument moderne*" as an epigraph. But the modern novelist, unlike the modern painter, sculptor, or poet, cannot absolutely divest himself of realism: the modernist novel is inevitably a hybrid form. Only through the illusion that he is in some sense "telling it as it was" can the novelist sustain the reader's attention and touch his heart. The self-reflexiveness of modern art, its aggressive avowal of materials (cf. Maurice Denis's provocative injunction of 1890: "Remember that a picture—before being a battle horse or a nude woman or some anecdote—is essentially a flat surface covered over with colors in a certain order") can extend only partially to narrative literature. Kundera's work deepens our sense of modernism as a force powerfully pulling at the novelist but never quite taking him over the border.

*The New York Review of Books*, 1984

# The Trial of Alyosha

"$I$ HAVE always stressed the importance of convention in theater," Václav Havel wrote in 1981. "I have often realized, and stressed, that where everything is allowed, nothing has the power to surprise." *Letters to Olga*, the collection of letters Havel wrote to his wife while serving a four-and-one-half-year prison sentence at hard labor between 1979 and 1983, draws its own immense strength from the fact that almost nothing was allowed the writer. Havel's weekly letter to his wife—the only form of writing permitted him—was ruled by the following singular poetics: it could not be more than four pages long; it had to be written in a legible hand, with nothing crossed out or corrected; there could be no quotation marks or foreign expressions in it; margins were required to be a specific width; and, as for subject matter, it could not touch on any of the actualities of prison life and had to confine itself to "family matters." Whether the letter got through or not depended on the whim of an "absolutist and much feared, half-demented warden" (as Havel later described him in the long interview with Karel Hvížďala published here as *Disturbing the Peace*).

For many, probably most, writers, such conditions would not recommend themselves, but for Havel, the writer of absurdist dramas, they could not have been more propitious. They restored to him precisely what was intended to be taken from him: his occupation as a writer. They compelled him to function as an artist where, under less extreme conditions of censorship, he would probably have functioned merely as a good letter

✦ LETTERS TO OLGA: JUNE 1979–SEPTEMBER 1982 (New York: Alfred A. Knopf, 1988), by Václav Havel, translated by Paul Wilson.

writer; they elicited from him a strange, unclassifiable, inad-
vertent masterpiece, a work that I believe will outlive his plays
and essays.

For Havel, the half-demented warden was like one of those
great, strict teachers who prod us into achievements we did not
know we were capable of. He forced Havel into modes of writing that it would not have occurred to him to attempt if left to
his own devices, most significantly the autobiographical mode.
The proscription against describing prison life was not as uncomfortable for Havel as it might have been for another writer.
As he was later to say to Hvížďala, commenting on his realization that he would probably never write about the prison
experience, "I am not a narrative author; I can't write stories,
and always forget them anyway. . . . I'm no Hrabal." Havel's
initial solution to the problem of what to write about when you
can't write about the single glaring fact of your life was to follow
his natural bent toward philosophical reflection. In his youth,
he had come under the influence of phenomenology and exis-
tentialism via the Czech philosopher Jan Patočka (a student of
Heidegger and Husserl), and he welcomed the opportunity to
work on hard metaphysical problems in his letters. (The letters
were being circulated among a group of friends and colleagues,
and portions of them read more like papers for a Heidegger
colloquium than like letters to a spouse. Early in the correspondence Havel actually formed the intention of publishing
the essayist segments of his letters, and he wrote them with
that object in mind.) But presently the warden, perhaps growing
suspicious that "existence-in-the-world" and "thrownness" were
code terms for dissident mischief, or simply getting bored, sent
word down that Havel was to stop writing his philosophic
meditations and to write only about himself. This edict had
momentous literary consequences.

At first, Havel fretted about the impossible task he had been
set. "It is neither my nature nor my habit to concern myself
seriously and out loud with myself," he wrote to Olga.

My aversion to "disrobing in public" was a factor in my decision to stop writing poetry and start writing plays, a genre in which the persona of the author is best concealed, since in drama he speaks only through the mouths of others, and his work, therefore, is about as objectified as it can get.

Havel goes on to ponder the problem of self-description:

When a person describes himself, it is as though he were not merely saying that he is a certain way, but that he is consciously so, and that in fact (though he claims the opposite) that is how he wishes to be. . . . In describing oneself, one is already somehow stylizing oneself. Of course, being aware of the accursed fact does not encourage one to try it.

Havel finds an ingenious and elegant solution to the problem of writing about himself: he proposes to write about his moods—"eight bad moods and seven good ones." In this way, he sneaks into autobiography through the back door, as it were, eluding the self-censorship at the main entrance and maintaining the objectifying stance toward himself of the playwright and essayist. The self-portrait that emerges from the letters about the fifteen moods is striking in its evocativeness: we feel we have met this man before, or someone like him. Finally we realize who he is: a character out of nineteenth-century Russian literature. Havel has stylized himself along the lines of a Levin, an Alyosha, a Laevsky. He employs the devices of realism— absent from his minimalist absurdist plays—to render a character in whom touching, ordinary humanness and extraordinary capacity for moral thought are uniquely fused. This character has, improbably, been transplanted to the stage of world politics, where its like has perhaps never been seen before.

In a tribute to Havel published in the January 29, 1990, issue of *The New Republic*, Milan Kundera struggles with the problem presented to skeptical minds by the phenomenon of Havel. "I have always been especially allergic to the remark attributed (wrongly, I think) to Goethe: 'A life should resemble a work of art.' It is because life is formless and does not resemble a work of art that man needs art," Kundera writes. He goes on to allow that there are rare cases where "comparing a life to a work of art is justified," and he counts Havel's life as "one gradual, continuous process [that] gives the impression of a perfect compositional unity." But I think that Kundera errs in excepting Havel's life from the general formlessness that gives art its necessity. He mistakes Havel's narrative of his life for the life itself, paying him the tribute we sometimes pay our great novelists and playwrights when we believe in the existence of their characters and count what has happened to these characters among the real occurrences of life. The great characters of literature cause us to look at ourselves in ways we don't ordinarily do; they cause us to ask ourselves some of the same questions they have been urgently asking themselves. The hero of *Letters to Olga* produces this effect on the reader, causing even so astute a reader as Kundera to believe that he exists outside the pages of the book (and of its sequel: Havel's speeches, interviews, and public appearances). A closer look at Havel's narrative of his life—like all close looks at all narratives—heightens our sense of its subjective and wrought character.

A leading motif of Havel's narrative is the motif of good fortune. Havel sees himself as lucky, as someone who was dealt a good hand at birth and whose luck has always held. Everything that has happened to him, however bad it may seem at first, turns out for the best in the end; his misfortunes are blessings in disguise. This cheerful way of imagining his history was already in place ten years before the writing of *Letters to Olga*. In the spring of 1968, speaking to Antonin J. Liehm* of the hardships that he and his family suffered after the Com-

---

* A collection of interviews with Czech writers, *The Politics of Culture*, edited by Liehm (Grove, 1972).

munist *Putsch* of 1948 (Havel's father was a wealthy entrepreneur whose money and property were confiscated and whose sons were barred from *Gymnasium* and university), Havel characterizes them not only as "a most valuable bit of education for which I shall always be grateful both to my bourgeois ancestry as well as to the new regime" but as the prerequisite to becoming a writer:

> If it hadn't been for February [Havel tells Liehm] I would probably have graduated from the English *Gymnasium*, gone on to study philosophy at the university, attended Professor Cerný's lectures on comparative literature, and after graduation I would have ridden around in an imported sports car without having done the least thing to deserve it. In short, I would have been a cross between an educated man—far more educated than I am now—and a member of the *jeunesse dorée*. I doubt, however, that I would have become a writer.

In *Letters to Olga*, Havel fleshes out the vision of his life as a series of lucky escapes from comfortable mediocrity (through the agency of adversity) with an account of his childhood during the Second World War in a Moravian village, where, in a kind of foreshadowing of the trouble he was to have with the Communist regime, he was ostracized by the village children for his wealth and privileges; he was also made miserable for being fat. Havel traces his feeling of being "in a fundamental and essential way a little bit 'outside the order of the world' " to this early actual experience of not belonging and connects the self-doubt he perpetually feels to this formative bad period. At the same time, he writes, the feeling of being an outsider has been "a life-long wellspring of energy directed at continually improving my self-definition" and "a decisive force behind everything worthwhile I have managed to accomplish." Havel further notes that his perks as "a gentleman's son" paradoxically made an egalitarian of him by instilling in him a feeling of shame for having more than others without deserving to. Giving the paradox yet another turn, he credits his high-bourgeois background with providing a guide for extricating himself from hopeless situations (among them the hopeless situation of being the son of a bourgeois in a new Communist society), citing as invaluable elements of the middle-class entrepreneurial legacy "the ability to take risks, the courage to start all over again from nothing, the ever-vital hope and élan to begin new enterprises." Havel writes about all this with such authority that one never stops to think that being rich and fat doesn't necessarily lead to being socially aware, gifted, and good.

Being sentenced to prison is the culminating "blessing" of Havel's narrative of good fortune. Before serving the sentence, while in detention in a Prague jail, Havel writes to Olga of his eagerness to begin his new life and—allowing that "this is a little like the hopes with which Dostoevsky's heroes go off to prison"—weaves a fantasy of self-renewal that is also a little like the hopes with which people go off to writing colonies and weight-reducing ranches. He wants to find his way back to a mellower, less tense, and less earnest version of himself. "In recent years I have been living a strange, unnatural, exclusive, and somewhat 'greenhouse' existence," he writes of his life as a famous dissident. "Now this will change. I will be one of many tiny, helpless ants. . . . I will be one of a multitude, and no one will expect anything of me or pay any special attention to me." And "I don't want to change myself. I want to be myself in a better way." And "I'd like to return at the age of forty-eight not as an irascible old man—which in some ways I've already become—but rather as the cheerful fellow I once was." He also grandly plans to improve his English, learn German, study the Bible, and write two plays during his prison term. At the prison camp, where he is put to work at cruelly taxing physical labor, making heavy steel mesh with a spot welder, he soon concedes the absurdity of his daydreams. "In many ways . . . prison life is incomparably harder than anything I have ever experienced before," he writes, and "My aim now is far more modest: to return as unscarred by the experience as possible, which means, much as I went in." But eventually, in a letter reflecting on where he is after serving three years of the sentence, he picks up the thread of the original optimistic narrative. "All things considered, it seems increasingly clear that my prison term is merely a necessary and inevitable phase of my life," one which provides "the chance to prove—to myself, to those around me, and to God—that I am not a lightweight as many may have seen me, that I stand behind what I do, that I mean it seriously, and that I can take the consequences." In his last letter before release (he was let out a few months early because of a serious illness) he tells Olga that "it's strange, but I may well be happier now than at any time in recent years."

But Havel is too intelligent and too self-aware a man—and too modern a writer—to draw his self-portrait only in terms of his sense of being lucky and acquitting himself well. He also portrays himself as a man who is so tormented by guilt that the only alleviation for his torment is to be in prison, receiving his just punishment. Something Havel did gnaws at him and will not give him peace. Three years into his sentence, in a letter of July 25, 1982, Havel makes his "confession." By now he has been transferred out of the half-demented warden's labor camp into a camp whose warden is evidently more lenient or, at any rate, more willing to accept Heideggerian philosophy as a "family matter," and he is once again wrestling—week by week, four-page letter by four-page letter—with the question of what it all means. Whether or not one is able to follow Havel's dense and difficult meditation (I sometimes could not follow it, and often would not), one is aware of the brilliance of the writer's timing in making his revelation in its woolly midst.

Five years earlier, in 1977, when Havel was arrested for the first time—for his Charter 77 activities—he sent the public prosecutor a request for release which, he says, he formulated

in a way that at the time seemed extremely tactical and cunning: while saying nothing I did not believe or that wasn't true, I simply "overlooked" the fact that truth lies not only in what is said, but also in who says it, and to whom, why, how and under what circumstances it is expressed. Thanks to this minor "oversight" (more precisely, this minor self-deception), what I said came dangerously close—by chance, as it were—to what the authorities wanted to hear.

Four months later, in May, when Havel was released, the authorities took the "weapon that amounted to a heaven-sent gift," "voluntarily and quite pointlessly" handed to them, and (with appropriate "recastings," "additions," and "widespread publicity") used it to make it appear that he had given in under pressure and betrayed the Charter movement to save his own skin. Havel continues:

> All my worst fears were more than fully realized: I came out of prison discredited, to confront a world that seemed to me one enormous, supremely justified rebuke. No one knows what I went through in that darkest period of my life. . . . There were weeks, months, years, in fact, of silent desperation, self-castigation, shame, inner humiliation, reproach and uncomprehending questioning. For a while I escaped from a world I felt too embarrassed to face into gloomy isolation, taking masochistic delight in endless orgies of self-blame. And then for a while I fled this inner hell into frantic activity through which I tried to drown out my anguish and, at the same time, to "rehabilitate" myself somehow. Naturally, I felt how tense and unnatural my behavior was, but I still couldn't shake that sensation. I felt best of all, relatively speaking, in prison: when I was locked up a second time [in 1978], I caught my breath a little.

In recalling the years of anguished self-reproach, Havel writes: "The central question I came back to again and again was this: How could it have happened? How could I have done something so transparently dubious?" He reviews the psychological explanations that presented themselves, none of which satisfied him or assuaged his guilt, because, as he now realizes, his self-examination

> was essentially only a desperate attempt to hide from myself the hard fact that the failure was mine—exclusively, essentially and fully mine—that is, was a failure of precisely that "I of my I" which then professes such astonishment at that failure, which tries to explain it away at all costs, inconspicuously shift its roots to the "non-I," put some distance between itself and the failure and thereby free itself. This dividing of my self . . . into an alien, prior and incomprehensible "I" that failed, and a living, present, genuine "I," genuinely mine, which does not understand and condemns the former "I" (bitter because it must bear the consequences of the former's actions)—all that was simply an unacknowledged attempt to lie my way out of my responsibility for myself and shift it onto someone else, as it were.

Now, three years into his third incarceration, Havel is able to look at the incident with equanimity and see it as a culminating illumination of his life:

> I have my failure to thank for the fact that for the first time in my life I stood—if I may be allowed such a comparison —directly in the study of the Lord God himself: never before had I looked into his face or heard his reproachful voice from such proximity, never had I stood before him in such profound embarrassment, so humiliated and confused, never before had I been so deeply ashamed or felt so powerfully how unseemly anything I could say in my own defense would be. And the most interesting thing about that confrontation, which in an utterly new way revealed my responsibility as responsibility "toward," was this: if my request had ended up in the chief prosecutor's wastebasket and I had come out of prison a hero, I might never have experienced it at all!

What had Havel actually written in his request for release? From everything we know about this courageous and transcendentally decent man we have reason to think that it could not have been so bad and that he was being much harder on himself than the case merited. However, nowhere in his long discussion of the incident (it entirely occupies two successive letters) does he tell us what the fatal statement was that gave the authorities their weapon and him his eventual epiphany. We have here a narrative of the progress of a soul in deep crisis—but a narrative that omits the "fact" on which the crisis is poised. Although censorship by the prison authorities was an ever-present concern of Havel's, the omission could also have a philosophical motive, one arising from Havel's acute sensitivity to the problem of factuality: his awareness that "the truth lies not only in what is said but also in who says it, and to whom, why, how, and under what circumstances." His experience with the prosecutor has made a kind of deconstructionist of him. He knows too much now about the fallacy of literal meaning to repeat the mistake he made in his request for release. As his enemies read it in too bad a light, we, his admirers, might read it in too good a light—one that would considerably blunt the force of, if not render nonsensical, his eloquent discourse on taking responsibility for failure. "What failure?" we might ask. "You didn't do anything wrong. Why are you carrying on so?"*

---

* What Havel later said to Hvížďala about the incident would support the theory that Havel's guilt was more irrational than real—was another instance of the psychological phenomenon, described by Primo Levi in *The Drowned and the Saved*, of the shame felt by the most blameless, and even the most righteous, of the survivors of the Nazi death camps. Havel told Hvížďala, "They said, for instance, that I'd given up the position of spokesman [for Charter 77] in prison, which wasn't true; the truth is that I had decided to resign (naturally my resignation would have been submitted to those who had entrusted me with the job in the first place, not to the police) for reasons which I still believe were reasonable. But I did not resign while in prison: I merely did the immensely stupid thing of not keeping my intention to resign a secret from my interrogator." A brief account of the incident also appears in *Charter 77 and Human Rights in Czechoslovakia* by H. Gordon Skilling (Allen and Unwin, 1981).

HAVEL had not planned to publish the letters in the form in which they have come to us. He had intended to publish only the essayist passages, omitting the personal portions—what he called "the matter-of-fact passages meant for Olga." But in preparing the letters for publication in 1984, Havel's friend Jan Lopatka decided to ignore Havel's instructions and to retain much of the personal material. This decision, like the censor's contribution, had important literary consequences. Havel himself immediately saw the merit of Lopatka's idea, which (as he tells Hvížďala) "makes it clear that the book is a book of letters from prison, not essays written in the peace and quiet of my study. The existential background of these meditations is uncovered and made present."

Paradoxically, it is this background of the matter-of-fact that gives the book its poetry, its quality of madeness and stylization, reminiscent of Havel's own well-made, stylized plays. The meditations are laid out on a grid of repetitions, recurrences, rituals: the weekly letter, Olga's trimonthly visit to the prison, the package she is allowed to bring of some unspecified but exact weight and size. Over and over, as in the refrain of a ballad, Havel returns to these points of connection to the outer world, to which Olga is the sole link, and permits us a remarkably intimate glimpse into his relationship with this all-too-important Other. Paul Wilson, in his excellent introduction (to his exemplary translation), notes that "some of the passages addressed specifically to Olga are unpleasantly finicky, fussy, lacking in warmth." Indeed, under the pressure of the unnatural situation between them created by his incarceration, Havel sometimes behaves toward Olga in a way strikingly akin to the behavior of the supine member of the psychoanalytic couple. Early in the correspondence, Havel's complaints and reproaches to Olga about her "infrequent and meager" letters (letter writing is evidently not Olga's strong suit) are like the complaints and reproaches of a new analytic patient who is in a fury about the frustrating incommunicativeness of his interlocutor. "Is it really impossible to write to me more often?" he asks. "Is it really such a problem to write to me every week?" "You must admit that a single page in six weeks is hardly enough." "I've finally got another little letter from you."

Over time, Havel comes to terms with his "analyst" and with the conditions of his encounter with her; finally the veil of transference lifts and Havel recognizes the woman behind it. His complaints about Olga's letters cease, as do his anxious preparations for and unrealistic expectations from the visits. In a letter about a visit Havel characterizes as a "mess" in his post-visit summing-up, he movingly writes that "my initial feeling of depression . . . (and my anger with myself because of it) was soon relegated to the background when a deeper, beneficial significance began to surface. . . . I realized that among people who really belong together there can be no embarrassment. They know each other so well, and are so familiar with how things really are, that such accidental external circumstances can't touch them in any way, let alone throw them off."

In the introduction Wilson quotes some remarkable comments that Havel made to Hvížďala about Olga:

Olga and I are very different. I'm a child of the middle class and ever the diffident intellectual. Olga's a working-class girl, very much her own person, sober, unsentimental, and she can even be somewhat mouthy and obnoxious; in other words, as we say, you can't get her drunk on a bun. I grew up in the loving and firm embrace of a dominant mother, and I needed an energetic woman beside me to turn to for advice and yet still be someone I could be in awe of. . . . In Olga, I found exactly what I needed: someone who could respond to my own mental instability, to offer sober criticism of my wilder ideas, provide private support for my public adventures. All my life, I've consulted with her in everything I do (the wags claim I even require her agreement to the sins through which I hurt her, and that I seek her advice in the problems my occasional emotional centrifugality bring me).

Havel also tells Hvížďala that "Olga and I have not professed love for each other for at least two hundred years, but we both feel that we are probably inseparable," and that Olga is the "main hero" of his book of prison letters, "though admittedly she's a hidden one." All this is present in the letters themselves: the dialectic of overestimation and resentment, tenderness and coldness, closeness and detachment, the sense of a relationship that is marked by idiosyncrasy, authenticity, and contradiction. What one marvels at when one marvels at the phenomenon of Havel is not that a writer has become president of Czechoslovakia but that a man who is not afraid of his own ambivalence has succeeded in public life.

Earlier I connected Havel to Russian literature. The Russian novelists knew in the most uncanny way how complicated we all are, how we don't add up; Havel has created his public persona in the spirit of these writers. He seems so human (in contrast to the simulacrum of a human being that the usual politician appears to be) because his knowledge of himself as a unique mixture of good and bad impulses is so manifest. In *Letters to Olga* we come even closer to this man who lets us come so close, and we receive confirmation and elaboration of the impressions of him we have formed from his essays, speeches, and television appearances. The plays are an exception to this unified body of self-expression. The early plays (*The Garden Party*, *The Memorandum*, *The Increased Difficulty of Concentration*), treating of the dehumanizing tendencies of the modern state, are the well-crafted, witty work of an A-plus student of absurdist drama. The later plays (*Largo Desolato* and *Temptation*) have a larger ambition. They attempt to look at the horror of (in the case of *Largo Desolato*) emotional breakdown beyond repair and of (in the case of *Temptation*) moral lapse beyond expiation. Both are more about the idea of it than the thing itself; they have a ponderous, schematic quality. From *Letters to Olga* we may gather how much more potent the optimistic view is for Havel's imagination. His is a comic vision. "I am not interested in why man commits evil," he writes in one of his philosophical meditations. "I want to know why he does good (here and there), or at least feels that he ought to." In the age of Auschwitz, this is an arresting preference, particularly for a man who has himself been persecuted most of his life by a harsh totalitarian state and who as he writes is being punished in a hard-labor camp for speaking out against its abuses. Those of us who do not share Havel's optimism about the human prospect must do him the honor of acknowledging that when he speaks of man's ability to triumph over adversity he speaks from a position of authority that, if we're lucky, we ourselves will never be in.

*The New York Review of Books*, 1990

# *Part* III

# The One-Way Mirror

ON a hot, clear day in July, I rang the doorbell of a small, neat house in one of those new suburbs where the trees on the streets are still short and spindly and the bushes that hug the sides of the houses are more evocative of the word "landscaping" than of greenness and shade. A middle-aged couple came to the door and greeted me in a friendly way. Beyond them I saw a teenage girl in jeans stirring a pot on the stove.

Although this was my first visit to the house and my first meeting with the Brauns (as I shall call them), it was not the first time I had seen them. For an hour a week over a period of eight weeks, I had sat behind a one-way mirror in an observation room in a psychiatric clinic and watched and listened to their sessions with a new breed of healer called a family therapist. The therapist was a young woman psychiatrist named Lee Combrinck-Graham, and the clinic was the Philadelphia Child Guidance Clinic. My presence in the observation room had been arranged by a leading figure in the family-therapy field, Salvador Minuchin, who was teaching Lee Combrinck-Graham and four other young psychiatrists how to do what he calls "structural" family therapy.

At the clinic, my first sight of the Brauns was of a couple at their wits' end. They backed into the treatment room angry and upset, futilely remonstrating with their daughter, Yvonne, who was still in the entryway, out of sight of the observers. "I am not going in," I could hear the girl say, in a stubborn, angry voice. "No way."

The parents coaxed, begged, and finally shouted at her.

"Yvonne, get in here this minute!" the father bellowed.

"Yvonne, why are you acting this way?" the mother said. "You promised you'd try it once."

"I did not," the girl said with cold rage. "I told you I did not want to come. I told you I wanted to go back to Dr. Horace."

Lee Combrinck-Graham, an attractive blonde with a brisk, cheerful manner, talked to the girl in a more evenhanded manner but with no greater success.

In the observation room, Minuchin, a wiry, swarthy man with a graying mustache, who speaks in an intense, authoritative way with an unplaceable foreign accent, frowned and said, "Lee can't win this. We must think of an alternative to offer the girl." He picked up a telephone and pushed a button sounding a buzzer in the treatment room. Lee got on her end of the phone, and Minuchin said to her, "What if the girl stays where she is—out of view—and we bring her a chair?"

Lee nodded, and Minuchin sent one of the students out with a chair to be placed in the entryway. The maneuver worked. The session proceeded, with the girl sitting out of sight but participating.

The facts of the case were these: The Brauns were a couple in their forties. He was a field supervisor for the telephone company, and she worked in a day-care center. They had two daughters—Estelle, now married and out of the house, and Yvonne, fifteen, a sophomore in high school. A few months earlier, Yvonne had become depressed and had stopped going to school. The parents took her to a Dr. Horace (as I shall call him), who gave her antidepressant drugs in increasingly high dosages and finally pronounced her condition to be one of psychotic depression, requiring hospitalization. The parents, concerned about the high dosages and looking for an alternative to hospitalization, remembered hearing about the family therapy that was being done at the Child Guidance Clinic. They called the clinic and were accepted for treatment by Lee, but on the condition that they lend themselves to being observed and videotaped, since the class time with Minuchin was the only time she had available. The parents accepted the stipulation, over the daughter's objection.

Now, in the treatment room, Lee embarked on a conversation with the Brauns, in which the parents—mostly the mother—talked about Yvonne's condition (how she stayed in her room for long periods of time, how the drugs affected her, how she didn't eat), and the girl sullenly answered questions from Lee about school and complained about her parents. "Why can't they leave me alone?" she said in a nasty, depressed, indrawn voice. "They're always hitting me and yelling at me. They come into my room and ask me if I want something. What I want is to be *left alone*."

After about five minutes, Minuchin began to grow restless and shift around in his swivel chair. "This isn't going in the right direction," he said. He abruptly got up and entered the treatment room. He introduced himself to the parents and to the offstage daughter, and then said to the mother, "I don't know. Maybe I'm wrong. But, frankly, I think the problem in this family is that you're treating your daughter like a baby. You won't let her grow up. You're behaving like someone who is in need of a baby." He turned to the husband. "I think you should try and help your wife to grow up, so your daughter can grow up," he said. "I think as things are now, your daughter cannot grow up." Minuchin returned to the observation room. The husband looked puzzled, and the wife was shaken. "If I'm doing a number on the kid, I want to know about it," Mrs. Braun said to Lee.

"Maybe *you* can comment on this, Mr. Braun," Lee said.

Mr. Braun began to complain about his wife. He said that she "screamed and hollered." Mrs. Braun began to cry. He went on to report that she had said she couldn't take it anymore and was going to leave. Mrs. Braun, through her tears, accused her husband of leaving everything to her; it was all too much for her, she said.

In the observation room, Minuchin listened to the argument and then said, "I'm going to attack the mother again." He reentered the treatment room and said sternly to Mrs. Braun, "I am concerned about what you are saying. I am concerned that when you leave here today your daughter will go crazy again. And I think the reason she will do it is to save your marriage. Children sometimes act in very weird ways to save their parents' marriage." He turned to the girl and said, "Yvonne, I suggest that you go quite crazy today, so that your parents can become concerned about you. Then things will be OK between them. You seem to be a good daughter, so you will go crazy, and your father will support your mother in taking care of you, and things will be OK." To the parents, he went on, "I think that your daughter is trying to save your marriage. It is a bizarre thing to say, I know. But sometimes children are so protective of their parents that they sacrifice themselves. I think that Yvonne has kind of perceived that you are at the deep end, and she is saving you by being crazy, so you will organize your-selves." He started to leave, and then, pausing in the doorway, he said to the girl, "You're a good daughter, and if you see a danger, go crazy."

The parents started talking about their marriage, and Lee told the girl that she could leave if she wanted to, since what her parents were saying didn't concern her. "Do you think you'll go crazy when you get home?" Lee asked her.

"I don't know," the girl said. "If Alex talks to me, I will."

"Who is Alex?"

"He's in my head."

"OK," Lee said, after a slight pause.

In the observation room, Minuchin creaked in his chair and shook his head. "That was a mistake. She shouldn't have let the girl go. The girl should have been made to stay, because she has to correct her mistaken notion that she is needed to save the marriage." He listened to the dialogue between the parents for a few minutes and then said impatiently, "The mood is too relaxed. They are now in a nonstressful session. You need stress for transformation." Once again he entered the treatment room, and once again he went on the attack. He said that the father patronized the mother and humored her and treated her like a child, and as a result the daughter was very childish. "I don't think your daughter is crazy. I don't see any signs of craziness but, rather, of childishness," he said. Then he left, and Lee left, too, after telling the parents to talk to each other.

Their dialogue was at once touching and artificial—stiff, careful, and overformal. They were conscious of being observed.

"What have I done wrong?" Mrs. Braun said.

"It may not be just you," Mr. Braun said. "Maybe it's me, too."

"We don't communicate," Mrs. Braun said.


FAMILY therapy emerged in the mid-fifties, when a number of people working with mental patients in different parts of the country began to reexamine a phenomenon that had plagued psychiatry since Mesmer's day. This was the strange way that a patient's relatives behaved as soon as he improved under psychotherapy. Unlike a cure achieved by a surgeon or an internist, psychiatric improvement was greeted by the sufferer's family not with relief and gratitude but with displeasure, suspicion, and anxiety, and sometimes even with the eruption of symptoms in another member of the family. Families either would pull the patient out of treatment (Freud reports several such cases) or, if they allowed treatment to continue, would subtly undermine its effects. Schizophrenics who had been helped by psychotherapy in the hospital would relapse soon after going home. Sometimes even a visit to the hospital by a relative would trigger psychotic behavior. Children and adolescents—who had nowhere to go but to their families—were particularly susceptible. To the people who were to become known as the pioneers of family therapy, it began to seem that the psychoanalyst's rule about relatives—the therapist should see only the patient, to avoid contaminating his therapeutic relationship—could profitably be ignored in certain cases, such as that of a hospitalized adolescent schizophrenic who was to return home. They began to call in the rest of the family.

This small, innocuous-looking step proved to have enormous consequences—was a leap, in fact, into a new field of psychotherapy. From the moment that there were more than two people in the treatment room, the therapist found himself obliged to think and behave in a different way. His focus necessarily shifted from its accustomed place within the individual psyche to a new place, *outside* and *between* people. From the early practitioners' accounts, one gathers that they did not so much invent family therapy as have it thrust on them. Coming in as protectors of a patient against his relatives, they remained as critics of the way that everyone in the family behaved—the patient included. The original view of the patient as the victim of a conspiracy to keep him sick yielded to the notion that the family itself was sick—that *it* needed treatment, rather than the "patient," who was only, and almost accidentally, an emblem of the family's disorder. An early family therapist named Don Jackson employed the term "family homeostasis" to express the constant force within each family that maintains the status quo, in the way that the thermostat of a heating system governs the temperature. All unhappy families, he thought, are alike in the ruthless destructiveness of their homeostasis, which exacts illness or misery from family members in order to keep going. When a member of this sort of family gets sick, it is in response to a threat to the family's equilibrium; when a psychiatrist intervenes and "cures" the patient, the family is thrown into a new disequilibrium and (like a thermostat activated by someone throwing open a window) gets to work to reestablish its balance.

This new view of the psychiatric symptom as a reflection of a current interpersonal situation, rather than of an inner conflict rooted in the past, was a radical shift in thinking about mental illness, and it brought therapists face-to-face with the question of what to do with their previous training. To many, the Freudian baggage of the unconscious, the id, the ego, the superego, repression, transference seemed more an encumbrance than a help; seeing themselves as mechanics at work on a dysfunctional system (though at work they more closely resemble traffic cops or stage directors or union arbitrators), they found the psychoanalyst's tools useless for the job. Other therapists believed that psychoanalytic concepts could be pressed into service for family therapy. From the start, practitioners in the family field have been split on this issue, one group seeing family therapy as a total break with psychoanalytically oriented individual therapy, and the other seeing it as an evolutionary phenomenon, a logical next step in the revision of Freud expressed by Harry Stack Sullivan, Karen Horney, Erich Fromm, and other "interpersonal" analysts. Whether one group helps people more than the other is not known; studies of family-therapy results are as inconclusive as studies of the results of all other forms of therapy, tending only to confirm the thought that in therapy everything succeeds if the therapist is convinced it will. But the non-Freudian family therapists—sometimes called the communications, or systems, group—have one visible advantage over the Freudians: they have produced a body of theoretic writing that is lucid, logical, orderly, and persuasive to an outsider, while the psychoanalytic writings are muddled and inchoate, as if the writers were trying to multiply horses by oranges.

Perhaps the most difficult idea for even the most radical of the communications thinkers to shed was a notion basic not only to psychoanalysis but to humanistic thinking in general: that change comes about through understanding—that if you delve deep enough into yourself and gain enough insight into your motivations you will be equipped to deal with practically any problem of living. Advanced thinking in family therapy denies this, maintaining that change comes about in some other way and is achieved without the awareness of the person being changed. The techniques of family therapy, consequently, are designed not to get people to understand their behavior but simply to get them—sometimes even by trickery or manipulation—to change it. As Jay Haley, the leading theorist of the communications school, rather cynically wrote in a 1971 paper, "Talking to family members about understanding each other is necessary, because something must be talked about and families expect this form of discussion, but change really comes about through interactional processes set off when a therapist intervenes actively and directively in particular ways in a family system, and quite independently of the awareness of the participants about how they have been behaving." Or, as the family therapist Carl Whitaker once said, "This business of 'If you figure it out, that will solve it' is the sorriest I ever heard of. I believe that insight is a by-product of change. You have to go past it to see what it is."

Another shibboleth of psychiatry that has been set on its head by family therapy is the patient's right to privacy and confidentiality. Early in the movement, the use of tape recorders and one-way mirrors became a regular practice, and within the last five years the videotaping of sessions has been commonplace. This makes it possible to teach family therapy as therapy has never before been taught. Individual therapy had been (and largely continues to be) taught by hearsay: the student hears from his teachers what they do in their practice, and the supervisor hears from his student how he is doing in treating *his* patients, with everybody depending on notes taken during or after sessions. In contrast, family therapy is taught by direct observation: students learn by watching tapes of senior therapists at work, and by being observed, in turn, at their work. The feeling among family therapists is that it is crucially important to remove the filter of a biased consciousness through which descriptions of therapy have traditionally been transmitted to students. It has even been argued that, far from depriving the patient of his civil rights, the open session actually protects them. As Augustus Napier maintains in his introduction to *The Book of Family Therapy*, "Our insistence on visibility and openness . . . may be instrumental to a search for equality and for common purpose among people, [since] the tyrannies of groups over individuals, and the conspiracies of individuals against themselves, and even the maintenance of incompetence and inaction, are dependent on secrecy." In another section of this essay, Napier exults over family therapy's break with psychoanalysis:

> We are, families and therapists, in pursuit of the moment, in pursuit of confrontation and embrace and dialogue in the clarion, crisp now. We suspect the unseen, the unseeable: psychoanalysis' reverence for the past and for the metaphysics of internal dialogue fades; families and therapists meet together and discover hopefulness in understanding and experiencing the present. . . . This faith in the present—perhaps it is not faith, but the realization that it is all we have—may have occurred because we have less faith in understanding, or more interest in experience, or because we realized that the examination of the past was a form of mysticism, because it was forever hypothetical and also lifeless.

This passage, reminiscent of much writing in the sixties by young and youngish people, belongs to what was perhaps the most vital, and was certainly the most self-conscious, period of the family-therapy movement. By the sixties, the various isolated groups and solitary workers had learned of one another's existence and, whatever their theoretical differences, were banded together, remaining united throughout the decade by a sense of common revolutionary cause. Today, looking back on the period of family therapy's efflorescence, one can see the many sociological, psychological, political, and economic factors that favored it and that make its emergence seem a kind of historical inevitability. But there may be reason, too, to attribute the special character and form that family therapy assumed to a historical accident. This was the appearance in the field of a man who had no business being there, who has since left it (for work with dolphins!), but who briefly lent it the intellectual dazzle that large, eccentric minds shed wherever they alight, and who radically altered its future course. He was the English anthropologist Gregory Bateson, who stumbled into family therapy by way of a project dealing with paradox in human and animal communication, for which he received a Rockefeller Foundation grant in the fall of 1952.

The starting point for the project, Bateson has recalled, was a visit to the Fleishhacker Zoo, in San Francisco, in January of that year. In the course of checking out some notions he had formed about the signals that are exchanged between animals, Bateson came across a familiar phenomenon: the sight of two young monkeys engaged in a playful fight. As he watched their mock combat, he was put in mind of the paradoxes that Bertrand Russell and Alfred North Whitehead cited in *Principia Mathematica*—such as the statement of Epimenides the Cretan that "all Cretans are liars"—and for the resolution of which they devised their Theory of Logical Types. The monkeys were going through all the motions of combat and yet were not hurting or killing each other. Something was passing between them to indicate that they were only pretending to fight. But in their message "This is play" Bateson detected a contradiction of the Epimenides sort: translated into the language of logic, the monkeys' message became: "These actions in which we now engage do not denote what would be denoted by those actions which these actions denote"—in other words, "The playful nip denotes the bite, but it does not denote what would be denoted by the bite." Russell and Whitehead had put their finger on the problem that is posed by an impossible statement like this; by breaking the statement down, they showed that it consists of, first, a statement and, second, a statement about that statement—both of which, however, are treated as if they were a single statement and as if they existed on the same level of abstraction. The Theory of Logical Types is essentially a prohibition against ambiguity. ("The appearance of contradiction is always due to the presence of words embodying a concealed typical ambiguity, and the solution of the apparent contradiction lies in bringing the concealed ambiguity to light," Russell and Whitehead wrote.) The theory establishes a hierarchy of "types," or levels, of abstraction, and forbids the yoking of a lower level with a higher level.

But what is inadmissible in formal logic is pervasive in life, Bateson felt. Using Russell and Whitehead's analytical description of logical contradiction as his point of departure, he collected further instances of paradoxical communication. Together with two young men who joined him in 1953 (one was Jay Haley, then a graduate student at Stanford, and the other was John Weakland, a cultural anthropologist and former chemical engineer), he studied otters playing, mongoloid children in a group, a ventriloquist and his dummy, the training of Seeing Eye dogs, and the utterances of a schizophrenic patient. The study of special or disturbed modes of communication led to a general theory of communication, which states that in all human (and in much nonhuman) communication there is no such thing as a simple message. Rather, every message is qualified by another message, on another level of abstraction. A paradox of S. I. Hayakawa's came to the team's attention—

---

ALL STATEMENTS WITHIN THIS
FRAME ARE UNTRUE

---

—and coincidentally supplied it with the formulation that every message is "framed" by another. For example, if a person says "I am glad to see you," he necessarily "frames," or qualifies, the statement by his tone of voice and by the expression on his face, which may confirm and augment its content ("Boy, *am* I glad to see you!") or may contradict it ("Ugh, I wish I were elsewhere"). Given the complexity of communication, paradox (the illegitimate merging of levels of abstraction) is a regular, ineluctable occurrence in life. It is the matrix of such significant human phenomena as humor, fantasy, ritual, fiction, and the peculiar ritualized game of psychotherapy. "Our central thesis may be summed up as a statement of the necessity of the paradoxes of abstraction," Bateson wrote in the concluding paragraph of a paper called "A Theory of Play and Fantasy" (1955). "It is not merely bad natural history to suggest that people might or should obey the Theory of Logical Types in their communications; their failure to do this is not due to mere carelessness or ignorance. Rather, we believe that the paradoxes of abstraction must make their appearance in all communication more complex than that of mood-signals, and that without these paradoxes the evolution of communication would be at an end. Life would then be an endless interchange of stylized messages, a game with rigid rules, unrelieved by change or humor."

In the fall of 1954, the Rockefeller grant ended and was not renewed. The Bateson group then decided (fatefully for family therapy) to focus on schizophrenic communication, which they felt would be not only intrinsically interesting but a more attractive lure for grant money than the general communications project. The Josiah Macy, Jr., Foundation took the bait, and the famous Double Bind hypothesis was born of the four-year grant it bestowed.

The Double Bind (first described by Bateson, Haley, Weakland, and a new member of the team, Don Jackson, in a 1956 paper called "Toward a Theory of Schizophrenia") gave a sinister twist to the paradoxes of "Play and Fantasy." What had been the spice of life became—as applied to schizophrenia—a horrible repetitive pattern that led inevitably to pathology. A child, it was hypothesized, has a mother who is made anxious by closeness and affection. When the child approaches her, she instinctively recoils. But she cannot tolerate the idea of herself as an unloving, rejecting parent, so when the child, in response to her withdrawal, himself withdraws, she hastens to qualify the first message of heartfelt repugnance with a new, contradictory one of simulated lovingness. This again puts the child in the wrong. He is caught in a double bind—a situation of no alternatives—since whichever message he chooses to obey, he will be disobeying the other. He is in the position of the person who is told "I command you to disobey me," or (an example used in the paper) in that of the Zen pupil whose master holds a stick over his head and says fiercely, "If you say this stick is real, I will hit you with it; if you say the stick is not real, I will hit you with it; and if you say nothing, I'll hit you with it." But, unlike the Zen pupil, who achieves enlightenment when he "sees" alternatives beyond those posed by the master (like grabbing the stick), the child can't "leave the field"—can't *not* care about the relationship between himself and his mother— and consequently, as the paper puts it, "must live in a universe where the sequences of events are such that his unconventional communicational habits will be in some sense appropriate." The schizophrenic's confusion of the literal and the metaphoric is an acquired, adaptive mechanism—a pitiful but fitting defense against what the paper calls "feeling so terribly on the spot at all times."

The notion that the schizophrenic's bizarre patterns of thought and utterance came out of his dealings with his parents rather than out of something disturbed within himself—that the whole mystifying condition of schizophrenia was essentially a result of family interaction (the mother's "binding" of the victim required complicity on the part of the father and siblings)—was a radical idea whose time had come. Other investigators—among them Frieda Fromm-Reichmann, Theodore Lidz, Murray Bowen, and Lyman Wynne—had arrived or were arriving at similar conclusions. And the idea that schizophrenia could be cured by getting the patient and his family together in a room and somehow talking them out of their strange and terrible way of dealing with one another fell on fertile ground in this country. It spoke to our optimism and our pragmatism—to our belief that if you shake and jiggle and poke at something long enough it will work again.

In addition to ferreting out the family as (reformable) culprit, Bateson and his colleagues blamed the hospitals for a good part of the schizophrenic's plight. The essence of the anti-psychiatry movement was already present in the Double Bind paper: "Since hospitals exist for the benefit of their personnel as well as—as much as—more than—for the patient's benefit, there will be contradictions at times in sequences where actions are taken 'benevolently' for the patient when actually they are intended to keep the staff more comfortable. We would assume that whenever the system is organized for hospital purposes and it is announced to the patient that the actions are for *his* benefit, then the schizophrenogenic situation is being perpetuated. This kind of deception will provoke the patient to respond to it as a double-bind situation, and his response will be schizophrenic." (This quietly angry passage, like others in the paper, reflects Bateson's English origin. It shows how much the Double Bind concept owes to the special English feeling about hypocrisy as the most deadly of sins against one's fellows and oneself; other nationalities take hypocrisy less seriously, and consequently have produced no Swifts, Butlers, Orwells, or Batesons.)

The initial high hopes for the Double Bind theory as a kind of Cuisinart through which psychoses could be run and dispatched have given way to a more modest estimate of its clinical uses. (A lot of misunderstanding and confusion arose out of the paper's example of the unloving mother, which was meant merely to illustrate the kind of thing that could happen—to be but one of an infinity of possible double-bind situations—but was taken to be *the* double bind. Frieda Fromm-Reichmann's earlier hypothesis about a "schizophrenogenic mother" promoted this misapprehension.) The consensus today about schizophrenia is that it is a complex syndrome, like diabetes, which cannot be "cured" but may be controlled by a combination of chemical, psychological, and social interventions. In a paper entitled "Family and Social Management of Schizophrenia" (1975), C. Christian Beels, a leading teacher and practitioner in the second generation of family therapists, concedes that "the family therapy of schizophrenia has neither been well developed in practice nor had much demonstrable success," and goes on to say that "there is almost nobody writing today who advances family therapy by itself as the treatment of choice for schizophrenia." The chief importance of the Double Bind is now felt to be that it gave shape and structure and theoretical backbone to the amorphous clinical findings of the early family-therapy practitioners—it propelled communications theory into the mainstream of psychiatric thinking and put family therapy on the map of intellectual history, where no other therapy since psychoanalysis has appeared. Without Bateson, family therapy might well have become just another of the well-meaning, soft-headed systems of helping people which this country spawns like its gadgets, and which do as much good as the good-heartedness and charisma of their practitioners permit but have no intellectual rigor.

Bateson did not remain to preside over the revolution that communications theory brought to psychiatry—in a testy foreword to a 1976 anthology called *Double Bind: The Foundation of the Communicational Approach to the Family*, he wrote, "I must confess that I was bored and disgusted by the Augean muddle of conventional psychiatric thinking, by my colleagues' obsession with power, by the dumb cruelty of the families which (as we used to say) 'contained' schizophrenia, and appalled by the richness of the available data"—and in 1963 he went off to the Oceanic Institute, in Hawaii. It fell to Jay Haley to be the Saint Paul of the communications movement, and, like Paul's version of Christianity, Haley's version of communications theory offered some significant deviations from the thinking of its founder. In another place in *Double Bind*, Bateson speaks of "the very real epistemological differences" that developed between him and Haley during the project years: "As I saw it, he believed in the validity of the metaphor of 'power' in human relations. I believed then—and today believe even more strongly—that the *myth* of power always corrupts, because it proposes always a false (though conventional) epistemology. I believe that all such metaphors derived from pleroma and applied to creatura are antiheuristic. They are a groping in a wrong direction, and the direction is not less wrong or less socially pathogenic because the associated mythology is in part self-validating among those who believe it and act upon it." This passage not only casts light on the quarrel between Bateson and Haley which Bateson hinted at in speaking of his colleagues' "obsession with power" but also conveys something of the special quality of Bateson's thinking: the abashing originality of his ideas, the quirky beauty of his character, and the difficulty of his writing. The difficulty is not an impossibility, and people who have read the collection of Bateson's writings called *Steps to an Ecology of Mind* (1972) will have a better handle on the passage above, because (bearing out the title) everything Bateson has written is in some way connected to everything else, and the more of him you read, the more you understand.

The trouble one has to take over Bateson—like the trouble one has to take over a hard poem—is worth it; indeed, in trying to find a pace at which to read Bateson's work it is helpful to think of it as poetry rather than exposition. But for the task of conveying the communications viewpoint to psychiatrists, social workers, clinical psychologists, and other professionals who haven't the time or the patience to unravel Bateson's knotted thought no better person could have been found than Haley, who is one of the most readable writers in the social science field. He may be too readable. Haley's style is so lucid, his tone so natural and agreeable, his wit so nice, his language so unpretentious and untechnical, his arguments so logical, that he invites mistrust: if it's that easy, it can't be sound. In our intellectual tradition, a certain difficulty is supposed to attend serious intellectual endeavor. A serious thinker should sound as if he were mumbling to himself (Bateson magnificently fulfills this requirement), not as if he were playing to the gallery. Freud offers an instance of an easy and charming writer who gets around the problem of his readability by constantly letting the reader in on the difficulty he has had in arriving at the ideas he is finally able to set down; while reading Freud, one always has the sense of being in the presence of someone more honest, rigorous, and morally scrupulous than anyone else. Reading Haley, in contrast, is like being in the bedroom of a charming cad; one feels at once beguiled and wary.

*Strategies of Psychotherapy* (1963) is perhaps the most beguiling and wary-making of Haley's works. In it, he takes the core concept of communications theory—that no message is simple, but is always framed, or qualified, by other messages, which affirm or negate it—and expands it into the notion that every communication reflects a struggle for control of a relationship. Haley works into his argument an earlier concept of Bateson's (one that Bateson formed during an anthropological expedition to New Guinea with Margaret Mead, who was then his wife), of "symmetrical" and "complementary" types of relationship— the former describing behavior between peers (behavior of a matching, exchanging, or competitive sort), and the latter describing behavior between unequal parties (involving give-and-take, dependency and nurturance, superiority and inferiority). Haley sees the issue of the struggle for control of the relationship (which is implicit in every verbal and nonverbal message) as the *definition* of the relationship—will it be symmetrical or complementary?—with each party struggling to be the author of the definition. Seen in communications terms, something as insignificant as an observation about the weather by one of two people who have just been introduced to each other can become the first volley in a momentous power struggle. The second person can reply with another observation about the weather, and thus concede defeat, since he is letting the first person define the relationship—is accepting the first person's idea of it as one in which only neutral subjects will be talked about. Or he can challenge the definition by replying with an observation about the trouble he is having making love to his wife, or, even more disconcertingly, by saying, "I wonder why you are talking about the weather. You must want to put some distance between us."

This kind of jockeying for control, according to Haley, goes on in every relationship. In normal relationships, people work out a modus vivendi that more or less suits them. The psychiatric symptom, from the communications point of view, is a reflection of a kind of perversion of the struggle for control; instead of coming right out and frankly fighting for control, the symptomatic person denies that he is in any fight at all. Haley describes the pathological relationship that can result:

> When one person circumscribes the behavior of another while denying that he is doing so, the relationship begins to be rather peculiar. For example, when a wife requires her husband to be home every night because she has anxiety attacks when she is left alone, he cannot acknowledge that she is controlling his behavior, because *she* is not requiring him to be home—the anxiety is, and her behavior is involuntary. Neither can he refuse to let her control his behavior, for the same reason. When a person is offered two directives which conflict with each other and which demand a response, he can respond by indicating he is not responding to a directive. The formal term for such a communication sequence as it is described here is a paradox.

We're back at Russell and Whitehead—only now the emphasis has shifted from the etiology of mental disorder in paradox to the cure of mental disorder *by* paradox—a kind of homeopathic soul medicine, in which like is used to vanquish like. The idea of a therapeutic double bind was briefly touched on in "Toward a Theory of Schizophrenia":

Dr. Frieda Fromm-Reichmann was treating a young woman who from the age of seven had built a highly complex religion of her own, replete with powerful gods. She was very schizophrenic, and quite hesitant about entering into a therapeutic situation. At the beginning of the treatment she said, "God R says I shouldn't talk with you." Dr. Fromm-Reichmann replied, "Look, let's get something into the record. To me God R doesn't exist, and that whole world of yours doesn't exist. To you it does, and far be it from me to think that I can take that away from you. . . . So I'm willing to talk with you in terms of that world, if only you know I do it so that we have an understanding that it doesn't exist for me. Now go to God R and tell him that we have to talk and that he should give you permission. Also you must tell him that I am a doctor, and that you have lived with him in his kingdom now from seven to sixteen—that's nine years—and he hasn't helped you. So now he must permit me to try and see whether you and I can do that job. Tell him that I am a doctor and this is what I want to try."

The therapist has her patient in a "therapeutic double bind." If the patient is rendered doubtful about her belief in her god, then she is agreeing with Dr. Fromm-Reichmann, and is admitting her attachment to therapy. If she insists that God R is real, then she must tell him that Dr. Fromm-Reichmann is "more powerful" than he—again admitting her involvement with the therapist.

In *Strategies of Psychotherapy*, Haley develops the thesis that all forms of therapy—hypnosis, psychoanalysis, marriage therapy, family therapy, the treatment of schizophrenics—are variants on the single theme of paradoxical maneuver: the therapist forces the patient into a box from which his only escape is to change. Hypnosis represents the most naked expression of this benevolent power struggle—the trance being the patient's way of escaping from the double-bind situation he has been put into by the hypnotist. (Haley's thinking was shaped a good deal by his association during the Rockefeller project with a hypnotist named Milton H. Erickson, from whom the group derived its conception of the hypnotic trance as a product of the *relationship* between the hypnotist and the subject; Haley was also much dazzled by Erickson's unorthodox therapy methods (sometimes conducted with and sometimes without hypnosis), which cured people of their symptoms very quickly—largely by recourse to the kind of benign knavery that good fairies permit themselves and that conventional psychiatrists frown on. (Haley describes these methods in a book called *Uncommon Therapy*; the cases, as Richard Rabkin has commented, read like *Mission: Impossible* episodes.)

Psychoanalysis would seem to be the most inner-directed therapy and the one least open to trickery, but as reinterpreted by Haley it only amplifies his view of therapy as an exercise in power politics. Freud is politely dispatched:

> One cannot read Freud without admiring his tenacity and skill as he traces a patient's ideas through all their symbolic ramifications. There is no intent in this chapter to disagree with Freud's formulations about individual personality development or his analysis of symbolic material. Rather, it will be suggested that the exploration of the human psyche may be irrelevant to therapeutic change. Although Freud assumed that the patient's self-exploration produced change, it is argued here that change occurs as a product of the interpersonal context of that exploration, rather than the self-awareness which is brought about in the patient.

> Thus, the concern of psychoanalysis with dreams, free association, memory, fantasy, is mere window dressing ("something must be talked about") for the struggle between analyst and patient over control of the relationship—which the analyst always wins, since the deck is not only stacked in his favor but

(and this is the crucial thing) stacked in such a way as to allow the analyst to utterly deny that he is winning the struggle, or even that there is one. Than this there is no more crushing put-down.

> Ideally [the therapist] should be able to *let* the patient appear to be in the superior position when the patient insists [Haley writes]. Whenever a therapist demands that a patient behave in a certain way he is likely to be defeated, but whenever he *permits* the patient to behave in a certain way he is continuing to define his position as superior. For example, a patient may insist that his non-directive therapist talk to him. Should the therapist argue that he does not want to and the patient must talk, he will be at a disadvantage. However, he may say, "I wonder why you're so disturbed at my not talking" or "I'll be glad to talk, but it's how *you* see the problem that is important," and then he is accepting the patient's demand while still circumscribing the patient's behavior.

Psychoanalysis bombards the patient with paradoxes:

> The patient is asked to be spontaneous and responsive to a man who is unresponsive and unspontaneous; yet the therapist will suggest that the difficulty the patient has dealing with him is relevant to his difficulties in having satisfactory relationships with other people. The patient is taught that he must assume that the therapist will make comments which do not represent his true feelings. . . . Yet, at the same time, if the patient indicates that the therapist is not sincere with him, the therapist will wonder with him what could be the origin of such an idea. The relationship the patient faces is like no other in human life; but within that framework the therapist will "wonder" why the patient does not respond to him in ordinary ways.

A few years of this sort of thing leaves the patient feeling as "terribly on the spot" as the schizophrenic. But, unlike the schizophrenogenic mother, who is herself driven and suffering, the psychoanalyst is the cool, deliberate, Prospero-like author of a benevolent ordeal. He is tormenting the patient for the patient's own good. He is provoking and goading him into change, forcing him to go outside his usual (symptomatic) ways of dealing with people, since they have been so manifestly unsuccessful with the analyst. At the end of the analysis, the patient may think that he has learned something about himself ("Where id was, there shall ego be"), but in fact—and in common with patients of hypnotists, marriage therapists, family therapists, and brief therapists—he has simply learned not to knock his head against a wall. As Haley puts it at the end of a facetious piece called "The Art of Psychoanalysis" (tagged on to *Strategies* as an epilogue), in which psychoanalysis is discussed in terms of Stephen Potter's *One-Upmanship*:

> the analyst succeeds in topping the patient again and again as the years pass. Ultimately, a remarkable thing happens. The patient rather casually tries to get one-up, the analyst places him one-down, and the patient does not become disturbed by this. He has reached a point where he does not *really* care whether the analyst is in control of the relationship or whether he is in control. In other words, he is cured. The analyst then dismisses him, timing this maneuver just before the patient is ready to announce that he is leaving.

In 1967, on the invitation of Salvador Minuchin, the recently appointed director of the Child Guidance Clinic, Haley moved from Palo Alto, California—where he had been practicing hypnosis and brief therapy with no formal training but with characteristic élan and confidence, and also jauntily editing *Family Process*, a journal he had founded with Don Jackson and Nathan Ackerman to publish writings about family therapy—and came to Philadelphia. Minuchin was transforming a conventional child-guidance clinic into a place where a child problem was considered a family problem, and was gathering like-minded people around him. In 1969, the clinic received a grant for a project which greatly appealed to Haley's sense of the outré, and which he has cited as "the most interesting family-therapy training I have done." The project was to take eight poor blacks and Puerto Ricans off the street—people who had had no previous professional training, were unacquainted with psychology or psychiatry, and had not gone past high school—and to make them into full family therapists in two years' time. They would then go back to the ghetto and train others in the same way. The eight men and women selected from the sixty who applied were chosen for their personal qualities and experiences, since they had no academic degrees or professional credentials and consequently, as Haley has written, had less to unlearn than their middle-class professional counterparts would have had. The project succeeded—in five years' time, thirty therapists had been trained and sent into the black community—but it became a casualty of President Nixon's economic policy; when funds were withdrawn from community mental-health programs, paraprofessionals could not compete with Ph.D.s and M.D.s for the few remaining positions.

The line leading from *Principia Mathematica* to the ghetto therapist who probably had never even heard of Russell and Whitehead and yet was casually employing maneuvers in his work that derived from their thinking is pleasing to trace. It gives one a whiff of the process by which the most difficult, abstruse, incomprehensible, and useless idea may filter down into life to become one of its useful commonplaces. However, the process by which Pure Thought is brought into the muddy mess of life is considerably expedited when there is a human figure on which the popular imagination can fix—a Man to associate with the Idea. Psychoanalysis had such a figure in Freud, and the rapidity with which radical Freudian theory became conventional women's-magazine wisdom surely owed much to the tight hold that Freud kept on the reins of the movement and to the impression of unity and simplicity that he was able to convey to the informed public. Family therapy has no comparable figure, and accordingly its public image has been slow to take shape. (The name hasn't helped: "family therapist" sounds like a euphemism for someone on the staff of a funeral "home.") Minuchin is only one of a large constellation of leading practitioners, teachers, and writers, who respect or hate one another's work, as the case may be, but tacitly agree that the field has no single superstar. Murray Bowen, Carl Whitaker, Virginia Satir, John Bell, Lyman Wynne, Ivan Boszormenyi-Nagy, James Framo are some of today's other major figures (the untimely deaths of Nathan Ackerman and Don Jackson have removed their names from the roster), whose activities resemble a system of planets spinning in orderly orbits around—nothing. Each of these major figures has something that greatly or slightly differentiates him from the others. Minuchin's specialty has been his work with poor black and Puerto Rican families and, lately, with the families of anorectic girls. He has published three books—*Families of the Slums*, written with four colleagues, which came out of the experimental family work he launched at the Wiltwyck School for delinquent boys; *Families and Family Therapy*, which deals with his "structural" theory and technique of family therapy; and *Psychosomatic Families*, which concerns his work with anorectics. However, it is as a clinician rather than as a theoretician that Minuchin has gained renown. Not everybody equally likes what he does—there are those who object to him as a "manipulator"— but no one disputes his dazzling effectiveness or denies his position as a kind of Horowitz or Pavarotti of family therapy. Speaking of Minuchin as a performing artist is not so farfetched. In recent years, he has traveled to hospitals and teaching centers to present demonstration sessions that are, in effect, performances. At these events, he will meet with a family he has never before laid eyes on, and about whom, as often as not, he has received only the sketchiest information, and he will work with them for ninety minutes while an audience in a nearby auditorium watches the proceedings over closed-circuit television.

My first view of Minuchin was at such an event, which featured one of his most celebrated shticks. This is the serving of lunch to an anorectic and her family, governed by a special, drastic technique that Minuchin has developed to bring things to a crisis. As the audience watched with horrified fascination, Minuchin directed the parents of an emaciated fourteen-year-old girl to make her eat, "or she will die." The parents coaxed, cajoled, threatened, yelled, and finally brutally stuffed food down the throat of the sobbing and slobbering child while Minuchin dispassionately observed the scene. After what seemed like an eternity, he motioned to the parents to stop the torture. The girl collapsed into the arms of her mother, who held her like a baby as she wept. "Your daughter will eat now," Minuchin said in a tired voice.

Not all of Minuchin's demonstrations are as violent as this, but most are no less dramatic and compelling. The unedited videotapes of his sessions confound one's notions about the difference between art and life. Life is supposed to be disorderly, boring, fragmented, repetitive, in need of drastic editing. Everyone who has watched home movies or listened to tape recordings knows that. But watching a Minuchin session, or a tape of it, is like being at a tightly constructed, well-directed, magnificently acted play. Without appearing to be doing anything out of the ordinary, Minuchin has an extraordinary effect on the people who come into his therapeutic presence. After a brief initial period of backing and filling, the family commences to act out a scenario, to present the drama of its life together, in a larger-than-life, more-orderly-than-life, less-redundant-than-life manner. Minuchin immediately, instinctively, intuitively seems to sniff out the elements of the family members' way of dealing with one another, and is able to "direct" them in the enactment of characteristic scenes ("transactions") from the marriage and parenthood that aren't working well and need repair.

What seems spontaneous and unpremeditated, however, is more artful than it looks. In *Families and Family Therapy*, Minuchin analyzes the therapy he does in terms of two main types of intervention: the "accommodation operation" and the "restructuring operation." Accommodation operations are designed to gain the therapist an entrée into the family system; they are overtures of the friendly, ingratiating, tell-me-about-yourself sort that we all make when we are trying to get to know someone or are trying to get someone to like us—except that we do it unthinkingly and often unsuccessfully, whereas Minuchin does it consciously and with almost unfailing success. "As a therapist, I tend to act like a distant relative," he has written. "I like to tell anecdotes about my own experiences and thinking, and to include things I have read or heard that are relevant to the particular family. I try to assimilate the family's language and to build metaphors using the family's language and myths. These methods telescope time, investing an encounter between strangers with the affect of an encounter between old acquaintances." Only when the therapist has successfully negotiated the entrée (Minuchin compares him to the anthropologist who must join the culture he has come to study) can he go on to perform the "restructuring operations" that are the object of structural family therapy—"the dramatic interventions that confront and challenge a family" and force it to change. Accordingly, he says, the therapist must "maintain himself in a position of leadership within the therapeutic unit. He must resist being sucked into the family system. He must adapt himself sufficiently to the family organization to be able to enter it, but he must also maintain the freedom to make interventions that challenge the family organization, forcing its members to accommodate to him in ways that will facilitate movement toward the therapeutic goals."

On a Tuesday afternoon, after attending one of Minuchin's classes at the Child Guidance Clinic, I sat talking with him in his office. He was wearing checked slacks and a short-sleeved sports shirt—typical of the easy, non-intimidating dress of the clinic staff. (Younger male therapists wore jeans, and women therapists wore casual skirts and sweaters.) "Well," he said to me with a smile, "how is it for you, entering this world where we do all kinds of pushing people around? How does it reverberate with your own experience?"

I said it was different from my experience in psychoanalysis.

"Psychoanalysis is a nineteenth-century concept," Minuchin said. "It's a product of the romantic idea of the hero and his struggle against society; it is about man *out* of context. Today, we are in a historical period in which we cannot conceive of nonrelated things. Ecology, ethology, cybernetics, systems, structural family therapy, are just different manifestations of a concern for the relatedness of our resources. Family therapy will take over psychiatry in one or two decades, because it is about man *in* context. It is a therapy that belongs to our century, while individual therapy belongs to the nineteenth century. This is not a pejorative. It is simply that things evolve and change, and during any historical period certain ways of looking at and responding to life begin to crop up everywhere. Family therapy is to psychiatry what Pinter is to theater and ecology is to natural science."

At one lecture I attended, Minuchin had made a joke indicating that he himself had once been in analysis. I asked him if he regretted it.

"Oh, no," Minuchin said. "It was a very valuable experience. But, you see, I am a healthy person." He went on, "The analysts discovered something interesting and went overboard. They discovered the importance of the early years of life and how these create certain channels and eliminate others. But then they closed everything off. What they had discovered remained a closed and unchangeable dynamic structure.

"The analyst says that the mother-father-child triangle becomes internalized—that the drama is played inside the child. The family therapist says that the drama of mother-father-child is also played in *reality*—that these characters are real. When we have a person in family therapy who has forgotten that the real characters also exist, who is concerned only with observing the drama within himself, we push him out into the scenario of the real thing. We say, 'Don't look inside.' We say, 'Deal with outside reality, and if this changes, you will change inside.'

"When I have very seriously ill patients who are obsessive—seriously ill people are obsessive by definition; they become obsessed with the significance of their internal drama, and reify it, crystallize it, stabilize it, as if the drama had no alternatives—I put them in contact with a real scenario. The analyst does quite the opposite. He says, 'Let's look at your animus, let's look at your ghosts, and, through your contact with me, let's look at how your ghosts can change.' To me, in very seriously ill patients this is a mistake, because it keeps them crystallized around the non-change that their obsessiveness is. And the reason family therapy is so successful with seriously ill patients is precisely that the patient needs to get involved in dealing with life, needs to shed his obsessiveness and the ritualization of his thinking. I put people into stress. I make them survive in real life. With the anorectic girl you saw at the lecture—she had not eaten for two months and had been living on fantasies of I don't know what—I didn't ask about those fantasies. I never ask about fantasies. What I do with anorectics is so simple it should have been invented long ago. The anorectic is obsessed with her hopelessness, inadequacy, wickedness, ugliness. I incite an interpersonal conflict that makes her stop thinking about how terrible she is and start thinking about what bastards her parents are. At that demonstration, I said to the parents, '*Make* her eat,' and when they did she had to deal with them as people. Previously, the parents had been saying 'We control you because we love you.' In the position I put them in, they were finally saying 'Goddam it, you eat! Let's stop this crap about love or no love, and you eat, goddam it!' That freed her. She could then eat or not eat; she could be angry at them as clearly delineated figures."

I asked Minuchin if the girl had been cured. He said that she had, and that 86 percent of the anorexia cases he has treated by his methods have been successful, in contrast to the 60 percent cure rate of psychoanalytic therapy. He derives his figure from fifty anorexia cases he has been following up for five years, he said, and he added, "Ways of evaluating and measuring success in psychological healing are fuzzy and inconclusive. What we have are competing systems of belief. The scream therapist says, 'We are better than the transactional analyst,' who says, 'We are better than the group therapist,' who says, 'We are better than the sex therapist,' and so on. And because patients are indoctrinated with the philosophy of their respective healers, they will usually say 'Yes, I am feeling better' or 'Yes, I am feeling less anxious.' I want it to be demonstrated that what we do is useful not because we believe it is useful but because a follow-up of patients has shown it to be useful. My interest in psychosomatics"—Minuchin has worked with diabetics and asthmatics as well as with anorectics—"is partly based on the fact that in psychosomatics we have an area where evaluation of results is no longer so soft. We don't need to ask anything as vague as 'Are you feeling better?' or 'Are you less anxious?' or 'Are you more in harmony with yourself?' Instead, by changing the family organization we have, in the case of psychosomatic diabetes and asthma, controlled the illness, and, in the case of anorexia, cured it, and this is a breakthrough."

I asked Minuchin if he felt similarly satisfied with his work with the poor black and Puerto Rican families of the boys at Wiltwyck. He sighed and shook his head. "Psychiatry sometimes presents itself as if it knew the answers to social problems, as if it could save people from the tragedies of poverty. What we do when we bring psychiatry to the slums is to put Band-Aids on people who require major surgery. We are not surgeons. We work with a mother on how to feel more competent with her children when she is living on an income that makes it impossible to be competent. If you are raising four children on three thousand dollars a year, you have problems that don't exist for someone who has thirty thousand dollars a year. We operate as if the problem were psychological, because the only thing we have is Band-Aids. There is a story about the Russo-Japanese War. The Russians had only iodine, and the Japanese had only aspirin, so when a Russian soldier had a headache he was given iodine, and when a Japanese soldier had a bleeding wound he was given aspirin—because these were the only things they had. Psychiatry is the only thing we have, so that's the thing we give. We are not revolutionaries, and we are not even reformers; we are accommodators."

In his youth, however, Minuchin *was* a revolutionary. He was born in 1921 in a small village in Argentina, the son of a Jewish couple whose parents had emigrated from Russia through an organization called the Jewish Colonization Association, formed by the philanthropist Baron Maurice de Hirsch. "My given name, Salvador, is a strange one for a Jewish boy," Minuchin said. "I think it reflects my parents' total lack of assimilation into the community. They didn't care what my name in Spanish was, as long as my Jewish name was the one they wanted. My Jewish name is Schmerl, and how this became Salvador is a process my parents were obviously not involved in, since no Jewish parents would deliberately call their son 'Savior.' " Minuchin's childhood was marked by the happiness and the easy security of life in a large extended family (he writes in *Families and Family Therapy*, "Like an inhabitant of Chinatown, when I walked the street I felt a hundred cousins were watching me") and by the misery and insecurity of being a Jew in a Catholic, anti-Semitic culture. He remembers graffiti reading "Be a good Argentine: kill a Jew," and street fights with boys who called him a dirty Jew. He fought, paradoxically, out of the Spanish sense of honor, which demands that an insult be met by an attack. "Even if you were kicked and defeated, you were clean," Minuchin recalls. "And to this day I prefer to attack when backed into a corner." He began his medical studies at the university in Córdoba in 1939, a few years before Perón came into power, and while still in training he became active in a leftist anti-Perón student coalition. One of his activities—writing slogans in tar on the walls of an official's house—landed him in jail for three months. "That was a lovely period," he says. "At that time in Argentina, jail was the place to be. It was where all the most interesting people were." Minuchin finished his medical studies in 1947 and was about to open a practice in pediatrics when war broke out in Israel. He immediately sold his equipment and got on a boat with a group of forty other Zionist volunteers. He served in the Israeli Army as a doctor. After the war, he came to New York to train as a child psychiatrist, and then, after meeting and marrying Patricia Pitluck (now a professor of psychology at Temple University), he returned with her to Israel. He worked there with Youth Aliyah, an organization that concerned itself with the displaced children of first the Holocaust and then the emigration of Jews from Arab countries to Israel. It was while doing this work that Minuchin's interest in families began, but it wasn't until 1958, a few years after he and Patricia (and their son, the first of two children) returned to America and he was working at Wiltwyck, that he took his first real step into family therapy.

"I began as an intake psychiatrist at Wiltwyck and saw the kids come in," Minuchin recalls. "Then, two years later, I was switched to the outpatient service, and I saw many of the same kids, now back with their families in Harlem. They were not very different, even though two years had elapsed and the people at Wiltwyck were very good people. We must be doing something wrong, I thought. At this point, I read an article by Don Jackson or Virginia Satir or somebody, and I said to my colleagues, 'Let's begin to see families,' and we did. It was a great adventure. We didn't know anything. And since we didn't know anything, we invented everything. We broke through a wall in our treatment room and put in a one-way mirror and began to observe one another and to build a theory out of nothing. We were working with a social group that was called unreachable—the disorganized, multi-problem black family. The people doing family therapy then—Nathan Ackerman and the Palo Alto group and others—were working with middle-class families, and had developed concepts of intervention that required a level of verbal sophistication that our families were not on. We had to develop new concepts and new techniques. My technique of enactment—the bringing of problems into the room and acting them out—came from this period. I was trained by my poor families to work with concrete metaphors, to use things here and now. We didn't read a lot, and we didn't know much about what other people were thinking, but one nice thing about this period was that everyone in the psychiatric establishment felt that what we were doing was absolutely right. The establishment had dismissed Nathan Ackerman's work in middle-class family therapy, saying that it was superficial, that it didn't have psychological depth, that it lacked seriousness. He was competing with them, and they felt threatened. But we were working in a no-man's-land of poor families who had frustrated all previous attempts to reach them—so we were applauded."

"There is something elitist in this," I said.

Minuchin shrugged. "The mental-health field *is* elitist," he said. "If you have a poor person who is not very verbal in the hospital for depression, and if you have a more articulate middle-class person in the hospital for depression, the inarticulate poor person will get shock treatment and the middle-class person will get psychotherapy."

When Minuchin took over the Philadelphia Child Guidance Clinic, in 1965, there were eight or ten people on the staff, and it was situated in the heart of the city's black ghetto; ten years later, there were 225 people on the staff, and the clinic was part of the handsome, modern new Children's Hospital complex, on the University of Pennsylvania campus. In 1975, Minuchin, who had become more interested in teaching and writing than in running such a big and cumbersome operation, stepped down as director. "I feel that ten years is as long as anyone should stay in one job," he told me. His Tuesday class is part of a training program that the clinic offers to outsiders who want to learn how to do family therapy. The course costs two thousand dollars a year and is open to people in "helping professions"—psychiatrists, psychologists, social workers, ministers, nurses, nuns, priests. It is hard to get into; last year, twenty-five students were selected out of eighty-two applicants. The faculty, along with Minuchin, includes Marianne Walters, a forty-eight-year-old social worker, whom he hired in 1969, and Stephen Greenstein, a thirty-nine-year-old psychologist and former student of Minuchin's. (Haley was on the faculty until 1976, when he moved to Washington to run a family-therapy institute there with his second wife, Cloe Madanes.) The core of the course is therapy itself. Students are almost instantly plunged into doing what they have come to learn to do, working under the supervision of a teacher and the observation of the other students. They learn on families who have come in for treatment, the way hospital interns learn on clinic patients. Although the teachers try to select people with either experience in or aptitude for the work—people who won't go all to pieces when confronted with a family—they occasionally miscalculate. During one of Marianne Walters's classes, I saw an intelligent, articulate, self-possessed young woman student reduced to a jelly of hesitation, inaudibility, and inconsequence by the family she had been assigned to treat. She was like an actor with a bad case of stagefright, and the teacher had to take over the session; the girl would probably have to find a more congenial line of work. Minuchin selects the ablest or most advanced people for himself; the five students in his Tuesday class all behaved coolly and seemed comfortable in their work. Along with Lee Combrinck-Graham, they were Giovanna Todini, a thirty-one-year-old child psychiatrist from Rome, here on a Fulbright; Gottlieb Guntern, a thirty-nine-year-old psychiatrist from Switzerland, director of a psychiatric clinic in Brig; Stephen Cole, thirty-seven, a psychiatrist from New York; and Anthony Bottone, thirty-nine, also a psychiatrist from New York. That the class was composed entirely of psychiatrists was uncharacteristic, an unusual shake of the dice; generally, classes are more of a mix of psychologists, social workers, and such.

AT Lee's second session with the Brauns, Yvonne again remained out of sight in the entryway, but her parents seemed different: easier, less tense, less oppressed. Minuchin and the rest of the class settled down in the observation room.

"What case is this?" Minuchin asked.

Giovanna told him.

"Oh, yes," he said, and he began to chat with Gottlieb.

In the treatment room, the Brauns told Lee that Yvonne was back in school, going out with friends, and taking less medication.

"How much is she taking?" Lee asked.

"Even less than what you said to take," Mr. Braun said.

Minuchin, still chatting with Gottlieb, pressed the buzzer. "The girl should take care of her own medication," he said into the telephone. "It is her business, not the parents'." He resumed his conversation with Gottlieb.

Lee said to the parents, "It would be a good idea if Yvonne

took care of her own medication from now on. She's old enough to do that." She turned to the girl. "OK, Yvonne?"

"OK," the girl said, in a dull, expressionless voice.

"Something has changed with you two," Lee said to the parents.

"Something has," the mother agreed brightly. "We found out that Yvonne has wings."

"That's right," the father said.

The parents gave an account of their daughter's happy teenage activities and of their own enlightened parental attitudes—which Yvonne, in the entryway, bitterly, nastily, and utterly repudiated. Lee gently pointed out the difference between the parents' giving their daughter more freedom and their speaking for her. She asked the Brauns how things were between them. The husband proudly cited an incident illustrating his grasp of a suggestion made the previous week—that if he was irritated by something his wife did he should tell her about it. This something concerned a magazine she had left on a table. He went on to reminisce about his childhood in a small town in the South, where "nothing happened and people just worked and went to bed." He continued, "I didn't have much education, and I don't read enough, and so"—getting to the point of the rambling narrative—"the reason I don't talk enough to my wife is because I don't have enough to talk about."

The wife said that, for her part, she didn't see why there had to be a constant line of communication. "Why is it wrong if you don't communicate?" she asked. "That doctor popped in here last week and said our marriage was bad. I don't understand it."

Lee said smoothly, "I can't account for what Dr. Minuchin says and does. But you did have some complaints about each other last week."

The wife murmured that they had been under a lot of stress that week.

Minuchin had stopped chatting and was watching the case

with an ironic look on his face. "This wife must be challenged," he said, and went into the treatment room. He extended his hand to the husband. "I congratulate you on letting your wife know when there is something you don't like. It is a very good thing that you are able to do that." He continued in this vein for a few minutes, and then returned to the observation room.

The husband, emboldened by Minuchin, began to attack his wife. He accused her of being pretentious. "You are always trying to impress me," he said. "For instance, you come home and tell me about something that happened at your day-care center. Then a week later I hear you telling someone else about it, and it's all different. I can't stand a phony. You either do or you don't. Tell it like it is. Don't decorate things to make yourself look better."

The wife, stung to tears, defended herself. "I don't decorate," she said. "If I tell a mother at the center that she's a rotten parent, she *is* a rotten parent."

A psychoanalyst would pounce on this non sequitur. He would point out to Mrs. Braun that she had unconsciously selected the "rotten parent" example because her own rotten parenting was on her mind. He would try to unearth the irrational roots of her guilt. But the family therapist is not interested in unconscious content. He is often not even interested in surface content. He is trying to change patterns of behavior rather than to correct skewed perceptions, and for him the important thing in the passage above is the change in pattern it represents: the fact that the husband, perhaps for the first time in the marriage, is openly attacking the wife. Accordingly, Lee offered no interpretation of the wife's statement, and, as Minuchin watched approvingly, the quarrel between the spouses was allowed to grow in intensity and presently to subside into trivial squabbling. But at this point Minuchin began to squirm impatiently in his chair. "Lee should now bring the girl into the discussion," he said, frowning. "If she keeps on leaving the girl out, she is asking the parents to stop coming."

Lee did not include the girl in the conversation, so Minuchin himself got up and went to talk to Yvonne in the entryway. She once again complained, in her gratingly depressed voice, about her parents' intrusiveness. "I want them to leave me alone," she said.

"No," Minuchin suddenly said. "You want them to treat you like a little girl."

"I do not."

"You look so big and act so little," Minuchin said tauntingly. "You are so pretty and you look so seductive, but you act as though you were eight years old. You look like eighteen and you act like eight."

"Leave me alone," the girl said.

"Why?" Minuchin said. "Why should I leave you alone?"

"Just leave me alone," the girl said desperately, beginning to cry.

"No, I will not," Minuchin said. "Look how childish you are. Look how you're acting. This is the way an eight-year-old acts. This is not the way a fifteen-year-old acts."

"Leave me alone," the girl said, growing hysterical.

"No."

Minuchin continued to goad the girl until she lost control of herself and began to scream and pound the walls of the entryway with her fists. Then Minuchin turned to the parents in the treatment room. "See?" he said. "She is having a tantrum, like a small child. Your daughter has the body of a woman, but she acts very young. She needs to grow up. She needs to be fifteen. But she has the anger of a little girl, an anger that says, 'Do something for me without my asking.' "

The parents, accepting the re-labeling of their daughter's behavior as childish rather than sick, began to imitate Minuchin's harsh manner and to pick on her.

"Just leave me alone," Yvonne repeated.

"Why should they leave you alone?" Minuchin said. "They're concerned because you don't act fifteen. You're acting childish and too young." To the parents he said, "Maybe when she is fifteen you will give her her rights. But not now. Now she is acting like a little girl. She is not fifteen."

Lee, suddenly and surprisingly, said to Minuchin, "I think you're being unfair. She's not so young. She can act fifteen."

"I disagree."

"I disagree with *you*. She can. I've seen her behaving reasonably."

"OK. We disagree," Minuchin said with a shrug, and walked out of the treatment room. At the door, he delivered this parting shot to the parents: "You two people are growing up, and she is scared."

Back in the observation room, Minuchin said to the rest of the class, "The girl is dressed like a whore. She'll go out on a one-night stand and get herself pregnant." He added, "The way Lee challenged me was absolutely correct."

When the session ended, the students returned to Minuchin's office. Since there were no more cases scheduled for that day, Minuchin asked, "Who would like to show a tape? Gottlieb, maybe we will look at the session you did last week."

Gottlieb, a tall, thin, bearded man wearing tight jeans and high-heeled clogs, buried his face in his hands. "God, not that mess," he said in a deep, heavily accented voice. But he got up and put a tape on the machine. The case involved a welfare couple and a child. The woman was middle-aged and prone to psychotic breakdowns, for which she had been hospitalized; the man, her second husband, was an alcoholic; and the boy had anxiety attacks that kept him out of school. Gottlieb had previously worked successfully with this hopeless family—Minuchin has characterized him as one of the most brilliant students he has ever taught—but the session in question had been a disaster. He had repeatedly got into losing battles. Early in the session, when things were already going badly, Minuchin had intervened and said to the mother—as the students in the observation room laughed heartily—"I am not a family therapist. I am a child psychiatrist. Tell me what is the matter with your son—what are his symptoms?" Now, as the class watched this intervention on the tape, Minuchin said to Gottlieb, "Did you understand my message here?"

"Not completely," Gottlieb said. "My head was in a mist. My thinking was very blurred during that session."

"You didn't understand that I was saying to you, 'Enter the family through the child'?" Minuchin asked, and turned off the set.

"Obviously not."

"OK. I thought the message was clear. And when you went in the other direction—when you continued to argue with the father—then I said to myself, 'Gottlieb is in a power operation with me, or he would have adopted my suggestion of going through the child.' "

"No, I was not in a power operation with you," Gottlieb protested. "I was blurred. I felt I was in a swamp. I felt that every move I made was wrong, but I didn't know what I was doing wrong."

"You have some kind of a set about power," Minuchin said. "You antagonized the mother, and you antagonized the husband, and you antagonized the child. You got into a power operation with all of them, and then with me."

"It was all very strange," Gottlieb said. "I saw your thing. I understood it when you were there, but when you left, all at once I was in a swamp again."

"There is something else here you should understand," Minuchin said. "This family was dealing with you in a special way. There is something in your makeup that made it possible for this family to suck you into power operations with it. They transact only in terms of power. Let's watch some more of the tape with this in mind."

The class watched an episode in which the mother truculently told Gottlieb about the boy's anxiety attacks in school. She said that the boy liked school but didn't attend, because "his fear comes on in the lunchroom."

The boy, who had not spoken before, now piped up and

corrected his mother. "It could be anywhere," he said. "Not just the lunchroom."

Gottlieb turned to the boy and said, "Do you know anybody else who is afraid of being in a crowd?"

"I don't know," the boy said.

"Other boys?" Gottlieb asked.

"I don't know," the boy said again.

"Or grownups?" Gottlieb persisted.

"I don't know," the boy said. And, for good measure, anticipating the next question, he put in another "I don't know."

"I think you know," Gottlieb said.

"No, I don't."

("You're lost," Minuchin said to Gottlieb's figure on the screen.)

"I think you know," Gottlieb repeated.

"Know what?" the boy asked, with triumphant malice.

Minuchin switched off the set. "Look how the boy completely organized your behavior," he said.

Gottlieb grimaced in exasperation. "What makes me angry is that I fell so easily into that pit."

"When the boy said, 'It could be anywhere,' he was collaborating with you," Minuchin said. "But then he betrayed you."

"You say he was collaborating, but my feeling was that he was not. It's been clear from the beginning that he becomes fearful at night exactly when the mother and stepfather go to bed. His maneuver is to separate them in the bedroom. So when he stepped in and said, 'It could be anywhere,' I thought—"

"You think too much," Minuchin interrupted. "When I say he collaborated, I mean that he was being cooperative in volunteering information. That's all. Then you asked him your question, and look what happened to you."

"It was a difficult question," Steve Cole said.

"I don't think it was difficult," Minuchin said.

"The question made the boy feel disloyal to his mother,

because he knows she has the same problem," Gottlieb said. "I pushed him too far."

"You think too much," Minuchin repeated. "Look, if a child says to me, 'I don't know,' and I ask him a second time and he again says, 'I don't know'—then I forget my cognitive schemes and I say to myself, 'This kid is defeating me, and I need to shift.' Let's put the tape a little forward. I want to show you how I handle the same situation."

The episode began with the entrance of Minuchin. He calmed the mother, who was yelling at Gottlieb. The stepfather had already walked out of the session. Minuchin turned to the boy, who was chewing bubble gum, and said that gum chewing disturbed him. The mother chimed in to deplore the boy's constant chewing.

"No, no," Minuchin said gently to the mother. "This is between me and Jimmy. You stay out of it." Turning to the boy, he said, "Jimmy, throw the bubble gum away."

Giovanna turned off the set. "I don't understand this intervention," she said. "I don't understand why you did that."

Minuchin smiled. "Can you accept it if I tell you that I just hate gum chewing, that I find gum an impossible thing, that I can't stand it—pure and simple?"

"But," Giovanna said in exasperation, "here is a situation where everyone is in a power operation, and you come in and do a power operation yourself."

"But with a little difference," Gottlieb said dryly. "He wins."

"I won because I wouldn't accept the mother's coming in and made it purely between me and the boy," Minuchin said. "But when I told the boy that I was disturbed by his gum-chewing, that was no dynamic thing. I just don't like gum-chewing."

"But it *became* dynamic," Giovanna said, and turned on the set. The class watched the boy throw the gum into a wastebasket. Minuchin said, "Thank you. Thank you very much, Jimmy. That was very good of you to do that. How old are you?"

"I don't know," the boy said.

"How old are you?" Minuchin said again.

"I don't know," the boy repeated.

"You don't know how old you are," Minuchin said. "OK. That's very nice." He turned to the mother and said, "You are worried because you have a son who doesn't know how old he is. Your concern is legitimate. . . ."

Minuchin switched off the set. "In this family, the traps are continuous, and it is useful to get caught, to get a feeling of how the system works," he told the class. "But it is essential to get out."

During lunch, which was brought in from the hospital's cafeteria and eaten in Minuchin's office, a general discussion developed out of Gottlieb's debacle.

GOTTLIEB: The strategy that worked so well before Christmas no longer worked. I learned from this session that you never put your foot in the same river twice. I see in retrospect that things had improved too fast. When healing processes go too fast, there must be something wrong. After three sessions with such a complicated family, I would never again think I had done a good job.

MINUCHIN: What happens in therapy is that you intervene in a system as a powerful stranger and produce a kind of disarray, which leads to a kind of transformation. People feel very happy with the changes that have occurred with your support. But then you disappear, and the system reverts to its previous way of being.

GIOVANNA: Yes; I have seen families where there is a tremendous change in the first three sessions, and then there is a relapse.

MINUCHIN: The question is: What is change? In individual therapy, we looked at change in terms of the symptom-bearer. In family therapy, we want to change the patterns that support a certain kind of behavior. The therapist will create certain changes by his entrance, and then he needs to make the changes operate in his absence.

GOTTLIEB: The problem is one of the learning process. If the family doesn't have time to learn how to be different, it cannot change.

MINUCHIN: The issue is the difference between learning and change. When you enter a family, what you are doing is trying to rearrange a sequence among people. If you are able to do that, the family will change, and learning will come later.

LEE: So you are saying that it is necessary for the family to change its structure before it can learn.

GOTTLIEB: But people *have* to learn in order to change. All your teaching to make us better therapists—your speaking with us, supervising us, discussing our tapes. How the hell do you think we would change if we didn't learn? I really think that learning theory has to be integrated—

MINUCHIN: My dear Dr. Gottlieb Guntern, I am talking about the difference between system change and individual learning. I am not discussing learning theory. I am saying that learning theory is related to individual memory and cognition, but in systems you have transactions, interrelationship patterns, and so on. You do not need learning to change that.

After the class dispersed, Minuchin said to me, "In what you saw today with Gottlieb, I was saying to him, 'Look at the way you get into conflict, and look at the way I avoid the same situation.' And when this happens again he will not behave automatically, because it will have become an area of self-observation. Braulio Montalvo has compared the training of the therapist to the training of the samurai. You train and train and train, and then you forget your training and the sword becomes an extension of the hand. Like any well-trained professional, the therapist needs to have the kind of trained spontaneity that allows him to say at some point, 'I can allow this part of myself to be free.' For example, let's say that a child insults his father. I feel that this is wrong. I feel a certain element of discomfort in myself. Then I ask myself, 'Shall I act on this feeling? Will it be useful?' And if I think it will, I angrily attack the boy. Indeed, I permit the feeling of discomfort to balloon into indignation. I put myself in motion, and I deliberately do not control what happens after that, because it is more effective when I do not. But I could equally well have *not* become indignant. I could have said, 'No, this would not be useful at this point,' and have done something else."

Minuchin said that he did not object to having the term "manipulator" used about him. "I consider the people who have come to therapy as people who have got stuck for lack of alternatives. They come to me in order to increase their possibilities, and it is my function as a therapist to use myself as an instrument to help them, and that is clearly manipulation. When you go to a psychoanalyst and he puts you on a couch, he is manipulating you. He is creating a particular set of circumstances in which you are invited to participate in a particular way. It is not wrong. But no analyst will accept the term 'manipulation' as descriptive of what he does, because the word has become a pejorative when used about interpersonal transactions, though in science it remains a respected term.

"In some ways I am a technocrat, since I believe in precise learning. But I also believe in imagination, poetry, and wisdom. It is a tragedy that many people who become therapists do not have wisdom. Like Jacob, you need to have struggled with God, and maybe if you haven't succeeded too well in your struggle you will be more respectful of other people's lame ways of dealing with life. You will not try to impose your way of being a spouse, your way of being a parent. You will accept differences. There is a lack of wisdom in all fields of therapy. Psychoanalytic schools often accept people who are very, very bright but not wise. How you select candidates is an extremely important issue, because therapists become people who give other people rules of life. I despair sometimes because we have young people who get their M.D.s or Ph.D.s, finish their training, but have no experience of life whatever. They are single people with no children, and suddenly they are experts on how to raise a family. I wish there were a way of telling people,

'Don't go to a therapist who hasn't had at least the experience you have had. If you have a problem when you're in your middle fifties, do not accept a therapist who is thirty.' "

WHEN the Brauns appeared the following week, the girl came into the treatment room, and—as if to illustrate the students' discussion of too rapid change—she was transformed. She talked in a fresh, mildly inane young voice, with no trace in it of depressed sullenness. She wore jeans and a high-school T-shirt, and she seemed like a normal slightly boy-crazy high school girl as she chattered to Lee about a boy she liked in her class. The parents seemed calm and happy. They only occasionally betrayed their nervousness by laughing too much.

In the observation room, Minuchin nudged me and said, "Don't believe what you see." But he watched approvingly as Lee guided the scenario along a strategic track that, as she later explained, would "strengthen the parents as a pair, disengage the daughter from them, and hook her up with her peers." Lee saw the girl's depression as a reflection of a developmental crisis in a family that was too "enmeshed"—whose members could not differentiate themselves from one another. (In *Families of the Slums*, Minuchin first offered his categories of the "enmeshed" and the "disengaged" families. The members of the first are too mixed up with one another, and the members of the second are too rigidly separated; the first is usually ethnic, and the second is usually WASP.) Lee spelled some of this out to the Brauns: "You've raised one child, and she's left home, which is what is supposed to happen in families. Families are supposed to come apart. But it's painful and hard on the parents, and when there is another child left at home the parents instinctively cling to that child. The child, in turn, clings to the parents by being too involved with them and by worrying about them." To Yvonne, Lee said, "You have a lot to do, Yvonne. And I don't think you have a lot of time left over for worrying about your parents—or you shouldn't have. The problem is: How are you going to change so you don't use up so much of your time and your energy worrying about them? Because if you don't feel that the time you spend on yourself is legitimately yours—if you always feel that you should be doing something for *them* or worrying about *them*—then you'll do something very strange and very dangerous to yourself." She paused. "Like go out and get yourself knocked up."

"Nah," the girl said. "No way."

"OK. If you can plan your life, and if you can think about it, then that sort of thing won't happen. But if you feel you have to grab time, that you—"

"No way, no way," the girl scoffed. "They know that if I don't have the wedding ring or the engagement ring on my finger they don't touch me."

Lee playfully questioned the girl about how far she would let a boy go, maintaining a light tone. The subjects that came up during the period were seen as life problems rather than as pathology: this family's problems were the problems of other families with adolescents. Nothing was said about the girl's depression, her voices, her sickness.

"Lee has learned to be less central and intrusive," Minuchin said. He got up and entered the treatment room, where he talked in a friendly, bantering way to the parents. He then got down to the business he had entered the session to do, suddenly turning to Yvonne.

MINUCHIN: Who is this fellow Alex?

YVONNE: Alex tells me what to do, sort of. When I was sick, he was trying to help. He's just something that comes to me.

MINUCHIN: He's a voice inside of you?

YVONNE: Yes.

MINUCHIN: How do you know his name is Alex?

YVONNE: I don't know. It's just . . . you know . . .

MINUCHIN: I prefer Moishe myself. When I had a voice, I called it Moishe. It's more friendly. Alex has a ring of detachment in it. It's kind of too WASPY for me. How do you imagine Alex to be? Is he tall and lanky?

YVONNE: No, he's like a mist, sort of, with a lot of colors.

MINUCHIN: A disembodied voice?

YVONNE: Yes.

MINUCHIN: My goodness! Is he a lot of little dots, like that Impressionist painter—you know, what's his name?

LEE: Seurat.

MINUCHIN: Yes. Do you smoke pot?

YVONNE: No.

MINUCHIN: Do you take LSD?

YVONNE: No.

MINUCHIN: OK. So the voice came to you when you were sick? And you've lost it now?

YVONNE: No, he's still here.

MINUCHIN: Can you call him on command?

YVONNE: No. He just comes when he wants to.

MINUCHIN: Then he's like Mother. He's overbearing. You cannot control him.

YVONNE: No, he's not overbearing.

MINUCHIN: You know, one of the nice things about voices is that you can call them and they come. If you cannot control them, they're not fun. They can become like parents. Tell me, is he friendly?

YVONNE: Yes.

MINUCHIN: Is he bright?

YVONNE: He's interesting, but he's not bright.

MINUCHIN: Is he wise?

YVONNE: To a certain extent.

MINUCHIN: That's nice. If you are going to have voices, it's nice that your voices should be interesting and wise. So. What do you talk about together? Issues of life?

YVONNE: We contemplate the universe most of the time.

LEE: I think you're being a little sarcastic.

YVONNE: No, I'm not.

MINUCHIN: No, she is not.

The buzzer from the observation room sounded at this point.

In the observation room, the students had been discussing Minuchin as they watched him in the session. "He's a master at seducing and manipulating," Gottlieb said admiringly.

"I think I'll become a pediatrician," Giovanna said. "I'll never learn to do what he does."

"When I am doing a session, I always feel that the family is waiting for the moment when he will come in—like the Lone Ranger," Steve said.

"Look how he is re-labelling the voice the girl hears, making it seem normal to hear voices," Anthony said.

"He has such a smartness and lightness," Gottlieb said. "His easy manner persuades the family that it is easy to change. We think we can imitate him, but we just learn some tricks."

Steve was struck with an idea. "Let's buzz him and tell him he's doing well," he said. The group was enthusiastic, and Steve pressed the buzzer.

Minuchin, looking a little surprised, picked up the phone.

"The group wants to tell you that you're doing well," Steve said.

Minuchin put down the phone and returned to the Brauns. "They told me I am being too intrusive," he informed them. He sat down and pointedly said nothing. The rest of the session was curiously flat and quiet. Minuchin let the tight drama he had been constructing fall from his hand. Everything slackened. It was as if a member of the audience at a play had stood up at a crucial point and shattered the illusion by complimenting an actor on his performance.

In the observation room, the students were chastened. They realized that they had acted rashly, that they had been put in their place, and that something complicated had happened.

"Sal is a master in power struggles," Gottlieb said finally. "He has to win. Look how he's defeated us."

"I don't see that," Anthony said.

"If he had accepted our praise, he would have accepted the reversal of the teacher-student relationship, and this he could not do," Gottlieb said. "So he re-labelled our praise criticism, and in that way kept his superior position. He was not too intrusive. So he withdrew and spoiled the session to teach us a lesson."

"You read too much Haley," Anthony said.

"Gottlieb is right," Giovanna said. "It was a power operation."

"I guess we shouldn't have done it," Steve said. "His message really meant that *we* were intrusive."

"He was right," Anthony said.

"He's a sly fox," Gottlieb said.

LEE saw the Brauns three more times. By the final session, Yvonne had completely stopped taking drugs, had caught up on her schoolwork, was going out with a boy she liked, and seemed cheerful and content. Only one reminder of her condition of two months earlier emerged during the session, and this was her remark that she still sometimes saw the Angel of Death—sitting on the roof of a building or standing under a streetlamp. "But it doesn't bother me anymore," she said. Lee asked the girl what she would do if she got depressed again. She thought, and then replied, "I'll get my father to take me to the shopping mall, and I'll buy a lot of clothes and records and things. That will keep me from getting depressed."

"OK," Lee said, and dismissed the case.

IT was a month later that I went to see the Brauns at home. I arrived late in the afternoon, and Mr. Braun, after greeting me and leading me into the kitchen, brought out a cocktail shaker and mixed some Manhattans. Following an abortive attempt by Mrs. Braun to move the party into the coldly immaculate living room, where obviously no one ever sat, we settled down around a table in the middle of the pleasant, still sunny room. Yvonne remained at the stove, poking at things in pots.

I asked the family what they thought of the treatment they had received in Philadelphia. The parents were enthusiastic about Lee, Minuchin, and family therapy. They said that it had changed their relationship with each other, and that now, for the first time in their marriage, they could communicate. "We sometimes lie in bed together just holding hands," Mrs. Braun said. As if overcome by the memory of these intimate moments, she reached over and took her husband's hand and stroked it tenderly and nervously. Mr. Braun looked uncomfortable, and though he didn't pull his hand away, he was clearly waiting for an opportunity to do so tactfully.

"We were all criticized," Mrs. Braun said complacently, "and we all deserved it."

Mr. Braun, glancing at his hand as if it were an extremely unpleasant sight, corroborated his wife's view of the treatment as criticism and correction. They felt that they had been rebuked and chastised, he said, and were now doing things better.

"In the car going to the clinic, we would make bets on who Minuchin would pick on that day," Mrs. Braun recalled. "He was hardest on me and Yvonne. You got off pretty lightly."

"What did you think of the treatment, Yvonne?" I asked. The girl had not joined the conversation. She remained at the stove, as she had remained in the entryway.

"It was helpful," she acknowledged. "But I still prefer Dr. Horace."

"Yvonne, that man drugged you so you didn't know if you were coming or going," Mr. Braun said, finally removing his hand and pouring himself another Manhattan.

"We were worried sick by those high dosages," Mrs. Braun said.

"I liked him," the girl insisted. "He understood me. I could relate to him."

"He was going to put you away in a mental institution," her father said.

The girl bit her lip and said nothing.

"How did you like Minuchin?" I asked Yvonne.

"I sometimes wanted to go home and get a knife and come back and kill him," she said. "But I guess he was right to do what he did. He drove me sane."

Mrs. Braun asked Yvonne to set the table, and the girl obediently got out some place mats and put them on the table. Knives and forks, flower-decorated plates, and glasses of iced tea appeared, and then platters and serving dishes of ham, fried chicken, scalloped potatoes, peas and carrots, coleslaw, gravy, and bread and butter were set in the middle of the table. Yvonne sat with a weight-watcher's scale in front of her, on which she weighed boiled chicken and vegetables brought from the stove. She said she was trying to lose ten pounds. I chatted with her about diets and then casually asked her how things were at home. Were her parents giving her the privacy and independence she had wanted?

"Yes, they treat me better," she said. "They don't come into my room anymore, and they don't beat me anymore, like they used to."

"Yvonne!" her mother said.

"What do you mean, 'beat' you?" I asked. "Do you mean they beat you in arguments—defeated you?"

"No, I mean they hit me," the girl said, nastily and tearfully. "Slapped me and yelled at me."

"Yvonne, that's not true," Mrs. Braun said tremulously.

Mr. Braun glared wrathfully at his daughter.

Good God, I thought, they think this is a family-therapy session. They're going to have a horrible scene. I clumsily but pointedly changed the subject, and the parents recalled themselves. The girl withdrew into herself again, playing the role of the "good child." She spoke only when spoken to, obeyed her parents, helped to clear the table. At the end of the meal, as turgid Italian pastries were passed around, she sat bleakly peeling an orange. The father helped himself to a second pastry and, with a satisfied smile, told me about an electric guitar that he had given his daughter as a surprise for her birthday. "She had asked me for an electric guitar, and I told her I'd have to think about it, and then I told her that I had decided *not* to get it for her. When she got home from school on her birthday, the guitar was waiting for her on her bed. I had got her just the one she wanted."

The girl dropped her second bombshell. "It was not the one I wanted," she said.

"What do you mean?" the father said, the smile gone from his face.

"I wanted the gray-and-white one, and you got me the black-and-white one."

"Is there something the matter with the guitar I got you?"

"No. It's just that the gray-and-white one was better."

"I thought I got you the one you wanted."

"No. It was close. But it was a little cheaper and a little less good than the gray-and-white one."

The father was visibly upset. The girl sullenly ate her orange. I asked her if she would play the guitar for us. OK, she said. She went into her small, neat room—bed with printed-patch-work spread, chest of drawers, chair, rock-star posters, TV set—and brought out the black-and-white electric guitar. We went into the immaculate living room, and the girl plugged in her guitar and played a Simon and Garfunkel song. She played slowly and carefully and nicely.

I looked around the living room, with its new furniture, pristine draperies, a few symmetrically arranged figurines, a white pot of African violets, a large TV set, and two pictures. One was a reproduction of a religious painting, and the other was a tinted formal wedding photograph taken in the fifties. It showed a pair of thin, awkwardly young kids—he with a crew cut, and she in a curled hairdo of the day and dark-red lipstick—who faintly resembled the heavy, settled middle-aged couple sitting across from me. I looked from the parents to the sad, squelched child stolidly playing her electric guitar.

"I thought that was the one she wanted," the father said to no one in particular.

*The New Yorker*, 1978

# A Girl of the Zeitgeist

ROSALIND Krauss's loft, on Greene Street, is one of the
most beautiful living places in New York. Its beauty has
a dark, forceful, willful character. Each piece of furniture and
every object of use or decoration has evidently had to pass a
severe test before being admitted into this disdainfully interesting room—a long, mildly begloomed rectangle with tall windows at either end, a *sachlich* white kitchen area in the center,
a study, and a sleeping balcony. An arrangement of geometric
dark-blue armchairs around a coffee table forms the loft's sitting
room, also furnished with, among other rarities, an antique
armchair on splayed, carved feet and upholstered in a dark
William Morris fabric; an assertive all-black Minimalist shaped-
felt piece; a strange black-and-white photograph of ocean water;
and a gold owl-shaped Art Deco table clock. But perhaps even
stronger than the room's aura of commanding originality is its
sense of absences, its evocation of all the things that have been
excluded, have been found wanting, have failed to capture the
interest of Rosalind Krauss—which are most of the things in
the world, the things of "good taste" and fashion and consumerism, the things we see in stores and in one another's houses.
No one can leave this loft without feeling a little rebuked: one's
own house suddenly seems cluttered, inchoate, banal. Similarly, Rosalind Krauss's personality—she is quick, sharp, cross,
tense, bracingly derisive, fearlessly uncharitable—makes one's
own "niceness" seem somehow dreary and anachronistic. She
infuses fresh life and meaning into the old phrase about not
suffering fools gladly.

I have come to her loft to talk with her about the history of
the magazine *Artforum*. I am preparing an article about the

magazine's present editor, Ingrid Sischy, and have been speaking with some of the old guard—the people who were at the magazine in the early seventies, when it was such a formidable critical force in the art world as to give rise to the expression "*Artforum* Mafia." The editor then was Philip Leider, followed by John Coplans, and the editorial board included, along with Krauss, Annette Michelson, Lawrence Alloway, Max Kozloff, Barbara Rose, Peter Plagens, Robert Pincus-Witten, and Joseph Masheck. In 1975, Krauss and Michelson left *Artforum* to found *October*, a taut, Eurotropic intellectual journal, which they have coedited since then. In addition, Krauss has been a professor of art history at Hunter College since 1975 and has written vanguard art criticism since the sixties. Her writing has a hard-edged, dense opacity; it gives no quarter, it is utterly indifferent to the reader's contemptible little cries for help. (Another art critic, Carter Ratcliff, told me, "I remember one of the writers at *Artforum* in the old days—I think it was Annette Michelson—saying, with a kind of pride, that *Artforum* was the only American journal that seemed to be translated from the German.") I am therefore surprised by the plain, entertaining way in which Rosalind Krauss speaks, as she sits in the Morris chair with the gold clock beside her on a little table—a Minerva with her owl. She is a handsome, dark-haired, elegant woman in her mid-forties, reminiscing, with a sort of peevish relish, about the bad feeling that existed among the contributing editors of *Artforum* in the seventies: "Lawrence Alloway was forever sneering at me and Annette for being formalists and elitists and not understanding the social mission of art. There was also a quite unpleasant quality emanating from Max Kozloff. He was always very busy being superior—I could never understand why. He, too, had this attitude that the rest of us were not aware of art's high social function. Neither Annette nor I would buy into this simplistic opposition that they set up between formal invention and the social mission of art. Our position was that the social destiny, responsibility—whatever—of art is not necessarily at war with some kind of formal intelligence through which art might operate, and that to set up that kind of opposition is profitless. It's dumb. I remember having all these stupid arguments with Lawrence, saying things like 'Why are you interested in art in the first place?' and pointing out that presumably one gets involved with this rather particular, rather esoteric form of expression because one has had some kind of powerful experience with it—and that presumably this powerful experience then makes you want to go on and think about it and learn about it and write about it. But you must have at some point been ravished, been seduced, been taken in. And it's this experience that is probably what one calls an aesthetic experience. And it probably doesn't have very much to do with the message."

Rosalind Krauss pours tea from a clear-glass Bauhaus-design teapot into thin white porcelain cups and asks me if I have heard about "the Lynda Benglis thing." I have. It is a famous incident. In the November 1974 issue of *Artforum*, an advertisement appeared—a two-page spread, in color—that caused readers to disbelieve their eyes. It showed a naked young woman, the artist Lynda Benglis, with close-cropped hair and white-rimmed harlequin sunglasses, standing with her breasts assertively thrust out, one arm and hand akimbo and the other hand clutching an enormous dildo pressed against her crotch. The ad not only caused a stir among the *Artforum* readership but impelled five of the editors—Krauss, Michelson, Masheck, and (for once aligned with Krauss and Michelson) Alloway and Kozloff—to write a letter, published in a subsequent issue, stating that they wished to publicly dissociate themselves from the ad, to protest its "extreme vulgarity" and its subversion of the aims of the women's-liberation movement, and to condemn the magazine's complicity with an act of exploitation and self-promotion. An article about Lynda Benglis, written by Pincus-Witten, had appeared in the same issue as the notorious ad. According to the Alloway-Kozloff-Krauss-Michelson-Masheck letter, "Ms. Benglis, knowing that the issue was to carry an essay on her work, had submitted her photograph in color for inclusion in the editorial matter of the magazine, proposing it as a 'centerfold' and offering to pay for the expenses of that inclusion. John Coplans, the editor, correctly refused this solicitation on the grounds that *Artforum* does not sell its editorial space. Its final inclusion in the magazine was therefore as a paid advertisement, by some arrangement between the artist and her gallery."

Rosalind Krauss recrosses her handsomely shod feet, which are stretched out on the coffee table before her, and says, "We thought the position represented by that ad was so degraded. We read it as saying that art writers are whores."

I had heard that in addition to the Benglis affair there had been a struggle between Coplans and some of his editors over the issue of "decommodified" art vis-à-vis advertising. Many of the most advanced artists of the seventies—the people doing conceptual art, performance art, film and video art, multiples —were deliberately creating work that had little, if any, market value. Their work constituted a kind of protest against the fact that unique, one-of-a-kind art objects, possessed of an "aura," which could be bought and sold for huge sums of money—i.e., commodities—were still being made in our "age of mechanical reproduction" (as Walter Benjamin identified it in his classic essay). Coplans, who had become editor in 1972 and was trying to keep the magazine financially afloat (when he took over, *Artforum* could barely pay its printing bill), was felt to be selling out to advertisers by turning down articles on (unmarketable) film and performance and conceptual art in favor of articles on (marketable) painting and sculpture.

"Yes," Rosalind Krauss says. "That's how we felt. And one of the things that Annette and I have done with *October* is to free ourselves from that. We've never had a single piece of gallery advertising. But our theory about John's courting of the dealers and gallery owners, which was certainly why Annette and I thought that various projects of ours were not acceptable to John—that theory failed in the light of what John subsequently did. Because John's policies in the last years of his editorship alienated every advertiser. He accepted Max's position and carried on in a way that had to do with becoming this—I don't know—this *Novy*-left type, dumping on the art market, and writing all kinds of attacks on it, and running the magazine absolutely contrary to the interests of the dealers and the advertisers, to the point that the owner, Charlie Cowles, simply sacked him."

I ask Rosalind Krauss what she thinks of the present *Artforum*. She replies, "I just got so bored with it that I stopped subscribing. I've just not looked at it. I'm just not interested in it. Ingrid's sensibility just doesn't interest me."

I ask her what she thought of Thomas McEvilley's critique of William Rubin and Kirk Varnedoe's primitivism show at the Museum of Modern Art—to whose two-volume catalogue she had contributed an essay on Giacometti. The controversial McEvilley article appeared in the November 1984 issue of *Artforum*.

"I thought it was very stupid," she says. "I think Tom McEvilley is a very stupid writer. I think he's pretentious and awful. His piece seemed to be primarily involved in trying—as Tom McEvilley always seems to be trying—to present himself as some sort of expert while misrepresenting what the museum was doing."

"Did you read the exchange of letters that Rubin and Varnedoe had with McEvilley?"

"Yes. And I must say I found it very unpleasant, because you couldn't tell which side was the more horrible. On the one hand, you had Rubin and Varnedoe sounding like complete assholes and, on the other, you had McEvilley doing his hideousness. I have never been able to finish a piece by McEvilley. He seems to be another Donald Kuspit. He's a slightly better writer than Donald Kuspit. But his lessons on Plato and things like that—they drive me crazy. I think, God! And I just can't stand it."


JOHN Coplans's loft, on Cedar Street, has the look of a place inhabited by a man who no longer lives with a woman. There are ill-defined living and work areas (after being fired from *Artforum*, Coplans became a photographer, and the loft serves as his studio and darkroom as well as his living quarters), punctuated by untidy mounds of things on which a gray-striped cat perches proprietorially. The furniture is spare and of simple modern character. Coplans is a man of sixty-six, with curly gray hair and with black eyebrows that give his eyes a kind of glaring gaze. He speaks with a British accent in a vigorous, incisive, almost military way. (I later learn that he was in fact a British Army officer.) At the same time, there is something ingratiating and self-depreciating in his manner. Coplans leads me to a table strewn with papers and books, brings a bottle of seltzer water and two glasses, and talks about the early history of *Artforum*, in California.

The magazine, he says, was founded in San Francisco in 1962 by John Irwin, a salesman for a printing company who had formed the desire to start an art magazine—"a sweet, naive guy, in his early thirties, who had very little idea of what he was doing." Coplans had recently come to San Francisco—he had gone to art school in London after leaving the Army and was now a painter and occasional art teacher—and he was with the magazine from the start, serving as an adviser to the wide-eyed Irwin and writing reviews and articles. But Irwin's most important recruit was a brilliantly intelligent young man named Philip Leider, a law-school dropout who had briefly been the director of a San Francisco gallery that showed Coplans's paintings and was now employed as a social worker in the San Francisco welfare department. Within a few months of his joining the magazine, Leider was asked by Irwin to become the magazine's managing editor (and its only paid staff member), and then its editor—a position he held for the next seven years. But even as early as 1964 the magazine was failing financially. It was rescued the next year by the publishing magnate Gardner Cowles and his stepson, Charles Cowles, who had just left Stanford and was looking for something to do. Charles Cowles became publisher. (Irwin, when last heard from by Coplans, was running a dry-cleaning business in Cleveland.) "Gardner Cowles provided the magazine with an annual subsidy and Charlie with a job and a position in the world," Coplans says. "But Phil Leider couldn't stand Charlie, who was concerned with social position and with the prestige of being publisher, and was indifferent to the everyday minutiae of publishing. Phil was the kind of intense human being who could sit for five years in this tiny office next door to Charlie Cowles and never say a word to him. Phil came out of a quite poor, nonintellectual Jewish immigrant family—Jewish immigrant in the most traditional sense: high morality and very involved with Jewishness itself. He got through college by writing papers for other people, at five or ten dollars apiece. He got a master's degree in English and then served in the Army, where he worked as a typist—he was one of the fastest typists the Army had. Later, he went to law school, but he sheered off from that. Phil was always wary, alert, and skeptical. He had no personal ambition; he was not a careerist in the American sense. He wanted nothing to do with power or money. He lived with his wife and children in the simplest way. Furniture was just plain, straightforward furniture, like mine—whatever could be bought cheap, like office furniture. He loathed and hated decoration, social ambition, careerism, making money. He dressed simply but neatly, in a black suit. The whole orientation of his life was his family. I've rarely come across a man so involved with his wife—they used to read together every night—and with his children. His only aberration was that every year he and his wife would drive down to Las Vegas, and he would take maybe a hundred dollars and gamble as long as the money lasted. Then he would come home; he had purged himself of frivolity for the year. He was an enormously articulate man, and he couldn't stand inarticulateness in others. He was offended by it, by the dumbness of artists. His best friends eventually were the artist Frank Stella and the art historian Michael Fried, two of the most articulate men in the American art world. I took to the guy tremendously; I really liked him, and he saw in me someone deeply strange and felt that there could be some dialogue between us. I have to say that he didn't trust me, really, because as time went on he thought—and he may have been right—that I was too interested in power. He saw in me some aspect of worldly ambition that he backed away from.

"I am a self-educated man. I was raised in South and East Africa, in a Russian-Jewish family, and I left school when I was sixteen. I joined the British Air Force and then the British Army, for a total of eight years of military service. I didn't go to college, but I wanted to learn everything. I was curious. I became an art historian. I taught art history at the University of California at Irvine. I became a museum curator at the Pasadena Art Museum, a writer, an editor. When I was editor of *Artforum*, I had half a dozen editors on my board. They were always quarreling with each other. They all hated each other. They were strong people, all academically very well trained, all extremely knowledgeable, the most experienced writers and critics in America, who had all gone through the various evolutions of art since the fifties. And now here's this young lady Ingrid Sischy, who goes in at about twenty-five and has been learning everything on the job and trying to find out what to do. She has no background in American art—this moment in art is all she can deal with—and she doesn't have the range of people I had. She's got a little board. She's got Germano Celant, who's a European, hardly ever here; and this Frenchman whom I simply don't know; and Edit deAk, a young woman like herself; and Thomas McEvilley, who is first-rate, absolutely first-rate; and a books editor who is a lightweight."

As Coplans talks, my eye is drawn to a large black-and-white photograph on the opposite wall of a male torso and genitals. It is part of a series of photographs that Coplans has taken of his own naked body, which are soon to be shown at the Pace/ MacGill Gallery here and have already been exhibited in Paris. Coplans gets up and shows me other pictures in the series: brutally searching examinations of an aging, sedentary, hirsute body, which refer both to ancient sculpture and to twentieth-century art and photography and have an appearance of monumentality and solemnity that almost obscures their underlying, disturbing exhibitionism. I am therefore not surprised by Coplans's subsequent unrepentant recollections of the Lynda Benglis incident:

"The ad was in response to Robert Morris's photograph of himself as a macho German, wearing a steel helmet and iron chains over bare muscles, which he used as a poster for a show of his work at Castelli/Sonnabend. This was her message to him. She wanted it to run in *Artforum*, and I said to her, 'Look, the editorial content of the magazine can't be interfered with in any way. We don't allow any artist to have a role in what is published. I'm sorry, but you just can't have this in the magazine.' So she said, 'Well, can I do an ad?,' and I said, 'There is a publisher, and you'll have to ask him. I don't interfere with him, and he doesn't interfere with me. Go to Charlie Cowles and ask him.' Then Charlie came to me and said, 'What do I do?' I said, 'Charlie, make a decision. I will not be put in the position where you don't make a decision. You have to face the art world and the artists. I'm not saying anything. Make a decision.' After about three days of heavy sweating, Cowles came to me and said, 'I can't *not* publish it. They would hate me.' I said, 'That's right, Charlie.' So he said, 'All right, we'll run it.' I made up the magazine and sent it down to the printer, and the printer refused to print the ad. So Charlie said to me, 'It's solved. I'm off the hook.' And I said, 'No, Charlie, you're not off the hook. Those printers have no right to refuse to print, and our lawyer will tell them so. They can't select what's going to appear in the magazine.' So I went down to the printer, and the head of the printing firm was a former brigadier general in the U.S. Army, and I'm a former Army officer, too, and I said, 'Come on, General, you know you can't do this.' He was a nice guy, actually. I said, 'We have a contract with you. Don't let's have to go to law.' So the general said, 'All right.' I went back to Charlie, and I said, 'Charlie, it's going to be printed. I insisted that it had to be printed as a matter of principle.' Now, I was obviously interested in seeing that ad get published. My position was that every woman had the right to make her individual choice as to how she faced her womanhood. This was an artist, and she had made this choice, and I was determined to protect her choice. Annette Michelson and Ros and Max thought it was obscene, that it was too sexually explicit. They were wholly opposed to me. Whether I was right or wrong I don't know."

ROBERT Pincus-Witten is a short, fresh-faced man with a sleek, well-tended look about him, who seems younger than his fifty-odd years, and who speaks with the accent of that nonexistent aristocratic European country from which so many bookish New York boys have emigrated. Pincus-Witten is a professor of art history at Queens College and teaches at the City University Graduate School. He was one of Coplans's gang of contributing editors, and for the last ten years he has been writing a column for *Arts* in the form of a journal. I first talked to him at a gathering of artists, collectors, curators, art-magazine editors, and critics at Marian Goodman's apartment after an opening of Anselm Kiefer's work at the Goodman Gallery, and I retain an image of him slightly bent over the buffet table as he helped himself, with a serious, responsible, almost sacerdotal air, to delicious, expensive food. Later, we talk further over lunch at a Japanese restaurant near the graduate school. He speaks of Rosalind Krauss, who is a fellow-member of the graduate faculty, with grumpy familiarity: "Ros is a full professor, and she tends to pout in order to get her own way. She receives extraordinary academic consideration. She teaches only two courses a semester, instead of the three that the rest of us teach. She's a very attractive person, and many of the seemingly better students—I don't know if they actually are better—are drawn to her glamour. What happens is that she tends to be condescending, though not cruel, to students she doesn't think are intellectually desirable, so those students, as it were, become the students who come to one. They are not intellectually undesirable, but they walk around with this feeling of rejection and intellectual disparagement. Rosalind tends to attract a certain kind of stylishly intellectual student. Some of them are not particularly well prepared. I myself am more interested in general cultural knowledge than in the interpretative skills of the new dispensation, under which the truth of Derrida, the truth of de Saussure—what have you—are replacing the truth of Greenberg. The kids who can do this deconstruction talk are doing the eighties' equivalent of the fifties' Greenbergian formalist talk. It disturbs me. When I examine them, they have very little general knowledge. They have methodology, but they don't know the monuments. I happen to be interested in monuments. When one supports a certain radical position, one should know the conservative position that one is rejecting. What troubles me is the unexamined adoption of a radical stance. These kids still believe in a class struggle without realizing that they have made an a priori judgment that capitalism and its fruits are evil. I'm not happy with that, so I'm considered an archconservative. And it shocks me, because these are such privileged kids."

I ask Pincus-Witten if he feels a kinship with the New Right.

He replies, "No, I feel a kinship with something much older: the aristocracy of the intellect, the aristocracy of sensibility. The others, they're just Rotarians. They're bowling teams, whether they're bowling teams of the right or the left. I know that I must always remain an outsider. I feel a fundamental alienation that is not materialistic or class-oriented, and that's why I don't join anybody. Ingrid Sischy is another person who doesn't belong to any team or party, and that's why there is a thread of identification between her and me. Ingrid is very anarchic, and that's why she is resented by some sectors of the art community. Her reluctance to adopt a party line is viewed as a *retardataire* form of bourgeois privilege and opens her to a dated form of criticism that seems to come from fifty years ago. The fact that she can be interested in any style that might be regarded as involved with commodification—or what her critics imagine to be commodification—identifies her in their minds as an enemy of the class struggle. I find it quite astonishing that people who embrace such textbook theories still have no trouble being owners of co-ops or putting copyright marks at the bottom of their writings. They're stuck in a paradoxical situation that renders their absolutism ludicrous. Ingrid is odd. She can get curious *idées fixes*. She is very interested in popular culture. I remember one conversation I had with her and some fairly glamorous people when she was telling us about the tragedy of an extremely popular pop singer—the one who wears a glove. His tragedy was the built-in supersedence of his prestige by another extremely popular pop singer, named Prince. And it was simply impossible for me to think of that as even remotely entering the sphere of tragedy. She was reading tragedy in connection with some issues in popular culture, and I was reading it in terms of, you know, hubris, nemesis, the idle cruelty of the gods. What was nice about the conversation was that on some level Ingrid was closer to what the conversation was really about than I was with my high-flown stuff. When I first met Ingrid, I was struck by how young she was and how she wasn't conventionally pretty—she didn't look like Gloria Steinem. I've known Ingrid for six years now, and I've never seen her behave badly or coldly or curtly. I've never seen her even be short. I've never seen her behave in an ugly way—ever."

. . .

BARBARA Rose's loft, on Sullivan Street, with its mirror-filled walls, soft-gray carpeting, curved black sofa, mirror-topped coffee table, abstract and Oriental art, and fur-covered bed, looks more like a Park Avenue co-op than like a downtown living space, and Barbara Rose herself—a thin, pretty, somewhat jumpy woman of around fifty, with apricot-colored hair and wearing a loose, stylish light-blue wool dress and high heels—has a decided uptown aspect. When I arrive, she is talking on the telephone, and throughout my visit the telephone (which she sets to have answered by machine) rings frequently, with a discreet, rasping electronic sound. Barbara Rose's speech puts me in mind of simultaneous translation: she speaks very rapidly and a bit remotely, as if dealing with someone else's text. Since leaving *Artforum*, she has taught art history at several universities, has been a museum curator, and has written art criticism for *Partisan Review*, *Art in America*, and *Vogue*. "The art world today is not a serious world," she says. "Art today is an aspect of decor, of entertainment. It's like gourmet food. In the sixties, I would invite people over—I was married to Frank Stella then—and there would be raging fights. Of course, people like Barnett Newman and Ad Reinhardt were alive then. They were major intellectuals. There's nobody like them today. There are a few artists who are intellectuals, but most artists have become professionals. They're like cloak-and-suiters—they make this product, it's the thing they do. It's not about the agony and the ecstasy, or whatever, anymore; it's middle-class, it's bourgeois. There used to be a sharp demarcation between the bourgeois world and the art world. The bourgeois world was Other, its values were Other. You didn't have anything to do with these people; you didn't see them socially, you certainly didn't have dinner with them. But now that's all artists want to do—be invited to fancy restaurants and discothèques. And there are all those people from the suburbs. How do they get a foothold in Manhattan? They get involved with art. They're out there in New Jersey and Long Island collecting Major Works. And all those ladies running around with—you know—the briefcases and the slides. The people who are talking about art today are the people who twenty years ago were talking about— What were those people talking about twenty years ago? They were talking about big cars. I find the art world today very much like suburbia, and I'm not interested in the values of suburbia or its life style or its aspirations. I left suburbia many years ago, and I don't want to go back.

"At *Artforum* in the sixties and seventies, we were talking to each other and we were talking to a group of artists who could understand us—Robert Morris, Donald Judd, Claes Oldenburg, Jasper Johns, the remaining Abstract Expressionists. They were people of high intellectual caliber—I mean major intellectuals, not dodos. We had all been formed by the same educational process. We were all trained art historians, and we all had a background in philosophy and aesthetics. We knew what we were talking about. Annette and Max and I had been pupils of Meyer Schapiro at Columbia, and Michael Fried and Rosalind had been at Harvard. Frank and Michael, who were undergraduates at Princeton together, went to hear Clement Greenberg lecture, and they were converted immediately to the Greenberg doctrine, because it offered a coherent way of looking at art. Nothing else did. Harold Rosenberg wrote, but nobody serious took him seriously—it was sociology; it wasn't art criticism. It had nothing to do with aesthetics, it had no background in art history, it was off the top of the head. It was fine for a general audience, but for people who had been trained in aesthetics and art history it seemed very hollow, and it had nothing whatever to do with actually looking at art. Whereas Greenberg looked at art. Now, he was a strict formalist, but he really shone in comparison with Harold, particularly at that time. We were all very impressed by Wittgenstein and by Anglo-

American philosophy and by linguistic analysis and the veri-fication principle—by that school of philosophy, which fitted perfectly with Greenberg's way of thinking—and Harold just simply didn't seem to have any philosophical underpinning to his thinking.

"After 1967, when Philip Leider moved the magazine to New York, there was a lot of hanging out together. You had a sense of not being isolated. You were talking to other people. It might be only five people, but you were talking to somebody, and you knew who you were talking to. I would write an article knowing that what I was basically doing was having a fight with Michael. We were a group of people who had had the same kind of education addressing the same topics from different points of view. The magazine had coherence, which the culture had at that point, too. There was then such a thing as a core curriculum, there was such a thing as a liberal-arts, humanistic education, there was such a thing as a thorough art-history education. These things don't exist anymore. The people in-volved in the art world don't have them. The new *Artforum* is a media magazine; it's totally media-oriented. There's no real criticism in it, or almost none. McEvilley writes criticism, and John Yau writes criticism, but I haven't found anything else that I would call criticism in the new *Artforum*. It's some kind of writing—some strange kind of writing—but it's not criticism. It's Rene Ricard doing whatever it is that Rene Ricard does. I mean, it's something weird, and a lot of the people can't write. They have no background; they don't know what they're talking about, if they're talking about anything.

"We were literary people—academic literary people. We didn't watch television. If we were interested in cinema—which Annette and I were—it was on the level of avant-garde film, not Hollywood. And we didn't like junk. There wasn't this horrible leveling, where everything is as important as every-thing else. There was a sense of the hierarchy of values. We felt that we had to make a distinction between Mickey Mouse and Henry James. There's a generation now that feels you don't have to make that distinction. Mickey Mouse, Henry James, Marcel Duchamp, Talking Heads, Mozart, *Amadeus*—it's all going on at the same time, and it all kind of means the same thing. For that, you have Andy Warhol to thank. I also think Susan Sontag was very influential in giving permission to so-called educated people to watch trash. Her article 'Against Interpretation' said that this idea of highbrow and lowbrow didn't matter any longer—you could just love everything that was going on, you could be positive and optimistic and just love it all.

"I used to be able to earn a living as an art critic. I got paid a lot of money by *Art in America*, because there was a differential, you see: if you were a very popular writer or were considered a very good writer, you got paid more money. Then, all of a sudden, the great era of democracy came to *Art in America*, and they started paying everybody the same. So I said, 'Forget it—I have too much experience, and I'm not going to write for the same amount of money you pay my students.' I don't believe in democracy in art. I think that when elitism got a bad name in this country, it was the beginning of the end for American culture. The only interest the *New Criterion* has is its pretension of being an elitist magazine. Unfortunately, it's not. What it is is just a strange kind of dinosaur. It has such a clear party line that it's just not an interesting magazine. In fact, it's extremely boring. But its goal—the reconstruction of what was once a consensus of educated people—is correct."

THE party at Marian Goodman's apartment where I first talked to Robert Pincus-Witten began with a certain—as Pincus-Witten would say—*déconfiture*. Almost everyone there had heard about, if not actually seen, a confrontation that had taken place between two of the party guests an hour before, at the

Anselm Kiefer opening. The opening had been an enormous one, with hundreds of viewers on hand drinking bad champagne, and the confrontation had taken place in an alcove off the main, museum-size room, so that not too many people actually witnessed it. Those who did—I among them—were stunned by what had suddenly erupted in their midst. At one moment, Richard Serra and Ingrid Sischy were having a normal conversation; at the next, Serra, his face contorted with fury, was jabbing a finger at Sischy's face and abusing her with a stream of invective. "I think he would have hit me if I'd been a man," Sischy said later. "I was very glad I wasn't." Sischy —a short, very young-looking person with cropped, dark, wavy hair, a round, clear, olive-skinned face, and large glasses, who was wearing tapered stretch pants and a tailored shirt—stood facing Serra, occasionally putting in a quiet word and showing no emotion beyond a reddening of her face. Like the other bystanders, I stood transfixed, catching some of the words but not able to understand what Serra's tirade was about or what had so enraged him. This was the first time I had seen Richard Serra, and he didn't fit the image I had formed. From his massive, thrusting sculpture, his difficult, theory-laden writing, his reputation as a major artist, and the name Serra itself, I had imagined a large, dark, saturnine man—a sort of intellectual-conquistador type, emanating an air of vast, heroic indifference. The actual Serra looked like someone from a small American rural community: a short man with a craggy, surly face, receding gray hair, and pale eyes rimmed by light eyelashes. He was wearing a long black shirt over black trousers and under a black leather jacket—an artist's costume—but his aura was of rough small-town America rather than of bohemia. I have seen men like him standing beside pickup trucks in wintry landscapes, locked in slow, obdurate, implacable argument; I have heard that voice, that aggrieved intonation of flat unyieldingness and threat, that conviction of being right, and that suspicion of being put upon; I know that closed yet oddly sly expression.

Sischy stood her ground, letting Serra's abuse rain down on her without flinching, and finally he stalked off, and she un-clenched her fingers. I shared a taxi with her to the Goodman party, and I at last learned what she had said to trigger the explosion. It had had to do with the "Tilted Arc" controversy, which was then at its most intense.

In 1979, Richard Serra received a $175,000 commission from the federal program called Art-in-Architecture—whereby one-half of one percent of the cost of a new building goes for public art—to create a sculpture for the circular plaza in front of the glossy and ugly forty-one-story Jacob K. Javits Federal Build-ing, on Foley Square, and in 1981 he fulfilled the commission by sinking a seventy-three-ton curved steel wall, twelve feet high and a hundred and twenty feet long, into the paving of the plaza, positioning it so that it seemed to be arrogantly turn-ing its back on the bland fountain that had previously been the plaza's focal point and in every other way declaring its contempt for the characterless place it had been chosen to embellish. "Tilted Arc," as Serra called his work, brutally dominated the plaza and confirmed the worst suspicions of the building's fed-eral employees as to the unlovable nuttiness of modern artists. The wall blocked the view of the street and bisected the plaza like a kind of Berlin Wall, and as time went on and its surface acquired a patina of rust, graffiti, and—if one witness at a public hearing held in March of 1985 was to be believed—pee, it looked less and less like a work of art to the federal workers and more and more like a forgotten piece of industrial debris that someone would eventually come and cart away. The hearing was called by William Diamond, the regional administrator of the General Services Administration, which is the Washington agency that runs Art-in-Architecture; it was a somewhat belated response to a petition submitted three years earlier by thirteen hundred federal workers in and around the Javits building, asking for the removal of the Serra piece. It has been said, and it has not been denied, that the hearing was a kind of Stalin trial—that a decision to recommend removal of the sculpture had already been made by Diamond and his four-man panel—and, indeed, after three days of testimony such a recommendation was handed down, even though the testimony had been predominantly pro-sculpture. It has also been observed that the art world, which appeared to be solidly behind Serra at the hearing, was in fact in a state of anxious division over the paradox-fraught controversy. For this was no simple case of a philistine public's hostility to an artwork it didn't understand. The public's objection was only secondarily aesthetic. The primary objection was to the way the sculpture had moved in on the plaza and turned it from a place of benign, ordinary workaday recreation into a kind of dire sculpture garden of the Age of Orwell. "The placement of the sculpture will change the space of the plaza," Serra had told an interviewer in 1980. "After the piece is created, the space will be understood primarily as a function of the sculpture." The disconcerting thought that the public might, after all, prefer eating lunch and hanging out to interacting with a piece of Minimalist sculpture evidently never crossed his mind. What troubled many people in the art world—people who ordinarily would have sprung to the defense of avant-garde art against philistine attack—was the touching *reasonableness* of the federal employees' wish to have their plaza restored to them. Although a few people at the hearing made the obligatory hysterical references to Nazi book-burning, most of the pro-Serra speakers were quiet and thoughtful, well aware of the pitfalls and traps that lurk in the vicinity of any position that puts the claims of avant-garde art ahead of those of a clerk or a secretary who wants to hold a Health Fair outside the building where he or she works.

The coeditors of *October* and a younger colleague, Douglas Crimp, were among the most delicate treaders in the pro-Serra party. Annette Michelson pointed out Serra's working-class origin and read a statement from him saying, in part, "As a kid, I worked in steel mills . . . and my work could have something to do on the personal level with the fact that my father was a factory worker all his life." (From Michelson's testimony, one would not have suspected that Serra also went to college at the University of California, to graduate school at Yale, and then to Italy on a Fulbright.) She went on to say that Serra was concerned that working people "be confronted with an art which . . . does not necessarily confirm their beliefs or impose second-class or third-rate qualities on them" and that "the working man and the office worker be presented with that same kind of challenge that the middle-class and upper-class art patrons have found so interesting."

Rosalind Krauss, accordingly, paid all the spectators present the compliment of speaking to them almost as she might have spoken to a seminar of her students at the graduate school. In her elegant lecture on, as the transcript has it, "minibalist" sculpture (the phonetic spellings that leap off the pages of the transcript—"Grancoozi," "Saint Gordons," "DeSuveral," "DeEppilo," "Modelwell," "Manwhole"—testify to the gap that exists between the ordinary *literate* American and the tiny group of people who are the advanced art public), Krauss told the group:

> The kind of vector that Tilted Arc explores is that of vision. More specifically: what it means for vision to be invested with a purpose, so that if we look out into space, it is not just a vacant stare that we cast in front of us but an act of looking that expects to find an object, a direction, a goal. This is purposiveness of vision, or, to use another term, vision's intentionality. For the spectator of Tilted Arc, this sculpture is constantly mapping a kind of projectile of the gaze that starts at one end of Federal Plaza and, like the embodiment of the concept of visual perspective, maps the path across the plaza that the spectator will take. In this sweep, which is simultaneously visual and corporeal, Tilted Arc describes the body's relation to forward motion—to the fact that if we move

ahead it is because our eyes have already reached out in order
to connect us with the place to which we intend to go.

Evidently, not everyone was up to the stern challenge of
Krauss's discourse; after she had spoken, Diamond had to ad-
monish the audience, "Please, no negative comments."

As for Douglas Crimp, who lives a few blocks from the
Federal Building, he said that although he considered "Tilted
Arc" the "most interesting and beautiful public sculpture in my
neighborhood," he had to acknowledge that "my experience
evidently differs from that of many people who live and work
in the area of 'Tilted Arc.' " However, he went on, "I believe
that this hearing is a calculated manipulation of the public.
. . . What makes me feel manipulated is that I am forced to
argue for art as against some other social function. I am asked
to line up on the side of sculpture against, say, those who are
on the side of concerts or maybe picnic tables."

What Sischy had said to Serra at the Kiefer opening—which
took place a few weeks after the hearing—was that she was *not*
lined up on his side in the "Tilted Arc" controversy. He had
begun talking to her about the case, comfortably assuming that
she was one of his supporters, and she had felt constrained to
disabuse him. "I felt I couldn't just stand there and say, 'Yeah,
yeah, it's terrible,' " she told me. "It would have been a kind
of betrayal of my job to get drawn into a conversation where
it was assumed that I was one of a gang of outraged people. I
knew that if I didn't say anything and then commissioned an
article on the thing I would feel like a hypocrite. As an editor,
I felt that it was necessary to claim not neutrality—there is no
neutrality—but that this was still an open book. So I said, 'The
whole thing is very complicated.' And there was like a minute
of surprise on Richard's part—which there shouldn't have
been—and then he flooded out with all this stuff. Calling me
a capitalist, saying that I sucked up to advertisers, telling me
that I was a fascist, because 'you believe in petition signing.' I

guess he thought I was a fascist because I found significance in the fact that thirteen hundred people had signed the petition. He said, 'You don't know what it's like to have your work on trial'—as if those of us who are trying to do something or make something weren't on trial all the time. He said, 'You don't know what it's like to be betrayed by your country. It was my government, and I believed in it. I believed in art and government. Don't you understand that I've been betrayed?' But how can he or I or any of us be so angry about a betrayal over an object? The betrayal wasn't Vietnam. How could we dare to be so naive and personal?

"Everything in my head and body says that we can't go around undoing works of art because people have signed petitions. But what do you do when people really don't want something? There's more than one liberty involved here. And I think that if we ever get to the point of believing that avant-garde art is so sacrosanct that we can't undo a decision, then it's all over. The worst thing we could do is to feel that our decisions are so sacred, and our committees of experts are so sacred, and avant-garde art is so sacred, that the very notion that something should be debated causes us to invoke all those horrifying, atrocious episodes in history."

I asked Sischy how she felt during Serra's attack.

"I felt OK," she said. "*Before* he attacked me, I felt nervous and anxious—when he thought I was part of his gang, on the side of those who were saying that this was like a bookburning. I felt like a hypocrite then. But once I'd told him where I stood, I felt OK. I felt as though I'd had a job to do and I'd done it. But he wasn't able to listen to me. It just never occurred to him that I might have something to say. He was abusive in the most extraordinary way."

"It was as if he were yelling not at you but at some fantasy figure," I said. "Who do you think you represented to him?"

"It wasn't me, in the sense that you mean, but in another sense it *was* me. You have to remember that I haven't been overly obedient to the tyranny of this particular avant-garde. I think I've been a great disappointment to people like Richard. I've turned down articles on works like Richard's. This avant-garde was the power structure that ruled the art world and was never questioned—an authoritative, massive power structure. Its rule was that painting was dead—it was just decadent picturemaking, the regressive act—and all one could do was produce heroic works of abstraction, accompanied by a great deal of terminology. There wasn't room for anything else. My interest in painting—particularly in European painting—as opposed to heroic structures was offensive to them. When I ran articles on Kiefer and Clemente and Schnabel in *Artforum*, I'm told, artists like Richard felt that I'd done something devastating. There wasn't much bridge building going on between the avant-garde and the world outside, and I think my bridge building drove—and drives—people like Richard Serra mad."

INGRID Sischy became editor of *Artforum* at the age of twenty-seven. She was offered the job by Anthony Korner, a forty-year-old English former banker, and Amy Baker Sandback, a thirty-eight-year-old art historian and artbook publisher. They had jointly bought the magazine from Charles Cowles in 1979 and had decided to replace the editor they had inherited, Joseph Masheck, who had succeeded Coplans. Masheck, an art historian, was probably the most scholarly and the least impossible of Coplans's gang of warring contributing editors, and under his editorship the magazine entered a period of calm enervation and dry academicism. With the troublemakers gone (Krauss, Michelson, Rose, Pincus-Witten, Alloway, and Kozloff had all left), *Artforum* seemed somehow to have lost its reason for being; it was as if all the air had slowly leaked out of it. At the time that Korner and Sandback were acquiring it, Sischy was finishing a fifteen-month curatorial internship under John Szarkowski in the Photography Department of the Museum of

Modern Art. Before that, she had worked as the director of an organization called Printed Matter, which had been formed by a group of artists, critics, and publishers—among them Sol LeWitt, Pat Steir, Lucy Lippard, and, fatefully, Amy Baker Sandback—to publish and distribute what they called "artists' books," as distinguished from artbooks. Artists' books were a pleasing expression of the decommodification ideology: where artbooks are about art, artists' books are themselves art of a sort—art that is mindful of its social responsibility, art that refuses to be a precious commodity, art that is cheap, multiple, and without aura. "They had a great idea, but they didn't know how to do it, and they all had other jobs," Sischy has said of the board members of Printed Matter. Sischy didn't know how to do it, either—she had had no experience running a business—but she made it her job to turn Printed Matter into a proper, self-sustaining small business, which it has remained to this day. I once watched Sischy chop tomatoes. She took a small paring knife and, in the most inefficient manner imaginable, with agonizing slowness, proceeded to fill a bowl, tiny piece by tiny piece, with chopped tomatoes. Obviously, no one had ever taught her the technique of chopping vegetables, but this had in no way deterred her from doing it in whatever way she could or prevented her from arriving at her goal. She is less afraid than anyone I have ever met of expending energy unnecessarily. While at Printed Matter, in order to convince the Internal Revenue Service of the legitimacy of the organization's claim to be nonprofit, she dragged twenty cartons of records down to the IRS office. (They were records of pitifully small transactions: in Sischy's day, the average sale at Printed Matter was five dollars; today, it is ten dollars.) At *Artforum*, she will think nothing of spending a whole night in the office working with a writer whose piece is going to press the next day, ministering to him like a kind of night nurse.

When Sischy first took up her duties at *Artforum*, a few days before Christmas, 1979, the next issue of the magazine was due at the printer's in two weeks. (She had been unable to start any sooner because of two exhibitions she was committed to do for the Modern.) "Everyone was about to go off for the Christmas holidays and probably was not very thrilled at the sight of me," Sischy recalls. "I think people were shocked at the thought of working for a young woman they had never heard of, as against an established academic man. After they were gone, I sat there looking at this pile of articles that were ready to go into the issue, and I just couldn't do it. I thought to myself, If this thing isn't going to suck you up, if it's not going to kill you, the only way you can do it—even though it will irritate everyone, because you go so slowly—is to take one step at a time and do only what you know and feel secure about. The minute you do something that isn't yourself, the minute you publish something you can't stand, the minute you answer somebody faster than you want to, it's all over. I'm positive it is. So I looked at those manuscripts, and I said to Amy and Tony, 'I don't think I can publish these things.' I said, 'If I'm coming in here, and I'm this new person, I've got to say right away who I am and do what I have to do, even if it's going to be crazy or stupid or two months late.' And Amy, quite rightly, said, 'Look, it can't be two months late. Because that's a part of what they'll know about you—that you're someone who can't get the magazine out. It's got to be on time.' So I said, 'OK. That makes sense.' We went to Amy's house for lunch and talked about what to do. The only things I knew were artists' books and projects and photographs. I didn't know how to deal with eighty manuscripts by art historians, but I did know contemporary art, and I knew artists. So I said, 'Why don't we make a whole issue of new art? And let's not get famous artists, who will do a little doodle—let's get people who have a real commitment to the printed page.' So we made lists. It was pointed out to me that we had to have a finished pile of material in two weeks. I also knew it had to be pretty good. I didn't think it had to be great. I mean, I would already have been happy if I could have figured out how to get the typesetter on the phone. I didn't even know what a typesetter was. The only thing I had was this ability to relate to people. So I called people up and told them what I wanted them to do, and they said, 'Great! When do you want it?'—thinking I would say in a month—and I said, 'In a week.' And something must have happened in these phone conversations, because every one of them came through."

When the issue—the issue of February 1980—arrived on the newsstands, it caused a great stir. It was utterly unlike any previous issue of *Artforum*. The contributors included the photographer William Wegman, the English conceptual artists Gilbert and George, the German conceptual artist Joseph Beuys, the performance artist Laurie Anderson, the editors of the radical-feminist magazine *Heresies*, and the editors of the art journal *Just Another Asshole*, and the whole thing had an impudent, aggressively unbuttoned, improvised, yet oddly poised air.

Sischy had happened to take over the editorship of *Artforum* at exactly the start of the new decade, and the appearance of an untried, unbookish, unknown, very young woman at the helm of a magazine whose three previous editors had been older men of parts, and whose atmosphere, even in its recent, least successful, manifestation, was that of a powerful and exclusive men's club (notwithstanding its women contributors, who possibly even contributed to that atmosphere), was a kind of portent of the astonishing developments in art that the eighties were to witness. In the abrupt transformation of *Artforum*'s format from a predictable high-art austerity to an unpredictable sort of underground-press grunginess/flashiness may be read the changes that were to transform the quiet and stable New York art world of the seventies—with its Minimalist and post-Minimalist stars surrounded by familiar constellations of conceptual, performance, video, and film artists—into today's unsettling, incoherent postmodern art universe. One has to remind oneself, of course, that every present is disorderly, that art history is an artifact of time, and that certain temperaments tolerate chaos better than others. Barbara Rose, for example, found the present as threatening twenty years ago as she finds it today; the following passage, from a piece by Rose entitled "How to Murder an Avant Garde," was published in *Artforum* in November 1965:

> Today, there is no "scene." Although the slick magazines have invented a fictional scene for public consumption, the experimental artist is more alone than he has been since the thirties. There are many disturbing signs: among art students, one perceives a "make-it" mentality conditioned by mass press descriptions of artistic high-life. . . . There are other bad omens. As the pace becomes more frantic and distinctions are blurred, values are equally obscured. . . . Pseudo-art writing in mass magazines confuses issues, imputes artists' motives while supposedly honoring them. . . . Having lost their common purpose on being accepted into the Establishment, and now rapidly losing their center as galleries and museums and exhibitions proliferate, is it any wonder that avant-garde artists are experiencing a crisis of identity?

The cover of Sischy's first issue was a reproduction of the cover of the first issue of an avant-garde magazine of the forties called *VVV*, which styled itself a magazine of "poetry, plastic arts, anthropology, sociology, psychology," and numbered André Breton, Max Ernst, André Masson, William Carlos Williams, Claude Lévi-Strauss, Harold Rosenberg, Arthur Cravan, and Lionel Abel among its contributors. The *VVV* cover, by Max Ernst, was an Ernstian design of mysterious figures and diagrams from some abstruse, invented science, which surrounded the three *V*'s in black, on a green background. Sischy had borrowed the original cover from David Hare, *VVV*'s former editor. Someone who had not come from John Szarkowski's Photography Department might not have been as overjoyed as

Sischy was by the cigarette burn and the spills that stained it, but she correctly gauged the surreal beauty that these ghostly traces of a past life would assume when photographed, and also the sense of quotation marks that they would help impart to the notion of a cover about a cover. There was in addition a special personal fittingness to the unretouched, worn, dog-eared appearance of Sischy's first cover. Among the people in positions of power in the cultural institutions of this city—book publishers, magazine editors, newspaper executives, museum directors and curators, theater producers—there has developed a style of dealing with staff which is noted for its informality, directness, simplicity, ordinariness. The pompous, self-important boss who puts a glacial distance between himself and his underlings, the petty tyrant who surrounds himself with cowed secretaries, is so rarely seen today that he is almost an endearing anachronism (in the upper-middle-class establishment of which we speak, that is). In this context, Sischy's way of running her magazine as "a kind of kibbutz" (in the words of the critic Donald Kuspit) is not all that remarkable. If there are some things Sischy does that editors of other magazines don't do— like running out of the office several times a day to the luncheonette across the street to get coffee and pastry for the staff—her relations with her employees are, in general, only slightly more egalitarian than the norm.

Where Sischy *is* outré is in her obsessive, almost fetishistic concern with questions of ethics. She sees moral dilemmas everywhere—and, of course, there are moral dilemmas everywhere, only most of us prefer not to see them as such and simply accept the little evasions, equivocations, and compromises that soften the fabric of social life, that grease the machinery of living and working, that make reality less of a constant struggle with ourselves and with others. Sischy, however, rejoices in the struggle; she is like someone walking through a minefield who has taken a course in mine detection. She positively enjoys staring into the abyss and drawing back just in time. Once, at Printed Matter, she received a telephone call from a museum curator who wanted to buy a copy of *The Xerox Book*, a collection of work by seven conceptual artists, published in 1968, which had been very successful and had become something of a collector's item. "Our last copy had just been ordered by somebody," Sischy told me. "So I said to the curator, 'Sorry, it's gone.' And the curator said, 'Ingrid, we'll give you a lot of money for a copy.' We were really in deep financial trouble then, and the museum was talking, I think, a minimum of a thousand dollars. But I thought, How dare they? And I told them I had just sold it for twenty-five dollars, first come, first served, and hung up."

In the presence of such shining rectitude, one cannot—worm that one is—but feel a little resentful. One can even, if one pursues this cynical train of thought far enough, summon up a bit of sympathy for Richard Serra. Who does she think she is? Why does she always have to behave better than everyone else? There are times when the heroines of Henry James's novels provoke just such coarse thoughts—moments when the thread of sympathetic attention snaps and we fretfully wonder why these girls have always to be so ridiculously fine. But if Sischy's moral imagination is of a feverishness to invoke the spirits of Fleda Vetch and Milly Theale, her atmosphere is very different from that surrounding those tense, exquisite intelligences. She has an incongruous, almost Mediterranean easiness and dailiness. The momentary irritation one feels with her when one believes she is riding her ethical hobbyhorse too hard (I remember once standing with her outside an Italian airport sulkily watching everyone else get a taxi while we, at her insistence, honorably waited our turn behind a pair of utterly baffled Japanese) is swept away by the disarming agreeableness of her company. Her capacity for enjoyment is movingly large. She is a kind of reverse Jewish princess: she goes through life gratefully accepting the pleasures and amenities that come her way, and if they are not the particular pleasures and amenities she ordered—well, so much the better. Her relationship to the world of consumer objects is almost bizarrely attenuated. (If a person could be likened to a work of decommodified art, Sischy would be that person.) She has no credit cards, no charge accounts, no savings account (until last year, she had no checking account), no car, no driver's license; she doesn't even have a handbag, and stuffs her money and the tiny scraps of paper that serve her as an address book into a bulging wallet, which she awkwardly carries in her hand, like a kid on the way to a show. She uses no makeup and wears the plainest of clothes: the knit pants and shirt are her uniform. She has no possessions to speak of—she has never bought a painting, a sculpture, a photograph, a decorative object, or a piece of furniture or jewelry. All her belongings (mostly books and papers) fit into a trunk that she brought to the house of the woman she lives with when she moved in four years ago, and that she has yet to unpack.

The not yet unpacked trunk is a fitting metaphor for Sischy. As a child, she was twice uprooted—first from South Africa, at the age of nine, and then from Scotland, at the age of fifteen. She was born in 1952 in Johannesburg, the youngest of three children (she has two brothers, one a doctor and the other a lawyer) of a Jewish professional family. Her father, Benjamin Sischy, is a physician, and her mother, Claire Sischy, is a retired speech therapist. The family emigrated to Edinburgh in 1961, after the Sharpeville massacre, and again in 1967, to Rochester, New York, where Dr. Sischy took a position in oncological research at Highland Hospital. In Edinburgh, Ingrid went to a famous private school for girls, George Watson's Ladies' College; in Rochester, she went to public high school; and in 1973, she graduated from Sarah Lawrence College. In all three places, she became a leader very quickly and easily. "My ability to adjust got to be a family joke: we'd move to a new country, and within six months—at most, a year—I'd be president of the class, and eventually president of the school," she told me almost ruefully.

Sischy speaks of her parents with affection and approval bordering on reverence, and she once told me how, as a child of such a socially conscious family, she was able to reconcile herself to the apparently socially useless work that she does now. "For my parents, art was something that you did after the day's work," she said. "I grew up with the assumption that I would go into a profession like theirs—one that did some social good every day. When I took this job, I realized that the only way for me to do it was as if I were going to medical school. I worked sixteen hours a day, the way I saw my father work, and the way I saw my brother work when he was a resident, and I still work that way. I'm still serving my residency." She went on, "I used to have the fantasy that I would do this work for a few years and then one day I'd stop and dedicate the rest of my life to South Africa. But more and more I have come to understand that to edit an art magazine today is to participate in all of today's social, economic, and political discourses. Nowhere was this clearer to me than in the primitivism show."

THOMAS McEvilley's attack, in the November 1984 issue of *Artforum*, on the Museum of Modern Art's major exhibition " 'Primitivism' in 20th Century Art: Affinity of the Tribal and the Modern" made an extraordinary impression on the art world. There was something about the piece that was instantly recognized as more deeply threatening to the status quo than it is usual for a critique of a museum show to be—and not least aware of the threat was William Rubin, the director of the show, and also the director of the museum's Department of Painting and Sculpture. The article had a sort of dangerous luster, and this quality was also present in the two replies that McEvilley, a classicist turned art historian and critic, wrote to the letters that Rubin felt impelled to address to the editor of *Artforum*. (Kirk Varnedoe, codirector of the exhibition, joined the fray for the first round of correspondence and prudently dropped out for the second.) McEvilley's article was like the knocking on the door dreaded by Ibsen's master builder—the sound of the younger generation coming to crush the older one—and drew its power as much from the urgency of its Oedipal subtext as from the cogency of its manifest argument. Other reviews just as critical and as well argued as McEvilley's—Arthur Danto's devastating one in the *Nation*, for example—didn't get under Rubin's skin as McEvilley's did. (With one exception: an earlier piece, by Michael Peppiatt, published in *Connaissance des Arts*, caused Rubin to threaten to sue the magazine—it remained calm—when it refused to publish his long riposte, which was accompanied by fourteen color illustrations.) What also may have contributed—indeed, must have contributed—to the specially charged atmosphere of the McEvilley article was the intense pressure under which it was produced. It was written, revised, and prepared for publication in just eleven days. Sischy told me how this had come about. She and McEvilley had gone to the opening of the primitivism show together, with the understanding that he would write about it if he felt moved to do so after seeing it. "As I walked through the show, I had a really creepy feeling that here, yet again, was a case of two objects looking the same but not meaning the same," Sischy told me. "As I went along, I began to feel that yet again the Other was being used to service us. Yet again. Practically a thesis had been written on the label below a Brancusi work, but it was enough to say of the primitive sculpture beside it, 'From North Africa.' All the research had gone into the Brancusi, while the other thing was being used once again simply for affirmation of our values. A supposed honor was being bestowed on primitive work—the honor of saying, 'Hey! It's as good as art! We'll even call it art.' But now we know that a different set of questions needs to be asked about how we assimilate another culture. Tom had the same feelings—maybe even stronger. So we went to the Plaza and had about five drinks, and after the drinks Tom said, 'Look, can we get the review into the next issue?' and I said, 'Tom, the issue is all designed. It's going to the printer in four days.' And he said, 'Well, what do you think?' and I said, 'It would be incredible to come out with the piece while the show is still so new. Let me think about it.' And I had another drink and said, 'I've thought about it.' I went to the office the next day and asked Amy and Tony whether it would be possible to open up the magazine and add an article a week late, which is an insane thing to do. But Tony and Amy agreed that in this case it would be a great thing to do. So Tom wrote the piece in four days, and then we sat in my office for seven days and seven nights working on it."

The article, entitled "Doctor Lawyer Indian Chief: ' "Primitivism" in 20th Century Art' at the Museum of Modern Art in 1984," not only bore down heavily on the ethnocentricity of which Sischy (among others) was so painfully conscious ("This exhibition shows Western egotism still as unbridled as in the centuries of colonialism and souvenirism") but denied that it was any longer interesting to see modernist paintings and sculptures juxtaposed with tribal objects to which they bear formal resemblances. That sort of thing, McEvilley said, was all very well in 1938, when Robert Goldwater published his classic text *Primitivism in Modern Painting*, but today such a way of thinking is a pitiful anachronism. Writing of MoMA as "the temple of formalist Modernism," McEvilley characterized the primitivism show as a sort of last-ditch stand by the museum against the incursions of advanced thought:

Whereas the esthetics of [formalist Modernism] had been seen as higher criteria by which other styles were to be judged, now, in quite respectable quarters, they began to appear as just another style. For a while, like Pre-Raphaelitism or the Ashcan School, they had served certain needs and exercised hegemony; those needs passing, their hegemony was passing also. But the collection of the Museum of Modern Art is predominantly based on the idea that formalist Modernism will never pass, will never lose its self-validating power. Not a relative, conditioned thing, subject to transient causes and effects, it is to be above the web of natural and cultural change; this is its supposed essence. After several years of sustained attack, such a credo needs a defender and a new defense. How brilliant to attempt to revalidate classical Modernist esthetics by stepping outside their usual realm of discourse and bringing to bear upon them a vast, foreign sector of the world. By demonstrating that the "innocent" creativity of primitives naturally expresses a Modernist esthetic feeling, one may seem to have demonstrated once again that Modernism itself is both innocent and universal.

Rubin, he went on to say, made "highly inappropriate claims about the intentions of tribal cultures without letting them have their say, except through the mute presence of their unexplained religious objects, which are misleadingly presented as art objects." And he continued:

In their native contexts these objects were invested with feelings of awe and dread, not of esthetic ennoblement. They were seen usually in motion, at night, in closed dark spaces, by flickering torchlight. Their viewers were under the influence of ritual, communal identification feelings, and often alcohol or drugs; above all, they were activated by the presence within or among the objects themselves of the shaman, acting out the usually terrifying power represented by the mask or icon. What was at stake for the viewer was not esthetic appreciation but loss of self in identification with and support of the shamanic performance. The Modernist works in the show serve completely different functions, and were made to be perceived from a completely different stance. If you or I were a native tribal artisan or spectator walking through the halls of MoMA, we would see an entirely different show from the one we see as 20th-century New Yorkers. We would see primarily not form but content, and not art but religion or magic.

The gauntlet flung down by McEvilley was picked up by Rubin in a long reply that *Artforum* published in its issue of February 1985, together with a shorter reply from Varnedoe. Rubin started out by complimenting McEvilley for being "fair-minded" and for maintaining "a high level of discourse" but quickly went on to say that "notwithstanding his evidently good intentions, his review is interwoven with sufficient misconceptions, internal inconsistencies, and simple errors of fact that—given its seriousness—it should not go unchallenged." The chief factual error of which Rubin accused McEvilley—an accusation that developed into one of the most excruciatingly particularized squabbles about a matter of doubtful significance ever published—concerned the number of objects in a pair of vitrines at the Centre Pompidou, in Paris. McEvilley, to illustrate his dismissal of the idea of the primitivism show as "not new or startling in the least," cited (among other examples) an exhibition of "about one hundred tribal objects" from the Musée de l'Homme which the Centre Pompidou had placed in meaningful proximity to its modern-art collection shortly after it opened, in 1977, and left up for about five years. Rubin challenged the figure one hundred. He said that "a rapid check reveals that . . . the two vitrines at the Centre Pompidou together never contained more than twenty or so objects." I will spare the readers of this essay what the readers of *Artforum* had to endure in order to finally learn that neither contestant's figure was strictly accurate: in one of the sixteen footnotes that Rubin appended to his second reply, he confessed that according to a list he had just received from the Musée de l'Homme there had been as many as fifty-two objects in the vitrines. As one of the readers who did not fall by the wayside in the battle of the vitrines, I can report that, despite my boredom with the particulars of the debate, I was kept going by the passionate intensity with which it was conducted. Clearly, each man had more at stake than being right or wrong about a number. The number had become a kind of objective correlative for the anxiety each man felt about his position. Rubin frankly told me later, "McEvilley was at great pains to show that the exhibition was old hat, and since I had spent five years and a pile of money on it, I took it ill. Some of our trustees are readers of *Artforum*. I didn't want them to think that I had gone to all this trouble and expense just to do a rerun of something that had already been done." McEvilley, for his part, felt that his position as challenger of the establishment was threatened by the insinuation that he couldn't get his facts straight, and he displayed a kind of young man's anger over being corrected by an elder. (Actually, McEvilley isn't so young—he is forty-seven, to Rubin's fifty-nine—but in the psychodrama of his encounter with Rubin he fell easily into the role of the impetuous young Jack the Giant Killer, just as Rubin, by position and temperament, was a natural for the role of the giant.)

In his reply to Rubin and Varnedoe, McEvilley adopted a provocatively folksy tone. "I'm the one who barked these grouchy bears out of the woods, so I guess I have to listen to their howling and gnashing of teeth," he wrote. "In a sense, it's a chance in a lifetime. We rarely see these bears out in the open—especially the big one." McEvilley quickly dispatched the little bear, as he maddeningly called Varnedoe:

> The whole-cloth 19th-centuryism of Varnedoe's thought is revealed in a display of comedic ignorance. He quotes me as using the term "intentionalities" and notes parenthetically that this is "a word [McEvilley] favors as a substitute for the simpler 'intentions.' " He evidently doesn't recognize that "intentionality" is a technical term in the philosophy of Edmund Husserl and in the whole phenomenological movement.

Rubin, in his second letter, saw an opportunity to avenge Varnedoe's honor, and he gleefully pounced on it:

> I can only envy McEvilley's authority in art history, anthropology, linguistics, phenomenology, and literary theory, and sympathize with his need to mock the comedic ignorance

of those less accomplished than he. Alas, as but a poor art historian, I can only hope that after a professional lifetime in this field I know something about *it*, at least. . . . McEvilley asks us to consider that "the charioteer of Delphi, ca. 470 B.C., for example, was seen totally [*sic*] differently in classical Greece from the way we see him now. He was not alone in that noble, self-sufficient serenity of transcendental, angelic whiteness that we see." Perhaps I should take it less amiss to find my own ideas being transformed beyond recognition by McEvilley when I discover that he can also somehow transform this familiar monument of introductory art history from a bronze into a marble.

I am afraid that almost all of McEvilley's art-historical assertions come from the same quarry as the marble charioteer.

But Rubin's triumph was short-lived. McEvilley retorted:

Hibernation can be a productive method—one can go into solitude and come back with understanding—or it can cloud the mind with dreams of scrambled facts, of fabricated evidence and marble charioteers. "The charioteer of Delphi," I wrote, "ca. 470 B.C., for example, was seen totally differently in classical Greece from the way we now see him. He was not alone in that noble, self-sufficient serenity of transcendental, angelic whiteness that we see." The word "marble" is Rubin's, not mine, and comes up in his claim that I misreported the classical bronze as a marble work—after which he exercises his wit against me by referring to "the marble charioteer." Rubin never deals with the question of why I brought the charioteer up in the first place. My point was about the manipulation of the object through its context; we now see the work alone on a pedestal in a white room in the Delphi archaeological museum, in the typical kind of installation with which we relate to works from other cultures or times by isolating them so that they are available to receive our projections. The charioteer is decontextualized in this artificial white atmosphere and made meaningless in terms of his native context, function, and intention. I drew the analogy in my initial article as a criticism of the installation of the primitive works at MoMA, where, similarly, fragments of complex pieces were isolated in such a way as to render them meaningless in their own terms, as if indeed they had no terms of their own. Rubin chose to ignore this issue, as well as others that related to the example of the charioteer, and instead to argue a point of physical detail that would not have affected the argument in any way even if he had gotten it right.

If Rubin did himself no good by engaging in these scholastic skirmishes, his greatest disservice to himself was his writing to *Artforum* at all, thus giving McEvilley a second, and then a third, chance to score off the primitivism show. McEvilley's original critique was probably not as airtight as it might have been if he had had more than four days in which to write it. Now Rubin had afforded him more time, and perhaps even more motivation, to shine. Taking his argument against a universal aesthetic to another level, McEvilley listed three periods in the history of the West's relationship to tribal art. In the first period, primitive objects were "denied the status of art, as if it was an honor that they did not deserve." In the second, primitive objects were thought "formally and intellectually 'good enough' to be called art." And in the third, which is the present period, "one may begin to look at the tribal objects from the point of view of their own culture and to realize that, whatever they are, they fall in between the categories on our grid." McEvilley chastised Rubin for being stuck in the second period. He accused him of presenting "a value system that had been firmly in place for sixty years as if it were a terrific new discovery," and of treating the primitive objects in the show "as if they had nothing to do with any living societies except ours, as if they were pretty objects and no more, there for us to do with as we like." In his first letter, Rubin complained that

McEvilley had missed the point of the show, which was to study tribal works from the point of view of the pioneer modernists. "Of course the tribal objects in our show are decontextualized," Rubin snapped, adding, "In fact, they are more than that; they are *recontextualized*, within the framework of Western art and culture. *And that is what our particular story is all about.* McEvilley simply refuses to accept the fact that our story is not about 'the Other,' but about ourselves." But McEvilley stubbornly insisted that "to really be about *us*, the show would have to be about the evolution in our relationship to the Other." He wrote:

> We no longer live in a separate world. Our tribal view of art history as primarily or exclusively European or Eurocentric will become increasingly harmful as it cuts us off from the emerging Third World and isolates us from the global culture which already is in its early stages. We must have values that can include the rest of the world when the moment comes—and the moment is upon us. Civilization transcends geography, and if history holds one person in this global village, it holds another. In fact, if one of us is privileged over the other in art-historical terms it is the so-called primitive object-makers, through whose legacy we got our last big ride outside our own point of view, and called it Modern art.

A FEW months after the publication of the final round of the McEvilley-Rubin exchange, I pay a call on Rubin at his office in the Museum of Modern Art. In his embodiment of all the clichés about men in positions of power, Rubin is an almost allegorical figure. To make an appointment with him requires prolonged conversation with a secretary ("Mr. Rubin has asked me to get as much information about his calls as possible, so that he may judge the urgency of returning them"), and to enter his office is to immediately experience a feeling of diminishment, in the same strange way that entering a Gothic cathedral gives one a feeling of exaltation. Rubin is extremely well dressed and well groomed, with a dark, assertive, attractive face; he sits behind an enormous, immaculate desk in a large white room that commands a spectacular view of the museum's sculpture garden and a panorama of New York buildings, and is fitted out with spare, expensive modern furniture, abstract paintings, and an African sculpture. In spite of the dossier of information I have left with the secretary, he does not know who I am and why I have come. Once my identity and purpose have been reestablished, I ask him the two questions I have come to ask: Was he satisfied with the treatment he received from *Artforum*, and was he satisfied with his performance in his two letters to the editor?

Rubin replies yes to both questions. "The people at *Artforum* were at great pains to be fair, though I think they were reluctant when we said we wanted to write a second letter," he says. "Ingrid would have liked to say no, but we made certain points about misstatements, and then she realized that the matter couldn't just be left there. I feel very secure in thinking that students and other people reading this exchange ten years from now are going to come down on our side. If I didn't feel that way, I would have to accept criticism that would put five years of work into question. Not that there aren't things in my exhibition which I wouldn't have done differently. Sure there are. And not that I'm saying that all the criticisms of the exhibition were wrong. I think there was good criticism even in McEvilley's article. But McEvilley wanted a different exhibition altogether. Someone in the department here said to me, 'McEvilley would have liked to be invited to do the exhibition.' That's the sort of thing you run into in this work. Since we invited people from all over to participate in the exhibition, to write articles for the catalogue, McEvilley may have felt that the museum overlooked him. There may have been personal offense taken. Frankly, Kirk and I found McEvilley's replies to the letters much worse than his original article. We deeply felt the absence of *politesse* in the thing about the bears."

A few days after this meeting, to my surprise, Rubin telephones me and says he would like to speak to me again. Evidently under some compulsion to do everything twice, he says that he has had some further thoughts over the weekend about the McEvilley exchange and wishes to share them with me. When I arrive in his office, he hands me a three-by-five file card on which the following list has been typed:

> Bears
> Shoddy arguers
> Poverty of intellect
> 19th-century
> minds
> Childish tactics
> Arrogance
> Cheapest  .   .   .
> tactics

Rubin has spent the weekend reviewing his exchanges with McEvilley and evidently no longer feels satisfied with himself. He tells me he feels that McEvilley has bested him through "rhetorical devices," examples of which he has typed out on the card. "McEvilley went down claiming that he never did or said a single thing that was wrong," Rubin says. "At least I admitted that I was wrong about the number of objects in the vitrines, though I don't think I was as wrong as McEvilley believes. The point is, these rhetorical devices that he has obviously studied somewhere are for winning arguments, not for getting to the truth. I never studied rhetoric, so I'm disadvantaged to that extent. It may be that McEvilley is emotionally so offended by the very conception of the show that he can't see straight. And I think it kind of shocked him, and hurt him, that he was being questioned at all. The tone of his reaction seems to me to contain not a little anger at being called on to defend himself. His interest only in winning an argument is how I explain his unwillingness to see if there is a common ground. I'm only human. If someone uses invective on me, and slithery techniques to prove he's always right, I'm going to come straight back—I'm not going to try and find common ground either. But I think there *is* common ground. I don't think McEvilley really believes half these extreme things he says."

Like a teacher handing out reading material to a class, Rubin hands me a pack of Xeroxes he has made of McEvilley's article, of his letters and Varnedoe's, of McEvilley's replies to them, of various other reviews of the primitivism show, and of an exchange in *Artforum* in 1967 between him and Harold Rosenberg over a piece Rubin wrote on Jackson Pollock, which McEvilley cited in his second reply. Referring to a set of Xeroxes of his own, which I notice are extensively underlined, Rubin proceeds, like one of Borges's obsessed men, to go over the entire exchange, point by point. He continues this rite of self-justification for the next two hours, touching yet again on the dread vitrines, and also on the other exhibition that McEvilley cited—that of the Menil Collection in the Grand Palais in 1984. "McEvilley dismisses our show as old hat because it was done before, in the Menil show," he tells me. "Then I write in to say that in the Menil show there were only two juxtaposed examples of primitive art and modern art, and that all the rest of the tribal art was shown separately, in its own area. And how does McEvilley respond to this? He responds by *blinding the reader*, in effect: 'The fact that Rubin can neither growl away nor live with is that the tribal objects were not shown *entirely* in their own separate area,' he writes. By the time you get to this, your head is dizzy. You would have to be much more clearheaded than anyone is likely to be at this point to see that what he's saying is just ridiculous. It's so tricky and slimy."

The telephone rings, and the secretary announces Rubin's next appointment. Rubin looks at his watch and says to me,

"I'll just race through this." Then, in a moment of apparent uncertainty, he lets the pack of Xeroxes fall from his hand. He takes off his glasses, rubs his eyes, and seems to be hovering on the edge of seeing the absurdity and futility of the proceedings. Then he puts his glasses back on and resolutely picks up the Xeroxes.

ONE afternoon in April 1985, I deliberately arrive late at the Upper West Side apartment of the artist Lucas Samaras, where I am meeting Sischy and Amy Baker Sandback, the president of *Artforum*. I want to make sure that I am not the first to arrive: I have never met Samaras, but his mysterious, aggressive work—menacing black boxes lined with pins, strange objects made of bright-colored yarns, fantastic pieces of painted furniture, photographs of his own leering face and contorted naked body—though it has a sort of creepy fascination, has made me instinctively feel that this is not a man I want to be alone with. I am late, but the others are even later, and I am met at the door by a tall, thin, dour man in his forties with a graying beard, who ushers me into the apartment with a resigned air and motions for me to sit on a sofa whose cushion is a tangle of colored yarns encased in a plastic cover. The place is like an enchanter's workshop, filled with rolls of sparkling metallic fabrics, collections of broken wineglasses, jars of rhinestones, long sticks to which plastic brides and grooms are affixed, sinister clay figures, a wall of necklaces, a weirdly shaped handmade table and chairs, all bearing the Samaras signature. But the place is also like one of those shabby, harshly orderly apartments inhabited by old women from Balkan countries; it lacks only the embroidered cloths and the religious kitsch to complete its authoritative dissociation from middle-class taste and fashion. When Samaras tells me that he is from Macedonia—he came here as a boy of eleven—I think, Of course, where else? He stares at me expressionlessly but not unkindly, and we fall into talk. I almost immediately realize that the dire persona that emerges from his work and the actual person who is Lucas Samaras bear the sort of relationship to each other that a lion bears to a house cat. Where the work glints with menace, irony, and disdain, the man is merely acerbic, willful, and a little needling. He says of Sischy that she is unique among editors he has known. "All the others are interested in power—they play power games. If they are women, they use their femininity to gain power. Ingrid is not interested in power."

Sischy and Sandback arrive with a vague, unrepentant story about a distrait taxi driver. Sandback is in her forties—a calm, soft-spoken, somewhat mysterious woman, with the air of a natural consoler about her, though at present she herself is in need of consolation, because of a new, profoundly regretted punk haircut. Both women are very animated with Samaras. I am struck by the change in Sischy's demeanor—how much lighter she is here. With me, she has always been rather serious and subdued. Now there is a lot of banter and laughter and kidding. The purpose of the visit is to make a selection from among Samaras's new acrylic paintings for an eight-page spread in the Summer issue of *Artforum*. The new paintings are a large collective portrait of the art world—a taxonomy of the dealers, curators, collectors, critics, artists, artists' wives, and failed artists who inhabit it. The paintings are all on thirty-six-by-twenty-four-inch canvas boards, and all are horribly grinning skulls. The groups are distinguished from one another largely by color and style of brush strokes, so that each is unpleasant in a slightly different way. The dealer skulls, for example, are done in slashing, sketchy, bright colors on a black background, the critics are done in a bleary gray-and-white, and the collectors are in thick, vividly colored strokes and have been given *two* mouths. During the two hours it takes to make the selection and agree on how to lay out the spread, Samaras serves tea and coffee and offers expensive chocolates; when Sischy says no to the chocolates because she is on a diet, he brings out three grapefruits, deftly peels them, cuts them into artful slices, and serves them in bowls with spoons, all with the sad, ironic air of one doing an avant-garde performance piece that may be beyond the grasp of the audience. The joshing and kidding continue as Samaras, Sischy, and Sandback regard the paintings that Samaras has spread out, though there is a tension beneath the surface. Sischy and Sandback will do everything to please the artist, up to a point, and Samaras, for whom it is extremely advantageous to be shown in *Artforum*, knows he must gauge where that point is and not push beyond it. However, as the afternoon wears on, the sense of cautious negotiation gives way to a rhythm of work, to a tide of interest in the task at hand, into which all three are drawn—and into which even I, who have no vested interest in the project whatever and was initially rather repelled by the paintings, now find myself drawn.

At Samaras's, Sischy behaves as if she had all the time in the world to spend on the project, but in fact she is almost calamitously behind schedule. There are only eight days left before the Summer issue of the magazine goes to the printer, and some of the writing that is going to appear in it has yet to be committed to paper. Thomas McEvilley has not yet finished a piece on Conceptual art, and Rene Ricard, a poet and a regular contributor, is still working on an article about an unknown figurative painter named Bill Rice, whose chief subject is homosexual black men. The unconventional art criticism of Ricard has been the cause of much of the grumbling among the older art-world intelligentsia about the new *Artforum*'s lack of seriousness. Here is an example of it, from Ricard's first contribution to the magazine—entitled "Not About Julian Schnabel"—in the Summer 1981 issue:

> When I wrote about Julian Schnabel's last show at the Mary Boone Gallery for *Art in America*, I became so embroiled in a distasteful episode with the gallery concerning my request for an exclusive on the picture I wanted to use as an illustration

that I vowed never to cover any painter represented by that gallery. I ignored Stephen Mueller's last show there and I really wanted to write about it. Now Julian has ascended to Leo Castelli—though he's splitting the bill with Boone—and I can leave personal feelings out of the picture, where they belong. Anyway, my responsibility is not to the painter, the dealer, or myself; it is to the pictures.

Nor was this the only treachery perpetrated by a dealer. I wanted to know how much a drawing Brice Marden had given me was worth. That very day, the person I'd asked (not at his current gallery) told Brice's best friend that I was selling his drawing. Next time I saw Brice the first thing he said was, "I hear you're selling my drawing!" As a point of fact I'd never part with it. I just wanted to know how much it was worth. For someone of my generation the possession of a Marden drawing is a big thing. I call it my de Kooning, and I *have* a de Kooning.


Ricard is thirty-nine years old, has published a book of poems that inevitably bring the verse of Frank O'Hara to mind in their emotional immediacy (though their descriptions of very rough homosexual sex are beyond anything O'Hara dared or cared to render), and at an early age was a member of Andy Warhol's Factory. He lives in a very bad, brutish tenement on East Twelfth Street, in an apartment that he keeps in a condition of aggressive squalor and disorder. He has no telephone, and it is unclear what he does to support himself. It is not his writing. Sischy has spoken to me about the gross financial inequalities of today's art world between the artists who have made it and the ones who haven't. "As for those of us who work in a reporting or critical way, our lives are a sort of joke in comparison to what we're dealing with," she added. "I'm lucky. I happen to live with someone who owns her own house. I'm in comfortable circumstances. But I know that most of our writers have nothing, and when I took this job I made it clear that I hoped to reach a point where writing about art would be taken seriously enough so that maybe we could provide some income for the writer. Our fee is now up to eight hundred dollars for a piece—and a writer may work for a year or more to earn it. So whenever I'm out with a writer the least I can do is make sure that there's a decent meal. It's crazy, but that's the level it's on."

For the past three days, Sischy has been going to Ricard's place in the evenings to work with him on his piece about Bill Rice, staying until two or three in the morning and somehow getting it out of him. On the day it is finished, I join her and Ricard for dinner at an East Village restaurant called Evelyne's. Ricard has brought along a friend named George Condo, an agreeable and short young artist, who is wearing a white shirt and a red crew-neck sweater under a dark suit that is two or three sizes too big for him, to indicate that he is not an Ivy League college student but an artist. Condo does luridly expressionistic paintings of heads on long necks, which are enjoying a vogue in Europe. Ricard is dressed in a gray sweatshirt over jeans; he is thin and wiry, his brow is deeply lined, his eyes are frightened, and his mouth is petulant. His voice is high-pitched, and in it there is spite, self-pity, self-parody, seduction, false innocence, anxiety. As he talks, he gesticulates wildly and reaches out to touch and stroke you. He dominates the conversation, but, unlike most people who are nakedly interested in themselves, he is also aware of what is going on with others, though in a specialized way. Certain things capture his interest: he comments on people's looks and clothes and mannerisms. When a woman at the next table takes out a compact and puts on lipstick, he says, "That's my favorite gesture in the world. I love it. It's so twenties. Isn't it the twenties?" A beautiful and elegant young woman wearing a pristine white linen suit, whom Ricard knows (and, bafflingly, introduces as "someone I was engaged to eight years ago"), joins our table, as does, when he arrives, the good-looking man—a curator of a small museum in Colorado—she has been waiting for at the bar. After introductions are made, the curator asks Sischy what she does. She replies, "I work in the editorial department of *Artforum* magazine." After the curator and the young woman have left for the Danceteria discothèque, Ricard turns exasperatedly on Sischy and says, "Why did you say that to him?" He does a mincing parody of Sischy saying "I work in the editorial department of *Artforum* magazine," and goes on, "Why didn't you say, 'I am Ingrid Sischy, *the editor of Artforum* magazine. I'm this big deal. I'm this powerful person. I'm the whole thing'? Telling him 'I work in the editorial department'! Come *on!*" Sischy quietly glares at Ricard, like the older sister of a child who is doing something embarrassing.

The dinner arrives, and Ricard eats it hungrily. He tells, as if for the first time, the story he told in "Not About Julian Schnabel" concerning the "exclusive" he lost at the hands of Mary Boone. He says that everyone he has ever written about has become a millionaire. "That's why everybody wants a Rene Ricard write-up," he explains. "It's like magic." Sischy looks pained. Condo politely suppresses a yawn. Ricard goes on to tell about an auction in New Jersey the previous day where two Picabias went for two hundred and three hundred dollars, respectively. "You made me miss that auction," he says to Sischy accusingly, and then, to me, "She made me stay here and work on my piece." I ask Sischy if it is true about the Picabias. She replies, "Whatever Rene says is true." But I remember a poem of his about malevolence—a litany of such acts of bad faith as

> *I've advised people to get haircuts that made them*
> *Look a mess, and poked fun behind their backs.*
> *I've convinced writers to destroy their best work.*
> *I've thrown people out of their own apartments*
> *I've sublet, and never paid the rent.*
> *I've conned young girls into giving me heirlooms to pawn.*

*I tease people who stutter. I like to talk dirty in front*
*Of old women.*
*I've talked nouveau-riches people into letting me throw*
*A party and then invited derelicts into their home,*
*Leaving it in shambles.*

The last line is "I made a lot of this up, but a lot of it is true."

During coffee, the conversation turns to Henry James, because Ricard has paraphrased a line from *The Portrait of a Lady* in the Bill Rice piece but cannot remember where in the novel it appears. Nor does he care. But Sischy is adamant about finding the line, so the paraphrase can be checked, and though I don't recognize the allusion, I offer to look for it in my copy of the novel at home. Condo politely yawns again. Ricard says that he admires James but feels constrained to add, "*I would never write fiction. It's lying.*" Sischy listens but does not join in the conversation. She once told me that she wasn't bookish. "Everyone I've ever been close to and loved and lived with has been a person who reads all the time," she said. "It would be very nice if I could say the same about myself. But the truth is I've never in my life been a reader." Among the things that she had not read, she astonishingly confessed, was the old *Artforum* itself. Until she became editor, seven years ago, she would buy the magazine but not read it. "Even now, if I wasn't forced to edit them I probably wouldn't read some of the things we publish," she said. This confession followed a confession of my own about finding much of the magazine unreadable. Sischy was sympathetic. "It's always been a problem, this troublesome writing we print," she said. "The bigger question is: How does one write about art? That's what the magazine has been struggling with—probably quite disastrously, in the end—for twenty-two years. How does one write about something that is basically mute? Any cliché about *Artforum* is always about its problem with writing. That is probably why I was brought in as editor—because I found much of *Artforum* unreadable myself. I never used to read the magazine, and when I look back I must have been mad to take on the job of editing this thing I couldn't read. It was like a penance for all those years of not reading it. And I still have the problem, which may be why the magazine is so damn nervous inside itself. That's why you see so many different kinds of writing in it. An object lesson I keep before me all the time is that of my mother, who picks up *Artforum*, who is completely brilliant, sophisticated, and complex, who wants to understand—and then *closes* it."

THERE is one contributor to the Summer issue about whom Sischy can feel easy, whose article will come in exactly on time, will not require all-night editing, and will never be anything less than a piece of workmanlike prose. This is Carter Ratcliff, who, like Ricard, is identified as a poet at the end of his articles in *Artforum* but is as far from the flamboyant Ricard as one can get. Ratcliff is cool, detached, impassive, reserved, rational, elliptical, grudgingly kind, pale—a sort of Alan Ladd of art criticism. He has written about art for over fifteen years, has published five book-length critical studies, five monographs, and two books of verse, and has taught modern art and criticism at Pratt, the School of Visual Arts, and Hunter. He is forty-five years old. His loft, on Beaver Street, is as clear and clean and uncluttered as the man. When I visit it, a few days after the dinner with Ricard, it has the appearance of a place that someone has just moved into and hasn't furnished yet, but Ratcliff mentions that he and his wife have lived there for a year. There is a new, highly polished light wood floor, two off-white sofas facing each other across a pale wood coffee table, a dining table and chairs at a remove, and nothing else. Ratcliff's study, filled with books and papers, looks more inhabited. Ratcliff offers no refreshment, and we sit and talk, facing each other on the two sofas.

Ratcliff writes for *Art in America* as well as for *Artforum*, and

I ask him whether there is any difference in the way he writes for each. He says, "Yes. My tone for *Artforum* is less formal. At *Art in America*, there is an ideal of responsible, properly organized, moderately political writing with a moderate tone —a kind of standard essay style that has survived into the present and that Ingrid simply isn't interested in. I find it annoying sometimes, but its influence isn't all that bad. I think, for example, that the Frank Stella piece I wrote for *Art in America* was far more convincing than the piece I did on Andy Warhol for *Artforum*, because I took more care to argue points in the Stella piece, whereas in the Warhol piece I felt freer to simply make assertions, or argue from an attitude, or have prejudices—as opposed to substantiating everything in a responsible manner. I'm not sure that in a collection of my pieces one could tell which article was written for which magazine. Maybe one could. But when I'm writing for *Artforum* I feel free to write in a way that is more direct and more responsible to what I feel and less responsible to some standard of rationality."

I ask, "Does this sense of permission to write more freely and less responsibly come from Ingrid directly, or do you get it from reading people like Ricard in the magazine and feeling, Well, if they can write like that so can I?"

"Both are true," Ratcliff says. "Just from reading the magazine, one gets the sense that Ingrid is encouraging individual voices. But, also, when Ingrid is talking over a project with you, or going over a text, often what she wants you to leave out is art-historical substantiation of a point, or an extended description. I'm fascinated by that absurdity—trying to describe what a painting is like. Both the description of art and the invocation of historical evidence are a kind of striving for proof: not direct proof but an attempt to impart an air of scientific rationality to one's writing—you know, all the apparatus of sounding as though you knew what you were talking about. But Ingrid is not interested in that. She's interested in an assertion of a point of view and in a tone of voice and in one's feeling about things. When we were going over the Warhol piece, I remember her saying it was too smooth. She was afraid that people wouldn't get the point. What she wanted to do in the editing was to leave things out and have it be a little choppier—to sort of wake up the reader, to have him make more leaps. I think she sees art writing as something declamatory and gestural; her ideal is not that of the well-wrought essay. She has a feeling that art-world readers need to be jolted, that they're not literary readers. I don't think she sees this as a fault on the part of art-world readers or writers. It's just that that's the way it is—it's basically a visual world, with visual concerns. Her own orientation is visual, and that strongly affects her idea of what is acceptable as a piece of writing. In a certain way, I think that Rene Ricard is the writer closest to Ingrid's vision of the magazine. I think she feels that *Artforum*'s function is to be on the spot when something newly pertinent pops up, and I think she feels that you can't, on the spot, come up with a considered argument about anything new. You can only say things that point in interesting ways. You can only strike illuminating postures in the vicinity of things. The sorts of things that she's interested in are not yet subjects for the responsible treatment they will eventually get in other magazines. She feels that *Art in America* is the magazine that stands off a little to the side and tries to get a rational view of things, while *Artforum* is more on the spot. She feels that it's not a problem if something sounds silly—that *Artforum* is a place where this kind of risk can be taken, where this kind of irresponsibility is possible. When everything is new and in flux, the writing should reflect that. It's not that she cultivates irrationality for its own sake; it's that she tries to deal with things very intensely and fully, still leaving them in their immediate state.

"I don't do that myself, so it's presumably not the only thing she's interested in. But it's what is at the center of the magazine. Rene Ricard and Edit deAk really keep track of the art world. They really know what's going on. There are other people who keep obsessive track of that world, but only within the framework of that tiny world itself, and they're very boring. Rene Ricard and Edit deAk, in their strange ways, are connected to many other worlds as well—a bewildering variety of them, especially in Ricard's case—and that's where their criticality comes in: from being outside. Ricard lives in a very strange world, with all kinds of very strange people. He is an ex-Warhol person, and his world is one I don't know very much about. He seems to have a strong art-historical background. And also—it's all very eccentric—he is involved with the side of the art world that has to do with collecting. All his personalities are available at once, so you get this strange refraction. What holds it all together, it seems, is the sort of ecstatic, fanlike involvement he has with one thing or another from moment to moment, so that his obsessions kind of recapitulate the whole art world. He's impossible, he's hopeless. He is someone who is always connected to someone else. There used to be Warhol; now there's Ingrid."

"He's supposed to be an important figure in the art world," I say. "But I find his significance elusive."

"Yes, very. Because you can't ever find the center of a Rene Ricard article. I'm not sure I know what he's talking about a lot of the time. He's this kind of gestural presence—the spirit of the new painting. And it's not just a question of someone coming along and saying that the new painting is great, because others have done that, and they don't occupy Ricard's position. These gestures he makes in the vicinity of the new painting seem to reflect something about it, seem to illuminate it in some way. He's a kind of messenger figure: he's bringing us news about the new painting, assuring us of its significance, or at least making a very strong claim for it. I think he's important, because if there hadn't been this irrational love that he, and maybe deAk, expressed for the new painting—and by 'irrational' I mean a love based not on argument and sober judgment but just on this really flamboyant embrace—then people's suspicions that the new painting is empty and calculating and manipulative might be stronger. I am almost swayed by Rene Ricard. I don't know him, and I don't pay all that much attention to him. But I do pause at the spectacle of his mad love for this new painting. I don't quite see it—I mean, I think that in many ways Schnabel's painting is banal and predictable—but the presence of Rene Ricard calls my judgment into question in some way.

"The other thing I think is important about Ricard is that he represents a kind of sordidness that it's important for the art world to believe that it is still capable of. The art world is supposed to be alienated, to be on the periphery—and it's not. In fact, it's very much integrated into the mainstream of culture. It's not that most people like art; rather, it's that the art world has found a secure place in ordinary life—which goes against all the avant-garde's claims to being adventurous and in opposition. At a time when artists bring in architects to design their lofts, a flaky character like Ricard is very important. He makes it more believable that art is odd and weird and challenging."

THOMAS LAWSON is another of Sischy's more dependable and quiet writers—personally quiet, that is. His writing is tough, sharp, hard-hitting, very cold-eyed. In the November 1984 issue of *Artforum*, Lawson published a short article ironically entitled "Hilton Kramer: An Appreciation," which had nothing good to say about Kramer. In one of its milder passages, Lawson wrote: "Kramer and the *Times* were a formidable combination. There, on a regular basis, he could press the authority of his opinions on those who were unable or unwilling to think for themselves; there his forceful mediocrity found its most congenial home." Earlier, in a piece published in the October 1981 issue of *Artforum*, entitled "Last Exit: Painting," Lawson had not scrupled to attack a fellow contributor to *Artforum*:

Rene Ricard, writing in these pages on Julian Schnabel, has offered petulant self-advertisement in the name of a reactionary expressionism, an endless celebration of the author's importance as a champion of the debasement of art to kitsch, fearful that anything more demanding might be no fun. The writing was mostly frivolous, but noisy, and must be considered a serious apologia for a certain anti-intellectual elite.

Lawson is a calm, fresh-faced, somewhat burly thirty-five-year-old Scotsman with a very level gaze, who came to New York in 1975 to pursue a career as an artist. During a conversation with him, I ask how he got into art criticism, and he replies, "Desperation. When I first arrived here, there was apparently no space for younger artists. There was a real doctrinaire thing going on. Every gallery was selling and every magazine was covering something called Post-Minimalism. Post-Minimalism was very systematic and black and low-performance, which was fine, but it was the only game in town. I began to meet other younger artists who had also just arrived and were also dissatisfied; the connective tissue between us was an interest in mass media. We felt that TV and the movies and advertising presented a problem and a challenge to visual artists that these Post-Minimalists were avoiding. What we did, first of all, was to perversely deny ourselves originality of any kind—and this denial runs the gamut of all young artists working today. Even artists who are not directly involved in appropriating mass-media imagery—Julian Schnabel, for instance— refuse to accept the idea that you have to invent. There is something melancholy about our work. If Pop Art represented a kind of optimistic acceptance of mass culture, ours is a kind of melancholic acceptance. We never had coherence as a movement. For some reason, this generation has a particularly high incidence of extreme individualism and of paranoia about one's peers. So there has never been much of a group. This all took place after 'the death of painting.' We had all been schooled in the idea that painting was finished, and the second perverse thing we did was to decide to paint. Since there's a deadness to mass-media imagery, there was a fittingness to our decision to work in a medium that we didn't have all that much conviction about. But, interestingly, once you start working in it you become more and more convinced by it. All these years later, painting actually seems interesting in itself, rather than a mere perverse challenge.

"Anyway, I started writing reviews for *Art in America* because I was so irritated with the situation. And soon I got a little name for myself as someone who could write quite acerbically about older art, who would throw a negative light on what was being shown, and who was something of a participant-champion of the new art. But then I had a falling-out with *Art in America*, though not to the point of exchanging words. David Salle and Cindy Sherman had shows that I desperately wanted to write about but wasn't allowed to, and I began to feel used, I began to feel like a hired gun. I'm really quite good at cutting away the pretensions that accrue around a body of work, and I had done this to some established artists, which was obviously what they liked at *Art in America*. But it wasn't exactly what I wanted to base a career on. My whole intention had been to be more constructive, and suddenly, with these two shows I wanted to do, I found myself being denied the opportunity. There had been a misperception at *Art in America* of my relations with Sherman and Salle—with whom I was neither friendly nor unfriendly. I do have sympathy for their work—I don't see anything wrong with that. I'm an advocate of partisan criticism. Most art writing is from an insider point of view; there is very little that has an Olympian distance. I remember once reading something about Harold Schonberg, the music critic of the *Times*—about a deadly, life-denying thing he did. He forbade himself any personal contact with musicians, on the ground that it might influence his judgment. He wouldn't even let his wife, who was a musician, have anything to do with them. Apart from the horror of that on the human level, I think it's just crazy. You learn so much by knowing what in fact musicians and artists are actually thinking about and talking about, instead of pretending to drop in from the sky."

Of his work with Sischy, Lawson says, "She's almost chameleonlike. When I talk to her, we appear to be in complete agreement. But then an issue of *Artforum* comes out and—" Lawson gestures his feeling of betrayal. He goes on to describe a strange evening he once spent at the old *Artforum* office, on Mulberry Street (it recently moved to Bleecker Street), working with Sischy late into the night on an article about to go to press, and being acutely conscious of the presence of Rene Ricard in another room. Sischy was like a doctor going back and forth between patients in cubicles. "She would spend half an hour with me, and be extremely helpful and sympathetic, and then she'd get up and say, 'I have to go and see how Rene is doing,' and presumably she'd be equally helpful and sympathetic to him," Lawson says. "There was no communication between Rene and me. We can barely talk to each other anyway, we're so opposed in our opinions and our life styles. But Ingrid could move back and forth between us all night with ease. The Feast of San Gennaro was going on that night, and all that fairground noise outside—the firecrackers and the hawkers and the venders—only accentuated the feeling of unreality which that night with Rene had for me."

For the past seven years, Lawson has been publishing a small art magazine of his own, called *Real Life*, with grants from the National Endowment for the Arts and the New York State Council on the Arts, which reflects, in its unpretentious format and its radical critical content, the no-frills avant-gardism of its editor. The following excerpt from an interview by Rex Reason with Peter Nagy and Alan Belcher, the directors of the Nature Morte Gallery, in the East Village, gives some sense of *Real Life*'s tone:

RR: You guys are so modern. What do you look for in an object? What qualities?

AB: Right now we like either black, white, or gray, or generic color.

PN: We're pretty anti-color.

RR: By generic you mean red as "red" rather than modulations of it?

AB: Yeah.

PN: So many people bring us slides that are just like Salle, Basquiat, or Roberto Juarez. These poor kids are out there going to the galleries and they say, "This is what I have to do to have a show." So they run home and paint them. We don't want that—we want stuff we've never seen in a gallery before.

RR: And what do you think is the best art? What influenced the shaping of your taste?

AB: Right now, we like pretty classic late modern stuff: Pop Art, Paolozzi, Indiana for logos, Duchamp, Manzoni, Beuys, Klein. Scarpitta's a favorite of mine.

PN: We think Op Art is highly underrated. Bridget Riley. That's corporate psychedelia, the orgasm of modernism.

AB: We started the gallery because we really just wanted to get our voices in.

PN: And chose the name "Nature Morte" for its Fifties-jazz, pseudo-continental appeal. Ersatz European. Franco-American Chef Boy-ar-dee.

AB: We wanted to be the Leper Gallery.

PN: But then I thought of the Wallet Gallery.


AFTER her three nights of ministering to Ricard at his place on Twelfth Street, Sischy begins a similar series of vigils with Thomas McEvilley at his place, on Clinton Street, near Houston. I attend one of these sessions, which begins in the late afternoon and goes on until two or three in the morning. (I do not last the course.) McEvilley is a thin, bearded man, harried-looking but cheerful, who wears old corduroys during the day and in the evening often appears in a dashing white suit that he bought in a secondhand-clothing store. As I look around his place, I am struck by its peculiar combination of poverty and electronics, which speaks of our coming predicament with a kind of satiric authority. The apartment is a former ground-floor shop, and McEvilley has painted over the show window jutting out into the street, both for privacy and in order to have more wall space for books: the tiny room is entirely lined with books in cheap commercial cases. It has a lairlike aspect. There is an orange shag rug on the floor, and the furniture is four chairs of the sort you see thrown out on the street. But on a huge desk near the ex-window is a word processor; classical music is playing from an advanced stereo system; and there is an electric coffeemaker on a rickety side table, in which McEvilley's girlfriend, Maura Sheehan, prepared an odd herbal drink before leaving for her studio—an identical space across the hall—where she is painting classical Greek-vase motifs on cracked automobile windshields.

McEvilley, as he once told me, sort of drifted into art criticism. He is a classicist by training (he has a Ph.D. in Greek and Latin) and some years ago shifted from the Classics Department of the University of St. Thomas to the Art and Art History Department of Rice University, in Houston, to which he actually commutes from New York during part of the school year. Before his critique of the primitivism show, he had done pieces on the Conceptual artists Yves Klein, Marina Abramović and Ulay, and James Lee Byars, as well as an article called "Art in the Dark," about extreme types of performance artists, among them people who subject themselves to very unpleasant ordeals, such as spending five days and nights in a two-by-three-foot locker without food, or sitting on a shelf in a gallery for twenty-two days. McEvilley said that he had dabbled in the genre himself, "but strictly as ordeal, not in an art context." He told me that he had spent a year sleeping only four hours a night

—a notion he had got from Buddhist monks—and that he had also experimented with fasting, vegetarianism, and meditation. However, one day he had caught himself feeling superior to other people because of these activities and had decided to curb them.

McEvilley began writing for Sischy's *Artforum* in 1981. "In the seventies, I couldn't stand the magazine," McEvilley said. "It was promoting Minimal art in overwhelming doses, and it had forced reductionist art modes on everybody with its aggressive ideological stance. Its power was undeniable—everyone knew the term *Artforum* Mafia, and used it." (A disaffected member of the Family—Max Kozloff, the critic and editor, now turned photographer—once spoke to me in a similar vein about the old *Artforum*. "The magazine was looked upon with a kind of delirious bitterness," he said. "It solaced the readership to know that there were people of such self-confidence and commitment at the helm, rendering such zippy and righteous judgments right and left. But if you were an artist they were not interested in—and they were interested in a very few artists, about whom they wrote repeatedly—then you found this a repellent phenomenon. You were put off by this *camarilla* of kingmakers and bully boys—or, as the case may be, bully women—who wrote in a hermetic language that they were partially inventing and who took themselves with ultra-seriousness. They used to say that *Artforum* was like Listerine: it tasted terrible, but it was good for you.")

McEvilley went on to speak of Sischy's ideological suppleness. "She's very sensitive to the Frankfurt school's perspective on the social function of art, and she wants to maintain that perspective in the magazine. But she has gone far beyond what I see as the naive hostility of the old regime to the art market—a hostility that I myself used to share, I should add. I came to the magazine with a poet's or a scholar's or a philosopher's antagonism to the market process. But Ingrid has pointed out to me very intelligently that in the past fifteen years, as the

major New York museums have withdrawn from what is happening in art, serious dealers have become terribly important.
They are the people who nurture contemporary art and bring
it to us."

Now I sit in a corner of McEvilley's living room diligently
jotting down snatches of the inscrutable dialogue going on between him and Sischy at the desk, punctuated by long silences
while McEvilley works at the word processor.

"Is the idea that self-sameness is the only reality? I don't
think so."

"Can I get rid of it?"

"Let's see. Later it becomes clear that . . . OK, let's take the
sentence out."

"OK."

" 'Preemptively.' What do you mean, 'preemptively'?"

McEvilley goes to the word processor and unknots a sentence.
Sischy looks it over. "It now reads as if Beuys is mad because
Duchamp got there first."

The telephone rings. McEvilley picks it up and hands it to
Sischy. It is Ricard. Sischy speaks to him in a motherly way.
She explains, as if speaking to a child, that she is busy at the
moment. "Rene, you *knew* I was going to be working with
Tom." She listens to him talk at length, occasionally interjecting
a "Great!" or a "Beautiful!" As soon as she can, she ends the
conversation and returns to the manuscript.

"Is Rene OK?" McEvilley asks.

"Yes."

"I thought he looked a little freaked the other day."

"Maybe he didn't have enough sleep," Sischy says, with the
dryness that I have come to recognize as her characteristic response to an invitation to be indiscreet.


A FEW days later, I run into Ricard himself at the recently
opened Palladium discothèque. The place is the creation of the

former owners of Studio 54, Steve Rubell and Ian Schrager, who, after finishing jail sentences for tax evasion, hired the eminent advanced Japanese architect Arata Isozaki to turn the old Academy of Music, on Fourteenth Street, into a state-of-the-art discothèque, and the result is now being hailed as an improbable triumph of architecture, art, and chic by the city's architecture critics, art critics, and arbiters of chic. The young artists who have done paintings on the walls and ceilings of the Palladium's various rooms and corridors—Francesco Clemente, Keith Haring, Kenny Scharf, and Jean-Michel Basquiat—are receiving renewed, wondering notice as nouveau-riche media stars from a press apparently still haunted by the idea of a revolutionary, marginal avant-garde; and the Palladium itself is being viewed as a kind of metaphor for the current state of art—the implosion of high and low culture into ever more grungily demotic and sleekly marketable forms. On this night, the Palladium has been turned over to a party for Keith Haring, and it is filled with beautifully and/or weirdly dressed people from the art world and its periphery. I come upon Ricard in a room that is apart from the discothèque proper, called the Mike Todd Room, which has a large bar, small marble-topped tables, and wire-back chairs, and is where the celebrities of the art world like to congregate. Ricard, resplendent in a white sharkskin suit, is sitting at one of the tables, in a state of high, almost incandescent excitement. As I glimpse him, I recall a passage, in a recent *Art in America* article on Watteau by the art historian Linda Nochlin, about the painting of the clown Gilles in the Louvre:

> You can see *Gilles* as a small, vague, white glow shining in the distance. As you draw nearer, the glow assumes a shape, a significance, and, finally, a vast authority. Grand in scale, looming in its frontal pose, half-sacred in its silky whiteness, it becomes the famous *Gilles*, Christ-like in his innocent exposure to the gibes of the crowd, the very prototype of the

tragic clown, the clown with the broken heart, avatar of Pier-rot Lunaire, *He Who Gets Slapped*, and Prince Myshkin—that whole galaxy of more or less holy fools whose existence has marked the art, literature, and film of the modern period.

Ricard beckons me to sit with him, gives orders for drinks to a passing waiter, and points out celebrities as they go by. "Isn't she *pretty*," he says of Marisol. Of another well-known artist he says, "He's a closet queen," adding, "*I'm* no closet queen." The poet Allen Ginsberg pauses at the table to chat with Ricard, and after he leaves, Ricard grumbles about what he took to be a piece of prospective *schnoring* on Ginsberg's part when he looked longingly at our drinks. Several times, I get up to leave, and each time Ricard clamps a hand on my arm. "So, what I was about to say," he begins, and I am obliged to stay. I ask him whether he has been writing poetry, and he replies, "The manuscript of my new poems is in Julian Schna-bel's safe. If you want to read them, go to Julian's house, get the manuscript, strap it to your person, and have it Xeroxed." As Ricard speaks, he keeps scanning the crowd for people he knows. I counterpropose that Ricard himself go to Schnabel's house and get the poems out of the safe. "Or are you too busy?" "I have too much to do, and I have nothing to do," he replies. I laugh and once again get up to leave, and once again I am prevented from doing so by Ricard's desperate clutch. I don't know why he wants me to stay—and I don't know why I do stay. I only know that I am drawn to this Factory-made Mysh-kin; he is an oddly familiar, possibly anachronistic figure. In his "Not About Julian Schnabel," Ricard wrote about a kind of line that "just gets tuckered out after a while," adding, "The beautiful charcoal smudges and style we can follow from Ma-tisse through de Kooning to Rivers, Serra, and, in its ultimate decadence, to Susan Rothenberg are perfect illustrations." He went on, "Judy Rifka told me that when she was in art school all her teachers drew that way. That was the way you were taught, and no matter how lousy the drawing was it always looked pretty good, like 'art.' " The conventional bohemianism that Ricard embodies may be going the way of the art line he so tellingly describes.

I RECEIVE an acute sense of the newer bohemianism during two visits I pay to the artist Sherrie Levine—first to her studio, in Little Italy, and then to her apartment, a few blocks away. The studio, on the second floor of a small, run-down commercial building, is a twelve-by-seven-foot room that has nothing in it but a table, four chairs, and a fan. If you know Levine's work, the studio is not a surprise but a kind of inevitability. She is a Conceptual artist, and the Conception for which she first became known, in the early eighties, is a series of twenty-one photographs entitled "After Walker Evans." The photographs bear an uncanny likeness to the famous Farm Security Administration photographs that Evans took of tenant-farmer families in Hale County, Alabama; in fact, they *are* those photographs. Levine wrote away for copies of the Evans photographs to the Library of Congress, which owns the negatives; had them recopied at a commercial lab; and then—following Duchamp—made them her own work simply by signing them. If Duchamp's signed urinals and snow shovels and bicycle wheels redefined art as whatever somebody designates as art, Levine absurdly extended the world of objects that are potential Readymades to include already designated works of art. "After Walker Evans" was succeeded by an "After J.M.W. Turner" series, which was exhibited in London in 1984; it consisted of twenty color reproductions of paintings by Turner which Levine had cut out of an artbook, signed, and had matted and framed. When I visit Levine in her studio, she is engaged in a third technique of appropriation: she is tracing reproductions of drawings and paintings by Matisse, Schiele, Léger, and Morandi, and then adding washes of watercolor.

Levine is a pleasant, unmannered woman in her late thirties, with dark, wavy hair, wearing a denim shirt and a gathered skirt, who delivers difficult explanations of her work with such an air of directness and naturalness as to almost cause one to feel that what she is saying is self-evident. Distinguishing between the rephotographed works and the cutout works, she says, "I used to think that the cutout things were the more extreme, but now I think that the rephotographed things are more transgressional. They're more mine. Ultimately, though, all my work is a feminist statement. It deals with the difficulty of being a woman who is trying to create images that are not a product of the expectations of male desire, in a culture that is primarily a celebration of male desire. What I do is to come at the problem through the back door; I appropriate images of male desire as a way of not being co-opted by that desire. I appropriate only the great modern male masters, and I choose only works that I love and value."

We are talking in Levine's apartment, on the fifth floor of an untended tenement—a single long room of bare-boned plainness, where she lives alone, with her cat. There is a bathtub in the kitchen area, and the sparse furniture has a bleak, cast-off character. We sit at the far end of the room, near the windows, in an area of incongruous conventional decorativeness—at a pale wood table, on which a vase of flowers and a spread of bread and cheese and Granny Smith apples has been pleasingly set out. The walls of the room are painted a dull gold. "When I moved in, I painted the walls this way, under the mistaken idea that it would make the place less depressing," Levine says. "It looks more depressing."

"I have heard your work described as melancholy, as a sort of depressed expression of the feeling that there is nothing left to do," I say.

"I wouldn't deny that there is a sadness in the work," Levine says, "though I don't think that's all there is."

"Do you feel that at another time you might have been doing

work of your own instead of appropriating the work of others?"

"Or not working at all. I might have been raising babies. I don't have any feeling of destiny about doing this, but it's a choice I've made. I've been an artist since I was a very young child. My mother gave me crayons to keep me quiet. It was an activity that has always emotionally sustained me. I enjoy the solitude of it. There was a period in which I considered becoming a filmmaker—I was very tempted, because in some ways movies are my first love—but then I realized that the communal activity of filmmaking was very different from the solitary activity of making a painting."

"With the tracing and painting you're doing now, you seem to be working your way back into conventional artmaking."

"Well, I never thought that what I was doing was anything *but* that. That's the irony. I have always regarded my work as conventional art objects. They are always presented that way—matted and framed. I have never considered myself anything but a gallery artist. Several years ago, some friends of mine were in Holland, and they were really excited because they saw this show and thought it was my show, and then realized that it was a Walker Evans show. Or sometimes I'm looking through a magazine, and I think, Oh, great, they've reproduced an image of mine, only to see that it's a real Matisse, not one of my appropriations. When I first started doing the appropriative work, a lot of the criticism written about it—much of it in *October*—was based on ideas of the Frankfurt school of philosophy, but somehow I felt that these sociological explanations coming out of Marx were insufficient. I had the intuition that if I started reading psychoanalytic theory I might find more satisfying explanations. Appropriating art is not all that different from wanting to appropriate your father's wife or your mother's husband. It's the same psychological mechanism: the Freudian idea that desire is triangular—you desire what the other desires."

"Are you able to support yourself from your work?"

"For the past few years, I have been. But it's been a long time coming. I'm thirty-nine years old. Previously, I did waitressing, commercial art, some teaching. At that time, my support systems were critical rather than financial. *October* was the earliest of these systems." Levine goes to a ramshackle metal cabinet and brings out some Xeroxes of writings about her work which appeared in *October* and elsewhere, along with some statements that she wrote herself to accompany exhibitions of her work. The statements are stiff and portentous. When, later in the conversation, Levine remarks that she is attracted to the painters of the sublime but can't conceive of herself doing such work, because "I just can't take myself that seriously," I tell her of my sense of the discrepancy between herself and the forbidding writer of the statements, who seems able to take herself *very* seriously.

Levine says, "I know. Many people have said they were surprised when they met me—how different I was from the writer of those statements. The tone of those things isn't right. I guess I get intimidated when I'm faced with writing."

One of Levine's early statements—quoted in part by Douglas Crimp in a 1980 article in *October*—has an arrestingly different character:

Since the door was only half closed, I got a jumbled view of my mother and father on the bed, one on top of the other. Mortified, hurt, horror-struck, I had the hateful sensation of having placed myself blindly and completely in unworthy hands. Instinctively and without effort, I divided myself, so to speak, into two persons, of whom one, the real, the genuine one, continued on her own account, while the other, a successful imitation of the first, was delegated to have relations with the world. My first self remains at a distance, impassive, ironical, and watching.

The surprise of this passage is followed by an even more astonishing revelation by Crimp: "Not only do we recognize this as a description of something we already know—the primal scene—but our recognition might extend even further, to the Moravia novel from which it has been lifted. For Levine's autobiographical statement is only a string of quotations pilfered from others."

Sherrie Levine's bleak little conceits have stirred the imaginations of some of the art world's most advanced thinkers. Rosalind Krauss, at the end of the extraordinary title essay of her book *The Originality of the Avant-Garde and Other Modernist Myths*, in which she magisterially makes her way (with a few French litter-bearers) through the thicket of the discourse on originality set in motion by Walter Benjamin's essay "The Work of Art in the Age of Mechanical Reproduction," holds up Levine's purloined photographs as a kind of master trope of postmodernism. Another theorist—the critic Benjamin H. D. Buchloh—in an *Artforum* article entitled "Allegorical Procedures: Appropriation and Montage in Contemporary Art," compliments Levine on being "the strongest negation within the gallery framework of the re-emergent dominance of the art commodity," adding, "Her work, melancholic and complacent in defeat, threatens within its very structure, mode of operation, and status the current reaffirmation of individual expressive creativity and its implicit reaffirmation of private property and enterprise." Buchloh goes on to say, "Baudelaire was wrong when he argued that the poetical was necessarily alien to female nature since melancholy was outside the female emotional experience. Enter the female dandy, whose disdain has been sharpened by the experience of phallocratic oppression, and whose sense of resistance to domination is therefore more acute than that of her male colleagues, if they still exist."

JULIAN Schnabel is believed to be the richest artist working in New York today (there are waiting lists for his paintings), so I am not surprised to learn—when Sischy takes me on a visit to his studio on White Street—that this is only an auxiliary studio to the main one, on Twentieth Street. (There is a third studio at Schnabel's country place, on Long Island.) Schnabel is a large, broad-shouldered man of thirty-five, with a fresh, clear, ruddy face, a direct gaze, and a natural, simple, friendly manner that inclines toward good-natured kidding. A pretty blond assistant meets us at the door and ushers us into a vast two-story loft, where Schnabel, who is wearing dark baggy trousers and a dark turtleneck sweater, awaits us. He leads us to one of two enormous paintings that are hanging loosely from beams high up and explains that it is painted on a tarpaulin from a truck that he came across on a trip to Mexico the previous year; the truck had broken down on the highway, and Schnabel bought the tarp from the driver for seventy dollars. "That's all I had on me—I would have given him more if I'd had it. I want you to look at those creases and folds, and at those patches." Schnabel adjusts lights to bring out the textures of the weatherworn brown tarp, on which he has painted, in broad strokes of white paint, a monstrous sort of primitive beast-man, with a leering face, an exposed rib cage, and a pair of clawlike extremities; at the top left, the letters "AZ" have been painted twice in red. In the late seventies, Schnabel began to attract notice with his "plate" paintings—he would affix a thick encrustation of crockery to the canvas before starting to paint—and the creased and patched tarpaulin is evidently another expression of his disinclination to start with a blank canvas (or, in Lawson's terms, to be original). An even more striking example of this refusal, which Schnabel shows us later at the main studio, is a series of paintings done on the stage sets of a Kabuki drama, which a friend sent him from Japan. These are six panels bearing delicately colored, stylized scenes of trees and flowers, over which, like a vandal, Schnabel has done brutish Expressionist drawings in thick, dark strokes. If Sherrie Levine's reverent little thefts are "transgressional," what are we to call Schnabel's rude violations? As Schnabel directs a strong young assistant to turn the heavy Kabuki sets this way and that, he keeps up a line of easy, agreeable, anecdotal patter about his work. What he says doesn't make too much sense; it isn't "hard," it's just talk—one has to say something to people who come to one's studio. Schnabel shows us an enormous amount of work—his output of the year—with the modestly pleased air of a successful entrepreneur. His energy and enterprise seem boundless; he tries all kinds of things in all kinds of figurative and abstract styles, and everything has a look of bigness and boldness and confidence. One work has a discrepant look of insignificance: it is a white shag rug on which a black-and-brown cross has been painted. I ask him about it, and he says something cheerfully vague about how the rug had been in a summer house he had rented and had got stained, so he bought it from the owner.

I recall the first time I met Schnabel, at the opening of the Museum of Modern Art's show of international contemporary painting, to which I had gone with Sischy: she and I were standing before a Schnabel abstraction—done on cowhide, with a pair of antlers sticking out of it—when Schnabel himself appeared. Positioning himself behind Sischy, with his hands on her shoulders, he gazed fondly at his work and said, "I bet you're the only person at this opening who is having her back rubbed by the artist whose picture she is standing in front of." Now, in the studio, he talks about the "objectness" of his work. I ask him if he is using the word in the sense in which Michael Fried used it in his famous essay "Art and Objecthood," first published in *Artforum* in 1967. Fried's difficult, profound meditation on the threat to art posed by what he called literalism (more commonly called Minimalism) is a sort of culminating aria, sung from the ground with the knife in the chest, of the enterprise known as formalist art criticism. It is an extraordinary performance—written in the driest, densest, most disdainful language, and yet permeated by an almost hysterical emotionality. As Fried's argument develops, it becomes a kind of allegory of good and evil—good being modernist painting and sculpture, which seek to transcend or "defeat" their "objecthood" (the canvas and paint, or the stone, metal, or wood they are made of) and thus achieve the "presentness" of true art; and evil being literalist painting and sculpture, which embrace their objecthood and thus degenerate into the inartistic condition of "theater." Schnabel says he doesn't know Fried's essay and asks me what it is about. After I tell him, he nods, and says with devastating carelessness, "All that is the language of another generation. We don't use language like that today. We're a different generation. We're interested in different things."

EDIT deAk lives on Wooster Street, in a loft (clearly not designed by an architect) with a shabby, functional, and only slightly, and rather haphazardly, funky appearance. She herself is a striking, good-looking woman of thirty-eight, with shoulder-length bright-red hair worn in bangs, who dresses in vivid, interesting clothes that have a sense of quotation marks around them. She speaks with an East European accent in a low, melodious voice, and as she speaks she has a trick of moving her stiffened right hand up and down, in a tender chopping gesture. She likes to play Nabokovian games with language (her speech and writing are filled with terms like "ego beaver" and "tour de farce"), though when she did gallery reviewing for *Artforum* in the seventies, she curbed her Pninisms and confined herself to straight, opaque Artspeak. But now, under Sischy's permissive reign, she denies herself very little and writes pieces entirely composed of epigrammatic, near-scrutable paragraphs, such as the following, which appeared in an article entitled "The Critic Sees Through the Cabbage Patch":

> In the contrast of scale, small imagery in large surroundings becomes all powerful when it is happening and speedily traversible when it is not. Tiny gland-sized figures, capable of being fondled, emphasize their secret porno charm as tiny emblems of hidden desires. Like makers of Oriental porn, the

Italian telescopes, allures, and funnels with a sense of security in codes which give comfort like the reliable conventions of the geisha. The German closes up; shoved in your face is a violent eruption reflecting our Judeo-Christian body guilt. They just can't mix. Sandro Chia has spread his work too thick. Dial *Q* and *A* (like in Questions and Answers) for Quotation and Appropriation. Dial *T* for Terminal Terminology. Again the terms engender a limitation on thinking about the issues. "Quotation" is anchored as a quicky, and Appropriation as mere antics. These terms are not comprehensive enough to deal with the realm involved: it makes it all seem like a klatch of bourgeois plagiarisms. We should be contending with counterfeit gestalt (Gesamtkunstpatch, in cabbage-patch terms). Asking, where has the original of the whole world disappeared to? Has Rammellzee taken it to the Van Allen Belt?

During the seventies, deAk and Walter Robinson, an artist, coedited a magazine named *Art-Rite*, a messy, impudent, sort of in-house organ of the New York avant-garde. Printed on newsprint, published irregularly, and run with an ironic sort of amateurism ("Unsolicited manuscripts are welcome, and you don't even have to enclose a self-addressed and stamped envelope to get them back," an editorial notice read), it observed the large and small movements of the advanced art scene of the seventies at a very close, somewhat blurring range. Although Sischy's *Artforum* is more formal, more professional, more like a real magazine than *Art-Rite* ever approached being, it has never entirely abjured the samizdat quality of *Art-Rite* and the other rakish little magazines of the period, such as *Heresies* and *Just Another Asshole*, whose spirit Sischy immediately recognized as her own. Attempting to characterize this spirit, and not doing too badly, Rene Ricard once remarked, "Ingrid put cheapness into *Artforum*." My own point of reference for the special demotic strain that runs through Sischy's magazine is the cover of the Summer 1981 issue, which she herself conceived. Other Sischy covers have made a bigger stir—for example, a famous cover featuring a sulky model wearing a remarkable long black evening dress (by the Japanese designer Issey Miyake) whose bodice was a kind of rattan cage—but this one shows Sischy putting the cheapness into *Artforum* in a particularly artful way. At first sight, it looks like a work by a postmodern Conceptualist; in fact, it is an arrangement of twelve blue-and-white paper takeout coffee containers. Eleven of them show a lumpish discus thrower posed beside a Doric column that supports a bowl containing the Olympic Flame; the twelfth container, centrally placed, is turned to show its other side, which bears the message "IT'S OUR PLEASURE TO SERVE YOU." Ricard's piece "Not About Julian Schnabel" appeared in that issue, and while Sischy was selecting the illustrations for it, she was suddenly struck by the preposterous similarity between a Schnabel painting called *Blue Nude with Sword* and the picture on the coffee container she was drinking from; the cover was the result.

When I visit deAk in her loft, she brings out a bottle of wine and two glasses and says, "I always thought I did *Art-Rite* to defy the idea of art magazines. I spent the best years of my life doing it, for free. In my mind, it was a project to undermine art. Mine is an anarchistic, negative feeling. I don't believe in anything until it is proven—and I don't like proving. *Artforum* is a magazine that comes out every month. My mentality is not used to that. I spent my entire life not being anybody, defying schedules, not having a job. At a moment when you are what job you do, people are constantly saying to me 'Who are you?' and it's a question I can't answer."

Another of deAk's nonremunerative activities was serving on the board of Printed Matter, which is where she met Sischy. "Ingrid sort of stabilized everything at Printed Matter," deAk recalls. "She got it out of chaos, out of the bowels of the board. There's no 'no' to her. When she was at Printed Matter, the two of us used to go and see if we could get corporate support for certain projects. I'll never forget the time when we went to the Xerox Corporation, in Rochester. I got up that morning to dress, and I was scared to death. I didn't know how you go in to see a corporation, so I put on the best dress I thought I had—all frills and shiny—and I looked like some kind of overdressed person who hadn't gone home the night before. As for Ingrid, she was wearing this badly cut three-piece man's blue suit. We were staying with Ingrid's parents, and when Ingrid's mother saw us coming down the stairs in the morning, ready to go on our executive trip, she just broke down laughing.

"Ingrid's father is one of the three doctors I've met whom I actually think of as a human being. He considers the totality of a person. The mother is brilliant, kind of filigreed, and fast, but with a soft edge, never stabbing. They're radical thinkers. Their ideology is really complex. They know so much. Their way of thinking is so much more contemporary than mine that I would have expected them to be weirdos, but they're not. They're completely regular people; they completely fit into society. They're exquisitely civilized.

"I had written for *Artforum* for four or five years before Ingrid came, so I knew the other regimes, and they were very different. Ingrid centered the whole operation on herself. The previous editor didn't. He was a very quiet person who sat at his desk, and the office was very quiet, and the manuscripts came in. He regarded the job as, sort of, 'OK, here is my desk, and here comes a manuscript, and I'll take care of it.' When Ingrid got into the office, there was no desk left unturned. She checked everything. The smallest note didn't leave that office without her checking it. She was even friends with the night cleaner. But when I say that she centered the whole operation on herself I don't mean that she was building herself up. If you look at the jobs that Ingrid has had, they were always concerned with the projects of others. She's just the opposite of a hustler. She's not going to hold up a cue card and say, 'This is what I am.' She will not guide you to her. She will show you the irrigated areas of the Nile. Her achievement is like that of the Nile—the fertilization of a certain area of culture."

A WEEK after the Summer issue has gone to press, Sischy takes me to the fifth-floor studio—in a commercial walk-up on Canal Street—of a pair of Russian-Jewish émigré artists named Alexander Melamid and Vitaly Komar, who collaborate on satiric paintings done in the style and employing the iconography of Socialist Realism. Melamid, a slight, thin, dark, quick man of around forty, wearing horn-rimmed glasses and jeans and running shoes, looks like any number of boyish New York Jewish or New York Italian men. Komar is fat, looks much older than Melamid but isn't, has a dark beard and small, cunning green eyes and red lips—a minor character out of Gogol, probably a horse trader.

The studio is bright, noisy from the traffic on Canal Street, and bare. Several large canvases are propped against a wall, their faces inward. (A year later, at a large SoHo gallery, I see them unveiled: brilliantly sharp-sighted pastiches of old, modernist, and last week's postmodernist paintings, with an occasional Stalin or Hitler thrown in as a kind of signature.) Komar and Melamid lead Sischy and me to a group of wooden chairs near the Canal Street window and bring a bottle of seltzer water and white plastic cups, and a basket of red apples that immediately evoke Mother Russia. After a minimal amount of desultory small talk, the two men abruptly plunge into a philosophical argument about the nature of time. Do we live in a space between past and future or are we perpetually in the past? Melamid argues that the present exists. No, Komar says, the present does not exist; there is only the past and the future. They argue back and forth, speaking very rapidly in accented English and gesticulating vehemently. Then, like a pair of house cats aimlessly walking away from a fight, they simply stop arguing. Melamid shrugs and says, "We always argue like this."

Komar smiles benignly. He speaks worse English than Melamid, who often corrects his pronunciation in a brotherly way.

Melamid tells us of the great discovery that he and Komar made in Russia before emigrating here, in 1978. While other Russian artists publicly did Socialist Realism and secretly worked in advanced modernist styles, he says, "it dawned on us that Socialist Realism could itself be a vehicle for avant-garde art." Komar tells of an American friend in Russia who brought them a can of Campbell's soup as a work of Conceptual art. "One day, there was nothing in the studio for a snack, so we ate the soup," he says. "It was not a bad snack." "It was bad," Melamid says. "It was not bad," Komar says. They start another animated debate, one that soon gets into art theory, the condition of art today, the situation of art in New York. As this argument, too, begins to peter out, Melamid sighs and says, "We sit here, and we talk, and I think, 'Where is *life* in all this? Life! Life!' We go at things obliquely, to the side," making a gesture of ineffectuality with his hand, "instead of straight, like this," pounding his fist into his palm. He continues, emotionally, "Last year, I woke up in a hotel room in Amsterdam. There was a woman in my bed. I looked in the mirror and saw that my eyebrows were gray. I saw that I was forty."

"You got that from Chekhov," I say to myself. I am no longer charmed by this pair. I find their performance tiresome, calculated. I look over at Sischy, who is enjoying herself, who thinks they are "great," and I ponder anew the question of authenticity that has been reverberating through the art world of the eighties. The feeling of mistrust that Komar and Melamid now arouse in me is the feeling that has been repeatedly expressed, within and without the art world, about the work of Julian Schnabel, David Salle, Francesco Clemente, Jean-Michel Basquiat, Keith Haring, Robert Longo, Cindy Sherman, and the other new stars who have emerged into prominence during the past five years. In a long poem, published in *The New York Review of Books* in March 1984, that was modeled on Pope's

"Dunciad" and entitled "The Sohoiad: or, The Masque of Art, A Satire in Heroic Couplets Drawn from Life," Robert Hughes, the art critic of *Time*, brought this feeling to a brilliant, splenetic apogee. Lashing out at artists, dealers, critics, curators, and collectors alike, he offered a vision of the contemporary art world as a Bosch-like inferno of greed, fraud, hype, and vacuity. After dispatching "Julian Snorkel," "Jean-Michel Basketcase," "David Silly," and "Keith Boring," among others (and treating Snorkel—"Poor SoHo's cynosure, the dealer's dream,/Much wind, slight talent, and vast self-esteem"—with special savagery), Hughes went on to mordantly inquire:

> Who are the patrons whose indulgent glance
> The painter craves, for whom the dealers dance?
> Expunge, young Tyro, the excessive hope
> Of gathering crumbs from *Humanist* or *Pope*:
> No *condottiere* holds his exigent sway
> Like MONTEFELTRO upon West Broadway—
> Instead, mild stockbrokers with blow-dried hair
> Stroll through the *soukh*, and passive snuff the air.
> Who are the men for whom this culture burgeons?
> Tanned regiments of well-shrunk *Dental*
>                             Surgeons . . .

When I showed the poem to Sischy, she was not amused. "Forgive my lack of a sense of humor," she said, "but what I see in that poem is just another reinforcement of stereotypes about the art world. It's like a Tom Stoppard play, where you have an entire Broadway audience snickering about things they haven't understood. It makes outsiders feel clever about things they know nothing about. *The New York Review* is a magazine I really respect—I respect its editors and I respect its audience—but this poem reflects the gap that exists between the serious literary audience and the serious art audience. Hughes's overwhelming message is that all of today's art is worthless, that the whole art world is a bunch of frauds and grotesques. I would agree with him that about half of what is being produced today is worthless, but I get worried when everything and everyone are lumped together and jeered at. That's too easy."

Sischy's fascination with what's difficult sometimes leads her into incoherence and opacity, as in a recent special issue of *Artforum* called "the light issue." It was conceived (according to an editorial by Sischy and Edit dcΛk) as a response to "the failure of the recent spate of big international shows to intelligently meet the development of contemporary art, and . . . their tendency instead to carelessly throw all 'the names' together in an expensive but cheap hanging spectacle of so-called international pluralism." The alternative it offered its readers was a survey of international art (the issue had no articles and was made up entirely of reproductions of paintings and photographs, some of them created specially for the issue), based on the common denominator of light. The issue left its readers utterly mystified. Since light, perforce, is the common denominator of *all* visual art, something other than the mere statement of this truism must have been intended—something less obvious and more particular to contemporary art—but to this day no one knows what it was. The light issue included, among other works, photographs by Joel Meyerowitz of moonlit water; ink-and-watercolor drawings by Agnes Martin of horizontal bands and lines; a Neo-Expressionist painting by Enzo Cucchi of a piano playing itself on a vast white plain; a cryptic five-panel figurative work by Komar and Melamid; a fold-out four-page spread by Francesco Clemente showing a pair of monstrous creatures emitting a sort of white gas from their posteriors; a photograph by Weegee of lightning in Manhattan; photographs of a set from Paul Schrader's film *Mishima*; a photograph of a starving African child vomiting. These were followed by a page of "shadow captions," whose explanatory texts only deepened the enigma of what all these works were doing together and what they were saying about light. The caption for Clemente's contribution, for example, read:

> The pink raybow of light dawns on you as the ribbon of the wrapping unfolds the tales of light about never being able to see all light at once. You can only get the heads and tails of this if you reshuffle the wrapping to cover the adjoining body of the riddle getting an ellipse of the senses; you have to have blindness to have insight.

The light issue has become a famous, interesting failure of Sischy's—people in the art community talk about it indulgently, as if speaking of the endearing foibles of a beloved, brilliant child. Sischy herself has no regrets about it, and of all the issues she has produced, it may be the one that most tellingly elucidates the character of her editorship. Its mysterious amorphousness is akin to her own boundless and restless energy. She is the Ariel of the art world, darting hither and yon, seeming to alight everywhere at once, causing peculiar things to happen, seeing connections that others cannot see, and working as if under orders from some Prospero of postmodernism, for whose Gesamtkunstpatchwork of end-of-the-century consciousness she is diligently gathering material from every corner of the globe as well as from every cranny of the East Village. Sischy not only travels to the big international art expositions, such as the Venice Biennale and the Kassel Documenta, but will impulsively get on a plane to check out a show in London or Paris that she thinks the magazine might want to review. She will spend a week in Spain or Italy recruiting reviewers and writers; she will fly out of town to give a talk at a museum or a university; she will journey to Japan on an exploratory mission for some possible future inscrutable special issue. While in New York, she tries to see as many as possible of the fifty or sixty gallery and museum shows that open every month, to attend as many openings and after-opening parties as possible, and to pay as many studio visits as she can.

During this ceaseless activity, Sischy remains unhurried, relaxed, and strangely detached. "In a world where all kinds of people—from editors to curators to collectors to dealers—want control, where control is of the essence, she doesn't seem to want it," the critic Donald Kuspit observes to me over a drink at a bar near Gramercy Park. Kuspit is a fifty-one-year-old professor of art history at Stony Brook who has been writing art criticism of a dense prolixity for *Art in America*, *Arts*, and *Art Criticism*, as well as for *Artforum*, for the past dozen years. He goes on, "She's not looking to be the Archimedes of the art world, with a lever that can move it. I think one of the things she realizes is that that whole way of thinking is obsolete. She's smart. There's a kind of canniness to her, what Hegel calls 'the cunning of reason'—insofar as there *is* reason in the art world. Frankly, I think the art world would be a terrible place without her. It would be a macabre place. Even as it is, it's a dreadful place. The megalomania that is rampant among artists is unbelievable, and so is the self-importance. Bankers must be the same, but the cry for attention from artists—the ruthlessness of their sense of what is due them—is extraordinary. When I first moved to art criticism, which was a natural extension of my work with Adorno in critical philosophy, I had a great need to concretize the importance of art. Now I go through bouts of wondering whether art isn't just a matter of fashion and glamour. The artists are getting younger by the minute, and, increasingly, anything with a little flip to it gets visibility. It used to be that when art was made, people would be unsure of its value until—slowly, through all kinds of critical discourse and debate—the art would acquire cultural significance. And *only then* would people arrive with money and say, 'I want that.' Now—and I think this started with Pop Art—there's money waiting like a big blotter to blot up art, so that the slightest bit of inkiness is sponged up. That's a very hard thing to keep a distance from. Ingrid walks around it. She doesn't let her magazine serve as a little subservient blotter for whatever powers there may be. She is fearless. Nobody owns her, yet she doesn't give offense because of that. I'm not saying that the editors of the other art magazines are owned, but somehow this free-spiritedness seems a more vivid part of Ingrid—almost as if she doesn't want to be owned even by herself."

DURING the year that Sischy and I have been meeting for interviews, she has been unsparingly frank about herself. She has confessed to me her feelings of self-doubt and inadequacy, she has told me stories of rejection and mortification, she has consistently judged herself severely. At the same time, she has not been altogether uncritical of me. I have not lived up to her expectations as an interlocutor. She fears that I do not understand her. As I ponder this tension between us, a story that she told me early in our acquaintance comes back to me with special weight. It was an account of a small humiliation—one of those social slights that few of us have not in our time endured—that she had suffered the previous day at a public lunch honoring a sculptor who had done a work for the city. Sischy had sat down at a table next to a stranger, a sleek, youngish man, who, as soon as they had exchanged names, turned away from her and began talking to the person on his other side. The guests at the lunch were from both the art world and the city government, and this man was a city politician. "He was clearly disappointed that someone who looked like me should have sat down next to him," Sischy told me. "I could see him thinking, 'What a waste of a lunch!' I considered getting up and going to sit with some people I knew at another table, but then I thought, 'No, I'll stay here.' A little later, a woman who had sat down on my other side asked me my name, and when I told her, she figured out who I was, and she was very interested. And then two people across from me figured me out, and they started talking to me. And eventually this guy, taking it all in, said, 'I'm terribly sorry—I didn't get your name.' So I told him again, and the woman beside me told him what I did, and his whole manner changed. He suddenly became very interested. But he'd lost me by then." Sischy told me this story with no special emphasis—she offered it as an example of the sexism that women still regularly encounter—but I obscurely felt it to have another dimension besides its overt one. Now, a year later, the latent meaning of the story becomes clear to me: it is a covert commentary on Sischy and me. I had formed the idea of writing about her after seeing *Artforum* change from a journal of lifeless opacity into a magazine of such wild and assertive contemporaneity that one could only imagine its editor to be some sort of strikingly modern type, some astonishing new female sensibility loosed in the world. And into my house had walked a pleasant, intelligent, unassuming, responsible, ethical young woman who had not a trace of the theatrical qualities I had confidently expected and from whom, like the politician at the lunch, I had evidently turned away in disappointment.

In a charming and artful essay of 1908 entitled "A Piece of Chalk," G. K. Chesterton writes about taking some brown paper and colored chalks to the Sussex downs on a fine summer day to do Chestertonian drawings of "devils and seraphim, and blind old gods that men worshipped before the dawn of right, and saints in robes of angry crimson, and seas of strange green, and all the sacred or monstrous symbols that look so well in bright colours on brown paper." But as he begins drawing, Chesterton realizes that he has left behind "a most exquisite and essential" chalk—his white chalk. He goes on:

> One of the wise and awful truths which this brown-paper art reveals is that . . . white is a colour. It is not a mere absence of colour; it is a shining and affirmative thing, as fierce as red, as definite as black. . . . Virtue is not the absence

of vices or the avoidance of moral dangers; virtue is a vivid and separate thing, like pain or a particular smell. Mercy does not mean not being cruel or sparing people revenge or punishment; it means a plain and positive thing like the sun, which one has either seen or not seen. Chastity does not mean abstention from sexual wrong; it means something flaming, like Joan of Arc. In a word, God paints in many colours; but He never paints so gorgeously, I had almost said so gaudily, as when He paints in white.

Since Chesterton wrote these buoyant words, the world has seen two world wars and a holocaust, and God seems to have switched to gray as the color of virtue—or decency, as we are now content to call it. The heroes and heroines of our time are the quiet, serious, obsessively hardworking people whose cumbersome abstentions from wrongdoing and sober avoidances of personal display have a seemliness that is like the wearing of drab colors to a funeral. In "Why I Write," George Orwell said, "In a peaceful age I might have written ornate or merely descriptive books, and might have remained almost unaware of my political loyalties. As it is, I have been forced into becoming a sort of pamphleteer." One feels about Sischy that at another time she, too, might have been less grave, less morally weighted down, and more vivid. She told me that as a child she had been extremely naughty and wild. What remains of this naughtiness and wildness finds expression in the astonishing covers, the assertive graphics, and the provocative special issues of *Artforum*. Just as Sischy's personal muteness is the by-product of an Orwellian sense of cultural crisis, so her vision of contemporary art is shaped first by societal concerns and only secondarily by aesthetic concerns. Her interest in the Neo-Expressionist painting that is coming out of Germany today, for example, is bound up less with the painting's aesthetic claims than with its reflection of the anguished attempt of young German artists and intellectuals to come to terms with the Nazi past. Sischy once said to me, "My greatest love is Conceptual art. I may be even more interested in thinking than in art." She added, "Rene and I used to have an argument. He'd say something like, 'Well, that work is really beautiful,' and I'd say, 'So?' and he'd say, 'Well, you hate art if you say "So?" about something being beautiful,' and I'd say—and I've come to realize that it's more complicated than this—'Well, maybe I just hate art when the only thing going for it is that it's beautiful.' "

*The New Yorker*, 1986

# The Window Washer

DANIEL Kumermann is a large bearded man of thirty-nine, with dark hair and full red lips, who dresses in jeans and dark-blue cotton shirts, wears wire-framed glasses, carries an unruly knapsack filled with books, papers, and odd items, and has about him an air of quiet certitude that is not without a trace of truculence. He lives on the outskirts of Prague with his wife and two children. He is a foreign-affairs journalist; until April of this year, he was a window washer. In 1978, he had signed the human-rights declaration Charter 77, and for the next twelve years he did menial work, as a great many of the other Charter signatories were obliged to do. When I first met him, in January 1990, he spoke contemptuously of Milan Kundera's novel *The Unbearable Lightness of Being*, whose hero, Tomas, a doctor, refuses to sign a statement of complicity with the Communist authorities, becomes a window washer, and spends an idyllic two years sleeping with the women whose windows he comes to clean.

"Kundera himself was never forced to work menially," Kumermann said, "and what he wrote about window washing was complete nonsense." He added, "It's very upsetting to meet Americans and when you tell them what you do they give you a lecherous look. In fact, washing windows is very unpleasant work, and the women you work for do not sleep with you. The women you wash windows for usually regard you as the lowest scum. Kundera writes completely outside of reality here."

"But his book is fiction," I said.

"I know. But everybody in the West reads Kundera's books as if they were accurate portrayals of life in Czechoslovakia under the Communists. If he writes nonsense and nobody reads it, all right. But his books are famous. Everybody reads them and thinks they are true. Actually, Kundera is not a Czech author anymore. He's become something like a French wit. He should write about France rather than about Czechoslovakia."

Kumermann was voicing a view of Kundera I had heard before; many of Kundera's countrymen had disliked and resented *The Unbearable Lightness of Being*, and the book's success in the West (Kundera emigrated to France in 1975) only exacerbated the sense of injury felt by those who had stayed in Czechoslovakia and had lived out the reality that Kundera "improved on" in his fable of totalitarianism. The reality had unexpectedly taken a novelistic turn of its own in late 1989, when the gray malaise of police-state existence was overnight transformed into feverish joy, and a shiningly good and intelligent man, Václav Havel, with a small group of fellow dissidents, rose to the leadership of the nation. Many Czech-Americans— I among them—flocked to Prague to participate in this heady moment.

I arrived in Prague in late December, on the morning of Havel's inauguration as President of the Republic. My parents had fled Czechoslovakia and the Nazis with my sister and me in 1939; in fact, all my close Prague relatives had emigrated to America before the Second World War. We were one of the few Jewish families in Prague who had had the extraordinary good fortune to survive intact. Now, fifty years later, I was back, carrying a long list of Prague writers, artists, academics, and editors, and of family friends and distant relatives as well. (The distant relatives on my list were either non-Jewish or sufficiently semi-Jewish to have been spared.) Kumermann's was one of the names on the list.

Everyone in Prague was in a state of manic excitement and frantic activity. Everyone was looking at his watch because he had to be somewhere in fifteen minutes, phones were constantly ringing, appointments were constantly being changed because something had suddenly come up, no one had enough sleep, no one had enough time. After years of nothing happening, something had happened—something beyond anyone's wildest imaginings. People said they felt they were in a wish-fulfillment dream, not in actual life. I had an appointment with Kumermann and his wife, Jarmila, at their apartment, and I arrived terribly late. My previous appointment had left me in a section of Prague where there were no cabs on the street, and a kind stranger had offered me a lift. But he turned out to have almost as poor a grasp of the geography of outlying Prague as I did, and, after long wanderings and blunderings, he brought me to the Kumermanns' door forty-five minutes past the appointed hour. Kumermann and Jarmila gave me tea at a round table in the dining area of their L-shaped living room, while one of the children and Kumermann's mother watched television in the living area, with the sound on quite high. Partly because of the loudness of the television but also because Kumermann insisted on speaking in English (as he later told me, he uses every opportunity to practice conversational English), while his wife and I spoke in Czech, the conversation was somewhat disjointed. On leaving, I again apologized for my lateness. Jarmila, a classically beautiful woman with honey-colored hair that she wears straight to the shoulders with bangs, and a melodious voice and gentle manner, said kindly, "It wasn't your fault."

Daniel Kumermann, standing a bit apart from us, said quietly but clearly, "It was her fault."

I looked at him with surprise and interest.

Jarmila said reproachfully, "How was it her fault, Daniel?"

"She should have taken a taxi at her hotel. A taxi driver wouldn't have had any trouble finding this place."

"You're right," I said. "But you're very strict."

"I suppose I am."

He accompanied me out of the apartment—he was on his way to meet someone at the Prague airport—and when we were on the street, walking in the dark toward the tram stop, he turned to me and said, in his abrupt, uninhibited way, "You're

Jewish, aren't you?" I nodded, and he went on, "I am half-Jewish—on my father's side. My father was an intellectual, and he married an uneducated woman who worked in an office. They separated when I was seventeen. I naturally gravitated toward my father's side. When I was twenty-two, I converted to Judaism and joined the Prague Jewish Community."

On the tram, Kumermann paid my fare, and when I offered to reimburse him he waved my money away and said, "You can repay me another way. Do you chew gum? No? Well, you can send me chewing-gum wrappers anyway. I collect them. I also collect comics. You can send me chewing-gum wrappers and comics from New York." We changed to the metro, and parted at Wenceslas Square. I went on to dinner with a professor from Charles University who had very polished manners, and when I returned to New York I told the friends who had given me the Kumermanns' address that I had liked her enormously but had not taken to him. Then, in April, I made a second trip to Prague, and in packing for it I oddly found myself putting in a number of chewing-gum packets and comic books.

KUMERMANN, I found on my return to Prague, was just starting a career in journalism. He had a job as an editor and writer on foreign affairs at a monthly magazine—one of the eighty-odd new publications that had emerged since December. We made a date for lunch, and I picked him up at his office on Pařížská Ulice, a street of handsome Art Nouveau buildings, which replaced a section of the old Jewish quarter when much of it was torn down in the early 1900s. His office—a room on the fourth floor, with high ceilings, tall, graceful windows, and ornate moldings—was furnished with fifties Soviet-modern office furniture of pale wood, a sofa and an armchair covered with a fabric of an ugly modernistic design, and a cheap green rug; the place had a bare, improvised look, as if furniture had been hastily dragged out of storerooms for occupants who had not yet properly moved in. Kumermann shared the office, and its only typewriter, with an older colleague, another former dissident who had done menial work. He was alone when I arrived, working at the typewriter. When I presented him with my gift of gum and comics, he glanced at each item expressionlessly and then thrust the lot into his knapsack. I said apologetically, "These must all be things you already have." He corrected me: "Not all of them."

The colleague came in, a man in his sixties with very pale skin and sandy hair and a pleasant manner. Kumermann somewhat grudgingly introduced me and then conversed with him about some magazine matter. When the colleague left, carrying a tape recorder he had taken from his desk, he paused in the doorway and addressed a courtly, mildly witty remark to me.

After he was gone, Kumermann said, "What a charmer. He must have been something with women when he was younger."

"I know the type," I said. "It was common among Czech émigrés when I was growing up in New York."

"I'm not that type," Kumermann said.

"I know," I said, and added, "This has struck me about you. You're more like a certain kind of New York Jew than like a Czech."

"Yes, I cultivate this Jewish thing as a kind of defense against the Czech milieu."

"So you feel you're a Jew rather than a Czech?"

"No, not *rather*. The Czech nation can be a very disappointing nation, so as a Jew I can say I don't belong to it. I know this is only a kind of escape, since, after all, my education was Czech; Czech is the language and culture to which I belong. But it was a particularly nice form of escape in the early seventies. In the sixties, Czechoslovakia became a country one could feel proud to belong to, but in the seventies everything dissolved into despair and loss of values and people turning coats. This is something that happens quite often in Czech history. The Czech nation is a great example of the phenomenon of surviving by giving up."

We went to lunch. Kumermann took me around the corner to Prague's only kosher eating place, in the Jewish Town Hall, which was built in the late sixteenth century (and reconstructed in the eighteenth) as the administrative and social center of the Prague Jewish Community, which now numbers around one thousand. (This number represents the people who have registered with the Community, most of whom are secular Jews. Before the war, there were forty-five thousand registered and unregistered Jews in Prague; today there are three thousand.) The restaurant serves inexpensive kosher food between eleven-thirty and two; foreign guests pay double what Czechs pay— thirty crowns (about a dollar) as against twelve to fifteen. The meals, Kumermann told me, are subsidized by the American Jewish Joint Distribution Committee, a philanthropic organization based in New York.

We hung up our coats on hooks along a wall of a small lobby in which announcements were posted and men in yarmulkes milled, and got in a line outside the dining hall. Kumermann pulled a yarmulke out of his knapsack and attached it to his head with bobby pins. When we reached the head of the line, an old woman at a counter took our money and handed each of us a bottle of mineral water, a small plate of salad, and a small plate of plain cake. We carried this to a table covered with a white tablecloth and set with glasses and white china soup bowls containing cutlery and paper napkins. In the middle of the table—it was Passover week—there was a platter of matzoth covered with a white cloth.

The dining hall was a large, somewhat somber high-ceilinged room with dark wood paneling, ornamented plaster columns painted beige, a balcony, and, at one end, a small proscenium-arch stage, on which stood a piano and a menorah. Posters of Israel were taped here and there onto the paneling, and near the entrance hung a black-and-white eight-by-ten framed photograph of Barbra Streisand, inscribed by her at the time of the filming of *Yentl* nearby. A single waitress moved deliberately and unhurriedly between the kitchen and the tables, bringing first a soup of mushrooms and vegetables and barley, then plates of beef and gravy and dumplings; she served the soup from a pot, ladling it out with a metal cup. The wait was fairly long, but people sat calmly and confidently; there was none of the tension and anxiety that slow service evokes in New York restaurants. I was to find this serenity about waiting characteristic of eating places throughout Prague. But the food at the Jewish Town Hall was uncharacteristically good—plain, wholesome, prepared with tact and grace, as if by a gifted home cook. Restaurant food in Prague today is generally dismal. There is a Czech word that nicely describes its dominant quality: *upatlaný*. Something is *upatlaný* when it has been handled too much, has lost all freshness and integrity, has a muddled, overcombined character. One gets the feeling that something is being hidden in the strange messes one finds on one's plate in Prague—there is much talk in Czechoslovakia today about poisonous chemicals in meat and about produce that has been grown in too much fertilizer—but one remembers that food in Czech restaurants in New York has never inspired confidence, either.

As we waited for our kosher lunch, Kumermann told me about his late father, Jaroslav Kumermann, who had escaped the Holocaust by going to Palestine in 1939 and joining the British Army there. "Before the war, he was quite rich," Kumermann said. "He was an assimilated Czech Jew who spent a lot of his time in Prague cafés in intellectual discussions. At the university, he unfortunately chose to study chemistry, which he never should have done, since he had no head for exact science. He should have studied the humanities. He was an only child, whose mother cared too much for him. He never finished anything. He tried various business ventures, at which he failed terribly, because he had no head for business, either. There was finally one thing he proved he could do, and that was selling insurance. He could talk well, he was a kind of charmer, so he managed to sell quite a lot of insurance. That's where he made his money. After the war, he returned to Prague—he found life in Palestine too harsh—but he was never able to establish himself again. When the Communists came, although he was never openly persecuted he had no chance to prove himself. There was no more insurance to sell. He couldn't succeed at anything. He wasn't even able to find a decent flat. I grew up in a two-room flat that had no water in it and a toilet outside. Because my father never got up enough inner strength—enough pushiness—to get a better flat, my mother finally moved away; she got some money for a flat from her sisters abroad. As I told you, my mother was a completely different person from my father. They didn't understand each other, they couldn't cooperate with each other."

The waitress poured out our soup, and Kumermann paused to eat a few spoonfuls. I asked him when and how he had come to join the Community.

"I was twenty-two when I first heard of it. Someone brought me to the Town Hall, and I started going to lectures here and services at the synagogue, and in a few months I was completely caught up in Judaism. I felt that this was it. Then I had to have this nice little operation."

"You weren't circumcised as a baby?"

"No. It isn't normally done here. So I had to have it done. It was performed in a hospital in Northern Bohemia where there was a Jewish surgeon. He even knew the *b'rachos*, so he said what it was necessary to say. Then I had a *tevilah* in the Vltava, and a bar mitzvah. Now they call me to minyan. Sometimes it's difficult to get a minyan here. When there are tourists, it's not a problem, but in winter, when there are few tourists and the old people who make up most of the congregation can't get out, they sometimes call me."

"How do you feel about being part of such a small group?" I asked.

"It suits my kind of personality better than being part of a majority," Kumermann said, not picking up my reference to the absent forty-two thousand. He went on, "After I joined the Community, I chewed out my father for not having introduced me to Judaism earlier. He always said, 'It's not safe. In every generation there is some problem with being Jewish.' But deep down he was glad I had become a Jew. He couldn't communicate it, but his Jewishness was important to him—it was him."

"How do you know the expression 'chewed out'?" I asked. At Kumermann's insistence, we always spoke English, of which he had a near-perfect command; he spoke with only a slight accent, and his mastery of colloquial language and nuance was remarkable. (His chief mistake was sometimes leaving out articles, which don't exist in Czech.)

"It comes from the comic strip *Beetle Bailey*," Kumermann replied. He told me that he had begun to collect comics when he was a boy. During the summer months, he and his mother were allowed to go to Vienna to visit his mother's mother and one of her sisters, and it was there that he first encountered Western comics—*Mickey Mouse, Donald Duck, Felix the Cat*. Later, the *Peanuts* strips provided an illumination. "Suddenly, I saw that there was an intellectual dimension to comics—there was more to them than providing pleasure for the youngest members of society. I saw that comics can comment on society as well as reflect it." When, as an English major at Charles University, he learned that there were serious American scholars of comics, he felt he had "intellectual clearance" for writing his master's thesis on comics as a cultural phenomenon. To do his research, he wrote everywhere. "I have an uncle in Connecticut, a doctor, who emigrated to America in 1964. He rejects comics as stupid, but he was willing to send two theoretical books about them. What I wrote in my thesis doesn't express my ideas now, because my sources were very limited. I wrote about comics that I knew were important but had never seen."

Kumermann accepted my offer of the beef and gravy on my plate, and went on to speculate that some of his fascination with comics might have derived from the Communists' dislike of them. "Comics were considered an imperialist diversion—against humanity, an opiate of the masses—and that may have been part of the attraction for me: my enemy's enemy."

I asked him when he had begun to think of the Communists as his enemy.

"Ever since I can remember, I have always considered Communists some kind of lower creatures. I always heard bad things about them at home. They were always tied to the word 'whore,' they were always something unspeakable. I never had any doubt about this regime being bad and the First Republic being good. We were very poor, and I blamed the Communists for that, though as I grew older and saw that there were people who lived much better than we did, I realized that our poverty was also due to my father's complete incompetence."

"You didn't openly rebel against the regime until later?"

"Let's say my rebellion was individual. I was always a bit choleric by nature, and when I was in the ninth grade and didn't like what a teacher did I sent him to ass—where you say 'Go to hell,' we say '*Jdi do prdele*,' or 'Go to ass.' I was always this kind of individual rebel."

"What happened when you said that to the teacher?"

"Nothing. He just didn't like me. He had never liked me before, and this didn't make him like me more. I was a kind of extravagant person. No teacher was ever undecided about me. Either they liked me very much or they hated me. When you look at the people who signed the Charter, you'll find that many of them had the same kinds of problems in school that I had. You suddenly realize that these people didn't just happen to be dissidents; they were determined to be dissidents. You don't choose it—it chooses you. There's a kind of mental predisposition among people who can't put up with false authority."

"Were you one of the original two hundred and forty-two signers of the Charter?"

"No," Kumermann said, and told of an initial period of equivocation. In 1977, he had a job as a computer programmer on a six-month trial basis, and, not wanting to immediately wreck his chances for a permanent position, he had placed himself in a special category of signers, whose names were kept secret. He lost the job anyway and, after failing to find permanent work in the field, openly resigned the Charter in the summer of 1978. Thereafter, only menial work was available to him. During the next twelve years, he was arrested five times and was taken in for interrogation more often than he can remember.

A woman with short blond curly hair stopped at our table, and she and Kumermann chatted amicably for a few minutes. After she left, Kumermann remarked, in his blunt way, "That's a girl I might have married."

"A fellow student?" I asked.

"Yes. She also studied English, and she is also Jewish. I was interested in her, but she didn't want to marry me. I was dating her, and she always said no, and we went on in this unsure way for months, and it was too much for me. When she changed her mind, I was already about to marry Jarmila. So it was a bit too late. Looking back at the last twelve years, I'm not sure if she could have stood the kind of life I've led."

I said, "These people who interrogated you—are they still around?"

"Yes," Kumermann said. "They are. It's funny—we have a kind of supermarket three tram stops away, and who should I see shopping there with his wife the other day but one of my interrogators. I said to myself, 'Should I go up to him and say "*Ještě pořád fizlujete?*" '—'Are you still spying?'—and then I thought, Forget it. He was one of the milder ones. I always had two. There was the one who dealt with the political side of it—the Charter—and the other, who dealt with the Jewish side of it."

"The Jewish side of it?"

"They had an anti-Jewish department. They called it the Anti-Zionist Department, actually. The political interrogator was very unpleasant, very rude, very aggressive. He never hit me, but he threatened to. He was not stupid, but he was crude and unpolished. The other one, the anti-Zionist one, was intelligent, polite, gentlemanly, always trying to catch you by reasoning. He was softer, but more dangerous. He was replaced by the one I met in the supermarket, who was just a plain idiot. He wasn't aggressive or bad; he didn't abuse me. He was just stupid. One day, he said to me—he was always trying to present himself as very clever and well educated—'Do you know how the ghetto came into existence?' I said, 'In sixteenth-century Venice, the Jews were forced to live in a certain area that was walled in.' And he said, 'No. The rich Jews fenced in the poor Jews, the better to parasite on them.' I said, 'That's not true. Even Marx wouldn't say so.' And he looked at me seriously and said, 'But I say so.' That was the end of the interrogation—he had put himself above Marx, and when the enormity of that sank in, there was nothing further he could say. In a way, it was great fun. Most of the Charter signers were accused of working with the CIA, and I was accused of working with the Israeli Mossad. They thought in James Bond terms. Also, they believed that America was ruled by Jews."

"They really believed this? They weren't just harassing you?"

"They really believed it. They had persuaded themselves of these conspiracy theories. What helped me quite a lot was that they could never accept the idea that any adult of sane mind would devote himself to comics and chewing-gum wrappers. They thought of me as an idiot, and finally they wrote me off. For the last six or seven years, they left me pretty much alone."

After lunch, Kumermann hurried back to his office to prepare for an interview he had been granted with Yasir Arafat, who was in Prague for talks with Havel. We agreed to meet again at his apartment the following afternoon.


THAT evening, I dined at the apartment of the professor with polished manners I had met in January. I will call him Egon

Valenta. He had not signed the Charter. Like the majority of the people in Prague who had demonstrated in Wenceslas Square during the incredible days of the velvet revolution, he and his wife—whom I will call Jana—did not have the serenity and the clear conscience of the opposition movement. The Valentas had been in what was called the "gray zone," between the active collaborationists and the dissidents. They had not done anything very bad, but they had not distinguished themselves, had taken no risks, and when that longest of long shots, the mangy nag of the dissidents, miraculously came in, they felt rueful about not having put their money on it. They felt obscurely ashamed, and disappointed in themselves. At our meeting in January, Valenta had adumbrated this complicated feeling to me, and now he and Jana elaborated on it. We sat in the living room of their apartment, on the Smetana embankment facing the Vltava, drinking vodka and eating little hors d'oeuvres of *upatlaný* canned crabmeat. The room was furnished with a combination of old things (glass-front bookcases, a vitrine of bibelots, a family portrait, a Persian carpet) and contemporary art and objects (abstract paintings, yarn wall hangings, tribal masks), along with a television set, stereo equipment, and the polyester lace curtains that are ubiquitous in Prague. The result was oddly depressing. As Kumermann's bare office had the look of a place that no one had taken possession of yet, the Valentas' fully furnished apartment had the aspect of a place whose inhabitants had already moved away: in both cases, the place and the inhabitants were not fully connected. The Valentas' one child, a twenty-four-year-old son, whom I will call Ivan, lived with them; until the early eighties, Egon Valenta's parents had also lived with them. The apartment was large, and by law, which allowed only a certain number of square metres to a person, the Valentas should have had to move, but they had been able to bribe an official and stay on. People in Prague spoke openly and unashamedly about the system of corruption by which the machinery of daily life creaked along.

"We are very tired," Valenta said, lighting his second cigarette in the ten minutes since my arrival. He is a man in his early sixties, short and of slight build, bald, with a patrician bearing and a deeply lined, still handsome face, out of which intelligence and self-mockery shine. Around the eyes there is a sort of baffled expression, the trace of a wince. He was wearing a black turtleneck sweater over gray flannel trousers. "Of course we rejoice in the change," he went on. "But for many of us it came too late. If it had happened ten years earlier, I might have been able to pick up the pieces of my life. Now I am too tired and too old."

Jana, a heavyset woman with permed blond hair, who is eight years younger than her husband, pressed me to take another hors d'oeuvre and, when I declined, anxiously offered a plate of cheese and crackers. She comes from a working-class background and was a typist at the university when she and Valenta met, in the late fifties; she now worked as a secretary at an industrial journal. Traces of great beauty are present in Jana's face, and so are the remains of a strong attachment between husband and wife. Valenta is another charmer, though at the moment he had an abstracted and harried air; there was a certain perfunctoriness about his flirtatiousness. Watching him, I inwardly smiled at the puritanical Kumermann's idea of his officemate as someone who had been beguiling to women "when he was younger"—as if charmers ever stopped being charming. Long ago, obviously, Valenta and Jana had made their pact of accommodation, and the air between them was calm, if a little murky.

"I'm no hero," Valenta said—gratuitously, since the identity of the heroes was never in question in Prague. He added vodka to my half-full glass and refilled his own empty one. "I was not in the active opposition. I belonged to no dissident group. I did not sign the Charter."

"Did you ever consider doing so?"

"No. I knew many of the signers and respected them. But I

never thought anything would come of it. I thought it was pure Don Quixotism. I thought, Why endanger Ivan's education, lose my job, risk Jana's job, when nothing can come of it? I was proved wrong. I miscalculated. Who would have expected a Gorbachev to come along and accelerate the end of the Communist system? I knew it would crumble from within, but I never expected it to happen in my lifetime."

Jana said, "We tried to live like decent people, but it wasn't always possible. We all did things we are ashamed of."

"Like what?" I wanted to ask, but didn't have the heart to.

Jana, who has a very pleasant voice and a direct, sincere manner, coupled with a sort of hostess's chronic nervousness, answered my unspoken question. "For example, a few years ago we were allowed to go to Munich for a conference in Egon's field. After the papers were read, there was a reception. Across the room we recognized one of our old friends from the university who had emigrated to West Germany in the seventies and was now working at Radio Free Europe. But we didn't dare go up to him and speak with him; we knew there were informers in the room. When our friend started in our direction, we silently walked away and pretended we didn't know him."

The story did not seem so shameful to me. The friend must have understood. Was the incident like a screen memory that hides a more painful recollection? Or were the guilt and shame that people like Valenta and Jana felt based on unrealistic expectations of themselves? Was Havel's example of moral purity too glaring a contrast for ordinary human weakness? Czechoslovakia now had a kind of perfect man as its President, a person truly deserving of a people's gratitude and admiration, and it is well known that children of perfect parents have a hard time; children of parents with feet of clay have less trouble overcoming their sense of inferiority and weakness. As the people of Czechoslovakia love Havel, they must on some level, one would think, also hate him and not wish him well. But among the many extraordinary aspects of the Havel phenomenon is that the man disarms even schadenfreude. No one can hate a man who is so free of pretension, so genuine in his humility about himself, so sincerely tolerant of frailty in others. He may be the first completely nonauthoritarian world leader in history. But if he makes people in distant places who read his writings feel displeased with themselves for not being as good as he is, one can imagine how he affects his own countrymen, especially those with bad consciences.

Over dinner, which continued at the coffee table—customary in Prague apartments, where separate dining rooms rarely exist anymore—the talk turned to Kundera. Valenta does not share the popular Czech view of Kundera as a kind of fallen angel. "He is simply our best contemporary writer," Valenta said. "In *The Book of Laughter and Forgetting* and *The Unbearable Lightness of Being*, he has rendered the reality of life here more vividly and more precisely than any other Czech writer. It does not matter that he wrote these books in France and that they are not works of realism. They are literature, and they are true."

When I quoted Kumermann's comments about Kundera, Valenta nodded impatiently and said, "Yes, people say things like that about Kundera. I've heard them all. But the resentment is about something else. As Oscar Wilde put it, 'The only thing that cannot be forgiven is talent.' " He added, "They also cannot forgive him for having had a life for fifteen years. They profess to prefer the novels of Škvorecký, who hasn't a tenth of Kundera's talent but has devoted his life in exile to the cause of dissident Czech writing." (Josef Škvorecký's publishing house in Toronto, called 68 Publishers, has been printing and distributing the work of banned Czech writers for the last twenty years.) "This is admirable, of course, and Škvorecký is a splendid fellow, of course, but it doesn't make him a great writer; it doesn't even make him a 'truer' writer than Kundera."

At the end of the evening, I declined Valenta's courtly offer to walk me back to my hotel. Prague is a small town, easy to find one's way around in. On learning that it was also entirely safe, I had been enjoying solitary walks at night through cobbled streets so empty and silent that one could hear one's footsteps. Tonight, before turning off the Smetana embankment and heading toward my hotel, near Wenceslas Square, I crossed the street and gazed up at Hradčany, the Prague Castle, rising from the far bank of the river like a mystical vision. The castle is in fact a collection of medieval and Renaissance structures—palaces, residences, churches, chapels—dominated by St. Vitus's Cathedral, one of the great Gothic cathedrals of Europe, which was now bathed in a delicate blue-green light. The surrounding buildings, which included the presidential palace, were illuminated by a golden light. Willows and fruit trees about to flower grew on the riverbank, forming the foreground of this ravishing night picture. I stood leaning against the balustrade of the embankment promenade, utterly alone, and feeling the special joy that adventitious aesthetic experience brings. Then my eye fell on a disagreeable sight on the riverbank below me. Glaring whitely out of the darkness was a disorderly pile of papers that someone had left strewn about on the grass. The sight of litter, unpleasing anywhere, is positively arresting in clean, orderly Prague. There is no refuse in Prague's streets, no windblown newspapers, no bottles, no dirty rags, no candy wrappers, no half-eaten pieces of pizza. During my previous visit, hundreds of thousands of people gathered in Wenceslas Square on New Year's Eve to celebrate the beginning of the post-Communist era, and thousands of bottles of champagne were drunk and then either smashed or left standing on the street in merry circles around the trees lining the square and in rows along the edges of the sidewalk. (Wenceslas Square is actually a long, wide boulevard of hotels, shops, cafés, and restaurants, with a statue of the saint on horseback at its uphill end.) On New Year's Day, between eight in the morning and noon, volunteer bands of citizens gathered in the square with twig brooms, swept up the broken glass, and helped load it and the thousands of bottles into city garbage trucks, so that by noon the square was completely restored to order and no trace remained of the revelry of the night before. As I stared with displeasure at the papers strewn on the riverbank, they underwent a transformation before my eyes and turned into the white feathers of a swan sitting on a nest she had unaccountably chosen to build on the grass just below the promenade. She gleamed out of the darkness, curving her neck and pecking at herself with affected unconcern, aware of me but sitting tight. When I looked up, the cathedral was gone. The blue-green light had been extinguished, and now only the buildings in the foreground were visible; one could make out, if one knew where to look, the faintest trace of the cathedral spires. Then the golden light went out too, and the whole vision disappeared. I moved on.

A little street off the embankment turned out to lead to the Theater on the Balustrade, where a performance of Havel's *Largo Desolato* was just letting out. Havel wrote this play—about a dissident leader who is having a nervous breakdown—in 1984, a year and a half after his release from a three-and-a-half-year prison term. It had been circulated in samizdat and had been produced in Germany and America but never in Czechoslovakia. Havel came to work at the Theater on the Balustrade as a stagehand in 1960 and soon became one of the shaping forces of its mordant, ironic spirit. It was here that he found his voice as a playwright; while associated with the theater, he wrote *The Garden Party*, *The Memorandum*, and *The Increased Difficulty of Concentration*, the absurdist plays on which his international reputation was based. The theater's great period—during which Jarry's *Ubu Roi*, Beckett's *Waiting for Godot*, Ionesco's one-act plays, and Havel's plays were produced, among others—coincided with the period of liberalization in Czechoslovakia that abruptly ended in August 1968, with the arrival of Russian tanks. (Havel left the theater shortly after the Russian invasion—for nonpolitical reasons, he has reported, though obviously, he further notes, he couldn't have lasted under the new dispensation, given "my various extra-theatrical activities.") In the autobiographical *Disturbing the Peace*, a book of essayistic responses to questions sent him in 1985 by Karel Hvížďala, a Czech journalist then living in exile in West Germany, Havel traces the history of the Theater on the Balustrade and that of other small, avant-garde Prague theaters of the sixties. "Life in Prague was different then," he observes. "Prague had not yet been buried under a landslide of general apathy and turned stiff and corpse-like under its weight. In other words—paradoxically—it made sense to deal with the absurdity of being, because things still mattered." After 1968, the Theater on the Balustrade, though retaining high standards of production and performance, lost its radical edge, as did every other cultural institution tolerated by the regime.

On the afternoon of December 31, 1989, I had been at a party held in the anteroom of the Theater on the Balustrade, at which many of the leading writers, artists, academics, and theater people of Prague were present, including Havel himself. He is a man of chunky build who looks younger than in his pictures and has a most winningly natural manner. He came to the party dressed in dark-gray denim jeans and a dark-blue sweater over a white shirt. He spoke softly, sincerely, easily to the people who approached him, drinking a beer, chain-smoking, gesturing a lot, often breaking into a wonderful smile. In his autobiographical writings (and, indirectly, in his plays), Havel has shown doubt-filled, anguished, neurotic sides of himself, but his public persona is that of a man who is remarkably comfortable with himself and knows how to be simple and direct without ever being glib. "Fortunately, my nature is such that I get on well with everyone," he wrote to his wife, Olga, while he was in detention in a crowded cell in the Prague Ruzyně jail, adding significantly, "And I'm able to suppress my various emotions." In the crowded cell of public life that Havel now inhabits, his gifts of self-control must serve him as well as they served him when he was incarcerated among murderers and thieves.

That New Year's Eve, I got another glimpse of Havel at a glittering party given by the Civic Forum, to which the whole Prague opposition movement and its members in exile had been invited. The atmosphere was something like that of an art opening in SoHo combined with a wedding in Astoria. People sat at long tables in an enormous hall, drinking champagne and happily listening to a terrible rock band. Just before midnight, Havel, wearing a suit, appeared on a stage, received an ecstatic ovation, and, in reply to a request for a speech, said good-humoredly, "I must remind you that what we are starting here is a democracy, not a monarchy." At midnight, the national anthem was played, and everyone stood up to sing and to cry. So much communal good feeling is rarely encountered, and on my second visit to Prague I was not encountering it. The city was sinking into what the critic Tzvetan Todorov has called "post-totalitarian depression"—a condition whose pathos was somehow only deepened by the hordes of tourists pouring into it.

I CONTINUED my night walk through small, empty, winding streets and then along Národní Třída, a wide thoroughfare, where I was joined by a few other strollers. I passed the place where on November 17, 1989, the police had savagely beaten peacefully demonstrating students with truncheons—the so-called massacre that roused the traditionally supine Czechs to action. Where Národní Třída approaches Wenceslas Square stands a handsome white six-story Art Nouveau building, which became the headquarters of the Civic Forum soon after its elegant rout of the Communists. (The Civic Forum's original headquarters had been the subterranean Magic Lantern Theater.) Street musicians had begun to perform in the open plaza in front of the building—under the Communists, street music was forbidden, as was another recently introduced Prague entertainment: *striptýz*—and when I arrived at the plaza an unusually large crowd was gathered around a pair of folk-rock singers, a young man and a young woman singing to the accompaniment of the young man's guitar. However, what had attracted the crowd was not the singing and playing, which were unremarkable, but an oddity: a very old woman, resembling one of the poor deranged creatures one sees wandering about the Upper West Side, had attached herself to the singers and was hopping about after them in a bizarre parody of rock dancing. The crowd laughed in a careless, good-natured way. The cruelty of the spectacle was blunted by the geniality of the performers; the pretty, rose-cheeked girl smiled encouragingly at the old woman and treated her more as a co-performer than as a freakish interloper. Earlier in the day, I had seen a crowd in Wenceslas Square gathered around another curiosity, this one a small demonstration that called itself a Protestní Žranice. ("Pig-out Protest" is the best I can do.) The protest took the form of a free distribution of food and drink to passersby: anyone who would accept them was handed a huge pallid hunk of boiled chicken wrapped in foil, a piece of bread, a slab of salami, and a beer. What was being protested, I learned from a man biting into his chicken, was the Communist Party's retention of money and property. The protester-distributors were some sort of ad hoc group, which wasn't running candidates in the coming election but—as my informant described it—"just does things for fun." The Protestní Žranice was evidently a takeoff on the Protestní Hladovka—hunger strike.

Back at the hotel, I turned on the television to one of the two Czech channels, which was showing a film about Robert Schumann and Clara Wieck. (Clara: "Did you write that?" Robert: "Unfortunately, no. Heine.") I investigated the other channel, which was broadcasting an interview with a young athlete who had won a prize in Athens ("How did you like Athens, Jiří?" "Very dirty. It's better in pictures"); switched back to Schumann (Mendelssohn: "Have more faith, Schumann"), back to the athlete ("What are your plans for the future, Jiří?" "To go on as before"); and finally alighted on a hazy but riveting *Swan Lake* from the Bolshoi on the Russian channel.

. . .

THE next day, a Saturday, I arrived at the Kumermanns' apartment at the appointed hour of five, this time taking a hotel taxi, whose driver, as Kumermann had predicted, found the address with little difficulty. Kumermann's apartment building is entirely without the architectural charm of the buildings in the city proper. It is a nine-story concrete structure of brutal plainness, resembling an American lower-income housing project in its mean, tiled lobby and general punitive air. But Kumermann and Jarmila are satisfied with their living quarters. During the first nine years of their marriage, they, and their two small children, lived with Kumermann's mother in a four-room apartment. The housing shortage in Prague is so acute, Jarmila told me, that their name would not have come up on the waiting list for an apartment in their lifetimes, and possibly not even in their children's. Ten years ago, Kumermann joined a building co-op, whose members, with their own hands, constructed their apartments within a prefabricated shell provided by the state. Construction was done after work hours and on weekends, and the project took six years to complete. Besides the living-dining area, the Kumermann apartment has a small entryway, a small kitchen, three bedrooms, and one bathroom. It is a pleasant place, reminiscent of young intellectuals' apartments in New York, filled with bright-covered books in pale-wood bookcases, modern furniture, posters, and photographs. When I came in, Kumermann was, as it happened, washing the living-room windows. "Jarmila has been after me for weeks to do them," he said with a smile. The television was on, and a folk-rock singer was singing a bouncy song called "Když má Čert Splín"— "When the Devil Has Spleen." Kumermann put away his sponge and turned down the sound of the television a little, but didn't turn it off. Jarmila came in from the kitchen to greet me and then went back to preparing dinner.

I asked Kumermann how the Arafat interview had gone. "Terrible," he said. "I was allowed four questions, and the answers he gave were not answers. They were harangues. They were packaged anti-Israel propaganda."

"What are you going to do?"

"I'll write an article about not getting the story." (He is not, I thought to myself, the first inexperienced journalist to think that such a story could be interesting.) "Do you want to hear the tape?" he asked. I said I did, and Kumermann played it. I was interested to hear Kumermann, always so confident and imperturbable with me, sounding cowed and helpless in the face of Arafat's practiced aggressivity.

Perhaps under the influence of this defeat, Kumermann now expressed his worries about his new career. "I'm almost thirty-nine, and I'm starting something I don't know whether I can do or not. Under normal circumstances, I would have tried myself at twenty-five. I would have found out then whether I could write or not. I did a little writing in samizdat, but that doesn't mean anything. In samizdat, there was no competition; everything was accepted. Now there is a great deal of competition." He glanced over at the television screen and added, "At almost thirty-nine, I don't have that much time left."

I mentioned Egon Valenta and his feeling that for him the change had come too late. "At sixty-three, he has more reason for concern than you do at thirty-nine," I said.

"No," Kumermann said. "I have more reason. If he is sixty-three, that means that in the 1960s—during the thaw—he was in his late thirties and therefore already had some experience of real life. Even the people who were kicked out of their professions in '68 and had to do manual work for twenty years—they at least already knew how to do something. But I never had a chance to prove myself. By now, I should either know I can't write or be assured about what I turn out. Thirty-nine is very late to be unsure about your abilities.

"People ten or more years younger than I am are better off, too. For example, the man who is the new editor in chief of

my magazine: at twenty-eight, he is an experienced and established journalist. Our generation had the experience of '68,
whereas his generation—he was seven in '68—grew up without
ever having to ask themselves certain questions. I heard that he
was a member of the internal party organization at his former
magazine. Last winter, when a petition protesting Havel's im-
prisonment was being passed around Prague"—Havel was
jailed for four months in 1989—"he signed it and in this way
evidently made up for his previous 'problems.' "

"What questions do you mean?"

"Well, for example, I happen to know a young editor on
another magazine—I've had frequent contacts with him over
the years because of a common interest in comics. Under the
Communists, he always looked at things very pragmatically.
He would say, 'This we can push through, and this we can't.'
He would try to get as much space as he could for what he
wanted to publish, not caring whom he had to deal with to get
it. For me, just the act of dealing with those top swine was
unpleasant—almost physically repulsive. But these younger
people never felt that very strongly. They thought, All right,
Communists are just part of reality—not a very pleasant reality, but something one can make one's peace with. This guy I
work for, the young editor in chief—I wouldn't hold what I've
heard against him as long as our contacts are OK. But I might
feel a bit touchy about it if we got into some kind of conflict over a moral issue. Then I might remember what I've
heard."

As Kumermann talked, he was stringing little colored beads
on short pieces of wire. He saw me glancing at them, and said,
"These are going to be rings. Have you noticed that I'm always
toying with something?"

"You never like to be idle?"

"No, I'm just neurotic. I'm always toying with something.
If I don't toy with something, I can't concentrate properly. If
I'm eating without doing something else—like reading—I get

nervous. Maybe it's not healthy, always having to do two things at once. I also do macramé. I usually do it when I listen to the radio or watch TV."

Kumermann worked silently for a few moments and then said, "I've always envied people who have one strong interest. I have a friend, a classmate from school, whose interest in archaeology began when he was thirteen. He is now a very important archaeologist; archaeology has always occupied most of his life. But I've done this, I've done that, and I've never really excelled at anything. I could probably be good at many things, but so far I haven't been excellent at anything. That is how you could describe my life to date, and I wonder if I'm going to end up like this."

"Doing a variety of things can be satisfying," I said.

"No. Not usually. Because it puts you in a position where, in whatever field you work in, there will always be people who are better than you. You are always trailing others. Maybe you can say, 'All right, that's nice,' but that's a rationalization."

Kumermann described the old *nomenklatura* system, under which all jobs were controlled by the Communists. "If you were not a member of the party, there were limits to your career. You could never be head of your department."

"Could you yourself have joined the party?"

"Sure. When I left the university, I was offered a very nice teaching position at this Communist school in the city—on just one little condition."

"That you join the party?"

"Yes."

"What would you have taught?"

"Marxist ideology." Kumermann finished his ring and added it to a large cluster of rings strung on a wire. "I'll tell you a nice example of how the *nomenklatura* worked. This archaeologist I was just telling you about: even before he finished school, he was already working for the Academy of Sciences, in the Department of Medieval Archaeology. Then, one day, the head of the department retired, and my friend was approached by the head of the academy's historical section, who said, 'According to *nomenklatura*, the head of the department must be a member of the party. You are not a member of the party, so you can't be head of the department. At the same time, it's impossible to have a department without a head. So here are your choices: one, you join the party and become head of the department or, two, you don't join the party and we abolish the department, because there is no head, and you lose your job.' It was a very easy choice for him to make. He told me all this when I once asked him if he was a party member. He felt he had to explain himself, he felt so unhappy and ashamed."

When Kumermann began to describe in detail some risky underground work he had done as a dissident, Jarmila came in from the kitchen and said, "Daniel, you shouldn't tell her this—not when there are Russians still on Czech soil."

Kumermann started to argue with her, then shrugged and said to me, "All right. I don't feel that way, but since Jarmila is nervous, just don't go into particulars about this."

Jarmila returned to the kitchen, and Kumermann went on to talk of his desire to travel and of his frustration at not having enough money to do so. This was a complaint I heard everywhere in Prague: the iron curtain had lifted, but the bars of economic actuality had come down in its place. Everyone was free to go where he pleased, and hardly anyone could afford to go anywhere. (Round-trip airfare to New York from Prague is the equivalent of perhaps ten months of Czech wages; dinner at a medium-priced restaurant in West Germany is the equivalent of two weeks of Czech wages.)

I asked Kumermann why it was important for him to travel. "Somehow, I just feel it is. In 1969, when I was eighteen, I was in Denmark for six weeks, and then in West Germany for three or four days, and after that, for nineteen years, I went nowhere. In 1988, I was allowed to go to London—they began allowing some of the lesser fry of the Charter signers to travel. One of the greatest inspirations for me was an American student I met twenty years ago at a hostel in Copenhagen. He had been in Vietnam before going back to school. Then he interrupted his studies to spend a year traveling around the world. He had a small backpack with him, and that was all—one change of clothes. He was always washing his things. When a garment fell apart on him, he bought a new one. He had saved up some money, and he had some kind of credit card he could use anywhere. Wherever he went, he always wore the same thing. Americans don't care very much about dressing, right? When people from here go to the West, they take fancy clothes with them. That's something Americans don't care about, right?"

I had learned not to try to disabuse Czechs of the fantastic ideas they held about America. On my first trip, I had spent much time in fruitless argument with them; now I simply nodded when Czechs delivered themselves of their immovable notions about us.

Kumermann went on to tell me about a trip abroad he was actually going to be able to make. The following week, Havel was flying to Israel to accept an honorary degree at the Hebrew University in Jerusalem, and Kumermann had got a seat on the presidential plane.

"How did that happen?" I asked.

"I just phoned. I was talking to someone in the President's office, trying to get the interview with Arafat, and I said, 'By the way, when Havel goes to Israel, would it be possible for me to get on the plane?' and he said, 'Yes; we have vacancies.' The only problem is that I have no place to stay in Jerusalem. Neither the government nor the magazine will pay my expenses. The magazine has some money, but they are careful who they give it to, and since I'm a beginner and haven't written anything important yet, they won't give it to me. If I go to Israel and write a good article, maybe my status on the magazine will change. I could write the article right now. I've already spent so much time learning about Israel that I could write a report about it without actually going there."

"You never know," I said. "You might run into some surprises."

"I feel it's the same with America. I've spent so much time learning about America that if I went there it would only be to recognize what I already know. You said you were impressed by my knowledge of colloquial American expressions. Well, I also know colloquial American realities. Like, say, at the Harvard Hillel they have a provocation—a sandwich called Blasphemy. Do you know what that is? All right, it's a ham-and-cheese sandwich. I remember these details."

I asked Kumermann if he would be reporting on Havel in Israel, and he said no. His plan was to get on the plane with Havel, and then leave the Havel group at the Lod airport, spend four days in Israel on his own, and rejoin the group to return to Prague. I asked him why the government was giving him what was essentially a free ride to Israel. "There are seats on the plane for journalists" was all he could say in explanation. He had sent express letters to friends in Israel asking if he could stay with them.

Jarmila came in to say that dinner was ready. The children were away for the weekend with their maternal grandmother, who lived in the country. The three of us sat in the dining area and ate an excellent chicken paprika. Jarmila did not speak much and had a put-upon air. She said she had not been feeling well, had been suffering from insomnia, and would go to bed early. I left right after dinner, aware that I had added to Jarmila's crossness by not finishing everything on my too generously heaped plate.

On Monday, Kumermann and I had another lunch date at the Jewish Town Hall. When we sat down, he asked me, "How much did you know as a child about the Holocaust?"

I said that I had learned about it after the Second World War, though on some level I felt I had always known about it. "What about you?"

341

"My parents didn't stress it very much. My father was hiding his Jewishness, so he didn't talk about it much. When he died, I found many books on the camps in his library. He had been obsessed with the subject. But as a child I mostly was influenced by the Communist propaganda, which said there were two Germanys—the bad Germany in the West and the good Germany in the East. East Germany had had nothing to do with the war. There had been no Nazis in East Germany. When I was about thirteen, my father got an official letter informing him that his mother had died at Treblinka. I got home before him, and I read the letter—it gave the date and number of the transport—but I didn't know then what it meant. It didn't seem unnatural that someone from our family had died in the war, because the Communists' propaganda always talked about the three hundred and sixty-five thousand Czechs killed in the war. Only, they didn't tell us that three hundred and twenty-five thousand of those people were Jewish. Slowly, the knowledge of the Holocaust crept over me. When I got involved with the Jewish Community, I came to see that I was part of the Holocaust, too—that I had been touched by it through my family. After my father died, I inherited his books about the camps and read some of them. There were books on every major camp—Auschwitz, Treblinka, Dachau, Belsen, Buchenwald—by survivors."

"How did this affect you?"

"Well, I wouldn't say it was a big emotional upheaval. It was more a reevaluation. Also, the more I learned about the Holocaust, the more sensitive I became to any hint of anti-Semitism; I realized that the Holocaust started with small independent islands of anti-Semitism in Germany. But, again, this was more a rational than an emotional reaction. You should realize that my life is based on rational analysis rather than on emotion. If I come to a rational conclusion, it influences my emotional side, more than the other way around. I'm a combination of choleric and theoretical. I don't react quickly. My feelings take a long time to develop, but then they may be stronger than those of people who have an immediate emotional reaction. This is hard on Jarmila, who is a very emotional person. She sometimes hates my logical analysis."

The waitress brought our lunch and as he ate Kumermann morosely told me of a serious hitch that had developed in his trip to Israel. The Israelis, he said, were now insisting that the journalists flying over with Havel participate in all Havel's activities and stay at his hotel, and demanded an advance payment of twenty-five hundred dollars to cover expenses. (Twenty-five hundred dollars is the equivalent of as much as two and a half years' salary.) *Rudé Právo*, the Communist paper, could conceivably cough up that kind of money, but no other publication could. So Kumermann would have to explore other ways of getting to Israel. One was to apply for a seat on an army plane that Havel had loaned to the Community to bring members to Israel during his visit; he was afraid, though, that he was applying too late. A second possibility—which made me stare at him in amazement—was to accept an invitation that Arafat had extended to him after the disastrous interview. On finishing his harangue for publication, Arafat had been all friendliness and had invited Kumermann to come to Israel as a guest of the PLO. A colleague of Kumermann's had received a similar invitation and had accepted.

"You would really go to Israel as a guest of the PLO?" I asked.

"Why not? I would still write something nasty about them." He looked at his watch and said he had better go talk to the people in the Community about getting on the army plane. I had an appointment late that afternoon to interview Jarmila at the apartment, and we parted until then.

DURING my first visit to Prague, I spent my days talking with people and my evenings at dinners and parties. I say "talking," but in fact I talked hardly at all; I mostly listened to monologues. One might have thought that after the years of isolation Czechs would be pressing foreign visitors for information about life in the West, but this was not so. Evidently, when people are let out of prison, before they can take in the vast, luminous universe "out there" they must first bear witness to the small, dark world they are leaving behind. In January, the Czechs, still rubbing their eyes in the too bright light, were all Ancient Mariners. By April, the general logorrhea was diminishing, and signs of curiosity about the outer world were beginning to appear, like snowdrops in February.

Perhaps because people now talked less—and also because I was intentionally seeing fewer people—I spent more time alone in Prague. My daily talks with Kumermann formed the structure of my journalistic enterprise. But another agenda also claimed my attention, and sometimes threatened to subvert the journalistic one. This was my quest for the Proustian sensations that would reconnect me to my early childhood in Prague, and illuminate—and possibly settle—the question of what coming to this place meant to me. I had two candidates for the madeleines that would release the flood of memories. One was an ice cream of ambrosial deliciousness I had a memory of eating with my father on the street in Prague. It was an ice cream lighter than American ice cream but milkier than sherbet, whose delicate, fresh, slightly and somehow arousingly commercial taste I have sometimes felt on the verge of—but never succeeded wholly in—encountering again. On Wenceslas Square I had seen strollers with ice cream cones, and there was something about the appearance of the ice cream that made me think it might be the madeleine ice cream. I bided my time, proleptically savoring the moment when I would walk into a certain shop I had noticed, in front of which there was always a line, and purchase my entrance into the kingdom of early childhood. The second madeleine would be a visit to the third-floor apartment on Vodičková Ulice where I had lived during the first five years of my life with my mother, father, and sister. The apartment was near my hotel, just off Wenceslas Square, in a six-story Art Nouveau building that had a café on the second floor. In January, I had walked into the building and started up the marble staircase, but the way to the third floor was barred by a metal gate, so I had left and not pursued the matter. Now, with more time and will, I had figured out how I could get into the apartment. But, as with the ice cream, I circled it, imagined it, and didn't rush into it.

I had taken to drinking afternoon coffee at the second-floor café, which in my parents' day had been an elegant establishment called Berger's. The café was no longer elegant and bore the generic name Cukrárna—"confectionery." It was dowdy and always crowded, the coffee wasn't good, and the pastries looked unappealing, but it had an agreeable and hospitable spirit. I had been a couple of times to the Café Slavia, on the river across from the National Theater, but neither its historical resonance as a famous intellectuals' hangout nor its aesthetic majesty (it is a vast room, with great, ornate windows looking out on the river and with a remarkable Symbolist painting at one end) was enough to counteract the tension that pervaded the place. There were too many West German youths with golden-blond punk hair, and American couples with sulky adolescent children, and elderly English librarians with puzzled expressions for the overworked waiters and waitresses to handle with grace, so the handling was done with the subtle sadism common to all places that are wildly successful. At my dowdy Cukrárna, there were few tourists, and the waitresses were efficient and benign. They wore uniforms of a permanently crumpled synthetic lavender fabric, with puffed sleeves and little white aprons, which were of a piece with the general gratuitous unattractiveness of the decor. On my first visit, I had sat at a table where two men were finishing their coffee (table sharing was customary at the Cukrárna), and one of them was studying his bill with indignation. "Seven crowns," he said.

"Last week, it was six." When a young waitress came to clear the cups, the man said to her, "Seven crowns, and they don't even give you water with the coffee." The waitress said nothing and walked away with the cups. But presently an older waitress appeared and said to the man, "So what's this about water?" He repeated, "Now they don't even give you water with the coffee." The waitress said, "When we served water, decent people would complain that it smelled." Then she went and got the man a glass of water.

On another visit to the Cukrárna, I got into conversation with a middle-aged man and woman at my table; he was a factory worker, and she was a telephone operator. They were not married—they were out on a date—and were a little skittish with each other. When the waitress came, they ordered white wine and did not rule out the possibility of a pastry later. In answer to my question about how they were getting along in the new order, the woman, who looked a little like Jana Valenta, said, "Life will probably be better for our children, but not for us. Things will probably get worse before they get better. But we love our President. Some people who are against him talk about how he speaks oddly—how he does something with his tongue, like a lisp. It's because they beat him up when he was in prison and damaged the roof of his mouth. That's why he speaks this way." (Havel has never written about being beaten in prison, nor does he speak with a lisp.)

I said provocatively, "We read in the newspapers in America that people in the former Communist countries don't know how to work."

Both the man and the woman chimed in to protest that this wasn't so. "We know how to work," the man said, "and we work very hard—those of us on the bottom. It's the people above us, the ones who do the paperwork, who don't work. That's why there is chaos." The woman said that at her previous job, at a dress factory, "we were worked so hard, they stood over us so much, that we couldn't even go to the toilet. If you went to the toilet and there was someone ahead of you, you had to go back to your place. They wouldn't give you the time to wait." The man said, "Much of what is made in the factory is defective"—as if no human agency were involved.

As he spoke, I recalled a passage in Havel's essay "The Power of the Powerless" that had made a strong impression on me. In 1974, after his plays were banned, Havel had worked in a brewery, and his immediate superior was

> a certain Š, a person well versed in the art of making beer. He was proud of his profession, and he wanted our brewery to brew good beer. He spent almost all his time at work, continually thinking up improvements, and he frequently made the rest of us feel uncomfortable because he assumed that we loved brewing as much as he did. In the midst of the slovenly indifference to work that socialism encourages, a more constructive worker would be difficult to imagine.

Havel goes on to tell the melancholy history of Š's quixotic attempts to rescue the brewery from the ruin it was being brought to by its incompetent manager, and about his final, desperate act of writing a letter to the manager's superior, "in which he attempted to analyze the brewery's difficulties [and] explained why it was the worst in the district and pointed to those responsible." But the manager had friends in high places and was able to get Š's letter labeled a "defamatory document" and Š himself a "political saboteur." Š was transferred to another brewery, where he was given work that required no skill. Havel writes:

> By speaking the truth, Š had stepped out of line, broken the rules, cast himself out, and he ended up as a sub-citizen, stigmatized as an enemy. He could now say anything he wanted, but he could never, as a matter of principle, expect

to be heard. He had become the "dissident" of the Eastern Bohemian Brewery.

I think this is a model case. . . . You do not become a "dissident" just because you decide one day to take up this most unusual career. You are thrown into it by your personal sense of responsibility combined with a complex set of external circumstances. . . . It begins as an attempt to do your work well, and ends with being branded an enemy of society.

But here, as in all his writings, Havel allows for the complexity and diversity of human experience even under totalitarianism. He writes:

I am far from believing that the only decent and responsible people are those who find themselves at odds with the existing social and political structures. After all, the brewmaster Š might have won his battle. . . . The manager, who was politically powerful but otherwise ignorant of beer, a man who loathed workers and was given to intrigue, might have been replaced, and conditions in the brewery might have been improved on the basis of Š's suggestions.

The Cukrárna was evidently a place where some Š had prevailed and set its agreeable tone and calmly efficient praxis. The older waitress's solicitude for the complaining customer reflected a fundamental decency and responsibility. Doubtless there were other workplaces where the better parts of human nature had prevailed over the worse ones even though the system was weighted toward the latter.

One day, I bought the ice cream cone and had a tour of the old apartment; of course, neither experience was significant. The ice cream was simply bad European ice cream, and on entering the apartment I felt not a shock but merely a small stir of recognition. Yes, this is where the dining room was, here was the kitchen, that room at the end of the hall was the nursery.

In the thirties, the place had been a standard bourgeois Prague apartment. Now it was a suite of offices belonging to an enterprise called the Prague Confectionery & Soda Company. Its director, a Mr. Švehla, took me around with a mildly resentful air; he didn't like the idea that all these rooms had been occupied by a single family. Although linoleum now covered the parquet floors, and one of the large rooms facing the street had been divided, the apartment was essentially intact, with its ornate ceiling moldings, and its tall windows looking out on Vodičková Ulice. But it evoked no memories. There was one room the director did not show me. It was next to the kitchen, on the side of the apartment facing an alley. Its door was locked, and it contained the office safe. The safes of childhood memory are similarly protected. One cannot get into them at will; one cannot pick their locks. One can only hope for an accident that leaves the door carelessly open for a few minutes, allowing one to slip in before the director is recalled to his duties.

My interview with Jarmila began badly. I had brought a present—some pansy plants in soil, which I had bought at a small farmers' market near the Old Town Square—and it created a problem: where and how to keep them until the weekend, when they would be taken to the family's plot in an allotment garden in an outlying district. Kumermann, who, like Jarmila, had come home from work a few minutes earlier, looked at the plants balefully and then said there was a pail on the balcony outside the living room where they could be kept. Jarmila went to the balcony, suddenly shrieked, and reappeared clutching her hand, in a fury at her son David, who had evidently left an open bottle of acid from his chemistry set on the balcony; she had knocked it over and spilled it on her hand. "This is the last straw," Jarmila said. "I've had it up to here with that boy's experiments." She went to wash her hand, and Kumermann called David from the bedroom. The boy, a shy, dark fifteen-year-old, appeared and said that the bottle had contained per-oxide, not acid. When Jarmila learned this, she was slightly mollified. The boy returned to his bedroom, and Kumermann went to the kitchen. Jarmila sank into an armchair, and we began the interview. Until now, Jarmila and I had always spoken Czech together—not because her English wasn't good (it was even better than Kumermann's: she was an English teacher by profession) but out of some shared instinctive feeling that Czech was the language of choice for our woman-to-woman rapport. Now, so I wouldn't have to translate when I wrote, we changed to English.

Jarmila said she was still exhausted and ill. She was still suffering from insomnia and over the last several months had been running a low-grade fever, for which no cause had been found. She said she had asked Kumermann to do the shopping and to cook dinner that day. I asked whether perhaps I shouldn't come back another time.

"No, it's OK. I can talk."

"Could it be something in the water?" I asked.

"No. No bacteria could survive in our water—it's so full of chlorine and other chemicals." She went on to speak of the neglect she felt to be inherent in the Czech medical system. The overworked clinic doctors, she believed, couldn't give her proper care.

"Are most Czech doctors women, as in Russia?" I asked.

"Yes."

"And does the medical profession here have the same low status it has in Russia?"

"It's a bit different here—different from the high status and money of America, but also different from Russia. Here the doctor gets a low salary—either the same as an ordinary worker or slightly lower, though a specialist may get a bit more. The average monthly salary of a doctor is between three thousand and thirty-five hundred crowns. Specialists may get four, five, or six thousand. But the social status of doctors is very high.

People look up to them; everyone wants the doctor to be his friend. The fact is, very often you have to give the doctor a bribe. We have a special word for it, *všimné*—it's the thing that makes the doctor notice you. People put the money in an envelope and give it to the doctor, and she just pockets it."

"Do you do it as you come in or as you are leaving?"

"You do it as you are leaving. I never do it. That is probably why I am so neglected. But other people do it. They say that if you need an operation, you have to do it."

"So this is the way doctors raise their incomes above the level of the worker."

"Yes. Some doctors make more than others. Gynecologists and obstetricians, for instance, make a lot of money. It is always better to pay the bribe and be sure that your child will be born safely."

"You paid the *všimné* when your children were born?"

"Yes. I paid a thousand crowns for each child, and I have never regretted it. Because the doctor did more than she would have done otherwise. For example, when I was taken to the hospital Daniel called the doctor, and she came to see me immediately, which was wonderful. Otherwise, I would have been left there without any help."

As we talked, Jarmila's spirits seemed to revive, and during a discussion of Prague sexual mores she became quite animated. In Prague, she told me, there were very few open homosexuals. She said that she herself knew only two gay men, and one of them lived in Finland. She added, "I've never heard of a lesbian in this country. We know what they are, but I've never met one."

I said that in America during the sixties, lesbianism had become a political gesture among feminists (as well as an agreeable alternative for women fed up with men), and it was now fairly commonplace, although not entirely without social stigma.

"That won't happen here," Jarmila said. "Not for a long time.

Because we still need our men. We simply can't live without them. We still need their salaries. Here, if you don't put two salaries together the family cannot exist."

I said, "What about two working women living together?"

Jarmila looked at me in bewilderment. "Two women? Two women living together? You mean women without children." She let the idea sink in and said, "Yes, that might be possible. But where would they live? We have a housing problem here. If you are single, it's extremely difficult to get a flat. You can't buy one, and you can't rent one through the state, so you usually live with your parents. So two women living together—that would be very rare."

I mentioned a lesbian couple I knew in New York who lived with the two children of one of the women from her prior marriage.

Jarmila again looked bewildered. "But how can the children cope with it? I can't imagine it. If I kicked out Daniel—and one day I will, probably, when I find the right woman—I just can't imagine how David and Míša would react to that. They would probably kick *me* out."

Daniel came in from the kitchen, where he could overhear our conversation. "Do you think you could find a woman who would put up with you?" he said.

"I could find many. All my women friends would be very glad to live with me. Well! Two women living together . . ." Jarmila stretched out in her chair and luxuriated in the idea. "Two women. It would be wonderful." Daniel picked up some papers from a desk and went into his bedroom. Jarmila continued, "But what about two men living together? Men are so lazy. They come home at night and sit down and pick up a newspaper or a book, or they watch television, or, if they have a car, they say, 'I must go have a look at the car,' and they lie under the car and have a little rest. Or they go to a pub. And the poor woman comes home from work and has to do the shopping and the cleaning and help the children with their homework and cook the dinner. She does everything. In my previous job, at a language school, I had to teach two evenings a week, and on Tuesdays and Thursdays I got home at eight-thirty. I thought it was terrible. Now I have a job where I come home every day at five o'clock. But, of course, it means that I have to cook the dinner every day, seven days a week. When I was at the language school, Daniel somehow took it as his duty to cook the dinner on Tuesdays and Thursdays, because there was no one else. But now he wouldn't think of doing it."

I ventured, "Maybe you could ask him to help you."

"No, I can't now. I started my new job in February, but for me it's not so new, since it's another teaching job. But Daniel started his new job this month, and for him everything is new. So I just can't ask him now. Last Tuesday, I got up at half past five and found him sitting at the desk here, sleeping. He had sat here the whole night. He has to work very hard, and it's important for him to succeed in his job. I've been teaching such a long time that I wouldn't mind being a window washer now. But he was a window washer for twelve years. It's a long time. He deserves something better."

"That's very nice of you—" I began.

Jarmila interrupted. "No, I'm not only being nice. I'm also fed up with having a husband who is a window washer and doesn't wash his own windows. Well, actually, he did wash the windows last Saturday. When he gets used to his job—if he ever does, and I'm not sure he ever will—then, of course, I can ask him to do more. But even when he was a window washer he did other things, so as not to go crazy. He read books and wrote articles and studied. He couldn't do any of this in the afternoon, after work, because the children were home then and were always asking him questions or wanting to do something with him. He did it all at night. He was also doing some work for Charter, all of which took a lot of time. When the revolution came, I thought, Now he will have regular hours and he will come home earlier. But he didn't. During the revolution, he started coming home at two in the morning and even later. Sometimes he didn't come home at all. Very often, I complained, and other women complained. The men went everywhere; they knew what was happening, and we didn't. They had no time to talk to us and tell us what was going on. Several times, I went alone to Wenceslas Square to take part in the big rallies—completely alone. I didn't like it. I'm scared of crowds. There were two hundred thousand people there."

Kumermann reappeared, and he and Jarmila had a brief, testy exchange. He told her he had to return to the office and would be back home at eight-thirty. He said he would bring back fried cheese for dinner and directed her to put the heat on under the potatoes at eight. She said sullenly that she didn't see how he could take the tram and the metro to his office and back and buy the cheese and still be home at eight-thirty. He shrugged and left.

"So you see. This is how it is almost every day. He simply announces he has to go somewhere, and he goes. Now he's leaving again. He said he was going to cook dinner, and he's not going to cook it. He says he will be back at half past eight. We will see whether he is back at half past eight."

I asked Jarmila whether she and Kumermann had been in accord about his signing the Charter. She replied, "Yes. We decided it jointly, and decided that only one of us should sign it, and that I wouldn't sign it. Daniel's mother was no good at looking after the children, and my parents lived in the country. We knew that if we were both taken away there would be no one to look after the children. So we decided that one was enough in our case." She went on to speak of her terror when the police would come early in the morning and take Kumermann away for interrogation. "He would come back very hungry, because he never ate anything in the prison."

"Was he afraid the food would be poisoned?"

"No. He was afraid it wouldn't be kosher."

"Does he eat only kosher food?"

"He sort of does and doesn't."

"Do you cook kosher food?"

"No. I don't know how to. But it's true, I don't use pork or ham."

Jarmila spoke of her teaching with confident satisfaction. "No one has ever fallen asleep in my class," she said. "When I left my previous job, the pupils were unhappy. I hadn't expected that. Czech students are not very lively. They just sit there and look at you. They listen, and they don't react. They laugh sometimes. I believe in laughter. If a lesson is quiet, if the pupils don't laugh at least five times, it's a waste of time. When they laugh they are learning, and when they don't laugh they are bored and not learning. But sometimes it is so difficult to wake them up and make them laugh."

At eight o'clock, I followed Jarmila into the kitchen. There was a pan on the stove in which neatly peeled and quartered potatoes sat covered in water; a handful of caraway seeds floated on the surface. "Well, he prepared the potatoes," Jarmila said grudgingly. She turned the gas on under the potatoes. At half past eight, she drained the potatoes and returned to the living room with a martyred air; then Kumermann came in, a few minutes later. He went into the kitchen, briskly prepared the fried cheese, sliced a couple of cucumbers, and called the children. Although the family usually ate together, Kumermann had thoughtfully decided to spare the shy children the ordeal of eating with a stranger from America, and fed them first; when they finished, they did their homework in the living room. The fried cheese was one of the best things I have ever eaten: slabs of a mild cheese coated with bread crumbs and egg, as if it were Wiener schnitzel, and lightly fried in oil. It was sold already breaded.

After dinner, Kumermann showed me his gum-wrapper collection. He brought out an album in which five hundred or so of his specimens were pasted, and a tea tin containing other examples of his twelve thousand wrappers. The album was an illumination. All my previous associations with gum wrappers had been unpleasant: the ugly sight of a chewing mouth, wads of gum stuck on soles of shoes or the bottoms of wastebaskets, crumpled-up wrappers on the floor of a car. Now I saw what a treasure of design lay embedded in Kumermann's collection. The variety of colors, typefaces, patterns, and illustrations changed my feeling of revulsion into one of delight. There were wrappers from India, Thailand, Egypt, Spain, Italy, France, Holland, Poland, Germany, Hungary, Iceland, Romania, England, Scotland, Finland. The carefully smoothed little paper rectangles were pasted on the pages in orderly rows, forming metapatterns that evoked the collages of Kurt Schwitters. Here, too, the unregarded flotsam and jetsam of commercial culture had been plucked out of their context and carried into the realm of the treasured. Walter Benjamin, in the most cited passage of his essay "The Work of Art in the Age of Mechanical Reproduction," speaks of the "aura" that distinguishes the unique art object from the mechanically made multiple. But a collection such as Kumermann's, like art in which mechanically reproduced images and patterns and texts figure, precisely invests the multiple with aura. In the context of its twelve thousand companion pieces, each gum wrapper acquired presence and aesthetic status. As I leafed through the album, I idly asked Kumermann if he had any Russian gum wrappers; he promptly delved into the tin and produced a pile of about fifty. The piles—neat and precise—had a charm of their own, though the album represented a higher stage of the wrappers' evolution from their humble origins on the world's candy counters.

Kumermann spoke of his long collecting career. "As far as I can remember, I always collected. When I was four, I had a collection of various pictures, and then, at eight, I started collecting matchboxes; in three years, I had several thousand. I gave up matchboxes for stamps, and by thirteen I had several thousand of them. I don't throw anything away, because I know somebody may be collecting it. For certain things I have regular

customers: I have a customer for everything relating to choc-
olate; he is a friend who has some fifty-five thousand chocolate-
related items. Another friend collects bottle caps. A collector
is best understood by another collector. There was this man in
the office of one of the companies whose windows I washed
who made regular trips to Egypt, and sometimes I succeeded
in squeezing something out of him, because he had two small
daughters to whom he brought Egyptian gum. A woman clerical
worker who sat next to him in the office would listen to my
conversations with him, and one day she said to me, 'Give me
advice on how to collect.' She was a recent widow and wanted
to fill her time with something. I told her, 'It's no use. If you
have to decide to be a collector, you'll never be one.' There are
collectors and there are gatherers, and the difference between
the two is that a collector collects even things he doesn't like,
whereas a gatherer collects only things he likes. A collector will
collect things he finds aesthetically distasteful, just for the sake
of completeness."

I got back to my hotel at around eleven, and then set out on
what had become a nightly walk to the river. When I reached
the riverbank, I found the nesting swan in a state of agitation.
Her neck was craning from side to side, and her wings were
thrashing about heavily. Something was moving in the grass,
and when I saw what it was my heart froze. Three rats were
scurrying around the nest, sometimes making audacious forays
into its outer edge, which the swan would fend off with her
bill and her wings. One particularly bold rat caused her to half
lift herself off the nest—revealing the eggs—as she hissed and
beat her wings. He scuttled away to a safe distance but was
soon back. I watched, anxious and upset, as the rats kept ap-
proaching the nest, and the swan—as if tethered to it—craned
and hissed and thrashed about. I was glad when another stroller
joined me at the balustrade, and we watched the scene together,
sharing its pathos and horror. Tonight, for some reason, the
mystical blue-green light of the cathedral was still on at eleven-

thirty. My companion left, and I soon made my way back to the hotel. I woke up several times that night and thought of the swan with dread and pity.

THE next day at noon, I picked up Kumermann, as usual, at his office, but when we arrived at the Jewish Town Hall we found the lunchroom closed, with no explanation; there was simply a sign saying LUNCHROOM CLOSED. We went to a local self-service grocery store and bought rolls for Kumermann and a yogurt for me, and walked over to a nearby square to eat our lunch on a bench. We could not find a seat, however. In addition to the usual Easter-holiday crowds, and the unusual post-velvet-revolution foreign journalists, businessmen, and curiosity-seekers, there were the tourists who had been drawn to the city by the impending visit of the Pope—the first papal visit ever. On Saturday, he was to appear at the Letná Plain, which could accommodate over a million people and was where the Communists had held their May Day parades. Kumermann proposed that we find somewhere to sit in nearby Charles University, and we walked over to an entrance a couple of blocks away. Kumermann led me with familiarity up a marble staircase and down a long corridor to a stone bench beneath a stately window, and we ate our lunch there. As faculty members went by, Kumermann would greet them, pointing out to me several former dissidents who had been kicked out after '68 and had been recently reinstated. One of the faculty members walking by—whom Kumermann did not know and to whom I did not make myself known—was Egon Valenta; he was accompanied by a small woman of around thirty, wearing a miniskirt and black tights, who was tossing a mane of prematurely gray hair and laughing up into his face in an intimate and proprietary manner. I was sure he had seen me, and I felt obscurely at fault, as one always does when these unwelcome encounters occur.

I said to Kumermann, "I have been reading Kafka's *Letters to Milena*, and this morning I came across a sentence where Kafka says that Czech is a more 'affectionate' language than German. It made me think about our talks and about the fact that we always speak English together. I probably have a different picture of you from the one I would have if we spoke Czech. Do you have the feeling that you are a different person in each of the languages?"

Kumermann considered. "Well, there are more precise emotional levels in Czech than in English, and various kinds of diminutives. Where in English there is only a single, rather primitive diminutive form of a word, in Czech there are several. That's about the difference."

"I feel there's more of a difference than that between the two languages. For instance, people with whom I have spoken in both Czech and English seem more playful in Czech."

"Yes, you can toy with Czech more than with English. And you can blur the boundaries of like and dislike, so as not to offend."

"You strike me as a very forthright person, who says what he thinks and never holds back. Do you seem less so in Czech?"

"No. In Czech I am the same. But I might put things in fancier, funnier words."

"I feel—and I've been allowing for it—that in English you're a much more gruff and plain-speaking person than you would be in Czech."

"I offend everyone around here, too."

I laughed. "So it wouldn't be doing you an injustice to describe you as a straightforward and no-nonsense type—as opposed, say, to your colleague the charmer, with his suavity and politesse?"

"Oh, I can be very polite, too. I may use bad language sometimes, but I still hope I'm not impolite or offensive to people in general."

"But you're a little argumentative."

"That's because you ask questions that need to be answered. That man in my office also has straightforward opinions. But when you saw him—and usually when I see him—it is in a situation where there is nothing at issue. So he can just toy— toy with words, toy with a situation. He makes jokes. I can make jokes, too, though I suppose I am more abusive in jokes than he is. But, basically, this is a different situation. Have you noticed I always say 'basically'? Because you are always trying to squeeze opinions from me, and these opinions are more or less radical. But that doesn't mean that I'm radical on a day-to-day basis. On a day-to-day basis, these questions don't come up."

"So in this unusual circumstance, where you are being, as it were, interrogated—"

"Yes, that's right. It is unusual. Normally, you can spend whole days when no serious issue comes up. When you don't have to assume any particular position all day. When"—Kumermann toyed—"you can just be charming."

As we were leaving the university, Kumermann did something he had never done before: he helped me with my coat. The gesture—clearly prompted by our conversation—touched and amused me. So he was a closet charmer after all. As we picked up the remains of our lunch, I asked him what I should do with the plastic spoon I had used to eat my yogurt. In the grocery, I had asked him if they provided spoons with the yogurt; he had given me a withering look and groped around in his knapsack until he found a pink plastic spoon. He now took it back from me, wiped it with his handkerchief, and restored it to the knapsack. He returned to his office to work on the Arafat story, and I headed for Vinohrady, a quiet residential neighborhood that began at the top of Wenceslas Square, where I had never seen any fellow tourists, and where there was a large old park.

On the way to the park, I passed handsome, solid nineteenth-century five-story apartment buildings in a state of gentle decay;

through their spacious front hallways I could glimpse romantic
vistas of lushly verdant backyards in which large trees grew.
In the almost empty park, I sat on a bench and thumbed through
a guidebook, trying to find the name of the park, where I
thought I might have been taken as a small child. As I thumbed,
I realized that I had slipped the wrong guidebook into my
handbag; instead of a guide to Prague, I had brought a guide
to the whole of Czechoslovakia. I continued leafing through it,
however, reading the title headings of lake regions, mountain
ranges, towns, and villages, and making trips to them in my
imagination. Some of the place names were familiar, having
figured in family history or in songs and stories of my childhood,
and one of them, the town Domažlice, haltingly brought to
mind a song my parents used to sing, a song I did not know I
knew anymore:

*Žádný neví co jsou Domažlice.*
*Žádný neví co je to Taus.*
*Taus je to německy, Domažlice česky.*
*Žádný neví co je to Taus.*

*No one knows what Domažlice is.*
*No one knows what Taus is.*
*Taus is German, Domažlice is Czech.*
*No one knows what Taus is.*

As this nonsense verse emerged—a relic of the Austro-
Hungarian Empire and its Germanifying geography—the door
of memory slowly swung open. What neither the ice cream nor
the visit to the apartment could achieve, the sight of "Domažlice" on the page had done. The agreeable fragrance of the
First Republic and of nineteenth- and early-twentieth-century
Czech folk and literary culture wafted out of the song, evoking
the atmosphere of my childhood years with startling poignancy.

The baggage of my Czech heritage, which I had refused to trail after me in my adopted country and had, as it were, left checked at the station, now stood massed before me, the lids open and the contents spilling out. Songs, stories, legends, jokes, anecdotes, reminiscences, poems, images came to me in a nostalgic rush. The indirection and playfulness of the Czech mind, with its distinctive vocabulary of tenderness—the qualities that have so endeared Czechs to foreigners and caused them to be regarded as the Minoans of Central Europe—were present to me as perhaps they had never been present before. The Czech part of my identity, which had always lain below the surface of my "real life" as an American child and American adult, and had affected it in subtle but palpable ways, now appeared to me with moving vividness. I rifled through the trunks with delight and affection and gratitude. My Jewishness was something else—a different order of influence, occupying a darker, less accessible region of my psyche. Like Kumermann's father, my parents fearfully played down the fact that we were Jewish. Only as an adult did I, again like Kumermann, claim my Jewish identity and form my sense of myself as a Jew, although, unlike Kumermann, I had not become a religious one. As I interrogated Kumermann about his life under the old and the new orders, my mind was never entirely removed from a period of time years before he was born, for whose horrors a string of place names has provided a kind of necessary, inadequate metonymy: Auschwitz, Dachau, Treblinka, Bergen-Belsen, Buchenwald, Theresienstadt, Ravensbrück. The Czechs, like the Hungarians, the Poles, the Romanians, the French, the Dutch—like everyone but the Danes—had not saved their Jews. Even my joy in the velvet revolution had ultimately been tempered by my (spared) Jew's awareness of this fact—by my need to keep the beguiling Czechs at a certain distance, lest the memory of the six million be dulled. The thorny, argumentative, emotionally closed Kumermann provided me with my defense against the danger.

. . .

I LEFT the park, and instead of going to the Cukrárna for my afternoon coffee I headed for the river, to see how the swan had survived her dreadful night. I was relieved to find her in place and unscathed. The rats were gone, and a pleasing daylight scene now greeted the passersby as they paused in their strolling to lean over the balustrade and gaze fondly down on the swan, who was fending off ducks and small birds in the grass with a composed, matter-of-fact air; the tense desperation of the night was gone.

When traveling, one is both more open to new impressions and more prone to blunt their force through the act of analogizing. We make the unfamiliar familiar through a kind of sleight of hand; the phrase "it is like" domesticates the exotic, gives us the illusion of having got our bearings, allows us to make ourselves at home when we are nowhere near it. My initial mistaking of the swan for papers strewn on the grass doubtless derived from some such familiarizing tendency of the mind, as did my subsequent association of her, on the night of the rats, with small, hemmed-in countries like Czechoslovakia, whose geography is their destiny, and whose condition is one of chronic stuckness. Now, as I watched the swan, confident and serene after her dark ordeal, yet another analogy offered itself: that of Havel himself, who had also weathered a bad passage and was now reaping the rewards of his fortitude and courage. In one of his letters to Olga from prison, Havel writes of friends who have emigrated and are "doing what they enjoy at last, they are involved in their work, free from endless complications, no doubt viewing our toiling and moiling as pointless now, while I, on the other hand, am deprived of all that, without the slightest chance of working in a theatre and revelling in the ideas that theatre has always inspired in me." But he adds that such thoughts "always end with a peculiar sensation of inner joy that I am where I should be, that I have not turned away from myself, that I have not bolted for the emergency exit, and that, for all the privations, I am rid of the worst privation of all (one that I have known myself, too): the feeling that I could not measure up to my task, though I may not have set it myself—at least not in this form and to this degree— but merely accepted it from the hand of fate, accident, and history."

I also thought of one of the émigrés—Milan Kundera—who had finally seen no point in hanging on in Czechoslovakia after his books were banned, and had viewed the work of the dissidents with skepticism and irony. One of the leitmotivs of *The Unbearable Lightness of Being*, and surely the aspect of the book that galled the Czech opposition more than any question of true-to-lifeness, was Kundera's pessimism about national and individual fate and his pitiless examination of the sentimentality and vulgarity and self-aggrandizement—he calls it kitsch—that can creep into the work of activist movements such as the one Havel headed. Already in 1969, when Kundera published an essay challenging Havel's position called "Radicalism and Exhibitionism," he was expressing the harsh, dark views that were to reach a culmination in *The Unbearable Lightness of Being*. There is a passage in the novel that most sharply reflects Kundera's skepticism. It concerns Tomas's refusal to sign the statement of complicity with the authorities (a retraction of a letter to the editor of a newspaper), which will cost him his job as a hospital surgeon and ultimately propel him into the world of window washing. Before making the decision, Tomas becomes aware of pressure from people who want him to sign—who, he notes with surprise, are not only people who have themselves compromised and collaborated but also people who refused to compromise and collaborate and have been persecuted:

> *Everyone* wanted him to write the retraction; it would make
> *everyone* happy! The people with the first type of reaction
> would be happy because by inflating cowardice, he would

make their actions seem commonplace and thereby give them back their lost honor. The people with the second type of reaction, who had come to consider their honor a special privilege never to be yielded, nurtured a secret love for the cowards, for without them their courage would soon erode into a trivial, monotonous grind admired by no one.

Through Havel's pure personal example and his simple, profound credo that one should "work for something because it is good, not just because it stands a chance to succeed," he imparted to this grind its transcendent beauty, and protected it against kitsch. In the glow of the velvet revolutions of Central Europe, Kundera's mordant psychology and sociology and his bleak view of the human prospect seemed carping and irrelevant. (Kundera himself came to none of the Czech inauguration events or New Year's celebrations; in January, he wrote a sincere, if somewhat nervous, tribute to Havel, published here in *The New Republic*, and in March he was said to have made a brief, secret visit to Prague.) But as time goes on and history reassumes its normal iron guise, Kundera's work may well regain its old power, and his use of the emergency exit may well seem less like a misstep and more like a fateful artistic choice.

On Saturday, following instructions from Kumermann, I took a tram out of Prague and disembarked at a desolate stop, three or four miles away, named Palmovka. A few minutes later, another tram disgorged Kumermann, who was carrying a bucket filled with dirt and the pansies I had brought. We were going to his allotment garden, where he worked on weekends. We waited for yet another tram, which came promptly (tram service is very good in Prague), and ten minutes later got out at an even more desolate stop. Kumermann led me across a highway abutting a large, ugly housing project that lowered over an empty wasteland. We came to a dirt road and followed it up a slope, passing small stucco houses with flowering fruit trees in their front gardens. After the road passed under a railroad, the landscape began to take on a more wildly rural aspect. Budding brush and tender early-spring flowers grew along the roadside. The temperature was mild, and the sky was an exciting mixture of fast-moving dark clouds and sudden piercing glints of sunlight. It was nice to be walking in the country in early spring, and I said so to Kumermann. "April is the cruelest month," he said in response. I nodded. We walked on, and I felt Kumermann struggle with himself—and lose. He simply couldn't not inquire, "Do you know who wrote that?"

"Yes," I said, and when Kumermann continued to look at me challengingly I added the name he needed to hear. Just then Kumermann reminded me of the endearing Mr. Spock, in the science-fiction television series *Star Trek*, who is half human and half Vulcan, and who allegorizes the pathos of a nature in which the capacity for reasoning and remembering is greater than the capacity for feeling and intuiting.

When we reached the top of the slope, the allotment garden came into view: a large tract of land divided into equal plots of about three thousand square feet, on which vegetables, flowers, and small fruit trees had been planted, and small houses built. Kumermann led me to his plot. There was a woodshed in one corner and, in the middle, the foundation of a projected small house. The garden had an unruly, unfinished character. There were piles of topsoil standing in weedy, uncultivated areas. In the planted part, strawberries rambled amid dandelions; there were also gooseberry, raspberry, and black-currant bushes, clumps of onions and chives, and a few infant fruit trees. I asked Kumermann where his garden ended. "It's easy to tell," he said. "Where it's orderly, it's not ours." It was true. The other gardens were traditional European kitchen gardens—rich, brown, weedless earth, the plants set in straight, neat rows. Kumermann told me that the messy appearance of his garden had led to bad feelings on the part of the other gardeners, and so had the fact that he had not yet built his "bungalow." According to the rules governing the allotment gardens, each holder of a plot had to build such a structure, and build it according to strict specifications. Kumermann said he felt no need to have a house in a garden forty minutes from his apartment—since he had no wish to sleep or eat there—and was taking his time fulfilling this contractual obligation. He had got the plot, for which there was a long waiting list, through the intervention of a friend in the bureaucracy, and through a five-hundred-crown bribe. "Basically, the difference between Western and Bolshevik systems is that in the West you do not meddle in other people's business unless you're asked," he said. "Isn't that right? But here they're always looking at your garden and always telling you what to do. All right—if it is messy here, that's my business. But they tell you it doesn't look nice and you should take better care of it. You should do this and you should do that. They consider it beautiful to have long rows of houses exactly the same—which I consider intolerable. Not only ugly but inhuman. But they like it, and there is no way to talk to them."

I asked him who the other gardeners were—people like him, who came out from Prague?

"No. Most of the people are from around here, which is what makes it so stupid to build the bungalows. It's only a short walk from their apartments to the garden—and still they want to spend their nights here. They come from one housing project and want to create another one. The system has penetrated so deep under their skin that they can't be human anymore." I refrained from challenging Kumermann's idea that conformity is an exclusively Communist trait and from pointing out that the desire to be like everyone else is no less human than the wish to be different. The orderly gardens of the neighbors did not seem sinister to me, nor did the undistinguished but inoffensive bungalows—cheap little wooden houses—while the anarchy of Kumermann's garden seemed pointless. Nature has her quiet, secret rules (we call them ecology), and the gardener has his more legible conventions (cultivation). To liken the rules of horticulture, which have evolved over centuries of trial and error, to totalitarian structures was to misunderstand the idea of a garden.

Kumermann went into the shed and changed into a pair of denim overalls. He began to plant the pansies, and when I asked if there was some work I could do he said the dandelions in the strawberry bed could be weeded, and handed me a weeding tool of unusual design. We worked quietly in different parts of the plot for about half an hour. Then the sky darkened, thunder sounded, and rain came down in a violent shower. We ran into the shed. In the dark I could make out disorderly tangles of implements and tools, coils of hose, boxes, buckets, cans, rags, clothes, blankets, debris. Kumermann put a dirty blanket on an upside-down pail for me to sit on, and sat on another pail himself. The rain pelted the roof and poured down in sheets. We chatted companionably. Deep feelings of coziness and security are aroused by the situation of taking shelter in a small, dark place during a storm. Like characters in nineteenth-century novels who are regularly obliged to seek shelter from the rain in summerhouses in order that the plot of their intimacy may go forward, so Kumermann and I drew closer together as we sat on our pails and watched the lightning flash and the rain come down. We speculated on the scene at the Letná Plain, where the Pope was even then blessing the multitudes. For the first time, he asked me questions about myself, and listened with interest as I told him about my family and my life in New York, and about my own garden in Massachusetts. But then, as the rain began to subside, we returned to our old, skewed journalistic dialogue.

I brought up the subject of Kumermann's invitation to Israel by the PLO, and told him of some second thoughts I had had about his response to it. "At first, I thought you were being a bit naive," I said. "You didn't seem to be aware that it's against journalistic practice to accept favors from people you intend to write about—that favors compromise you. But later I thought, That's all very well for me to say, coming, as I do, from a magazine that pays my expenses. Here in Prague, I realized, where magazines and newspapers have no money, journalists must take their opportunities as they come."

Kumermann heard only the first part of my comment. He said defensively, "First of all, I never took the PLO offer that seriously. Now my colleague says he's not sure he's going, either. But the main thing is that I see the PLO as killers and enemies, and consider Israel partly my own country. This view would not change if I accepted the PLO invitation."

"Ideally, your magazine would send you."

"But it is not possible at the moment."

"I know."

"If I take the ticket from the PLO and still don't write anything favorable to them—would that satisfy you?"

"Under normal circumstances, no. But I understand that you have to bend the rules of normal journalistic practice in the current economic situation."

"You could say that there is no normal journalistic practice in this country," Kumermann said. "So there is no bending of anything. The previous practice was to strictly follow the party rules." He added, "Maybe it's the American puristic approach that is behind your objection."

"We can afford our purism," I said. "We would probably do the same as you in your situation."

"It would be nice to see the world. Right now, we are dependent on the occasional trips that Havel makes, or on the occasional international seminar where journalists are invited. These are our only opportunities to report abroad."

Kumermann spoke contemptuously of the ignorance of the American journalists he had met in Prague. "They ask you such stupid questions. They don't do any basic research. 'How many people are there in Czechoslovakia?' They come unprepared. For all they know, they could be in Bulgaria."

"I have probably asked you some stupid questions," I said.

"Yes, some."

The rain stopped, and I told Kumermann that I had to get back to Prague for an appointment. I handed him his weeding tool, praising its efficacy. As he took it, he murmured something to the effect that I had probably pulled out the strawberries instead of the dandelions. When I looked at him uncertainly, he said, "That's an example of my unpleasant humor." He added, "I don't know—something drives me to it. Somebody says or does something, and I immediately find some kind of joke in it."

"Do you know the word 'needling'?" I asked.

"Yes. That describes it. Needling clears the field, in a way. Those who can't stand it soon get lost."

"So the people who like you are those who—"

"Yes, those who pass the test. Most people come and go."


THE next day, I went for Sunday lunch at the Valentas'. In daylight, their apartment did not have the incoherence and hauntedness of its evening aspect; the curtains were drawn back to let in sunlight, along with a breathtaking view of the river and the Hradčany. One could see why Havel had chosen not to move into the presidential residence at the castle and had remained in his apartment, on the embankment, a few blocks from the Valentas': to live where one can look at the castle is surely preferable to living in the castle itself, where one merely looks at one's old apartment. The Valentas' son was present this time, and the Valentas exhibited the tension and artificiality that parents whose children are a grief to them exhibit in their presence. At our previous meeting, Jana had told me of Ivan's troubled history with alcohol, drugs, and ulcers. He had been ill during high school, had dropped out of the university in his second year, and had been working—not for political reasons —at menial jobs ever since. He had a girlfriend whom Jana did not approve of—a woman twelve years older than he was, who had a ten-year-old son.

"She's not much," Jana had said. "A small, thin blonde, not pretty, washed out. She looks her age. He's at her place constantly."

"She's not a bad sort," Egon had said.

"She's too old for him," Jana had said.

Ivan came into the room a few minutes after I arrived. He was wearing jeans, a T-shirt marked "Indiana University," moccasins, and no socks. He was thin—too thin—with dark, curly hair that was already beginning to recede. He had his father's handsome features, but not his father's expression of European irony and animation; instead, he exhibited a kind of American blankness and lassitude. He was a beautiful, lost boy. The liaison with the faded divorcée almost had a ring of inevitability about it. His manner to me was polite and pleasant; nothing passed between him and his father; between him and his mother a complicated, painful, ongoing agon wearily played itself out, its most overt expression being a constant interrupting of each other, with sometimes the mother and sometimes the son prevailing. Valenta affected the air of a man so uninterested in youth that he was bored even by his own child. (I had heard that he was an extremely popular teacher—that his lectures were brilliant and his courses always oversubscribed.)

During lunch, Ivan drank a good deal of wine, smoked (as did both his parents), and ate almost nothing. I could see Jana tensely following the progress of his nonmeal and feel the effort it cost her not to urge him to eat. I asked him what he did. He said that he had changed jobs just before the revolution. His old job had been driving an ambulance. "What I saw at the hospital made me sick," he said. "Maybe things will be better now, but then it was completely corrupt. Only the people with money got decent care. The ambulance drivers were worse than anyone. They would extract money from the relatives of desperately ill people. Some of them would simply refuse to take sick people to the hospital if the relatives didn't pay up. Once—"

"But you didn't do that," Jana cut in.

Ivan did not yield. "—a man with a heart attack died on the way to the hospital, and the relatives complained about the driver, but nothing came of it. I finally couldn't stand it anymore. I now have a job driving a delivery van."

"The hospitals are scenes from hell," Jana said. "Last year, when Ivan had to have tests—"

It was Ivan's turn to interrupt. "I may do this for another year or so. Then I hope to go to Switzerland and study restaurant management. I have the fantasy of opening an ethnic restaurant in Prague."

Jana sighed, and dropped the matter of Ivan's tests. She cleared the table and would not let me help her. Valenta lit a cigarette. He watched Ivan pour himself a glass of wine, and then, with his elaborate courtesy, reached for the bottle and added wine to my glass.

"What kind of ethnic restaurant?" I asked.

"Vietnamese maybe. Or North African."

Valenta listened with an ironic expression. Jana came back from the kitchen carrying a plate of pastries. I recognized them as the blowsy cakes sold at the Cukrárna and at every other confectionery in Prague. The uniformity of Prague's food and consumer goods had only gradually registered on me. It had taken me some time to realize that the attractively and variously decorated food shops were in fact all filled with almost exactly the same limited goods. Tzvetan Todorov, in a memorable passage of an article on post-totalitarian depression, published in 1990 in *The New Republic*, reproves the glib critics of the consumerism of the former Soviet-satellite countries:

Several German intellectuals and politicians had hard words for their fellow-citizens who flung themselves on the West German shops as soon as they could. . . . These could only be the words of people who have forgotten, or never knew, the personal humiliation inflicted by the permanent lack of the most elementary consumer goods: the humiliation of silent and hostile lines, the humiliation inflicted on you by salespeople who seem angry to see you standing there, the humiliation of always having to buy what there is, not what you need. The systematic penury of material goods strikes a blow at the moral dignity of the individual. By throwing themselves on the shops of the West, the inhabitants of the East are not so much thinking of filling their stomachs as they are enjoying a freedom that the Western consumer does not feel because he is so accustomed to it.

When Jana offered the pastries, Ivan and Valenta refused, and I couldn't but accept one. As I ate it—and it wasn't as bad as it looked—I recalled a pastry I had eaten on my first trip to Prague, which was far worse than it looked. It had been offered to me by members of a macrobiotic cult whom I had met on the street in front of one of the video sets that the Civic Forum had placed on busy street corners to show key moments of the velvet revolution: the beating of the students, the rallies in Wenceslas Square, the inauguration of Havel, speeches of Havel. I got into conversation with a couple watching the documentary—a ruddy, friendly man and his thin, pasty-faced, unsmiling wife—who told me they were in Prague for the weekend, staying with their macrobiotic guru; they came from a village where they tended cows and calves at a factory farm. The next day, they had driven me to a villa in the suburbs where the guru lived—a twenty-four-year-old girl with braids, a doctor, who had come under the sway of the macrobiotic idea while at medical school and had gathered around herself a small band of believers. The villa belonged to the girl's parents—the father was a diplomat—who were away. The house had the look of a place whose owners were away. It was filthy and neglected; I caught a glimpse of a kitchen whose counters were loaded with piles of food-encrusted bowls and plates. The whole place evoked the atmosphere of American college dormitories, or the communes of the sixties. The girl in braids gave a lecture on the macrobiotic diet as a cure for and preventive of disease, citing studies and experiments done in Japan, America, Sweden, and elsewhere. (In the car, the couple had told me of the miraculous remission of the wife's terminal cancer after she went on the macrobiotic regimen.) As the guru held forth, in a mechanical, relentless little voice, other members of the cult wandered in and out. The macrobiotic movement had been one of the deviant movements suppressed by the Communists; now it could come out into the open, and its members could disseminate the macrobiotic theories and alert the nation to the dire effects of the regular Czech diet on the human organism. The unsmiling wife came in with a teapot, cups, and a plate of pastries. "You will see how good food can be without sugar," the husband said. The pastry was unbelievably awful—I remember rubberiness combined with a kind of dank, sweet, mealy staleness. The tea had an unfamiliar, punitive taste. These people, I thought, were like health cranks everywhere: innocent, well-intentioned, very boring people in the single-minded pursuit of their idea. I did not have to come to Prague to meet them. But, thinking of them again at the Valentas', I said to myself, "Yes, I did have to come to Prague to meet them, as I had to come to Prague to meet the Valentas." The narratives we call anthropology or travel writing or foreign journalism are created out of the tension between two ideas: "They are like us" and "They are different from us." The latter gives such narratives their status as repositories of new information about the world, while the former acts as a kind of brake on the alienation that comes from true difference. The field worker or travel writer or foreign correspondent, if he is honest with himself, is constantly confronted with the abashing incompleteness of his knowledge; even more disconcerting, he may suspect that this very incompleteness is what imparts to his narrative its requisite exoticism. After my return to America, I spoke with Kumermann on the telephone several times, and once he said, in his mocking manner, "I know you must be working for the CIA to ask me so many questions." The foreign correspondent/travel writer/anthropologist is indeed a kind of spy. The direct questions he asks are only a facade, behind which the operation of covert watching and listening is mounted; his work—like the work of all spies—is tied to contingency and marked by melancholy.

Jana brought in a tray of coffee, and Valenta switched on the radio. Every Sunday afternoon at two-fifteen, the President spoke on the radio for half an hour in an informal talk with an interviewer, and these talks were much liked and much listened to. They were recorded at the Lány Mansion, which had been Tomáš Masaryk's summer residence. Havel came on—his voice now as familiar to me as his face in the photographs that, after the events of November, had been pasted on every shopwindow in Prague. His voice is a deep baritone, with a somewhat toneless quality; what makes it recognizable and remarkable is that it is the voice of an individual speaking to other individuals, rather than that of a speaker addressing an audience. The self-relishing unction present in the voices of so many politicians is entirely absent from Havel's. He is direct, simple, clear, funny. He wears his learning lightly, but he wears it. He talks in a way that everyone can understand, using a plain vocabulary and forward-moving syntax, avoiding the sort of involuted, ironic floweriness that Czech intellectuals are prone to, but he is not folksy or condescending; he is authentic to an almost electrifying degree. The broadcast began with a question about ecology, to which Havel replied, "Here, as in everything, I turn to the moral dimension. We shouldn't just think of ourselves." He said he believed that if everyone behaved unselfishly and did his share, the country's grave environmental problems could be solved. He added that he did not believe that productivity and ecological concern are inimical. The centerpiece of the broadcast was Havel's answer to a criticism of himself. "People say I make too many trips abroad and don't take enough interest in the problems of this country," Havel said, and went on, "I have been President for one hundred and fifteen days. Of these days, I have spent thirteen abroad. That is not a very long time. But I believe I have accomplished more during those trips than I have accomplished at home, where I often think that what I do is useless. There are arguments between factions, I reconcile them; they argue again, I reconcile them again. In my trips abroad, I have none of this frustration. Rather, I have the sense that I am learning a great deal about my job. I want to stress that it isn't just tourism, it isn't just the wish to see foreign places, that motivates me. I have to learn how to be a President, and we all have to learn how to be citizens of a democracy. We can't ask people above us to do it for us." Then, with the artist's ability to get below the surface of things, Havel got below the surface of the criticism and to its essence, likening the complaints of his countrymen about his trips abroad to the hysterical anxiety of insecure children whose mother goes away for half an hour.

Later, thinking about the broadcast, I was struck by the fact that Havel had projected himself as a mother rather than as a father—and it struck me as being characteristic of him. His habit of forgiveness—the mother's riposte to the father's rule of law—is one of the signatures of his leadership. In 1977, after a four-month detention, he told an interviewer, "Try as I might, I was unable to feel any personal revulsion or hatred against my interrogators and jailers. Rather, I tried to understand them, and I must confess that at times I was even sorry for them." In *Letters to Olga*, he wrote, "I have different opinions of different people, but I cannot say that I hate anyone in the world. I have no intention of changing in that regard. If I did, it would mean that I had lost. Hatred has never been either my program or the point of departure for my actions." Since becoming President, Havel, following his nature, has made a number of conciliatory statements about Germany, which, almost alone of his public actions, have not been universally applauded. There are those who feel that it is not for him to forgive the Germans for the Holocaust—that here not a mother's mercy but a father's implacability is necessary.

After the broadcast, the tension between the three Valentas relaxed as they joined in praise of Havel.

"He's fantastic," Ivan said. During the program, his face had lost its torpor, and some animation still remained.

"Such a beautiful person," Jana said. "So human."

"Have you noticed that there are no Havel jokes?" Valenta said. "Not one. Which is unheard of. But Havel is beyond criticism—he's another Masaryk."

"Were there Masaryk jokes?" I asked.

Valenta thought. "Yes. There were Masaryk jokes."

Ivan looked at his watch and said he had to leave. It was clear from the look on Jana's face where he was going. I said I had to leave, too. I left with Ivan, and when I paused in the hallway to look back, the Valentas were standing in the door of the apartment, with the light and the view of Hradčany behind them, and something in their attitude suggested that they didn't know what they were going to do next.

ON my last night in Prague, I went with Kumermann to see Havel's *Largo Desolato* at the Theater on the Balustrade. My second cousin Vladimir Vodička, who is the theater's artistic director, had presented me with two coveted tickets (the play had been sold out since it opened, two weeks earlier), and I had invited Kumermann. His response to the invitation had been to ask if a third ticket could be found for Jarmila. I was torn between a feeling of annoyance and the thought that it was nice of him to think of Jarmila; however, another ticket could not be found, and Kumermann did not give up his to his wife. In honor of the occasion, he had put on a tweed jacket over his jeans and was wearing a tie. We met in the theater's anteroom, where my suave and genial one-quarter-Jewish cousin greeted us. I introduced Kumermann, and as they shook hands Kumermann said that though Vodička probably didn't remember him, they had met two or three years before, when Kumermann had come to the theater to wash windows. My cousin had to admit that he did not remember Kumermann's professional visit, and affably asked him what he was doing now. Kumermann told him, and the men chatted about the new Prague magazines and newspapers. Vodička invited us for a drink at the bar. He assured us, "You are going to enjoy yourselves tonight. Grossman is a genius." (Jan Grossman, the play's director, had been the Balustrade's head of drama during its seminal period, and had left the theater shortly after Havel did, in 1968.) I had seen *Largo Desolato* in New York, in a production at the Public Theater, and I had read the text, and I had not enjoyed myself. *Largo* is the first full-length play Havel wrote after his long prison term. As he describes it in *Disturbing the Peace*, it "examines what happens when the personification of resistance finds himself at the end of his tether." Although he drew on his own "post-prison despair" and "did put a bit of my own instability" into the main character, the play is not autobiographical, he says, but "has ambitions to be a human parable, and in that sense it's about man in general." He (somewhat Jesuitically) concludes, "And anyway, if I was as badly off as Kopřiva"—the main character—"I couldn't have written a thing, certainly not with any ironic distance, so, in fact, the very existence of this play argues against its being autobiographical."

In my previous encounters with it, the play had wearied and irritated me. Its dissident hero, who is cracking up under the strain of his noble work (his anxiety exacerbated by the expectations of his followers, the harassment of the secret police, and the sullenness of his girlfriend), put me off as a pretentious bore; the play's attempts at absurdist irony seemed leaden and mannered. Kumermann, who had read the play in samizdat, agreed with my estimate; like me, he felt that Havel's literary reputation would rest on his essays and on *Letters to Olga*, rather than on his plays.

We took our places in the tiny auditorium (it has only two hundred seats), and promptly at seven-thirty the lights dimmed (like Prague trains and trams, Prague plays and operas run on time), and as music sounded backstage—a thumping, raucous, speeded-up version of the Alla Turca finale of Mozart's Piano Sonata K. 331, in A major—the curtain went up. It was a red taffeta curtain with a ruffle on the bottom, and it didn't just go up but romped up, with a saucy and farcical air that matched the music's impudence. A sort of gasp of astonished delight arose from the audience, followed by laughter, which did not let up for the next two hours. Grossman is indeed a genius. Under his direction, an ensemble of gifted actors transformed Havel's inert text into an electrifying theatrical experience. The play was done like frothy French farce, at very high speed, with delicate, comic precision. (The set was merely a lot of doors and a floor strewn with cushions.) The horror of the protagonist's situation came out of the pores of the comedy, as it were. Where in the earnest New York production one had been bored by the man's self-absorption and had resented being asked to admire and pity him, here one only too gladly obeyed the production's imperative, which was simply to laugh at and with him. Jiří Bartoška's performance of Kopřiva was extraordinary: his rendering of a man having a nervous breakdown (his costume throughout was pajamas, and much of his time onstage was spent sprawled on the floor cushions) was entirely and horribly believable, because it was so close to the bone of ludicrous everyday unhappiness. Havel's remote parable—his cold play about "man in general"—now took on urgent immediacy. The sense that each person's life is unique and mysterious and lived in a particular way, so evident in Havel's essays and letters, had lain dormant in the text of *Largo*, waiting to be released on the stage. Havel has frequently written of the idea of theater as a communal experience. In *Letters to Olga*, he proposes that "seeing [a play] is more than just an act of perception, it is a form of human relationship. It is not only the actors onstage who make this event happen—through their living pres-

ence, their actions, and their lives—but the people in the audience as well." The phenomenon Havel describes occurred
that night in Prague, and occurred with special force. Added
to the usual electricity that theater can generate was the extra
voltage of the historical moment. It is not every day that you
can sit in a theater and laugh your head off at lines written by
the President of your country, and the audience was full of the
pleasure of that knowledge. The laughter was affectionate, fam-
ilial, and cathartic. When the lights came on after the first act,
I glanced over at Kumermann, and he was flushed and happy
and elated as I had never seen him before. In the dark, we had
already had the experience of shared delight, and now we agreed
on having to revise our estimate of Havel as playwright. Kumermann was particularly taken with the performances of the
actors who had played two secret policemen. "They were
perfect—just like the ones who interrogated me. The same
sliminess and stupidity."

The second (and last) act was as wonderful as the first. In
the lobby, we told my cousin he had been right, and thanked
him for a memorable evening. Outside, it was drizzling. Kumermann proposed to walk me to my hotel and then take the
metro home. On an impulse, I said, "Let me show you something," and I took him over to the river to see the swan. I half
hoped that she would no longer be there, that she had finally
hatched her eggs. But she was there, and so were the rats. As
she fended off the rats, the swan seemed less agitated than before
and her vigil less terrifying, or perhaps I was better braced for
the sight. I was not altogether unprepared for (though, all the
same, disappointed in) Kumermann's reaction to my offering,
which he received with the same apparent indifference with
which he had received my present of chewing gum and comics.
But as we left the embankment he said, in a kind of left-handed
gesture of reciprocity, "Let me show you something now," and
led me to a dark side street, where he pointed out a low, non-
descript building that might have been the offices of a small

business or manufacturing company but had no identifying marks. "That's the old security-police headquarters," he said. "That's where we were taken for interrogation." A few lights burned dimly within the depths of the building, and on the empty street outside there were a few cars with men in them who seemed vaguely connected to the building.

"What is going on there now?" I asked.

"I don't know," Kumermann said. He added, "I think the changes should have been more radical. The secret police should have been banned, and all its people thrown out. But the Civic Forum said, 'We don't want to be like them.' For a start, we should be more like them."

We turned in to Národní Třída, and as we approached Wenceslas Square a shared feeling of wanting to prolong the evening slowed our pace. At my hotel, we had a final drink and talk. Kumermann told me he thought he would be able to get to Israel on the Community's plane. He again fretted about his young editor in chief, with whom he was beginning to clash. "I'm afraid he's narrow-minded and we'll never agree." As we finished our drinks he said, "You said you liked my weeding tool. Would you like me to send you one?" I said I would like that very much. "All right, I had better be off." We embraced and said goodbye. I watched him shamble off with his heavy knapsack and his quick, grave tread.

Since then, we have spoken on the telephone a few times. In late April, he told me he had got to Israel (on a Community plane) and was working on an article about the trip. In mid-May, he reported that things had come to their anticipated unhappy head at his magazine, and that he had been fired. The young editor had turned down his Israel article and told him he did not have enough writing experience. Kumermann said he accepted the estimate of his work but resented being fired by someone he didn't respect. He also told me of a lesser misfortune: a trip that he and Jarmila had planned to East Berlin to visit museums had not come off, because on the eve of their departure Jarmila's passport could not be found. In our next conversation Kumermann reported that the passport had turned up five days later; it had fallen behind a drawer. ("It was my fault. Jarmila told me to look there, but I didn't look closely enough.") He also told me he had a new job, on a daily newspaper. In another conversation, he returned to the scene in his boyhood when he had read the official letter documenting his grandmother's death at Treblinka—this time articulating his sense of the transgression of his opening the letter ("the letter that I shouldn't have read—my father wasn't home and it was lying there and I opened it") but reiterating, "It didn't tell me anything. I didn't tie it to any evil, and I didn't have any feeling about it. I knew her picture on the wall—that was it." By mail, I have received from Kumermann a much cited article he had offered to send me, entitled "The Paradoxes of Milan Kundera," by Milan Jungmann, a Czech literary critic who also was a window washer (his tenure was thirteen years), and who was also at pains to point out that Prague women didn't sleep with their window washers. The weeding tool has not yet arrived.

*The New Yorker*, 1990